MOTOR RACING

The Drivers and Their Machines

WHITE STAR
PUBLISHERS

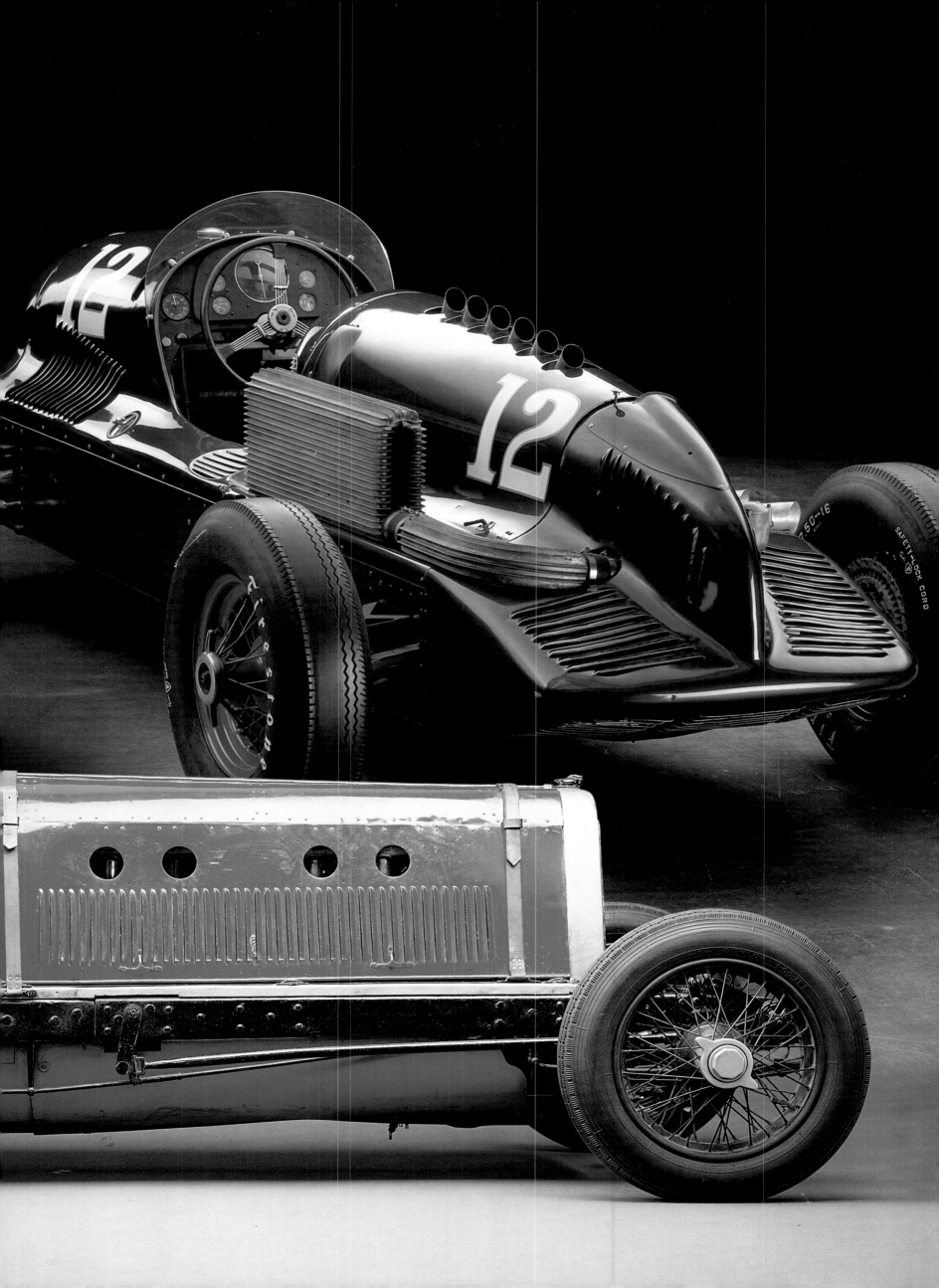

1 The red shadows of Formula 1: the Italian national livery has, over the years, become Ferrari's symbol.

2 top left The Italian driver Materassi, at the wheel of a Bugatti, tackling the Ponticello curve during the XVIII Targa Florio.

2-3 Mephistopheles, a Fiat F.B.4 racer, never passed unobserved in early 20th century races.

3 top right Millers were protagonists on the Indianapolis oval from the Twenties to the Forties.

4-5 Olivier Panis at the wheel of the Prost AP01 during the 1998 World Championship. The Frenchman drove the Professor's car to 11th place in the 1998 San Marino GP.

6 top left The culminating moment of a race is when the first car crosses the finish line with the race official waving the checkered flag.

6 bottom left The racing driver par excellence, the champion of champions, a man who treated his steeds with kid gloves: Juan Manuel Fangio.

6 right The Ferrari 158 F1 and John Surtees, two Formula 1 legends. The Italian manufacturer is the only one to have participated in every edition of the World Championship while the English driver is the only man to have won world titles on both two wheels (seven) and four (one).

6-7 The Kaiser of Formula 1 is Michael Schumacher, the only driver worthy of taking on the mantle of the late, great Ayrton Senna.

7 top left Argentina and Japan dominating the rally world: Carlos Sainz, winner of the 1992 World Rally Championship, at the wheel of a Toyota Celica.

7 top right Brazilians, quality rather than quantity: Emerson Fittipaldi preceded his compatriots Piquet and Senna to the World Championship title.

Text
Giuseppe Guzzardi
Enzo Rizzo

Editors
Valeria Manferto De Fabianis
Laura Accomazzo

Graphic design
Patrizia Balocco Lovisetti

Translation
Neil Davenport

English translation editor
Jay Lamm

North American edition
Managing editor: JoAnn Padgett
Project editor: Elizabeth McNulty

© 1999 White Star S.r.l.
Via Candido Sassone 24,
13100 Vercelli, Italy.

ISBN 88-8095-374-5

Printed in Italy

CONTENTS

PREFACE

It is said that humans were created from dust of the earth. While this may be true, in the case of racing drivers the Creator surely added a dose of engine oil.

Racing drivers are, without doubt, strange creatures, finding their *raison d'être*, fulfillment, and exaltation within an invisible tunnel tangible only when maximum speed is achieved. Then, and only then, do they detach themselves from the terrestrial world in a process something like what happens to an aircraft pilot—although in the latter case the detachment takes place in an immense soap bubble rather than a viscous tunnel.

It is probable that no one can effectively describe the sensations experienced by top drivers at the wheel—not even the drivers themselves. Those fortunate enough to have accompanied a true racing driver on a demonstration lap will know how far removed are the thought processes of even the most skillful ordinary driver from those of a pure racer, for whom the road is wider, the car is narrower, the curves are straighter and even the most anonymous of vehicles is transformed into a road-burner.

On the other hand, those who have had the experience of completing a flying lap on a racing circuit themselves will have gained at least a vague idea of the energy that courses through every nerve-end, that weakens and sets the knees trembling but strengthens and stills the hands, confuses the survival instinct but hones the projection of the vehicle along the Racing Line.

Over the course of more than a century of motor racing, much of the spirit and substance of the sport has changed, except for the drivers' desire to experience that extreme emotion at all costs. And, up until recent times, those costs were often perilously high—there were few pioneer racers who died of natural causes. Today, technology and strict regulations have reduced the risks for drivers and spectators, and this is without doubt a good thing.

At the same time, however, racing has lost something of its original purity.

This is unfortunately a phenomenon found in all sports. No longer spontaneous manifestations of the competitive spirit, they have become products of televised entertainment. In this sense motor racing, and especially Formula 1, CART and NASCAR, has led the way, bending to the whims and schedules of television before any other discipline.

The history of motor racing, however, remains rich in statistics, episodes, personalities and legends. It would be presumptuous of us to attempt to document it all and thus we shall restrict ourselves to a presentation of the essential historical framework of the principal competitions. We shall attempt, in moderation, to satisfy the thirst for dates and numbers and we shall try to describe the prerogatives, characteristics and salient aspects of the various championships.

Not so much a dedication but rather an honorable mention goes to all those enthusiasts with speed in their DNA who have never had the opportunity to display their suspected dexterity behind the wheel. We hope that they will always bear in mind the difference between racing circuits and everyday roads.

We also ask our readers to forgive our inevitable errors and omissions.—*The Authors*

8 top The cars that have taken part in the various sports-prototype championships are often hard to recognize. This photo shows a Ferrari 333SP that participated in the 1998 Le Mans 24 Hours.

8 bottom Parnelli Jones was one of the protagonists at Indianapolis between the Fifties and Seventies. He was the first driver to break the 150 mph threshold during qualifying for the race.

8-9 The minutes prior to the start of a race always require the utmost concentration on the part of the drivers. This photo portrays Tom Sneva, a driver with great experience, ready to face the grueling 1990 Indianapolis 500 in his March-Buick. Unfortunately he was forced to retire from the race.

9 top Frank Lockhart was one of the many drivers to have been killed attempting to go beyond human limits. The daring American driver won the Indianapolis 500 in 1926, but died two years later trying to break the land speed record of 207.5 mph.

THE PLAYTHING
OF BORED GENTLEMEN

The birth of motor racing virtually coincided with that of the car itself, in the last decade of the 19th century. The earliest events were exhibitions that, rather than rewarding a driver and car faster and stronger than others, aimed to demonstrate the reliability of the motorized carriage. The triumph of one model over another was not what was at stake so much as the success of the automobile itself.

The first drivers were often the men who actually designed and built the cars. Technical pioneers obsessed with the idea of combining the nascent technology of applied thermodynamics (thanks to which an engine miraculously transformed fuel into motion) with contemporary running gear and chassis, they battled the vibrations and stresses from which those strange quadricycles powered by steam,

10 top Felice Nazzaro, one of the most famous and daring of the pioneer drivers, seen tackling the Targa Florio. The Sicilian race snaked through the Madonie mountains behind Palermo. The photo was taken during the second edition held in 1907 and won by Nazzaro at the wheel of a Fiat.

10-11 Cars ready for the off. Races were started in various ways, but in some cases, as at Indianapolis or Brooklands (seen here), the cars were already lined up on grids. Note the smoke generated by the cars' screaming engines as the starter hurries to the edge of the track.

The origins

11 top left The process of changing tires and lubricating the hubs of a Renault on the occasion of the New York 24 Hours of 1909.

11 center left Following the pioneer phase, motor racing began to be organized around annual events, the Grands Prix. The first of these was organized by the Automobile Club of France at Le Mans in 1906. As the photo

shows this was still a road circuit, albeit closed to traffic. Shepard is seen negotiating the pharmacy corner with a Hotchkiss, but the race was eventually won for the first and only time by an Hungarian driver, Ferenc Szisz, with a Renault.

11 bottom left The protagonist in this early duel was no ordinary driver but one Henry Ford at the wheel of his Arrow 999 (left). In January 1904 the founder of the Ford Motor Company achieved a top speed of over 146 kph (90 mph).

electricity or with increasing frequency internal-combustion engines suffered.

Shortly afterward, however, cars came of age, becoming profitable, entertaining to drive and interesting to watch. Racing developed as a consequence of three needs: to improve the reliability of engines and ancillary components (brakes, suspension, transmissions); to distinguish individual models; to set the commercial wheels rolling by portraying the motor car heroically.

Our account will begin with this last factor. The young gentleman of the late nineteenth century, devoted to romantic success and challenge as an end in itself, immediately seized the opportunities offered by the new plaything. As happened at the same time for the athletic and gymnastic disciplines (the accounts of the New Olympic Games are full of enterprises of an exhibitory rather than sporting nature), the car soon proved to be an ideal means of proving one's manhood: Strength, stamina, skill, courage, recklessness and, even then, substantial financial resources were all required. In peacetime

there was nothing better for releasing pent-up aggression and relieving boredom.

Death? Since that of others served to feed the climate of risk and emotive tension that developed within the circus of speed, one's own was a risk worth running. Thus did the aristocracy and well-to-do of the time lend (and frequently donate) the flower of their youth to motor sport.

With regards to technological development it is clear that in the early decades the room for improvement was vast, and manufacturers with racing programs enjoyed alternating advantages. Today things are very different, and motor sport has become a very limited test bench due to restrictions imposed by the regulations, especially in the field of electronics. Experimentation takes place elsewhere, and any reference to the importance of racing for improving the breed smacks of hypocrisy or naiveté.

What instead has developed and taken on a primary role is the commercial and promotional aspect. At the dawn of motor racing history the great patriarchs of the automobile were unwilling to allow their vehicles to be used in those insane, useless and dangerous competitions. Nonetheless, virtually all manufacturers, past and present, eventually became involved in competition in one form or another.

Which were the first races and how and where were they held? There were many events on both sides of the Atlantic, spontaneous or carefully organized, before the first trophies were awarded and the first Grand Prix disputed. In the following chapters we shall look at a number of examples, while some of the great events that were born in this period (Indianapolis, Le Mans, the Targa Florio) will be discussed later.

Lack of space prevents us from recounting the stories and results of events that were not part of a championship program.

THE ACF RACES
THINGS ARE GETTING SERIOUS

Clearly, a book about the history of motor racing should start with the date of the first event that could be described as a "competition." But what do we mean by first competition? The first known meeting with some degree of official recognition during which two or more cars were pitted against each other in some form of contest? The date in question then can be none other than the 22nd of July, 1894, and the event the Paris-Rouen. In this case, however, the winning car was not the fastest (Count Jules de Dion's steam tractor), but rather those that covered the 80 km (50 mi.) "without danger" and while demonstrating "an ease of handling and economy," that is to say the Peugeots of Lemaître and Doriot. This was more of a regularity trial than a race.

Should we instead set the birth of motor racing at the date of the first organized competition, then we have to go back to the 20th of April, 1887. Unfortunately, on that occasion only one vehicle entered, another de Dion steam car. Lastly, should we prefer to mark the first true race backed up by an organizational structure, then the date moves forward to the 11th of June, 1895, when the first Paris-Bordeaux-Paris was held under the staging of the same Count de Dion. This is the true point at which the motor racing stopwatch was set running, and it has yet to stop.

But how could we ignore the episode of that first Paris-Rouen? We have no reliable documentation regarding the irascible French aristocrat's reaction when he was deprived of the victor's laurels, but we like to think that it was the humiliation he suffered on that occasion that triggered a mechanism that is still ticking today.

The unusual event was organized by the *Petit Journal* and attracted over a hundred hopeful drivers and constructors. All manner of vehicles are recorded in the entry details with cars powered by steam, petrol, pendulums, levers and compressed air, and this great variety led the organizers to set a qualifying test which reduced the field to 21 (only steam and petrol powered cars made it through to the event proper), with only 19 of those actually starting at first light on the 22nd of July 1894.

It is not hard to imagine the curiosity of the crowd that assembled at the Porte Mallot to see all these terrifying contraptions gathered together. The first to set off was Count Jules de Dion aboard an enormous steam car weighing two and a half tons and composed of a tractor and a carriage towed like a modern trailer.

12 top The photo shows the Panhard Levassor that won the Paris-Rouen race of 1894.

12 center This rare image shows a closed Panhard during the Paris-Rouen race of 1894, run over a distance of about 130 km (81 mi.).

12 bottom Count Jules de Dion took up the cause of motor racing but soon came into conflict with the organizers of the 1894 Paris-Rouen event. On the second of November, 1894, he held at his home the meeting out of which was born the French Automobile Club and the first regulated races. In 1910 de Dion resigned from the club he had founded following disputes over the organization of the Grand Prix.

The irrepressible Count deserves particular mention as a prototype of the aristocratic lover of entertainment, beautiful women and gambling. Inclined to duels and the taking of risks of all kinds, he enjoyed riches more than sufficient to allow him to indulge in expensive pastimes such as the nascent automobile.

On this occasion, however, the Count was out of luck. He was the first home, two and a half minutes ahead of his nearest rival—despite his vehicle at a certain point being bogged down in the loose road surface, despite wrong turns that led to a potato

field and despite the fact that in his arrogance he was the last to restart following the lunch break. All this notwithstanding, de Dion was disqualified because his car required a stoker to feed the boiler.

The first prize of 5000 francs was shared between the Peugeot of Lemaître and the Panhard-Levassor driven by Levassor himself, while de Dion was assigned the second prize of 2000 francs. His average speed worked out at 18.5 kph (11.5 mph). Among the spectators was no lesser figure than Gottlieb Daimler, whose engine, like those that followed, powered Emile Levassor's car.

In spite of the admiration expressed by jury and spectators alike, the epilogue to the event must have stung Count de Dion, as the nobleman organized a meeting for the following second of November during which, in the presence of constructors and financiers, he launched the idea of a Paris-Bordeaux-Paris challenge on the condition that no judges were to be appointed. One year and ten days later, the Auto Club de France, the patron of the first co-ordinated cycle of annual competitions, was founded in the same house.

The idea was daring; how could the Count hope that the same cars that struggled to complete the 127 km (80 mi.) between Paris and Rouen could cope with a distance of almost 1200 km (745 mi.)? Pure folly. The idea was nonetheless intriguing, partly because in contrast with other nations—the United States included—France was already fertile terrain for motor cars with a growing band of enthusiastic proselytizers. Why not make the attempt?

Thus was born the first true race between motor cars to boast at least minimal regulations: the cars

had to be able to carry more than two people and more than one driver could take the wheel. The riding mechanics could make necessary repairs in the presence of a race official and on the condition that they used only spare parts carried on the vehicle. In spite of de Dion's intentions to the contrary, these regulations still conditioned the final outcome.

The Paris-Bordeaux and return began on the 11th of June, 1895. Among the financiers were James Gordon Bennett and William Vanderbilt, who were subsequently to put up two trophies bearing their own names. Thanks in part to their patronage the prize fund reached 70,000 francs, 10 times that collected the previous year. This time, however, the event was a true race.

The 21 vehicles in the field, 14 petrol, six steam and one electric, paraded from the Arc de Triomphe to Versailles before heading off toward Bordeaux. On the first day of the race over three million spectators thronged the route.

The early leader of his own race was de Dion,

but his elephantine steam car broke down before reaching Tours. Emile Levassor aboard a Daimler-powered Panhard-Levassor inherited the lead in the grueling contest. At Ruffec, a little less than 200 km (124 mi.) north of Bordeaux he found his relief driver still asleep and so decided to press on alone. He reached Bordeaux three and a half hours ahead of his rivals after having driven through the night, and then set out again for Paris.

On his return to the capital around midday he was given a hero's welcome. He had driven for 48 hours and 48 minutes, establishing an extraordinary average night and day speed of 24 kph (15 mph). The second finisher, Rigoulot aboard a Peugeot, arrived almost six hours later.

However, both were disqualified because their

cars could carry only two people. First prize thus went to Koechlin with another Peugeot. Ironically, it was once again the regulations rather than the road that decreed a winner, and ironically the prize was once again scooped by a Peugeot.

On the 28th of November that year, one of the very earliest carmakers, Frank Duryea, won what was considered to be the first race held in the United States. The event was staged in terrible weather conditions that encouraged spectators to return home before the end of the race and Mueller aboard the second-placed Mueller-Benz suffered

from exposure. The American Motor League was founded on the first of the month, that is to say 11 days ahead of the French.

An organizational structure was evolving around motor racing and in Britain, Germany and Italy too, interest in the sport was growing. Returning to the races organized by the Auto Club de France, in 1896 the turning point was set on the Côte d'Azur at Marseille and the distance to be covered was increased to 1,700 km (1,056 mi.). In order to avoid the dangers of driving at night the route was divided into 10 sections that were to all intents and purposes the forebears of today's special rally stages. Thirty-two drivers lined up for the start including Jules de Dion, stubbornly at the wheel of a steam car but ultimately betrayed by tires unable to cope with

14 left This poster was printed by Renault in 1902 to publicize the victory of the "voiturette" constructed by Marcel that had beaten "all cars large and small." The ACF race again went beyond the French borders, this time as far as Vienna (on the first occasion in 1898 it had reached Amsterdam).

14-15 *These four cars were immortalized at the start of the third edition of the Paris-Bordeaux held in 1901 and won by Fournier with a Mors. From the left can be seen Louis and Marcel Renault, Dury and Cirüs.*

14 bottom *Marcel Renault aboard a car bearing his own name at Vienna at the 1902 race. He won by 13 minutes from Farman aboard a Panhard.*

15 top left and top right *Approaching Paris, Marcel Renault prepares to enjoy a well-earned triumph at Place de la Concorde following his victory in the 1902 Paris-Vienna race.*

15 bottom left *Louis Renault is portrayed here at a timing stage during the 1902 Paris-Vienna race.*

15 bottom right *An historic front page of Le Petit Journal, the periodical that organized the first French city-to-city race, the Paris-Rouen of 1894. This edition illustrated Fournier's victory aboard a Mors in the Paris-Berlin of 1901.*

the stresses of high-speed motoring. There were innumerable accidents, some caused by bad weather, and Levassor himself, while well in front, lost control of his car, ran over a dog and left the road. His injuries were serious enough for him to be hospitalized at Avignon and he never fully recovered, dying on the 14th of April, 1897. He was "avenged" by his test driver Mayade, who was first home to Paris at a then-remarkable average speed of just over 25 kph (15 mph).

In 1897, the Parisian race was joined by another enthralling contest run between Marseille and Nice (221 km/137 mi.), with an additional 17.6-km (11 mi.) stretch climbing (perhaps the first timed hillclimb?) to La Turbie above the Principality of Monaco.

The winner was an aristocrat at the wheel of a de Dion, but not the Count of the same name. This de Dion was instead Gaston de Chasseloup-Laubat, who finally succeeded in exploiting the power of the gigantic steam car both uphill and on the flat.

The "traditional" race departing from Paris had by now changed format and no longer included a return leg to the capital. The finish was set at Dieppe in Normandy, almost 170 km (106 mi.) from Bordeaux, which meant that the event could be completed in a single day. Victory went to one of the era's finest cars, a Bollée, a model founded by a father and his two sons who had the foresight to introduce a steering wheel in place of a tiller and the first wing-type profiles with a degree of aerodynamic effect. The car was driven by Jamin.

The newspapers of the time were quick to pick up on a story that emerged from this race: the train carrying the timing officials and journalists which departed immediately after the last car and that was due to arrive well ahead of the competitors actually arrived much later. Unbelievable as it must have been at the time, the car had beaten the train.

A new star emerged in 1898, Panhard, the friend and partner of Levassor who was in close contact through the extremely active wife of the latter with the automotive genius Gottlieb Daimler. It was aboard a Panhard that Fernand Charron won the second edition of the Marseille-Nice in 1898 in front of another two cars of the same model, and it was aboard a Panhard that de Knyff won the Paris-Bordeaux from another two Panhards (between these two races, the first recorded fatal motor racing accident occurred during the Course du Périgueux). Two Panhards also triumphed in the first international competition, the 1423-km (884 mi.) Paris-Amsterdam-Paris won by Charron.

In this case too, a curious story emerged from the race. In order to escape the attentions of the overbearing chief engineer of the police—a M. Bochet, who in virtue of an old bylaw claimed a right to inspect the participating cars—the start was moved to Villiers beyond his jurisdiction. The finish of the return leg after five days of spectacular racing

"classic" that consecrated the idol of the time, Fernand Charron, whose fame was equal to that of the all-conquering American ace Alexander Winton.

Taking into consideration contemporary road conditions, one can imagine the cloud of dust that must have been raised on the occasion of the first mass start, causing no lack of accidents. However, many of the 28 participating teams made it through to the half-way stage and the winner took less than half the time needed by Levassor to complete the first stage of the heroic 1895 race. This was a triumph for Charron and the Panhards (11 among the first 13). The brevity (560 km/ 438 mi.) of the race was justified by its coincidence with the organization of a great event, the Tour de France.

Never had there been a longer or more Pharaonic race: 2,160 km (1341 mi.), from Paris northeast to Nancy, then southeast to Grenoble and Périgueux

again risked being disrupted by the zealous M. Bochet, who threatened to arrest those drivers arriving in Paris aboard illegal cars. The finish was itself thus moved out of his reach to Montgeron.

The competition was so grueling that the drivers did not even have the strength to complete the traditional parade to Versailles. Worthy rivals of Charron were Léonce Girardot aboard a Panhard and Etienne Giraud with a Bollée.

In the meantime the power outputs of contemporary engines were boosted by the speed record attempts over the flying kilometer made by

Camille Jenatzy and Gaston de Chasseloup-Laubat: speeds rose dizzily from 65.6 kph (41 mph) to the insane average of 106.8 kph (66 mph). It is unnecessary to add that these head-to-head challenges made for great newstories, and that the reputation of the horseless carriages grew, with vast commercial implications.

This all took place toward the end of a century in which there had been a succession of events that had revolutionized Western life. Technology was triumphant and the automobile became the calling card of a century that promised progress and well-being. Art and culture, in the form of Futurism, were to record its development along with that of the airplane. The last year of the 19th century was actually one of firsts: the first woman racing driver, Madame Labrousse in the Paris-Spa; the first Tour de France; the first mass start, in the Paris-Bordeaux

not far from Bordeaux and the Atlantic Ocean. The route then headed northwest again to Nancy and further north toward Trouville before descending once more to Paris. The event was studded with accidents and mechanical failures, particularly to the wheels and suspension subjected to enormous stresses by road conditions bearing no resemblance to city streets or more frequently travelled routes. Charron had to drive 40 km (25 mi.) in reverse following the failure of a bearing. Panhards swept the board again, with the winner being another of the era's leading figures, René de Knyff, with an average speed of 48.3 kph (30 mph), followed by Girardot and de Chasseloup-Laubat.

In 1900 the ACF races culminated in July with the 1340-km (832 mi.) Paris-Toulouse-Paris won by Alfred Levegh aboard a Mors. The driver and model thus gained revenge for a victory never officially recognized in the first edition of the Gordon Bennett Trophy, held earlier that year. After three consecutive victories Panhard had to settle for third place.

The Paris-Bordeaux race was staged again in 1901 over a slightly shorter route (524 km/ 325 mi.) than the previous edition. A Mors again came home first, this time driven by another dashing hero, Henri Fournier, once Charron's talented riding mechanic, who was to enjoy further success on the other side of the Atlantic. Mors managed to extract 60 hp from its engine, half as much again as the Panhard.

In this edition of the Paris-Bordeaux the participants were classified according to the weight of their cars with categories for Cyclecars up to 250 kg (551 lb.), Voiturettes of from 250 to 400 kg (551–882 lb.), Light Cars from 400 to 600 kg (882–1,323 lb.) and Heavy Cars of over 650 kg (1,433 lb.; although in reality the most competitive

Panhard) and for the first time the leader board was occupied by brothers Louis and Marcel Renault. The latter won the race aboard a car bearing his own name, in spite of lapping the track on which the finish line was placed in the wrong direction. The fastest car in the event was the Mercedes driven by Count Zborowski, but the penalties he incurred relegated him to fourth overall. Second was Farman with the Panhard. Remarkably, a light car had beaten the heavyweight Panhard and Mercedes.

Shortly afterward an event was staged in Belgium, the Circuit des Ardennes, that is worthy of mention because it was the first known race run on a closed track to the benefit of public safety. The ACF instead decided to retain the epic road race formula — a great mistake — and in 1903 organized the ambitious Paris-Madrid race in three stages.

The Iberian capital was never reached,

such was the number and gravity of the accidents that occurred. The race was interrupted at the end of the first stage at Bordeaux. Among the victims were Marcel Renault and his mechanic. Victory in the Heavy Car category was assigned to the Mors of Fernand Gabriel and among the light cars to Louis Renault, who as soon as he reached Bordeaux withdrew his team and rushed to his dying brother's bedside.

This was not the end of road racing, but the massacre of drivers and spectators led to the ban of such events in the key motor-racing countries in favor of closed circuit events. The ACF races were abandoned. In spite of the cost in terms of human lives, which with hindsight can be seen to be no higher than in subsequent international events, the French era can be considered as the foundation of motor racing as a sport.

17 right This image highlights the radiator coils (top) that characterized racing cars at the turn of the century. This is the de Dietrich 45 hp driven by Charles Jarrot at the Bordeaux control point of the Paris-Madrid of 1903. The race was run by Ettore Bugatti for the first time, who drove a car of his own production. The race was interrupted at Bordeaux, the end of the first leg, with Jarrot finishing in fourth place.

racers weighed up to 1,500 kg/ 3,308 lb.).

Another important international event was staged that year, the 1,100-km (683 mi.) Paris-Berlin. It finished with a repeat victory for Fournier and Mors at an average speed of 70.7 kph (44 mph). These road races conducted at insane speeds included countless, frequently fatal accidents and there was great pressure within French political circles to see them banned. Legislation to this effect was proposed on two occasions but failed. The 1902 Paris-Vienna (985 km/ 612 mi.) took place with a record of 140 entries including William K. Vander-bilt, who two years later launched a similar event in the U.S.

The Panhards were now lighter and more powerful and thus more competitive with the fearsome Mors. Both models, however, were soon out of the running (with the exception of Farman's

HONOR ROLL

Year	Route/Circuit	Driver	Car	Time
1894	Paris-Rouen	Lemaitre	Peugeot	6h 51'30"
1895	Paris-Bordeaux-Paris	A. Koechlin	Peugeot	59h 48'
1896	Paris-Marseille-Paris	Mayade	Panhard	67h 48'58"
1896	Marseille-Nice	G.Chasseloup-Laubat	de Dion	7h 45'
1897	Paris-Dieppe	Jamin	Bollée	4h 13'33"
1898	Paris-Amsterdam-Paris	F. Charron	Panhard	33h 04'34"
1899	Paris-Bordeaux	F. Charron	Panhard	11h 43'20"
1899	Tour de France	R. de Knyff	Panhard	44h 43'39"
1900	Paris-Toulouse-Paris	A. Levegh	Mors	20h 50'09"
1901	Paris-Bordeaux	H. Fournier	Mors	6h 10'44"
1901	Paris-Berlin	H. Fournier	Mors	15h 33'06"
1902	Paris-Vienna	M. Renault	Renault	15h 47'44"
1903	Paris-Madrid*	F. Gabriel	Mors	5h 14'31"

interrupted at Bordeaux due to fatal accidents

THE GORDON BENNETT TROPHY
A NATIONAL CHALLENGE

James Gordon Bennett, publisher of the *New York Herald's* European Edition, had no connection with cars, racing or drivers. By the turn of the century, however, the great newspaper magnates had prosaically recognized the promotional value of heroic enterprises in all fields of human endeavor. They had also discovered that financing such enterprises and initiatives was good business: exclusive articles and reports published day by day created tension and interest around the event.

18 top This photo shows the front of a Panhard 50 hp of over 15 liters about to participate in the Gordon Bennett Trophy of 1904. Note the flat, wing-like mudguards and the steeply inclined radiator, predecessors of more sophisticated aerodynamic aids. On the right, the starting handle.

18 center The Gordon Bennett Trophy, 1903: the Mercedes 90 hp of the eventual winner Camille Jenatzy speeding along a straight road. The photo on the left portrays the Panhard team at the Gordon Bennett Trophy in 1903, held for the first time in Ireland at Athy. On the right René de Knyff can be seen; maybe his definitive retirement was due to his defeat by rival Jenatzy.

18 bottom The timing controls of the early races were similar to those of modern-day rallies. On the left, René de Knyff, second in the 1903 edition of the Gordon Bennett Trophy aboard a Panhard, alongside the timing officials with (on the right) the organizer's marquee.

Bennett was an archetypal modern entrepreneur of this kind: it was he who financed Stanley's expedition to the heart of Darkest Africa in search of Livingstone and with similar largess sponsored the first race organized by de Dion.

The organizational supremacy of the French began to become embarrassing, however, especially in such a promising field as that of the automobile. Bennett had strength, power, some knowledge of the sector and the ability to organize races on his own. Nineteen-hundred appeared to be the right moment and on the 14th of June his entrepreneurial spirit gave birth to the Gordon Bennett Trophy—an American in Paris no less. The regulations stated that each national Automobile Club could enter three cars constructed entirely in that country. The actual running of the event was entrusted to the ACF, the

Alexander Winton with a car bearing his own name. A Mors also raced, albeit unofficially because the French places had all been assigned. Mors was shortly to enjoy a brief period of domination in the sport and with Alfred Levegh at the wheel had the potential to win that first edition of the Gordon Bennett Trophy.

The 1901 event was also short of entries, so it was decided to hold the event in conjunction with the Automobile Club de France's Paris-Bordeaux race. The Gordon Bennett Trophy was awarded to Girardot, ninth in the ACF race aboard a Panhard 40 hp.

The following year the event was again held in conjunction with an ACF race, the Paris-Vienna, but over a shorter route finishing at Innsbruck (562 km/ 350 mi.). This time round the Panhard monopoly of the French team was broken with the inclusion of the talented Fournier's Mors. The French drivers were soon

19 top This photo shows the grandstands of the Taunus circuit, venue of the 1904 edition of the Gordon Bennett Trophy.

19 bottom left The cover of Le Petit Journal celebrating French success in the 1904 Gordon Bennett race, with Léon Théry at the wheel of a Richard-Brasier receiving the congratulations of Kaiser Wilhelm II.

19 bottom right The victories of Léon Théry were celebrated in Le Petit Parisien: the French driver is seen here about to win the trials for the Gordon Bennett Trophy of 1904 in the Argonne.

most experienced body, but the regulations stated that the following year's event would be staged in the country of origin of the winning car.

The first edition of the race was run between Paris and Lyons over a distance of 565 km (350 mi.) and the official winner of the race was France's most famous driver, Fernand Charron who once again beat Léonce Girardot. The cars were also French, the usual Panhards, no others managing to finish the race which the winner completed at an average speed of 62 kph (39 mph). The entry list had been short but of great interest: the French team included the resilient de Knyff as well as Charron and Girardot; representing Belgium there was Jenatzy, who was to enjoy glory under the banner of the Reich; while competing for Germany itself there was the son of Karl Benz, Eugene. The United States was represented by none other than record man sidelined by mechanical problems, however, and glory went to the Englishman Selwyn Edge and his Napier 50 hp, first home at an average speed of 50.9 kph (32 mph) despite being helped back onto the road by spectators after a crash. This first British victory in an international event was the spark that ignited enthusiasm for motor racing in the United Kingdom, enthusiasm that soon developed into unbridled passion.

As the regulations required, the publisher's trophy race was held the following year in perfidious Albion, on a circuit at Athy in Ireland: three laps of almost 200 km (124 mi.). It cannot be overlooked that the event was held less than two months after the ACF's catastrophic Paris-Madrid race which had been abandoned after a rash of serious accidents. We feel that apart from the name of the eventual winner, Camille Jenatzy aboard a Mercedes 90 hp, the 1903 edition of the Gordon Bennett Trophy should be remembered for two contrasting episodes. On the one hand René de Knyff's definitive retirement on being defeated by his Belgian rival, and on the other the discrimination against two talented drivers. The Gordon Bennett Trophy regulations stated that drivers and cars should be entered by a national automobile club of which they should be members. However, Otto Hieronymus and Christian Werner had been refused membership in the German

could have become one of the leading entrepreneurs in the automotive field but instead his name today is largely unknown; not that of his daughter, though, in whose honor Daimler-Benz began to call its cars Mercedes.

Returning to the Gordon Bennett Trophy, thanks to the pressure brought to bear by Jellinek, Hieronymus' entry was accepted, but not that of Werner. Fate eventually had a hand in settling the matter: a fire destroyed the German team's cars and the Automobile Club took the opportunity to change its plans and enter the aristocrat de Caters, a Belgian, Jenatzy and an American gentleman driver, Foxhall Keene. It was to be Camille Jenatzy who

20 top The pits at a race early this century: a number of mechanics are changing a wheel on the car with which Léon Théry won the Gordon Bennett race in 1905.

20 bottom This illustration by André Nevil taken from Historie de la locomotion *shows Théry who repeated his 1904 Gordon Bennett win the following year, the last edition sponsored by the publisher of the* New York Herald's European Edition.

Automobile Club on the grounds that they were "simple employees": a lack of pedigree in other words. As a consequence the German team was excluded from the race. They had on their side, however a formidable figure in Emil Jellinek, the German consul at Nice, undoubtedly one of the most acute minds in the history of the automobile.

Jellinek was not only an automotive enthusiast with considerable technical knowledge, but had also been one of the first to recognize the importance of racing to the commercial development of the sector. He acquired batches of cars directly from Daimler and became very influential within the company. His ideas proved to be well founded and there was little to be discussed with regards to the technical specifications he demanded. Had he wanted to he

would win the race, leading home the three French cars including that of de Knyff by 11 minutes.

A sporting gesture by de Caters is worthy of mention. He stopped to lend first aid to Jarrot but found him to be only slightly injured. After restarting he stopped again in front of the grandstand to reassure the crowd as to Jarrot's condition.

As per the regulations, the 1904 edition of the race was held in Germany. This was its golden age, partly because motor racing had been banned in much of Europe and the competitive aspirations of drivers and mechanics were focused on the 127-km (79 mi.) Hamburg circuit in the Taunus Forest. The competitors completed a total of four laps.

This time the Gordon Bennett Trophy was a form of World Championship and each nation, at

20-21 *The qualifying trials for the Gordon Bennett Trophy of 1905. The car in action at Clermont Ferrand is a Renault.*

21 top left This photograph shows one of the two Fiat 110 hp models at the start of the 1905 Gordon Bennett race. The leading Italian drivers, Nazzaro (seen here) and Cagno, had to settle for second and third places.

HONOR ROLL				
YEAR	ROUTE/CIRCUIT	DRIVER	CAR	TIME
1900	Paris-Lyon	F. Charron	Panhard 40 hp	9h 09'
1901	Paris-Bordeaux	L. Girardot	Panhard 40 hp	8h 50'59"
1902	Paris-Innsbruck	S. Edge	Napier 50 hp	11h 02'53"
1903	Athy	C. Jenatzy	Mercedes 90 hp	6h 39'
1904	Homburg	L. Théry	Richard-Brasier	5h 50'04"
1905	Circuit du Auvergne	L. Théry	Richard-Brasier	7h 02'43"

21 top center This photo shows the Mercedes of Camille Jenatzy during the 1905 Gordon Bennett Trophy. First in 1903 and second in 1904, the driver did not enjoy the same good fortune in 1905.

21 top right A Napier driven by MacDonald at the start of a qualifying trial for the 1905 Gordon Bennett race.

21 bottom right The photo shows a Renault GP during the 1905 Gordon Bennett Trophy. Note the front fairing, highly streamlined for the era.

least the most important of them, staged qualifying trials to select their teams.

The French raced in the Argonne (thanks to a government decree) when the Panhard challenge crumbled due to problems with their cooling systems. Léon Théry won with a Richard-Brasier. The British teams competed on the Isle of Man with former champion S. F. Edge winning aboard a Napier, the two Wolselys of Jarrot and Girling also qualifying. From Belgium came the champion Camille Jenatzy, de Caters again and the very young Fritz von Opel aboard a car of the same name that was very similar to the French Darracqs. Incidentally, out of Darracq's satellite assembly plant in Italy was soon to be born the Anonima Lombarda Fabbrica Automobili or A.L.F.A., the firm

which would play a leading role as Alfa Romeo.

Italy itself finally entered a strong team with the talented trio of Vincenzo Lancia, Alessandro Cagno and Luigi Storaro driving Fiats. Teams were also entered by Belgium and Austria, while the Swiss and United States entries were withdrawn.

Victory in the event went to Théry at an average speed of 87 kph (54 mph). There was an element of revenge in this triumph as the previous year Jenatzy had led home the Frenchman de Knyff by 11 minutes, this time it was a French driver who beat Jenatzy (aboard a Mercedes 60 hp) by the same margin.

Théry and the Richard-Brasier repeated their success in 1905, undoubtedly favored by their advance practice at length on the circuit at Clermont Ferrand. The Italian team put up a strong showing.

Nazzaro and Cagno finished second and third, respectively, while Lancia retired after his radiator was broken by a stone while in the lead. The best-placed Brit was Charles Rolls, who had founded the previous year, together with the brilliant Henry Royce, the firm of Rolls-Royce, designers and manufacturers of aviation engines and luxury automobiles.

The 1905 edition of the Gordon Bennett Trophy was the last, the event failing to survive the onset of modern racing—the age of the Grands Prix on dedicated (or at least closed and patrolled) circuits. On the horizon was the first golden age of motor racing, in our opinion the greatest and most enthralling, that was to last until the outbreak of the Second World War.

VANDERBILT CUP
THE AMERICAN CHALLENGE

While in the wake of developments in France, enthusiastically received motor racing events multiplied throughout Europe, in the United States interest in the sport had yet to take off. The sheer size of the country and the consequent complexity of the modernization of the road network inevitably delayed the motorization of the American giant. The years at the turn of the century were instead characterized by head-to-head duels and more frequently by attempts on the record for the mile (from a standing start, flying and in a closed loop). At the other extreme were marathon events testing the robustness of production cars destined for a

population who were pioneers by definition. These rallies captured a popular imagination hungry for feats of daring and adventure.

It was left to a rich young New Yorker, William K. Vanderbilt, to transfer the passion for true racing to the other side of the Atlantic Ocean. It was he who on the 27th of January, 1904, had taken the speed record to 147.5 kph (92 mph) at the wheel of a Mercedes 90 hp. Two weeks earlier Henry Ford had raised the record to 146.2 kph (91 mph) and on the 21st of July Louis Rigolly aboard a Gordon-Brillie became the first man to break the 100 mph barrier with a speed of exactly 166.7 kph (103.56 mph).

Vanderbilt had participated in the last of the Auto Club de France's great road races, the Paris-Madrid of 1903, intuiting the promotional value of the great automotive events for the manufacturing industry. He then ordered a large silver cup from the jeweller Tiffany and prepared regulations for an event that partially followed those of the Gordon Bennett Trophy (the first two editions were to be held in the USA).

The first edition of the Vanderbilt Cup was scheduled for the 8th of October, 1904 at Long Island, New York. The circuit was 45 km (28 mi.) long and was to be completed 10 times by the 18 cars entered. Thirteen of these were European and five American. The lineup included five Mercedes (the favorites), three Panhards, two Fiats, a Renault and a Packard. As had been the case with the early

European events, there was no lack of misadventures and vicissitudes including the objections of local people, some of whom scattered nails and broken glass along the route.

The event was won by the hero of the hour, George Heath, the first American to win a race in Europe, the Circuit des Ardennes. Heath was at the wheel of a Panhard 70 hp and completed the race at an average speed of 83.6 kph (52 mph). Second was the 19-year-old Albert Clément aboard another French car, a Clément-Bayard.

The second edition was firmly in the grasp of the Italian star Vincenzo Lancia aboard a Fiat until it was snatched from him at the end by Hémery with the Darracq 80 hp. The Italian driver was in the pits when he saw a large, slow but difficult to overtake Christie approaching. In order not to have to pass it Lancia hurriedly restarted but failed to take into account the Christie's wayward handling and in fact was rammed from behind with the Fiat's rear wheels being destroyed.

A Darracq, this time a 120 hp model driven by Wagner, triumphed again in 1906. The following year, however, the event was cancelled due to the intense controversy aroused by the slipshod organization of the American Automobile Association (AAA), which had been unable to prevent the crowd from invading the track following the arrival of the victor but before the other drivers had crossed the finish line.

There were further problems in 1908. In Europe, the new GP regulations were in open contradiction with the norms of the past and imposed a minimum weight of 1100 kg on the cars while the AAA remained faithful to the formula that indicated a maximum weight of 1200 kg. The protests of the European teams were in vain, and finding it impossible to modify their cars they were obliged to abandon the race, subsequently won by local driver George Robertson with a Locomobile. For the first time in the brief history of the Vanderbilt Cup the winner finished with an average speed of over 100 kph (62 mph).

From 1909 the Vanderbilt Cup was run in accordance with the Indy, rather than the GP, regulations, with engines of displacements between 4930 and 9830 cc. The race was won by Harry Grant with an Alco at an average speed of 101.1 kph (63 mph). It was a hollow victory, as the winner would have been Dawson aboard a Marmon had it not been for the spectators' deplorable habit of invading the track. This time it occurred two laps from the

end. The leading driver ploughed into the crowd and stopped to lend assistance to the injured. Grant passed and went on to win. However, Grant and the Alco repeated the feat the following season, raising the record average speed to 104.9 kph (65 mph). The 1910 edition is of note in that rather than by the AAA, it was organized by the Motor Club Holdings Company, jointly founded by the AAA and its eternal rival, the ACA (Automobile Club of America).

In 1911 the race moved from New York—Mr. Vanderbilt's home city—to Savannah, where the American Grand Prize was held under the patronage of an active local car club. Ralph Mulford won at the wheel of a Lozier, the victory crowning him as national champion. The event moved again in 1912, this time to Milwaukee. It was won by a driver who was to gain a great reputation in years to come, the Italo-American Ralph de Palma. It was de Palma who brought the Vanderbilt Cup to Mercedes' trophy cabinet for the first time, albeit with a non-works car prepared by the manufacturer for private entrants on the basis of the 37/90 hp, with a four-cylinder twin-spark engine featuring three valves per cylinder. De Palma was also to win the 1914 edition, but his 1912 car was unique in that it was the first to carry the Mercedes three-pointed star.

In 1913 the race was again cancelled, as was the American Grand Prize, because of the excessive cost

of organization and also because the public appeared to prefer races held on smaller closed circuits such as the Indianapolis Motor Speedway.

The race returned in 1914 and was held at the brand-new Santa Monica circuit in California. De Palma improvised a crafty strategy toward the end of the race when he saw that the leader Oldfield's tires were worn out. Even though his own were still in good condition he indicated to his pit crew that he intended to stop and replace them. Oldfield was thus lulled into a false sense of security, thinking that this would allow him to stop and change his tires without losing the lead. De Palma instead carried on to the finish and won by a minute and 20 seconds.

The European Grands Prix were brusquely interrupted by the outbreak of World War I while in

the U.S. racing continued for another two years. The Vanderbilt Cup was held at San Francisco and then at Santa Monica again, both races being dominated by Peugeots with the young Anglo-Italian Dario Resta at the wheel.

The trophy was then forgotten. The Americans preferred national championship events on smaller circuits that were veritable stadia like those used for football or baseball, with tracks frequently paved in wood that allowed the organizers closer control and significant economies of scale. The introduction of spectacular banked curves subsequently satisfied the public's thirst for speed and thrills.

The Vanderbilt Cup made a dramatic return in 1936 and 1937, now named after George Vanderbilt rather than William K. On both occasions the event

was held at the Roosevelt Airfield on Long Island. In 1936 the cup was won by a great driver at the wheel of a great car, Tazio Nuvolari and the Alfa Romeo 12C–36. The following year the winning combination was equally impressive (despite being held at the same time as the Belgian GP): Bernd Rosemeyer and the Auto Union Type C.

Vanderbilt never succeeded in his intention of giving the American industry an opportunity to compete with that of Europe, but he nonetheless made substantial contributions to a North American automotive sector that in those years was unfocused and unwilling to recognize the benefits of racing.

22-23 The New York 24-hour race of 1909, recognizable thanks to the fairing of the leading car, a Renault.

23 top right Bernd Rosemeyer heading toward victory with his Auto Union Type C Grand Prix car on Long Island's Roosevelt circuit in 1937.

23 bottom right A clear image of American triumph in the 1914 edition of the Vanderbilt Cup: Ralph de Palma, an Italo-American, crosses the finishing line to repeat his success of the previous year. The car was again a Mercedes 37/95.

22 left Vanderbilt tackling the replacement of a tire on his Red Devil. This was in 1901; three years later the millionaire organized the first race in the United States on Long Island.

22 top center Harry Grant at the wheel of an Alco crosses the line first in the 1909 edition of the Vanderbilt Cup.

22 top right Felice Nazzaro at the start of the 1905 Vanderbilt Cup. The Fiat driver was out of luck on this occasion, despite being one of the most experienced drivers and having a more powerful car than that of the winner.

22 center right Hémery's Darracq 80 hp flying to victory in the second edition of the Vanderbilt Cup in 1905 in which he achieved 99 kph (61 mph).

22 bottom right The Renault team at the New York 24 Hours in 1909. With the tires changed the hubs were lubricated and the driving team instructed. The first American events were organized with the benefit of European experience. Along with the Vanderbilt Cup there was also this 24-Hour race and the world's longest race, the New York-Paris held the previous year.

HONOR ROLL

Year	Venue	Driver	Car	Average speed
1904	Long Island	G. Heath	Panhard 70 hp	84 kph (52 mi.)
1905	Long Island	V. Hémery	Darracq 80 hp	99 (61)
1906	Long Island	L. Wagner	Darracq 120 hp	98.9 (56)
1908	Long Island	G. Robertson	Locomobile	103.6 (64)
1909	Long Island	H. Grant	Alco	101.1 (63)
1910	Long Island	H. Grant	Alco	104.9 (65)
1911	Savannah	R. Mulford	Lozier	119.2 (74)
1912	Milwaukee	R. de Palma	Mercedes	111 (69)
1914	S. Monica	R. de Palma	Mercedes	121.5 (75)
1915	S. Francisco	D. Resta	Peugeot L56EX-5	106.8 (66)
1916	S. Monica	D. Resta	Peugeot L56EX-5	140.3 (87)
1936	Long Island	T. Nuvolari	Alfa Romeo 12C	105.4 (65)
1937	Long Island	B. Rosemeyer	Auto Union Type C	132.3 (82)

1906-1950

THE BIRTH OF THE "GRAND PRIX"

The last edition of the Gordon Bennett Trophy was held in 1905 and finished in French hands through "manifest superiority," to use an expression that some years later was to be used by great cyclists and manufacturers of military equipment. In fact, in spite of the commitment and tenacity of many enthusiasts throughout the industrialized world, the first ten to 15 years of motor racing history presented a genteel and polite audience with an image of French grandeur favored by the implicit cast-iron pact between the

24 top left This starting grid is for the 1930 Monaco Grand Prix in which the Bugattis dominated, taking the first six places.

24 bottom left The Monaco circuit designed by the President of the local Automobile Club, Anthony Noghès, was inaugurated in 1929. This image shows the winner of the first Monaco GP, Williams, at the wheel of Bugatti number 12.

Automobile Club and the constructors (hence the ostracism of events such as the Gordon Bennett Trophy, even though it was under Parisian control).

This situation was not, however, to last much longer. Sales of cars in the rest of Europe and the United States increased exponentially, generating considerable commercial and social activity. While Karl Benz was reluctant to give way to his son and the directors of the firm and allow his machines to participate in such frivolities, Daimler (or rather Mercedes, under which name the German firm had raced since 1902), Fiat, Rolls-Royce and Opel devoted scientific interest to the study of technology applied to the improvement of performance. They

did so, however, by modifying their aim. While the racing drivers were still mostly members of a privileged elite, greater professionalism was asked of them and cases of mechanics, testers and technicians elected to the rank of driver became increasingly common.

While racing cars were still powered by titanic engines (some with displacements of over 15 liters), chassis and body dimensions tended to be reduced and specific power outputs increased.

Thus opened a new era in which the art of daring was transformed into the science of progress, drivers became full-time professionals and the first racing teams were organized. This

epic period began in 1906 and ended in the years immediately following the Second World War, when the experience gained until that point was distilled to create the magical Formula 1 category and the enduring drivers' and constructors' World Championships. Considering the first half of the century as the greatest, most dramatic and most genuine is, we feel, perfectly legitimate.

A blend of professionalism and enthusiasm, of economic interests and passion, of risk and success surrounded all motor racing events of the era and the sport became an instrument of political propaganda, a technological laboratory, a gravitational center of the *beau monde*, an

advertising medium and a passion inaccessible to the majority. Accidents, deaths and more or less severe injuries were like the dressing on a salad—a necessary evil with which to spice up the newspaper reports emphasizing the heroic courage of the champions. Until it was the turn of the champions to die, of course, whereupon they took their rightful place in the upper echelons of Valhalla.

Numerous major events were born in this period, almost all of the classic races in fact: the Indianapolis 500, the Targa Florio, the Mille Miglia, Le Mans and most of the national Grands Prix. It would be impossible to discuss them all and it probably would not help in maintaining a global overview of the fragmentary world of motor racing, which it has to be said extends in myriad directions. In this chapter we will therefore direct our attention to the events classified as "Grands Prix": races on closed circuits run according to international regulations. Subsequent chapters will deal with other great races while the many minor events that have indubitably contributed

memorable pages to the history of men and motors will on this occasion have to be ignored.

Two technological markers indicating the approach of a new era were the introduction of the cardan shaft first used in racing by Renault and the new Michelin wheels, which were heavier but easier to change. The adoption of this revolutionary concept was to prove profitable for both Renault and Fiat. Above all, however, there was growing interest on the part of the public, the organizers and the manufacturers in the so-called "voiturettes", cars smaller than those used in the Grands Prix but which captured the imagination with their close-fought battles and continual overtaking. This was an extremely important sector in an era of economic depression as it brought ordinary cars within the realm of motor sport. This type of racing could be compared with the modern-day NASCAR or Touring Car championships. There was a general tendency, however, to reduce engine displacements.

The sporting event that marked the dawn of the new automotive age was, perhaps inevitably,

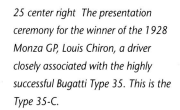

1906

the French GP held on the 26th of June, 1906, on a closed triangular circuit of 103 km (64 mi.) at Sarthe near Le Mans.

The organization of the event was entrusted to the local branch of the ACF, the Automobile Club de l'Ouest. The cardinal technical regulation was a weight limit of 1000 kg, with an additional 7 kg allowed for the magneto. Maximum fuel consumption was set at 30 liters per 100 km (62 mi.) and manufacturers were asked to direct the exhaust pipes upward so as not to asphyxiate competitors following behind and not to contribute to the cloud of dust raised by the cars' passage. The driver and mechanic were required to be aboard the car at all times. The event was run in two stages, each lasting a day; overnight the cars were locked in a compound patrolled by ACF officials, the first Grand Prix thus introducing the concept of the *parc fermé*. The entry list truly did great honor to the first Grand Prix. There were the usual French teams, Panhard, Renault and Darracq, joined by the powerful Mercedes and other formidable adversaries of the French cars such as the Fiats. Then there were the emerging Itala (which came to fame thanks to the exploits of Borghese, Barzini and Guizzardi in the mother of all rallies, the Peking-Paris), the Brasier, Clement-Bayard, De Dietrich, Gordon-Brillé, Gregoire and Hotchkiss.

After two days of furious racing the very first Grand Prix was won by a Hungarian, Ferenc Szisz, initially a mechanic and then a driver, with the Renault AK. He covered the 1,236 km (12 103-km laps [768 mi.; 12 64-mi. laps]) at an average speed of 101 kph (63 mph). Second was Felice Nazzaro while the fastest lap was recorded by Baras with a Brasier 105 hp. The French were forced to recognize, however, that an era was drawing to a close: Germany, Italy, the United States and Great Britain were now taking motor racing seriously.

26 top The Hungarian Szisz is at the wheel of the Renault AK with which he won the ACF GP in 1906.

26 center This document illustrates how the earliest GPs already featured organized teams in the pits.

27 bottom The episode portrayed in this painting was worthy of being recorded for posterity: the victory of the Renault AK in the first ACF Grand Prix, won by Ferenc Szisz. This event is generally accepted as the first international race organized under the Grand Prix formula.

26 bottom A photo showing the checking of the Michelin tires fitted to Szizs' Renault at the 1906 ACF GP.

27 top left The ACF GP of 1906: passing in front of the grandstand is George Heath, who finished sixth with a Panhard. Note the lavishly decorated stands.

27 top right This unusual car is the Hotchkiss with which Shepard completed just a few laps in the 1906 ACF Grand Prix.

27 center This photo shows the arrival of the winner of the 1906 ACF GP. The historic car carried the number 3A. In the foreground is the race steward; in the background the leader board, thanks to which reporters and spectators could easily follow the progress of the race. The board shows the number of competitors running, 17, of which at that moment Szisz, Clement and Nazzaro had completed the full number of laps.

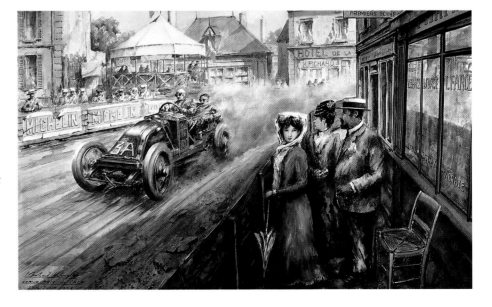

1907 1908

This was amply demonstrated in 1907, a magical year for Fiat. Felice Nazzaro, a driver who had been unlucky in the past and had suffered from mechanical problems, won the Targa Florio in Italy, the Kaiserprais in Germany and the Grand Prix de l'Automobile Club de France at Dieppe.

The second edition of the French GP was disputed over 10 laps of a 77-km (48-mi.) circuit. Although there had clearly been a generalized reduction in cylinder capacities, the crowd was able to admire the mastodontic Christie which had a total displacement approaching 20,000 cc. This time round the outcome of the event was decided by the regulation restricting fuel consumption to 30 liters per 100 km (62 mi.).

After the mid-way point victory was a private affair between Szisz and Nazzaro; the reigning champion attempted to conserve fuel but Nazzaro threw caution to the wind and leant on the accelerator, his daring eventually bearing fruit. It is not hard to imagine the disappointment of the

28 bottom left This photo shows the straight with the grandstands and pits at Dieppe which for the second year running was the venue of the ACF GP. The car in the foreground is a Fiat.

28 top right The 130 hp was one of the most successful racing Fiats. Thanks to drivers such as Nazzaro, Lancia and Cagno, Giovanni Agnelli's cars were, until the advent of the Mercedes, the French teams' greatest rivals.

28-29 In 1907 the Renault team had to defend the trophy won the previous year. Szisz is driving the car on the left, Richez, subsequently the victim of an accident, the one on the right. The Renaults were unable to match the Fiat 130 hp.

28 bottom right The Fiat driven by the winner of the 1907 ACF GP, Felice Nazzaro, recognizable by the race number F-2.

second-placed Hungarian who, when checking the contents of his fuel tank, realized that he too could have afforded to force the pace. Of course, in that era not only had telemetry and computerized instrumentation yet to be invented, but even the contemporary gravity feed gauges were unreliable. The year 1907 was also notable as that in which the first dedicated motor-racing track was inaugurated: The Brooklands circuit in England, which was laid out in the form of an irregular oval.

In 1908 the regulations were subjected to an apparently contradictory revolution. As mentioned earlier, there was increasing interest in voiturette racing, much to the satisfaction of manufacturers ever alert to the technological benefits for

production cars. The fact, however, that Grand Prix cars were restricted to a weight limit of 1000 kg had led to a stripping of the chassis rather than a reduction in the size of the cars. The ratio between the weight of the engine and the structure intended to support it was dangerously biased in favor of the former. Consequently, racing cars continued to be far removed from those produced in series. A controversial change was therefore made to the series' regulations. Rather than a maximum weight of 1000 kg, a minimum weight of 1100 kg was specified, and this in an era in which the maximum permitted weight for American races was 1200 kg! In order to reduce cylinder capacity and the size of engines, the regulations also specified that the

diameter of the pistons of four-cylinder engines should not exceed 155 mm (127 mm in the case of 6-cylinder units). These regulations were known as the Ostend Formula.

The ACF Grand Prix was again held at Dieppe. Forty-eight cars were entered, half of which were French. Once again, however, a foreigner won the race, Christian Lautenschlager with a Mercedes. At the time nobody could have imagined that the names on the podium prefigured the pact of steel that was to mark the history of the automobile: in second and third places were two Benzes (the sons of the great Karl had finally overcome the reluctance of their father, according to whom the car should serve solely as a means of transportation). It is curious to

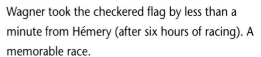

Wagner took the checkered flag by less than a minute from Hémery (after six hours of racing). A memorable race.

Henry Ford, a member of the ACA's technical commission, recognized that the technological gap between the Europeans and the North Americans could not be bridged by enthusiasm, inspiration or good will alone. There was an imperative need for great efforts to produce competitive cars, and in this respect the American industry received an unexpected boost from the European recession and the increasingly deep divide between the French manufacturers and the ACF. The boycott of the French GP by the national constructors led to the cancellation of the event. Renault's withdrawal from Grand Prix racing was to last until 1977.

This was a dark year for motor racing with no Grands Prix being held. However, a new blue ribbon

29 top Dieppe, 1907, the Fiat pits. The Italian firms were seeking revenge and Fiat entered Vincenzo Lancia, seen here pushing his car together with his mechanic Bordino, and Felice Nazzaro, both driving 130 hp's. It was the latter who won, overturning the result of the previous year when he finished second behind Szisz (second on this occasion).

note that the bookmakers were skeptical of the Mercedes' chances, quoting it at eight to one.

Testifying to the American predilection for dualism in the managing of sporting events that was also to be seen in basketball, football, boxing and baseball, 1908 was also marked by the first Grand Prix organized by the ACA (Automobile Club of America), the great rival to the AAA (American Automobile Association). Known as the American Grand Prize, the race was held near Savannah on a 40.5-km (25-mi.) circuit the drivers lapped 16 times. This was a major event and for perhaps the first time the teams participating represented the best of the automotive panorama in terms of avant-garde models and leading drivers. The honor of the United

States was upheld by Ralph de Palma, Bob Burman, Joe Seymour and Ralph Mulford among others, all contenders in the early Indianapolis races. The European contingent was equally impressive: Fiat could count on Nazzaro and Wagner, Benz on Hémery (despite the serious eye injury he had suffered at Dieppe) and Hanriot; and then there were the Italas of Cagno and Fournier, two drivers well acquainted with the victor's laurels.

It soon became clear that victory would be decided by a Western-style duel between Fiat and Benz. Despite de Palma's respectable showing the Americans were out of the picture, and the French were never in the hunt. Nazzaro was sidelined on the last lap by a blown tire and his teammate

29 bottom left Apart from the Grand Prix events, numerous other races were organized throughout Europe. In this case Berck is seen on the Taunus circuit competing for the 1907 Emperor's Cup.

29 bottom right A dramatic image from 1907: Richez crashed his Renault AK (race number R-3) exiting a fast curve. In the background is another car which also appears to be in difficulty: note the unnatural stance with respect to the middle of the curve and the generous opposite lock applied by the driver in an attempt to bring the rear wheels into line.

event did help to raise the sport's profile: in the United States "The Speedway" was born, the Indianapolis oval track nicknamed the Brickyard because after the inaugural races had pulverized the track surface, the group of entrepreneurs who owned it decided to repave the circuit with bricks (no fewer than 3,200,000 were used). This surface was retained until 1935 when asphalt was laid on all but one strip of the finishing straight, which remained paved in brick until 1961.

In a year of infrequent competition, the race against time and the birth of the Blitzen Benz, a steel monster bred to devour speed records and destined to become the benchmark for other models seeking similar glory, caught the imagination. The Blitzen boasted a total displacement of 21,500 cc divided among four cylinders of almost naval bore and stroke: 185 x 200 millimeters! This mammoth engine's 200 hp were transmitted through a two-speed gearbox.

The unbeatable Blitzen Benz was also sent across the ocean to break records and lay down challenges to the local champions like some medieval knight errant. Although it was an unofficial record, as it had been set in a single direction only rather than being the average speed of two opposing runs as required by the regulations, the maximum speed of 227.5 kph (141 mph) achieved by Bob Burman on the 23rd of April, 1911 is still impressive today. The record set in 1909 by the Benz works driver Hémery of 202.7 kph (126 mph), on the other hand, was officially recognized.

Fiat responded to the challenge with another monster, the S.76 300-hp Record. The total displacement was still greater than that of the Benz at 28,338 cc, with four cylinders and bore and stroke dimensions of 190 x 250 mm. Despite the car's name the maximum power output was "just" 290 hp. With the S.76, Fiat broke the Blitzen Benz's record in 1913 by reaching 213 kph (132 mph), but in this case too the speed had been achieved in a single direction only.

31 top left The cars competing in the ACF GP of 1908 lining up for the start.

31 top right This photo immortalizing the American driver David Bruce-Brown was in all probability taken at the American Grand Prize of 1911, won by Bruce-Brown with a Fiat S.74.

31 center Two drivers tackling the road bridge at Dieppe. The cars feature an innovation introduced by

the driver on the right, George Sizaire, who together with Louis Nardin developed independent front suspension, clearly visible in front of the radiator. Although this feature improved road-holding, it was ignored by most other constructors until the mid-1930s.

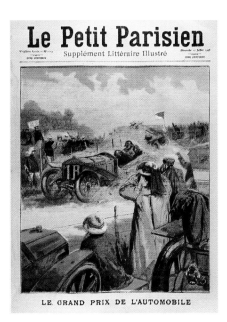

LE GRAND PRIX DE L'AUTOMOBILE

30 top Louis Wagner at the wheel of a Fiat on the occasion of the first race held in Russia: the St. Petersburg-Moscow of 1908. That year the great driver won the first GP not organized by the ACF, the American Grand Prize held at Savannah. The Russian race was instead won by Hémery at the wheel of a Benz.

30-31 This photo portrays the Mercedes team at the Dieppe GP of 1908 which saw the rise to stardom of Christian Lautenschlager.

30 bottom left This photo shows the classic pit-stop operations. The event was the Dieppe GP of 1908, the car a Benz. The driver is tightening the leather strap securing the spare tires while a mechanic is arriving with fuel. Note the trench behind which the other members of the team stood.

30 bottom, right Fritz Erte aboard a Benz won the Prinz-Heinrich-Fahrt held at Vienna in 1908.

31 bottom left Two cars tackling the fast curve of the Dieppe circuit used for the ACF GP in 1907, 1908 and 1912. The circuit was around 77 km (48 mi.) long and on the first two occasions (the photo is from 1908) was lapped 10 times, on the third 20.

31 bottom right This cover of Le Petit Parisien illustrates a spectacular episode from the third French GP, held at Dieppe in 1908.

EUROPE AND THE
UNITED STATES SEPARATE

1910
1911
1912

The ACF Grand Prix failed to take place in both 1910 and 1911, with only the American Grand Prize surviving in this period, given that the Vanderbilt Cup had abandoned the GP regulations in favor of the Indianapolis formula. This last event can be seen as the first crack that led to an increasingly deep chasm between Europe and North America.

As far as Grands Prix were concerned, the changes in the regulations were profound. Crisis or no crisis, the continual variations, especially those of a conceptual nature, could only harm the world of motor racing. But this situation was to be a constant and controversial feature of the regular Formula 1 World Championship from the 1950s onward. Modifications to the regulations were and still are the sporting authorities' most potent means of bringing pressure to bear on constructors. Had the regulations been left unchanged for a few years, the motor sport circuses on either side of the Atlantic would be much closer today.

Turning back to the racing, in 1910 the only competition that could be included in the list of the Grands Prix was the second edition of the American

33 top left Georges Boillot triumphed at Dieppe with a Peugeot L.76 in spite of breaking a universal joint on the penultimate lap. A French car and driver had not won the national Grand Prix since 1906.

33 top right The Peugeot racing team photographed at Amiens for the 1913 GP. Aboard the EX-5 is the driver of the moment, Georges Boillot, a member of the Charlatans team along with Goux and Zuccarelli. The Charlatans' project for the development of Peugeot racing cars was preferred to that of Bugatti.

33 center David Bruce-Brown, driver of the works Fiat S.74, wearing a face-mask during the 1912 edition of the Grand Prix de l'Automobile Club de France, the most important French race.

33 bottom right The S.74 seen here was also raced in America. In 1912 the Fiat team included Teddy Tetzlaff portrayed here, but the American Grand Prize was won by his teammate Caleb Bragg. Tetzlaff instead conquered an excellent second place at Indianapolis.

Grand Prize won by a Benz. The following year this race was organized by the Motor Club Holdings Company founded by the two rival automotive bodies, the AAA and the ACA. It was won by a Fiat S.74, the car that formed the basis of the above-mentioned S.76. The winning driver was the same as the previous year; David Bruce-Brown finished ahead of a Benz and a Mercedes, the Americans still unable to bring one of their own cars home first.

The ACF Grand Prix made its long-awaited return in 1912 to its natural home of Dieppe. It cannot be excluded that the renewed interest in racing was due to the hyperactivity of Robert Peugeot, who had created two rival teams working on the preparation of racing cars. One of these was led by a young Italian engineer who had emigrated to France, Ettore Bugatti. However, the prize went to the team of "Charlatans" composed of Boillot, driver and engineer; Goux, an amateur driver; and Zuccarelli, a driver and engineer formerly with Hispano-Suiza. The Charlatans' car achieved a speed of 183 kph (114 mph) against the 159.3 kph (99 mph) of Bugatti, racing head-to-head

The revived GP was held over 1,535 km (953 mi.) and was divided into two stages. Both the traditional GP monsters and the road-car derived voiturettes competed. This suited Peugeot and thus the French who kept faith with the larger cars, but only just: Georges Boillot won with a Peugeot L.76 that crossed the finishing line with only second and fourth gears remaining. The only restriction imposed by regulation was a maximum width of 175 cm.

That year the American Grand Prize changed venue: the Automobile Club of Savannah withdrew after being criticized for using forced labour and a proportional number of prison guards to prepare the circuit. The event was moved, like the Vanderbilt Cup, to the Wauwatosa circuit at Milwaukee.

The race was won by Bragg with a Fiat S.74, one of the most difficult combinations to beat in that period. The car was powered by a 14,137 cc engine developing 190 hp for a maximum speed of 165 kph (102 mph). During practice for the race the same type of car was being driven by the most popular American hero, David Bruce-Brown, when a blown tire cost him his life. Better luck was enjoyed by Vanderbilt Cup winner de Palma who in an

attempt to pass the leader left the road but got away with a broken leg.

In a curious alternation of fortunes, between 1908 and 1912 GP-style races were perpetuated by the American Grand Prize and, to a certain extent, the Vanderbilt Cup. In 1913, however, the two most important North American events collapsed under the weight of their organizational costs and the ball returned to the French court with the revived ACF GP and the French Grand Prix at Le Mans. Before proceeding with the narration of the events of those years, one point should be clarified. The Grand Prix Automobile Club de France—the oldest GP race—was the one that was eventually to give origin to the modern Formula 1 Grand Prix. It retained its original name until 1967, when it was simplified to Grand Prix de France. Under this name, events of lesser standing had been organized in competition with that of the ACF in 1911 (won by Hémery with a Fiat), 1912 (Zuccarelli, Peugeot) and 1913 (Bablot, Delage) and subsequently in 1934 and 1935.

Once again the regulations of the ACF Grand Prix were revised with the reintroduction of the 1,100 kg (2426 lb.) maximum weight, while the minimum weight was lowered to 800 kg (1,764 lb.). The fuel consumption limit was reduced: from 30 to 20 l/100 km (8 to 5 gal./62 mi.).

Lighter cars and less bulky engines equaled vehicles conceptually closer to production models. In the meantime, however, Grand Prix cars had become sleeker and more aerodynamic to the point where only roadsters (topless two-seaters with possibly a dickey seat) bore any resemblance to the

34 top This photo taken at Indianapolis shows a race held in 1910. Many American automotive events were held in conjunction with three national holidays; Memorial Day, Independence Day and Labor Day.

34 bottom The start of the Indianapolis 500 in 1912. The oval circuit was inaugurated in 1910 and from the following year the 500-mile race was held annually.

two-seater racing cars.

The cream of contemporary models was present at the GP held at Amiens: Peugeot, Delage, Opel, Sunbeam and Itala, but Fiat and Mercedes were notable for their absence. The "Charlatans" Peugeot team took a stranglehold on the race with Boillot first and Goux second. Tragically the third member Zuccarelli was killed during practice.

The Peugeot EX-5 designed by one of the most acute mechanical minds of the era, Ernest Henry, already featured twin overhead camshafts.

As far as the Grand Prix de France was concerned, it was run as an open event (thus not classifiable as a true "Formula" race), and was dominated by a pair of Delages driven by Ballot and Guyot.

In 1914 of the two traditional Grands Prix the first to be held was the American event, two days after the Vanderbilt Cup on the same very fast but demanding Santa Monica circuit. After a thrilling race the 250,000 spectators' dreams of local glory were finally answered as a trio of North American drivers stepped up to the podium with an American car, Pullen's Mercer, winning ahead of Balls with a Marmon and Taylor with an Alco.

The sport reached new heights of intensity with events such as the Targa Florio, the Vanderbilt Cup

and the Indianapolis 500 being ringed in red on the enthusiasts' calendars. The knives were sharpened for the French GP held on a circuit near Lyons. The single, albeit significant, regulation was a maximum cylinder capacity of 4.5 l.

Peugeot's success was hard for its rivals to accept, especially the Germans (it should not be forgotten that the outbreak of the First World War was imminent with the armies in a state of alert), who for some time had been going through a barren patch. The three Opels entered were joined by a squadron of five competitive Mercedes, fruits of the genius of Paul Daimler.

The race lived up to the straightforward France versus Germany script. Fiat, Nazzaro, Schneider, Delage and Alda became peripheral figures, bit-players, a silent chorus. The duel soon took on nationalistic metaphors until Boillot and Goux with their new Peugeots were eventually obliged to surrender to the overbearing might of the Daimler jewels. First was Christian Lautenschlager, winner of the 1908 edition, second Wagner, the winner of the American Grand Prize again in 1908, third Salzer. The German whitewash was ensured just 22 km (14 mi.) from the finish when a broken valve sidelined Boillot.

Following this spectacular triumph the curtain fell

on Grand Prix racing in Europe as it was replaced by a far crueler, more violent, divisive and destructive form of national rivalry.

In one way or another, however, the best European cars survived, after having suffered in that grueling, incomparable sporting episode, the ACF Grand Prix. Some were simply acquired, as in the case of the Peugeot EX-5 which the Anglo-Italian driver Dario Resta took to America and with which he subdued his rivals, and also the 1914 Grand Prix Mercedes—the car driven by Lautenschlager—which Ralph de Palma took to the States and drove to victory at Indianapolis in 1915. Others were acquired and cloned, like the two Peugeot EX-5s that the patron of the Indianapolis 500, Miles Carl Fisher, purchased and shipped to America. The cars were consigned to the Premier Motor Company with orders for three identical copies to be constructed (in reality the "clones" provided inferior performance). Some were even officially transferred, as in the case of the Peugeot L.45.

It was actually a Peugeot, the rejuvenated and big-hearted EX-5 famous for having introduced the twin-overhead cam engine, that won the 1915 edition of the American Grand Prize held at San Francisco on

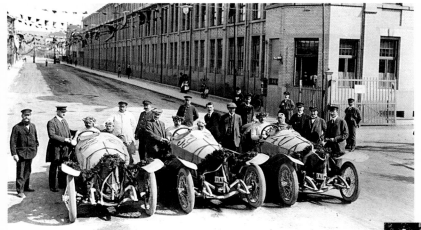

35 bottom left The Mercedes pits at the ACF GP of 1914. This race was a true Mercedes triumph: first Christian Lautenschlager, second Louis Wagner (in the picture), third Otto Salzer. Goux's Peugeot finished fourth, over four minutes behind the third-placed Mercedes.

35 bottom right Accidents of this kind were very frequent at Indianapolis. Cars exited one of the two curves leading into the main straights too quickly and the rear wheels tended to swing out as the car lost grip and drifted toward the outside of the track.

35 top A photo from 1914 recording the winners at Lyons: on the left Lautenschlager, like his teammates wearing a laurel wreath; in the center Salzer; and right, Wagner. The photo was taken at Untertürkheim, to which the drivers returned as they had departed– aboard the same cars they used in the race.

35 center Lautenschlager aboard a Mercedes GP flying toward victory in the ACF GP of 1914, held at Lyons for the first time. The 1914 Mercedes GP cars were mechanical jewels. Each cylinder was equipped with three valves, the total displacement was 4.5 litres and the engine produced 105 hp.

the occasion of the Panama-Pacific Exposition.

The following year the event returned to Santa Monica and the last two editions of the Grand Prize and the two Vanderbilt Cup races can be considered together as all four events were Peugeot victories, three obtained by the young Italian-born, English-raised driver Dario Resta. This was undisputed domination, and de Palma had to "settle" for victory in the Indianapolis 500 in 1915, an event won by Resta in 1916.

Returning for a moment to de Palma and his Mercedes; a second example of this racing masterpiece actually existed in the hands of Theodore Pilette and was to become ever more important than the Italo-American's machine. The car was acquired by Bentley and taken to England, where it was dismantled and its engine was "dissected" in the Rolls-Royce workshops. W.O. Bentley himself admitted at the end of the war that every British aviation engine used during the conflict was derived from that admirable technological concentrate. Any further comment is superfluous.

With European energies exhausted, in the U.S. the Grands Prix died unmourned. The public demonstrated a clear preference for races on the fast and compact Indianapolis-style ovals that were equipped with comfortable grandstands at all points, offering views of the whole track. Organizers were quite happy to satisfy this demand. The speedways allowed them to fill the stands with a paying public, offer accessory sevices, refreshments, secondary races and other entertainment and, lastly, immediate aid rather than the delayed rescue services that were the norm on the long European-style circuits. We have to wait until 1921 before the Grand Prix cars emerged once again in Europe. In America, the Indianapolis "wall" was not to be breached until 1959, when the U.S. Grand Prix at Sebring was included in the Formula 1 calendar.

HONOR ROLL

Grand Prix from 1906 to 1916

Year	Grand Prix	Venue	Driver	Car	Av. Speed kph (mph)
1906	ACF	Le Mans	F. Szisz	Renault AK	101 (63)
1907	ACF	Dieppe	F. Nazzaro	Fiat	113 (70)
1908	ACF	Dieppe	C. Lautenschlager	Mercedes	111 (69)
1908	American Grand Prize	Savannah	L. Wagner	Fiat	104.8 (65)
1910	American Grand Prize	Savannah	D. Bruce-Brown	Benz	113.6 (71)
1911	American Grand Prize	Savannah	D. Bruce-Brown	Fiat S.74	119.8 74)
1912	ACF	Dieppe	G. Boillot	Peugeot S.76	110.2 (68.4)
1912	American Grand Prize	Milwaukee	C. Bragg	Fiat S.74	110 (68.3)
1913	ACF	Amiens	G. Boillott	Peugeot EX-5	116.1 (72)
1914	American Grand Prize	S. Monica	E. Pullen	Mercer	124.4 (77)
1914	ACF	Lyon	C. Lautenschlager	Mercedes	105.4 (65)
1915	American Grand Prize	S. Francisco	D. Resta	Peugeot EX-5	90.1 (56)
1916	American Grand Prize	S. Monica	H. Wilcox-S. Aitken	Peugeot EX-5	137.9 (86)

1921
1922

36 top left A great small Fiat, the 501 SS Spider. Thanks to its lively 1.5-litre twin-cam engine this became the car to beat in its category in the early Twenties.

36 top right Pietro Bordino at the wheel of a Fiat 801. A former mechanic for Lancia, Nazzaro and de Palma, he was promoted to number one driver for the first edition of the Italian GP. Bordino kept the old fox Goux, aboard a Ballot rather than a Peugeot, at bay until his oil pump broke.

36 center left The cars line up for the start of the Le Mans GP for voiturettes in 1920.

36 center right A photo showing the refuelling of the Bugattis racing in the Le Mans voiturette event in 1920.

FIAT AND ALFA ROMEO TAKE CENTER STAGE

From an automotive point of view, too, the First World War left Europe as a whole licking its wounds: while prior to the outbreak of the war the domination of the European models had never been in doubt despite the best efforts of enthusiasts such as Vanderbilt, in the early 1920s the most dynamic force was the American industry. In fact, the first post-war Grand Prix, once again held on French soil, was won by the American Jimmy Murphy at the wheel of a Duesenberg (the first important racing car equipped with four-wheel hydraulic brakes), with de Palma second. The first European, Jules Goux, was third.

As Grand Prix racing got under way once more, so did the manipulation of the regulations. The maximum cylinder capacity was reduced to three liters and a maximum weight limit of 800 kg (1,764 lb.)was reintroduced.

Nineteen twenty-one saw the birth of another important event, the Italian Grand Prix, held that year at Montichiari near Brescia over 30 laps of a 17.2-km (11 mi.) circuit. In contrast with subsequent results in the era the first edition was won by a pair of French cars, the Ballots of Goux and Chassagne. This was, however, Ballot's

swansong as the firm withdrew from racing to concentrate on the production of touring cars. In third place was Louis Wagner, virtually a "home" driver given that he was traditionally associated with Fiat. He subsequently moved to Alfa Romeo, joining a team featuring natural leaders such as Ferrari, engineering brains such as Merosi, Jano and Bazzi and aces of the caliber of Ascari, Brilli-Peri and Campari. These are but a few of the fabulous talents who congregated around the four-leafed clover, the sporting symbol of the Milanese model that in 1926 passed under state control. We should not, however, deprive Fiat of two years of glory as it was thanks to the Turin firm that the European revival began.

The two-year period 1922-23 was marked by a number of firsts: in 1922 a number of major circuits were opened and the following year saw the introduction of notable technological innovations.

The Avus (an acronym for Automobil Verkehrs Und Übungstrasse) circuit was inaugurated in 1922,

with two long straights crossing Berlin linked by a very tight corner at one end (Südkurve) and a wider looping curve (Nordkurve) at the other.

Nineteen twenty-two also saw the debut of one of the most celebrated circuits in history, Monza. Built at the behest of the Automobile Club di Milano, which acquired a 30-year lease on part of a Royal Park recently donated to the Italian state, the track was prepared in less than four months and originally named Circuito di Milano.

Still on the subject of circuits, there was an important innovation with regards to the starting procedure at the ACF Grand Prix. For the first time the cars all started together. (The regulation that assigned pole position to the driver qualifying with the fastest time had yet to be approved, however.) New races were added to the calendar while another was erased: the Tourist Trophy abandoned the Isle of Man and disappeared for six years before reappearing in 1928 as an event for sports cars.

36 bottom Ettore Bugatti posing alongside E. Friederich in the pits on the occasion of the voiturette GP organized at Le Mans in 1920 and won by Friederich.

37 top The early Twenties were marked by the debut of Nuvolari, seen here with a helmet. He came to cars from a successful career racing motorcycles. His first car was an Ansaldo but he subsequently signed a contract with Alfa Romeo.

37 center The start line of the 1921 ACF GP. After an absence of eight years the most important continental GP promised the French crowd at Le Mans a French

victory: the Ballots were thought to be too good and everyone was expecting the winner's laurels to be presented to Goux and the American de Palma, also at the wheel of a Ballot. Instead, Murphy with the Duesenberg put the local cars in their place and Goux was only third.

37 bottom left The ACF GP of 1921: Murphy with the Duesenberg attacking de Palma aboard the Ballot. The former won the race with a broken radiator, two flat tires and a broken rib. Nonetheless, the crowd received him coldly, as this was the first time an important European race had been won by an American.

37 bottom center Jimmy Murphy's (right) victory in the ACF GP was widely publicized in the United States, but the functional American cars, fitted with hydraulic brakes for the first time, impressed European engineers and spectators, too.

37 bottom right The start of the 1921 ACF GP. On the line are two of the protagonists, Henry Segrave aboard the Anglo-French Sunbeam-Talbot-Darracq

(STD) with race number 10 alongside Murphy in the Duesenberg. A coincidence linked the two: Segrave, like the other Sunbeam drivers, was only able to race by financing himself because the firm lacked the necessary capital. Similarly, the four Duesenbergs were only entered at the last minute when sparkplug manufacturer Albert Champion, of French origins himself, provided the funds for the trip.

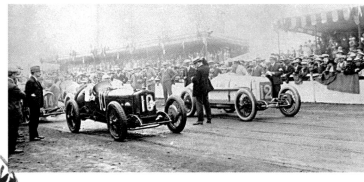

In 1923 the innovations concerned engine and suspension design. The Benz Tropfenwagens made their debuts and although they mustered only feeble resistance to the extremely powerful Fiats, they were highly influential nonetheless, thanks to the set-back location of their engines, their streamlined shape and their independent suspension. In this year, too, a Grand Prix was won for the first time by a supercharged car, a Fiat 805-405. Lastly, there was a widespread application of the aerodynamic principles of streamlining: Benz with droplet shapes, Fiat preferring the torpedo and Bugatti the all-enveloping "tank." The latter anticipated the concept of the "barchetta," a body style much in vogue for sports cars in the years to come. The merit for this development is largely due to Voisin, an aeronautical manufacturer that presented a pioneering car designed to create very little drag.

Fiat dominated on the tracks, taking two Grands Prix in 1922, the ACF and the Italian, with respectively the by now veteran Felice Nazzaro (his nephew died in the same race) and Bordino, who thus reached the peak of his career. In that year with the new two-liter

38 top left The Tropfenwagen Benz of 1923, of which the rolling chassis is seen here, was one of the strangest racing cars. This shot reveals the numerous perforations lightening the structure. The engine-gearbox assembly was located behind the driver's seat, together with the rear axle. The six-cylinder Benz developed around 90 hp.

38 top right Other unusual features of the Tropfenwagen that took part in the

Grand Prix of Europe held at Monza in 1923: the fan-shaped radiator behind the driver's seat allowed two, albeit very cramped, people to be carried.

38 center Among the many innovations of 1923 were the covered-wheel Bugatti "Tank" Type 32s seen here in the pits during the ACF GP of that year. Ernst Friederich (left) obtained the team's best placing: third with a T32.

1923

formula and a minimum weight of 650 kg (1,433 lb.), only the Bugattis managed to put up any real opposition.

In 1923 of the three Grands Prix disputed, two were claimed by Sunbeam and one by the supercharged Fiat 805. In reality the English cars were straight copies of the eight-cylinder Fiats, the designs of which were taken across the channel by the engineer Bertarone (shortly to move to Talbot). At Tours the ever itinerant ACF Grand Prix was won for the first time by an Englishman, Segrave. The Italian Grand Prix at Monza was instead won by Salamano with a Fiat. That race was significant as it marked the debut of the Mercedes designed not by Paul Daimler, who had in the meantime moved to Horch (the present-day Audi), but by Ferdinand Porsche, who

had arrived from Austro-Daimler bringing with him Alfred Neubauer, an average driver but a superb tactician. The season closed at Sitges with the first Spanish GP, won by Divo again at the wheel of a Sunbeam. The circuit proved to be so poorly constructed (the banked curves had an incorrect radius) that it was soon abandoned.

As a reflection of contemporary technological developments, engineers and mechanics were at the center of attention. Following the defection of Bertarone, Fiat was rocked by a second departure, that of Vittorio Jano, the designer of the 805. The great man who went on to create all kinds of mechanical jewels up to 1954 was unable to resist the persuasive eloquence of Enzo Ferrari who at all

38 bottom right Enzo Ferrari, prior to becoming team manager, director and eventually constructor, was a reasonable driver. This photo shows him aboard an Alfa Romeo following a victory on the Savio circuit in Emilia Romagna, the region of his birth.

costs wanted him with Bazzi at Alfa Romeo.

The team assembled by the legendary Enzo worked on a great car commissioned by Nicola Romeo and designed by Merosi, the P1—the only car truly capable of challenging the Fiats.

However, a dramatic event meant that Alfa's efforts were in vain. The driver Ugo Sivocci was killed during practice at Monza. Motor sport owes more to this figure than might be imagined, as it was in fact he who had persuaded Enzo Ferrari to devote himself to mechanical engineering and brought him to CMN (Costruzioni Meccaniche Nazionali). As a mark of respect the Alfa team withdrew from competition that year while Jano worked on the P2, soon to become the scourge of rival teams.

As for mechanics, Perkins, who rode alongside Guinness, was knocked out by a stone as he leaned out of the car to hold together the clutch with a belt, while Ferretti, Salamano's companion, reached the finish exhausted after being sent by his driver on a long run in search of a can of gas which he had to carry back himself by bicycle (to no avail, as the car refused to restart). At Monza Bodin's mechanic had to change gears in place of the driver, who had injured his arm in the previous Grand Prix.

The great adventure of the Le Mans 24 Hours also began in 1923, while the two-liter formula was adopted at Indianapolis.

38-39 The Fiat of Salamano refuelling during the European GP at Monza, which he won in 1923.

39 top right The cover of L'Illustrazione del Popolo *shows the welcome given to the three Fiat drivers following their success in the Italian GP held for the second time at Monza in 1923. No. 14 was driven by the winner Salamano, while the great Felice Nazzaro finished second. His former mechanic Pietro Bordino, now a fine driver, had to retire with a broken arm.*

39 center right The Fiat 805 that won the 1923 Italian GP. This supercharged model was derived from the 804 that the previous year had won in both France and Italy.

39 bottom right The Voiturette Grand Prix was organized at Brescia in 1923 in the wake of the successful events held at Le Mans. It was won by a past master, Alessandro Cagno—now 40 years of age—aboard a Fiat 803.

Thus we arrive at 1924; a year that promised to be exciting thanks to the eagerly awaited clash between Jano's Alfa Romeos and Porsche's Mercedes. The two teams came head-to-head at the Targa Florio (an event which the Alfa Romeo RL won in 1923). The German team won with Werner, while Ascari's Alfa was halted a few hundred meters from the finish with a broken engine. The driver and mechanic pushed the car home to take third place.

It was different at the Grands Prix. Of three races the P2s won two. The Italian GP was an epic: four Alfas in the first four places, driven respectively by Ascari, Wagner, Campari and Minoia.

After trailing the Alfas throughout, Mercedes withdrew following Zborowski's fatal accident. It was a tragic season elsewhere, too, with the deaths of

40 top This photo shows the formidable Alfa Romeo team at the French GP in 1924. The first car on the left is that of the winner Campari who got the better of two dangerous rivals driving 12-cylinder Delages, Albert Divo and Robert Benoist.

40 center Friederich's Bugatti tackling the corner of death during the ACF GP of 1924 held at Lyons. Together with the Alfa P2 and the Delage 2LCV, the Bugatti T35 was one of the leading cars of the era. This is testified by the trio of World Championships won by Alfa (1925), Bugatti (1926) and Delage (1927).

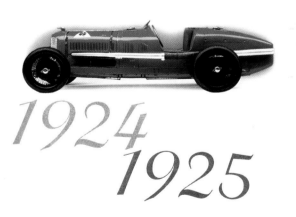

1924
1925

40 bottom left The Alfa Romeo P2, a Grand Prix thoroughbred, was one of the greatest cars produced by this Italian company, whose racing team was managed by Enzo Ferrari. Alfa won the first World Championship with this machine in 1925. The leading drivers were Ascari, Brilli-Peri and Campari.

40 bottom right The grandstand straight on the occasion of the Grand Prix of Europe (France) in 1924: Segrave is leading with the Sunbeam, one of the only pairings to put up serious opposition to the great Alfa Romeo team. On this occasion he finished fifth, but was to win the San Sebastian GP in Spain.

41 top left The cover of the Illustrazione del Popolo celebrating Giuseppe Campari's success in the 1924 ACF GP of Lyons aboard the Alfa Romeo P2. On that occasion the race was also the GP of Europe.

41 center This photo shows a driver, a mechanic and a team following a victory but gives no idea of the magnitude of Alfa's triumph that day. On the 19th of October, 1924, the team carrying the green cloverleaf monopolized the first four places with, in order, Antonio Ascari (in the photograph), Louis Wagner, Giuseppe Campari and Ferdinando Minoia.

Resta at Brooklands and Murphy at Syracuse. The high-speed circus thus lost three major players.

The results would suggest that there was little room for other teams. The Fiat team had been stripped of an exceptional generation of engineers and drivers and the French were struggling to regain their winning touch. The embers were still glowing, however, and Delage unveiled a V12 that was to score numerous victories, while Bugatti launched the car that was to go on to become one of the most successful Grand Prix cars and sports-racers of all time, the svelte Type 35.

Coincidences are part and parcel of the rhythm of history and in 1924 both Ferdinand Porsche and Enzo Ferrari received official recognition—an honorary degree from the University of Stuttgart and a nomination as *Commendatore* from Mussolini.

The Constructors' World Championship was organized for the first time in 1925 and held for four years (the 1928 edition was so muddled that an official winner was never declared). Quite rightly many critics disputed the legitimacy of such a title as a mark of global superiority, not so much because the winning drivers and models were undeserving, but because the regulations were ignored or at least manipulated due to their partiality and abstruseness.

The doubts were born out of the fact that the organizer was not an international association (such as the AIACR, the Association Internationale des Automobiles Clubs Reconnus), but a national body, the Automobile Club d'Italia (for this reason participation in the Italian GP was obligatory).

Frankly, we have no wish to associate Fascist Italy's desire to celebrate its national heroes with Alfa Romeo's eventual victory, as the model could count

on exceptional drivers, cunning strategies and a fabulous, unbeatable car in the P2. It was instead clear that sooner or later someone would decide to reward the season's most consistent drivers and most reliable cars. The idea was born in France and came from the editors of *L'Auto*, but it was a grave error to introduce regulations that were complicated and open to manipulation (or worse, the *suspicion* of manipulation).

It is worth stressing once again just how much damage muddled, complicated and all too frequently altered regulations have caused to motor sport. What should one make of a formula that rather than being based on the accumulation of points conferred the lowest number of points to the winner and the highest to the last placed competitor? In those early constructors' championships this was just what happened with the winner scoring one point, second place two, third three and fourth four. The eventual world champion was the manufacturer with the least number of points at the end of the season.

The exclusion of the German models from the 1925 edition due to disagreements with the international association deprived the first

41 bottom The photo above shows the Bugatti team from the French GP of 1924. The photo below portrays Ettore Bugatti, aboard a T35 together with his son Jean.

41 right A Shell poster from 1924. Producers of fuel, lubricants and tires were quick to take advantage of the use of their products in racing.

championship of leading contenders. The races that counted toward the title were the Indianapolis 500 and the Belgian (the first edition, held at Spa), ACF (Montlhéry) and Italian (Monza) Grands Prix. The final table saw Alfa Romeo triumphant with 13 points, followed by Duesenberg with 17 and Bugatti with 19. Alfa Romeo celebrated the victory by adding a laurel wreath to the radiator badge attached to all its cars.

In reality there were four GPs held in 1925, two won by Alfa Romeo and two by its worthy rival Delage. Alfa triumphed in Belgium and Italy with Ascari and Brilli-Peri respectively (the great Antonio Ascari tragically being killed in France between the two events), Delage taking the ACF with Robert Benoist and Alberto Divo and the Spanish GP with Divo and André Morel. Nevertheless, the strong

Delage team did not appear in the championship table because it did not enter the Italian GP.

Why the Spanish event was the only GP excluded from those valid for the championship is not known, although it may be presumed that it was the organizing body, the Automobile Club d'Italia, that snubbed the Catalan race.

The season's dominant cars were the P2 and the 2LCV with their every success being overwhelming and undisputed as each win was accompanied by, at least, a second place for the team. These two great cars had very different characters: the Delage boasted an extremely potent engine equipped with a Roots-type supercharger that developed 180 hp at 7000 rpm but its chassis was equal to such outputs. The P2 on the other hand developed a maximum power output of "just" 155 hp but was better balanced and

more driveable. The French engine was a 12-cylinder unit, the only one of its kind at the time, while the Italian car had a straight-Eight and was capable of a higher maximum speed, thanks in part to its lower weight: 750 (1654 lb.) vs. 1066 kg (2350 lb.).

The first Grand Prix of the year was held in Belgium at Spa. The only entrants were four Delages and three Alfa Romeos, with the former being wildly applauded while the later were ignored. When for various reasons the four Delages were forced to retire, Vittorio took revenge for the crowd's hostility by laying on a veritable banquet in the pits and calling in his drivers. During the unexpected lunch break the mechanics polished the cars, ignoring the spectators' catcalls and whistles. The drivers then calmly returned to the track and proceeded on their way to inevitable triumph.

42 top left A photograph of the inside of the Alfa pits at the Montlhéry circuit, the venue of the ACF GP for the first time in 1925. The smiling faces show that Ascari's tragic accident has not yet occurred.

42 bottom left This photograph with its strange excellent dynamism portrays a great champion racing toward his death: Antonio Ascari aboard an Alfa Romeo P2 at the ACF GP of 1925.

42 top right The straight in front of the grandstand at Monza. The 1925 race was won by Gastone Brilli-Peri from Giuseppe Campari paired with Giovanni Minozzi. The reserve driver was one Tazio Nuvolari, unable to race due to injury.

42 bottom right This image dramatically synthesizes the ACF GP of 1925: Ascari's Alfa No. 8 lies overturned as the dying driver is carried away.

42-43 This striking image succeeds in evoking the climate of competition. This is the Belgian GP of 1925 and the leading car is the eight-cylinder P2 driven by Ascari. He is followed by Campari in an identical car snapping at his heels. Behind them, with numbers 9 and 5 are probably two Delages, while Gastone Brilli-Peri is driving the third Alfa, No. 10. Only Ascari and Campari reached the finish.

In France the Grand Prix was held for the first time on the closed circuit at Montlhéry. The Delage victory was due to the withdrawal of the Alfa Romeo team following Ascari's fatal accident while he was in the lead. Involved in a furious battle with Alfa's second ace Giuseppe Campari, Ascari touched the track-side fence causing his car to roll a number of times. During his lap of honor Benoist, the first French Grand Prix winner for 12 years, laid a bouquet of flowers at the spot where Ascari crashed.

Alfa's absence meant that Delage had no opposition in Spain. Bugatti and Sunbeam were never competitive in these Grands Prix (although Bugatti did have the consolation of a Targa Florio victory), while Duesenberg's fine end-of-season placing was due to its home victory in the Indianapolis 500.

1925 1926

43 top left The Bugatti T39A Sport, developed from the GP Type 35, almost wiped the board in 1926. Bugatti won four GPs out of six, more than sufficient to take the World Championship. Note the all-metal artillery-style wheels.

43 top right This 1925 photo portrays two motor racing heavyweights: Giuseppe Campari alongside his team manager Enzo Ferrari.

43 right center Ascari acclaimed after his last victory at Spa-Francorchamps in the 1925 Belgian GP.

43 bottom right Rudolf Caracciola, one of the sport's leading figures, celebrates victory in the German GP of 1926. Then 25 years old, he had been racing since 1922. He engaged in incomparable duels with all the greats of his time, from Nuvolari to Rosemeyer.

New Formula against Germans and French

The two previous seasons had been rich in sporting events but a heavy price had been paid. In 1926 the international association of automobile clubs (AIACR) decided to further reduce the total displacement of Grand Prix engines to one and a half liters. The result was that the engineers and mechanics nonetheless managed to extract extremely high performance, achieving the remarkably high specific power output of 100 hp per liter, while the models with limited resources were eliminated by the need to redesign their engines. Take the sole 12-cylinder unit to be raced in a Grand Prix car the previous season mounted in a Delage: a decrease in total displacement of 25% could not be taken into consideration for such engine architecture and Delage had to work on the 15S8 project that was competitive but fraught with serious problems. The exhaust pipes running through the cockpit were responsible for

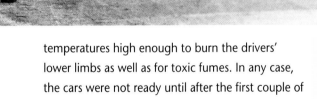

temperatures high enough to burn the drivers' lower limbs as well as for toxic fumes. In any case, the cars were not ready until after the first couple of Grands Prix.

It was Bugatti who took advantage of the situation, winning all the scheduled Grands Prix with the exception of those in Germany (Mercedes) and England (Delage), while Alfa Romeo and Sunbeam joined Fiat among the ranks of great models to have abandoned Grand Prix racing, thus seriously undermining the sport. Further innovations in 1926 included the single-seater cockpit and a minimum weight limit of 600 kg (1,323 lb.).

The first race of the season, the celebrated ACF Grand Prix, was rendered meaningless by the defection of Delage and Talbot as well as the models already mentioned. As a consequence the entire grid was composed of Bugattis.

However, in Germany a more flexible interpretation of the regulations allowed two-liter cars to participate and 46 teams entered. The race was won by a promising, likeable and daring youngster, Rudolf Caracciola, at the wheel of a privately-entered eight-cylinder Mercedes producing 150 hp and dating from 1924. Another private

44 left This photo shows the crowded start of the second edition of the German GP in 1927. Mercedes wiped the board: behind the winner Merz, Werner and Walb, second and third respectively, was the extremely talented lady-driver Elizabeth Junek at the wheel of a Bugatti, finishing fourth 30 minutes behind Walb. In 1928 the tenacious Junek conquered a third place in the Targa Florio, only missing victory due to fatigue.

44-45 The start of the 1927 Eröffnungsrennen at the Nürburgring: this was the first race held at the great German circuit. That year the beautiful and well balanced Mercedes S took European racing by storm. The S was derived from the K but was modified to make it more competitive in terms of handling and power. This race was a non-championship event; Caracciola (No. 1) won followed by Rosemeyer (2) and Von Mosch (3) at the wheel of a privately entered Mercedes-Benz.

44 bottom right Christian Werner, the winner of many races for Mercedes, particularly in the late Twenties, is seen here at the wheel of a Mercedes Sport. He was one of the leading drivers in the Mercedes team put together by Alfred Neubauer.

45 top left Rudolf Caracciola in action during the Eröffnungsrennen, the inaugural race at the Nürburgring in 1927.

45 bottom left Absent major manufacturers such as Renault, many of the smaller French models enjoyed success in touring car events or cate-

gories for smaller engine capacities. This well-preserved Amilcar from 1927 reflects the stylistic features of contemporary racing cars, including the pointed tail dear to Alfa Romeo and Bugatti, while the mudguards and the richly equipped and overly-attractive dashboard betray its touring nature. Note the exposed steel chassis longerons.

45 right The start line at the Grand Prix of Europe held on the 4th of September, 1927. Recognizable from the left are Kreis in a Cooper, Benoist with a Delage and Minoia with an OM.

For the first time, however, as well as the Constructors' Championship, it is legitimate to speak of a world champion driver, albeit one not officially recognized. The man in question was Robert Benoist who won all the European races valid for the title, an exploit that had never previously been managed by the Alfa Romeo or Bugatti drivers. And speaking of drivers, 1927 saw the retirement of Wagner, the only driver still racing who had taken part in the first French GP of 1906, and the debut of the Monégasque ace, Louis Chiron.

Ironically, as had already happened with the championship-winning Alfa Romeo team, at the end of the season Delage abandoned Grand Prix racing due to the latest variation in the regulations that signalled the end of the 1500-cc formula which,

while encouraging engineers to extract the utmost from their engines, had seriously compromised the number of models racing and therefore the level of competition. A more flexible formula was adopted that was based solely on the maximum permitted weight and the length of the races.

The World Championship was also abandoned in as much as the 1928 edition planned by the organizer was a victim of the complexity of its own regulations, sinking into oblivion without a winner even being designated—a worthy epilogue for a championship that started badly and finished worse. It should also be noted that Fiat took its final bow from Grand Prix racing, even though in 1927 the Turin engineers had prepared a competitive car, the 806.

entrant driving a Mercedes was Rosenberger, who while leading crashed due to the heavy rain and mowed down three timing officials. Caracciola instead seemed to sail serenely around the soaking track, earning himself the nickname *Regenmeister*, or Rain King. The winner of the Italian GP, indicated in the records as "Sabipa," was Jean Charavel.

In general terms it can be said that 1926 saw a partial revival in French fortunes as the models from that country won most of the races as well as the World Championship with Bugatti first and Delage second (no other team participated in sufficient events to be classified), but they were racing against modest and discontinuous opposition.

The situation was unchanged in 1927, although the maximum weight limit was raised to 600 kg (1,544 lb.). The dominant model was no longer Bugatti, which had in reality profited from the objective absence of adversaries in most events, but Delage with its technologically avant-garde cars prepared with painstaking care and born out of the stubborn determination of the French engineers to demonstrate that they were capable of producing an eight-cylinder engine at least as effective as the 12-cylinder unit from 1925.

Delage won in France, Spain, England and Italy, leaving its rivals with only the non-championship Grand Prix in Germany and the essentially unnoticed Indianapolis 500 overseas.

HONOR ROLL

Grands Prix from 1922 to 1927

YEAR	GRAND PRIX	VENUE	DRIVER	CAR	AV. SPEED KPH (MPH)
1921	ACF	Le Mans	J. Murphy	Duesenberg	137.9 (85.6)
1921	Italian	Brescia	J. Goux	Ballot	144.7 (89.9)
1922	ACF	Strasbourg	F. Nazzaro	Fiat 804	127.5 (79.2)
1922	Italian	Monza	P. Bordino	Fiat 804	139.9 (86.9)
1923	ACF	Tours	H. Segrave	Sunbeam	121.2 (75.3)
1923	Europe	Monza	C. Salamano	Fiat 805	146.5 (91)
1923	Spanish	Sitges	A. Divo	Sunbeam	156 (96.9)
1924	ACF	Lyons	G. Campari	Alfa R. P2	114.2 (70.9)
1924	Spanish	S. Sebastian	H. Segrave	Sunbeam	103.2 (64.1)
1924	Europe	Monza	A. Ascari	Alfa R. P2	158.9 (98.7)
1925	Belgian	Spa	A. Ascari	Alfa R. P2	120.5 (74.8)
1925	ACF	Montlhéry	R. Benoist/A. Divo	Delage 2LCV	112.2 (111.6)
1925	Italian	Monza	G. Brilli-Peri	Alfa R. P2	152.6 (94.7)
1925	Spanish	S. Sebastian	A. Divo/A. Morel	Delage 2LCV	123.5 (76.7)
1926	ACF	Miramas	J. Goux	Bugatti T39A	107.6 (66.8)
1926	German	Avus	R. Caracciola	Mercedes	134.7 (83.6)
1926	Europe	Lasarte	J. Goux	Bugatti T39A	116.4 (72.3)
1926	Spanish	Lasarte	M. Costantini	Bugatti T35	126.9 (78.8)
1926	British	Brooklands	R. Sénéchal/L. Wagner	Delage 15S8	115.3 (71.6)
1926	Italian	Monza	"Sabipa"	Bugatti T39A	138.2 (82.5)
1927	ACF	Montlhéry	R. Benoist	Delage 15S8	126 (78.2)
1927	German	Nürburgring	O. Mertz	Mercedes S	101.9 (63.3)
1927	Spanish	Lasarte	R. Benoist	Delage 15S8	132.8 (82.5)
1927	Italian	Monza	R. Benoist	Delage 15S8	173.9 (108)
1927	British	Brooklands	R. Benoist	Delage 15S8	137.7 (85.5)

46 top This color drawing from 1928 shows Albert Divo with his Delage at the Montlhéry circuit, venue of the ACF GP.

46 center left The 1928 German GP at the Nürburgring for Grand Prix cars was once again the scene of a Mercedes triumph, the team's cars finishing first, second, third

and fifth. Only two Bugattis could infiltrate the pack in fourth and sixth places driven by Gastone Brilli-Peri and Louis Chiron.

46 center right This image portrays Seibel with a Mercedes during the Nürburgring race. The German circuit snaked through the forests on the Eifel mountains.

46 bottom The photo immortalizes the triumphant Mercedes team at the German Grand Prix of 1928: on the left, wearing the laurel wreath, Christian Werner. On the right Rudolf Caracciola, who managed to repeat his win of two years earlier. The Mercedes SS was a development of the previous year's Sport. The Mercedes sports models of the period were both successful on the track and highly desired by private enthusiasts.

BUGATTI AND ALFA SHARE THE HONORS

Were there any sense in considering the 1928 World Championship as valid, the winning car and driver could be none other than Bugatti and Louis Chiron. But this was a muddled season with atypical races, as if the motor racing world had wished to anticipate by a year the economic chaos about to engulf the world. The regulations were changed yet again with the limit on total displacement that had accompanied Grand Prix racing since 1914 being abandoned, not to be reinstated until 1934. With the introduction of Formula Libre from 1928, the only restrictions concerned the minimum (550 kg/ 1,213 lb.) and maximum (750 kg/ 1,654 lb.) weight limits and the minimum length of the races (600 km/ 1,323 lb.).

A number of Grands Prix were thus reserved for sports cars while others were run according to a handicap formula. Only the Italian GP could be considered as a Formula-type race, the British and Belgian events not meeting the criteria. The race in Germany was won by a car with a total displacement of over seven liters when the previous year the maximum capacity had been just 1500 cc.

Despite the decline in the overall quality of the racing, 1928 was marked by the exploits of a number of legendary figures: Giuseppe Campari for Alfa Romeo, Rudolf Caracciola for Mercedes, Louis Chiron for Bugatti and Tazio Nuvolari for Maserati.

The season was marred, however, by a veritable massacre that took place during the Italian GP. Materassi crashed into the grandstand and died along with 22 spectators. The talented Pietro Bordino was also killed during practice for the Targa Florio: not a memorable year.

The supremacy of the supercharged Bugatti was confirmed in 1929. Chiron remained the driver to beat while his home city organized the opening race of the season, the first of the glorious series of Monaco Grands Prix. Chiron was not at Monte Carlo for that race and it was another Bugatti driver, William Grover-Williams (under the pseudonym W. Williams), who won with a naturally aspirated car and who repeated the feat in the French GP. Of five races, four were won by the remarkable Bugattis but the last, the ultra-fast Monza Grand Prix, saw the

47 top left Bugatti challenging for the Monaco GP, the home race of the team's leading driver Louis Chiron. The street circuit, still one of the Formula 1 World Championship's classics, was inaugurated in 1929

and Bugatti was present in force: five cars finishing in the first six places, with only the Mercedes SSK of Caracciola intruding in third place. The winner, Williams, is seen here aboard his Type 35B.

47 bottom left This photograph was taken immediately after the start of the first edition of the Monaco GP in 1929. The fore part of the start grid is crowded with Bugattis driven by Etancelin Dauvergne and Lehoux, but in the end Williams, Bouriano and "Philippe" resulted to be the best Bugatti's pilots.

47 top right Williams on a Bugatti enters a bend at the first edition of the Monaco GP in 1929. The race was too long at 100 laps for over 3 km (2 mi.), with continual corners and hairpin bends that demanded an infinite series of gear-changes. A few years later the race was restricted to 80 laps. On the left is the leader board indicating the lap number (the 30th) and the current running order of the first three drivers. Car number 34 belonged to Étancelin who later retired, while car number 12 was that of the winner William Grover–Williams.

ascendancy of another star and the future protagonist in furious duels with Tazio Nuvolari, Achille Varzi, who revived the fortunes of the "aging," albeit modified, Alfa Romeo P2.

Leon Duray was also present at Monza with two powerful front-wheel-drive eight-cylinder Millers that after the race he swapped, together with cash, for three Bugatti Sport Type 43s. Examination of the technical innovations contained in the Millers, which were dominating (although not for much longer) the American speedways, provided Bugatti with much useful information for the development of his Type 51 powered by a 2.3-liter, supercharged straight-Eight with twin overhead camshafts. The Type 51 made its presence felt as early as 1931 and was an enduring force in Grand Prix racing.

Another historic event took place in 1929 when Ferrari, having recovered from a serious nervous breakdown, formed his own team at Modena. Until 1932 he was able to count on works Alfas but when the Milanese firm withdrew from the direct management of its racing team, he raced the 8C 2300 Monza and Le Mans models as well as other

47 center right This photo illustrates a Bugatti pit-stop during the 1928 San Sebastian GP. Car number 9 was that of Benoist while Chiron's was number 7.

47 bottom right Louis Chiron, closely associated with the Bugatti Type 35, acclaimed on the occasion of his victory in the French GP held at Reims in 1928.

cars, including a number of Maseratis.

In the absence of Mercedes which had officially withdrawn from racing due to the deepening German economic crisis, the Bugatti supremacy was again evident in 1930 although there was greater competition, especially from Maserati (the firm winning its first Grand Prix) and Alfa Romeo. In particular, the Varzi-Maserati pairing enjoyed great success in the Italian and Spanish races. The other four Grands Prix, including the debut of the Czechoslovakian GP held at Brno, went to the Bugatti drivers at the wheel of blown and naturally aspirated versions of the redoubtable Type 35.

The Type 35 merits closer attention. It was powered by a straight-eight engine, initially naturally aspirated, with a cylinder capacity of 2261 cc and a maximum power output of 110 hp at 5000 rpm (140 hp at 5400 for the "B" version) and a maximum speed of 180 kph (112 mph; subsequently 210 kph/ 130 mph). Out of the Type 35 was born Type 45, in practice a twin-engined car:

48 top The T51 was one of the most successful cars built by the Italo-French Ettore Bugatti. This photo shows the slim front of the 1930 Gran Sport model that can be traced back to the Grand Prix T51. The horseshoe radiator design was retained into the 1930s and distinguished the Bugattis from the Mercedes (Greek temple), Alfa Romeos (rectangular with a honeycomb motif) and BMWs (double kidney). A classic headlamp arrangement was adopted.

its power unit consisted of two straight-8 blocks mounted on a single crankcase. It proved disappointing, as did a similar experiment by Alfa Romeo.

The P2 concluded its honorable career at Brno, driven to third place by Tazio Nuvolari. Varzi had earlier won the Targa Florio with this car, crossing the line in flames due to a fuel leak.

The P2, which the previous year had scored numerous wins, now enjoys a well-earned rest in the Museo Storico Alfa Romeo at Arese, Alfa's historic home close to Milan. Its long roll of honor includes a World Championship title, five wins and four second places in international Grands Prix, as well as wins in the minor Rome and Tunisia GPs, a Targa Florio, two Coppa Acerbos, two Circuito di Cremonas, a Targa Abruzzo and two Coppa Bordinos.

48-49 A rear three-quarters view of the Bugatti Gran Sport. The wings are slightly flared at the rear, a nod in the direction of aerodynamics. The classic Bugatti alloy wheels with eight flat spokes were retained despite the widespread use of wire wheels by Mercedes and the British constructors.

48 bottom This photograph highlights a number of features of the Bugatti T51 with which Achille Varzi won many races: the shape of the tail, triangular in plan and flat in profile, the guillotine windshield, the mirror attached to the strap fastening the spare wheel and the fuel filler caps.

49 top left The buildings of Monte Carlo act as a backdrop to drivers and mechanics involved in last-minute preparations prior to the start of the Monaco GP in 1930.

49 top right This photo shows a moment during an internecine battle between Bugattis: Two T35s are tackling the hairpin during the 1930 Monaco Grand Prix.

49 center right This poster publicized the second edition of the Monaco GP held on the sixth of April, 1930.

49 bottom The Monaco GP returned in 1930. While the first edition had already been characterized by the crushing supremacy of the Bugattis, in the second the blue cars almost wiped the board, conquering the first six places. The local hero, Louis Chiron, had to wait another year before winning in the principality. At the start can be seen the swarm of Bugattis, numbers 14, 18, 16, 28, 42, 20 and 26.

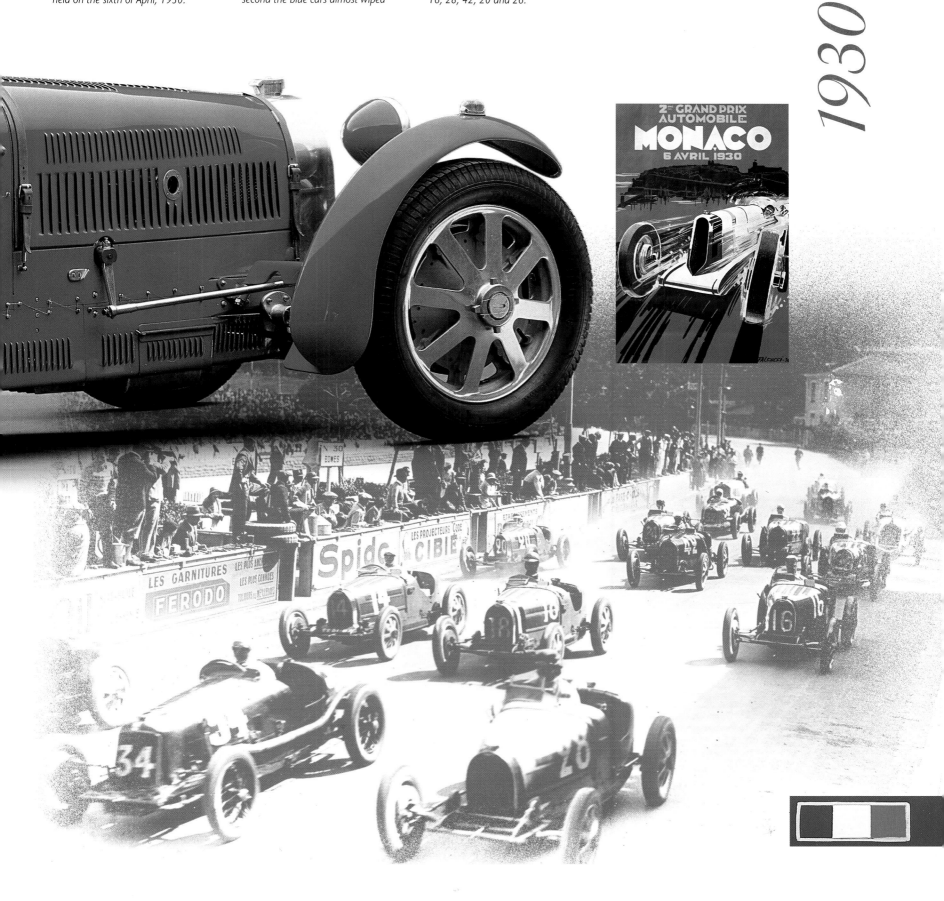

1930

2ᵉ GRAND PRIX AUTOMOBILE
MONACO
6 AVRIL 1930

50 top left *Achille Varzi posing with the cup won at the 1933 Monaco GP.*

50 top right *This group picture at the Monza GP is dated 1930, accepted with reservations given that Arcangeli, beaten by two-tenths of a second by*

Varzi, is missing. From left to right, from the third in overalls, Premoli: Brivio Sforza, Borzacchini, Campari, Senator Crespi, President of the Royal Automobile Club, and then Nuvolari, Étancelin, Caracciola, Varzi, Ruggeri and Ghersi.

50 center *Alfa Romeo won the Italian Grand Prix once again in 1931 with this car, the eight-cylinder 2300 Monza. The drivers of the winning car were two friends, Tazio Nuvolari and Giuseppe Campari.*

50 bottom *Caracciola wins the 1931 German GP. Although Alfa was close to perfecting its eight-cylinder car, the Maseratis were not always competitive and the Delages had disappeared, leaving Bugatti and Mercedes to share the honors. The 1931 event was Mercedes' own, although it was well balanced, Caracciola winning with the SSKL ahead of Chiron with the first Bugatti and Varzi with the second, then Nuvolari with the 8C Monza.*

1930 1931

There was a revolution in 1931. Cylinder-capacity restrictions having been abandoned, weight limits being relegated to the background and fuel-consumption figures being ignored, the regulations concentrated on the duration of the races: from this year onward Grands Prix were to last for at least 10 hours and consequently each car would require a team of two drivers who would alternate spells at the wheel. The Monaco GP was spared, and maintained its length of 100 laps equal to 318 km. In Germany and Czechoslovakia, too, the new formula was snubbed.

Both in Formula Libre races and the 10-hour events, the results went the way of the Bugatti Type 51. At Monte Carlo the model enjoyed a veritable triumph with Chiron finally able to complete a lap of honor on his home circuit after having beaten Caracciola with the Mercedes and Fagioli with the Maserati.

Alfa Romeo was highly active, however, and Jano unveiled the 8C 2300 which won at Monza (hence the Monza name, differentiating the model from the more road-going Le Mans) entrusted to an all-star pairing of Giuseppe Campari and Tazio Nuvolari, two great drivers who seen together had a comic effect— ruddy and robust the former, small and wiry the latter.

The 8C, derived from the successful six-cylinder 1750, was an extremely interesting and versatile car. The basic design allowed Jano to produce sports (four consecutive victories at Le Mans and three in the Targa Florio), touring (fine sales records) and Grand Prix cars by way of successive modifications of the cylinder capacity. The eight in-line cylinders were

51 left Spa, the European Grand Prix, 1930: the Bugatti team confirms its excellent state of form. This photograph shows Guy Bouriat who qualified in second place, at the weel of the car number 8 alongside the Mechanic Ernest Zihr. The race was won by the French ace Louis Chiron with the Bugattti number 9.

arranged in two separate blocks with gear trains between them driving the camshafts. This was a long-lived model that we shall encounter again later thanks to its numerous wins in various kinds of racing.

In the early Thirties, as well as aggressive, versatile cars Enzo Ferrari could count on an exceptional group of drivers: Arcangeli, Borzacchini, Campari, Chiron, Fagioli, Nuvolari and Varzi. The prancing horse, a tribute from Baroness Paolina Baracca, the mother of flying ace Francesco, appeared on the cars for the first time in this era, set on a canary yellow shield—the color of the city of Modena.

Mercedes, too, entered one of its all-time great cars—the SSKL, ultimately derived from the original Type S—for its home race, which it duly won. Here again we're faced with a breed worthy of a brief genealogical history that begins with a flashback. In 1928, the year of its maturity, the competition version of the Mercedes-Benz Type S was known as the 26/190/250 PS (the last two figures indicating the power output with and without supercharging). In a single year it scored 53 wins and set 17 records. It was a magnificent, imposing car ideal for a select and demanding clientele (as with the Alfas and Bugattis, there were touring versions or cars prepared for private entrants). The original model generated the SS and then the SSK, one of the most beautiful open cars of all time and still today one of the jewels of the Mercedes Museum in Stuttgart.

Recession struck Germany in 1929, however, and Mercedes was obliged to tackle both the crisis and the resignation of Ferdinand Porsche, who moved to Audi. The tenacious Alfred Neubauer, in effect the direct rival of the equally determined Enzo Ferrari, persuaded the Mercedes directors to discreetly and indirectly back a small team revolving around Caracciola. Wagner, the engineer provided by the manufacturer who was subsequently to become head of the Mercedes engine department, thus developed the SSKL, in which the L stood for *leicht*, or light-weight. Quite how is unknown, but he managed to pare away 125 kg (276 lb.) from the car, reducing its total weight to around 1,500 kg (3,308 lb.). The official name was the 27/240/300 PS, and this was the car with which Caracciola won the Mille Miglia and races at the Avus and the Nürburgring circuits.

Caracciola left Mercedes at the end of the season, promising to return at the first hint of renewed interest in racing. The SSKL's career concluded on a high note the following year thanks to another noble automotive hero, Manfred von Brauchitsch, who was determined to challenge lighter, more powerful rivals at Avus despite his lack of an equally potent car. He thus asked Baron Reinhard von Koenig-Fachsenfeld to design an aerodynamic fairing for the SSKL, thanks to which he scored a surprise victory, improving Caracciola's time from the previous year with a car developing an extra 30 hp. The heavyweight era was over, however, as the regulations were about to change with the reintroduction of a maximum weight limit. In this case too, as we shall see, Neubauer was to distinguish himself.

51 top right and center These pictures show mechanics at work in the Bugatti pits tackling the replacement of a wheel and refuelling during the ACF Grand Prix held at Montlhéry in 1931 that lasted 10 hours. The photograph at the top shows driver Albert Divo cleaning his windshield and Guy Bouriat observing the scene in the background. Unfortunately, both drivers, who alternated at the wheel of the Bugatti Type 51, were forced out of the race with mechanical problems.

51 bottom The poster for the Monaco Grand Prix of 1931. The illustrator has emphasized the chromatic contrast between the Bugatti blue and the Alfa Romeo red.

1930 1932

The decade marched to the tune of the intense struggle between Bugatti, Mercedes, Maserati and Alfa Romeo. Year 1932 saw the debut of the Alfa Tipo B, re-baptized the P3 to establish continuity with the unforgettable P2, the record of which it was to match: in only its second year the car scored 26 wins and 13 seconds out of 39 international races disputed. It won all the international events in which it took part between 1932 and 1934 with six 1-2-3 clean-sweeps, not to mention innumerable victories in minor races.

This remarkable car was powered by a straight-eight with twin cylinder blocks and two drive shafts, one per rear wheel, the driver sitting locked between the two. The initial displacement of 2300 cc was enlarged to 2654 cc. Up to 1935 the front end was fitted with a beam axle, subsequently abandoned in favor of fully independent suspension. The power output of 215 hp (equivalent to a specific output of 86 hp/l) was inferior to that of cars from previous years, but the engines were much less highly stressed and therefore more reliable. The strength of the P3 thus lay in its lightness, handling and road-holding.

The minimum race duration of 10 hours specified in the regulations became a maximum while the minimum was altered to five hours.

Following the Monaco GP won by Nuvolari from his teammate Caracciola, the Tipo B made a triumphant appearance at Monza. Nuvolari won by a lap from Fagioli in a Maserati; Borzacchini, Marinoni and Caracciola with the Alfa 8C Monzas of the Scuderia Ferrari; and Campari with the second Tipo B/P3. France saw an epic Alfa 1-2-3 with Nuvolari, Borzacchini and Caracciola beating three Bugattis driven by Chiron, Dreyfus and Williams. The feat was repeated in Germany with the finishing order this time reading Caracciola, Nuvolari and Borzacchini.

Suspicions regarding the finishing orders in Italy and Germany are legitimate. Mussolini and Hitler wanted "national" victories, and thus Caracciola and Nuvolari likely exchanged favors. Only in Czechoslovakia did Chiron and Bugatti manage to gain the upper hand, thanks to the absence of the all-conquering P3s. Alfa withdrew from competition at the end of 1932, delegating the management of the team's cars and drivers to Ferrari (although the P3s were only consigned to him mid-way through the 1933 season). In the meantime, Ferdinand Porsche had founded his own team.

52 left Varzi crosses the line first at Monza: this was the Italian GP of 1930 won by the Italian driver with a Maserati 26M.

52-53 The starting grid for the Italian Grand Prix of 1930. At that time up to five cars were lined up on each row, an arrangement subsequently abandoned for safety reasons. Pole position went to Arcangeli with the Maserati, with alongside him Borzacchini in the P2 and Fagioli with a second Maserati.

53 top left The two protagonists of the 1930 Italian GP were Luigi Arcangeli, on whose overalls can be seen the Maserati trident, and Achille Varzi, who beat his teammate by two tenths of a second.

53 center, left The start at Monte Carlo featured cars lined up three abreast. On the front row can be seen the Bugatti T51, by now mature but not yet dominant (it was to win the following year), driven by Grover–Williams, the Alfa 8C of Philippe Étancelin and the Maserati 26M of Amedeo Ruggeri. None of these drivers managed to finish in the top six.

53 bottom left Starace congratulating Varzi at the start of the Monza GP. In the early Thirties motor racing was an ideal stage for the Fascist authorities.

53 top right This Napier from the early Thirties boasts well-muscled styling and aggressive chromework.

53 bottom right By 1932 motor racing was a case of Nuvolari against the rest. This photograph portrays him during his victorious charge around the streets of Monte Carlo aboard the increasingly dominant Alfa 8C 2300 Monza. Rudolf Caracciola, second in this race, had also moved to Alfa due to the crisis that prevented Mercedes from continuing with its racing program. It was only later that Hitler ordered funds to be provided to support Mercedes and Auto Union as standard bearers of the Third Reich's automotive might.

In some ways better but mostly for worse, 1933 was the year of the drivers. Alfa's withdrawal conditioned the market, leaving many top names "unemployed." Ferrari signed Nuvolari but the friction between their two personalities soon led to divorce. Chiron was let go by Bugatti and formed a small private team with Caracciola. The latter, however, was the victim of a serious accident at Monaco that caused him to miss the rest of the season. By signing Varzi, Bugatti strengthened a team that already boasted proven drivers of the caliber of Williams, Divo and Dreyfus. Giuseppe Campari purchased his own Maserati but for the Grand Prix of Monza, staged just a few hours after the Italian GP, he was at the wheel of an Alfa 8C 2300 with which he engaged in a strenuous duel with Baconin Borzacchini in a Maserati. Both skidded on oil and crashed fatally, as soon did Czaikowski.

For the first time, from the Monaco GP grid positions were determined according to the lap times obtained during official practice. Until then, the starting order had been drawn according to team and the team managers assigned positions on the basis of the race strategy to be adopted.

This was not a fortunate year for Nuvolari. He lost at Monaco when his engine blew close to the finish, while he dominated in France until retiring with a

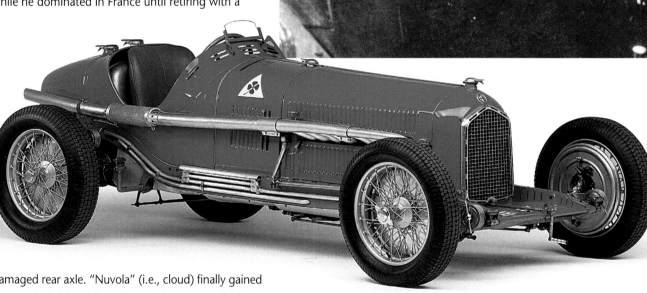

damaged rear axle. "Nuvola" (i.e., cloud) finally gained revenge in Belgium aboard a modified Maserati, while at Monza he was leading with just two laps to go when a rear tire blew and he had to settle for second place.

Meanwhile, the aggressiveness of the "traitor" Nuvolari had convinced Alfa to take the covers off the P3s and allow them to be driven in the final part of the season by Fagioli and Chiron. The two wiped the board, Fagioli winning the Italian GP at Monza and a few hours later Chiron taking Monza. One-two victories followed in Czechoslovakia and Spain. That year another prestigious model joined the world of competition, the British firm Jaguar, which took part in the Rally delle Alpi with the SS1.

It was a hard-fought, well balanced but confused and tragic year that concluded an era of great racing and alternating fortunes for the manufacturers involved in motor sport. On the horizon was a new era with a new maximum weight: 750 kg (1,654 lb.).

T. NUVOLARI

54 top In most photographs before or after a race or during practice, Nuvolari has a mocking smile. Here, however, he is seen in a serious mood at the wheel of a Maserati 8CM, perhaps because he is concentrating on the start of the Modena GP.

54 center The Alfa P3 in its debut season of 1932 won three consecutive GPs, scoring a 1-2-3 in Germany. Its eight-cylinder engine was divided into two groups of four cylinders, each with its own crankshaft.

54 bottom Nuvolari pushing his Alfa 8C 2300 Monza toward the finishing line after stopping on the penultimate lap of the Monaco GP in 1933.

55 top Following a brief intermission with the V4, Maserati challenged Bugatti and Alfa with this car, the 8CM, heir to the 26M. The engine had a total displacement of 2.9 l, just under the maximum allowed by the series. The photograph on the right shows the radiator of the Maserati 8CM with a fine mesh. Note the twin inclined suspension arms, still connected to the transverse link. An essential condition for this or other cars to win was the absence of the P3, against which not even the most talented of drivers could hope to compete. But the Alfas were gathering dust in their garage because the powers were reluctant to cede them to the Scuderia Ferrari, only relenting well into the '33 season.

With this car Nuvolari, in conflict with Ferrari who had taken over the management of the Alfa racing team, won the Belgian GP, giving even the Bugattis food for thought. Campari had also won a Grand Prix, the ACF event, with a Maserati he acquired privately. The day of his friend Tazio's triumph at Monza he lost his life in a futile head-to-head battle with Borzacchini when he skidded on spilt oil.

55 bottom Nuvolari acclaimed after having won the Italian GP in 1932. He was driving a car better suited to Grand Prix racing than the 8C 2300: the P3, so-called in the hope that it would follow in the footsteps of the P2.

HONOR ROLL

Grands Prix from 1928 to 1933

YEAR	GRAND PRIX	VENUE	DRIVER	CAR	AV. SPEED KPH (MPH)
1928	ACF	St. Gaudens	"W. Williams"	Bugatti T35C	105.6 (65.6)
1928	German	Nürburgring	R. Caracciola	Mercedes SS	103.4 (64.2)
1928	S. Sebastian	Lasarte	L. Chiron	Bugatti T35C	132.9 (82.5)
1928	Spanish	Lasarte	L. Chiron	Bugatti T35C	110.2 (68.4)
1928	Italian	Monza	L. Chiron	Bugatti T35C	159.9 (99.3)
1929	Monaco	Monte Carlo	"W. Williams"	Bugatti T35B	80.8 (50.2)
1929	ACF	Le Mans	"W. Williams"	Bugatti T35B	132.9 (82.5)
1929	German	Nürburgring	L. Chiron	Bugatti T35C	106.7 (66.3)
1929	Spanish	Lasarte	L. Chiron	Bugatti T35B	119.3 (74.1)
1929	Italian	Monza	A. Varzi	Alfa P2	187.7(116.6)
1930	Monaco	Monte Carlo	R. Dreyfus	Bugatti T35B	86.3 (53.6)
1930	Belgian	Spa	L. Chiron	Bugatti T35C	115.6 (71.8)
1930	Italian	Monza	A. Varzi	Maserati 26M	150.4 (93.4)
1930	ACF	Pau	P. Étancelin	Bugatti T35C	145.7 (90.5)
1930	Czech	Brno	H. zu Leiningen H. von Morgan	Bugatti T35B	101 (62.7)
1930	Spanish	Lasarte	A. Varzi	Maserati 26M	143.3 (89)
1931	Monaco	Monte Carlo	L. Chiron	Bugatti T51	87.1 (54.1)
1931	Italian	Monza	G. Campari/T. Nuvolari	Alfa 8C Monza	155 (96.3)
1931	ACF	Montlhéry	L. Chiron/A. Varzi	Bugatti T51	126.2 (78.3)
1931	Belgian	Spa	"W. Williams"/C. Conelli	Bugatti T51	130.8 (81.2)
1931	German	Nürburgring	R. Caracciola	Mercedes SSKL	108.2 (67.2)
1931	Czech	Brno	L. Chiron	Bugatti T51	117.9 (73.2)
1932	Monaco	Monte Carlo	T. Nuvolari	Alfa 8C Monza	89.8 (55.8)
1932	Italian	Monza	T. Nuvolari	Alfa P3	166 (103.1)
1932	ACF	Reims	T. Nuvolari	Alfa P3	144 (89.4)
1932	German	Nürburgring	R. Caracciola	Alfa P3	119 (73.9)
1932	Czech	Brno	L. Chiron	Bugatti T51	107.2 (66.6)
1933	Monaco	Monte Carlo	A. Varzi	Bugatti T51	91.8 (57)
1933	ACF	Montlhéry	G. Campari	Maserati 8C 3000	131.7 (81.8)
1933	Belgian	Spa	T. Nuvolari	Maserati 8C Monza	143.2 (88.9)
1933	Italian	Monza	L. Fagioli	Alfa P3	174.7(108.5)
1933	Czech	Brno	L. Chiron	Alfa P3	102.4 (63.6)
1933	Spanish	Lasarte	L. Chiron	Alfa P3	138.3 (85.9)

MERCEDES AND AUTO UNION DOMINATE

Apart from the new maximum weight limit of 750 kg (1,654 lb.; excluding fuel, oil, water and tires), the regulations also specified a minimum body width of 85 cm for Formula Libre races in 1934. Free choice was allowed with regards to fuel, while the minimum distance to be covered was 500 km. This formula remained unchanged until the end of the 1937 season. The teams turned their attention from the maximum increment of power output, perhaps through supercharging, to the development of lighter chassis, a factor hitherto mostly neglected.

It was immediately apparent that the sport's leading lights were determined to bore the enthusiasts with the whitewashes achieved by the Tipo B/P3 run by the Scuderia Ferrari in the first two races, at Monte Carlo (first four places) and in France (first three). The P3 already weighed much less than the 750-kg (1,654 lb.), but Maserati and Bugatti too could easily adapt their existing GP cars to the new regulations.

Alongside Chiron and Varzi, the Alfa team also included a promising young driver of Algerian origins, Guy Moll, who impressed in the Avus race which he won with an interesting streamlined version of the P3. Tragically Moll died shortly afterward while travelling at very high speed along the straight of the circuit at Pescara. Enzo Ferrari, never free with compliments, described him years later as one of the most talented drivers he had ever known.

After the first two races of the season a German whirlwind struck the world of GP racing with the return of Mercedes and the debut of the strange new Auto Unions, fruit of the genius of Ferdinand Porsche. The two firms shared the stated financial

incentive of 450,000 marks provided by the Ministry of Transport at the behest of Hitler who had recently come to power, although in reality, it was not much in comparison with the high operating costs of a GP team. Mussolini also provided lavish funds for Alfa Romeo (which was now under the wing of the state holding company IRI), but Alfa's research in the field of engines, while producing a range of excellent power units, had little coherency.

The surprise was sprung in Germany with Hans Stuck's victory at the wheel of the highly original Auto Union A, powered by a centrally mounted, offset, 16-cylinder engine with a total displacement of 4.4 l and a power output of almost 300 hp (subsequently increased to 375 hp). Second was Luigi Fagioli aboard the other newcomer, the Mercedes-Benz W25 with its 3.3-liter engine producing no less than 354 hp (430 in 1935). Even

57 top While the sports cars of the K-S series had shone in terms of beauty, sophistication and balance, in 1934 Mercedes-Benz played its ace of aces, the W25. A versatile, competitive car, just 10% of its design costs had been covered by the state contributions divided between Mercedes-Benz and Auto Union. Nonetheless, German pride was to produce this veritable thunderbolt which in the hands of Caracciola and Fagioli, seen here at Monza on the occasion of the 1934 Italian GP, was to dominate, announcing the second phase of the long Mercedes-Auto Union challenge.

57 center Refuelling Fagioli's Mercedes W25 during the Italian GP of 1934.

1934

56 top This image is both timeless and without place: anything just to experience the emotions of a Grand Prix, including rising at improbable hours, long queues in cars or buses or treks by bicycle. In this case the crowd has gathered for the German Grand Prix at the Avus circuit in 1934.

56 bottom The Alfa Tipo B/P3 in aerodynamic form in 1934. Note not only the vertical fin on the tail resembling the rudder of an aircraft, but also the streamlined droplets behind the wheels which in turn resemble aircraft undercarriage fairings. Another fascinating detail is the fencing-mask-type radiator grille dear to the American mass-volume designers.

57 bottom This photograph shows the aerodynamic version of the Alfa Romeo P3 or Tipo B with unusual stabilizing fins on the tail that unfortunately are covered here. The two men in the foreground on the right are Ing. Paravicini and Commendatore Jano. The latter was responsible for virtually the entire golden age of Alfa's sporting history in that he designed the most important cars. Ferrari dragged him into his team together with Bazzi. Discussing technical matters in front of the exposed engine are the two drivers Trossi and Guidotti and another great engineer, Gobbato.

a superficial glance at the new cars revealed radical differences compared with others in the field, quite apart from the Auto Union's engine location.

The German models gave some breathing space to their rivals in Belgium, where Bugatti scored a 1-2 (the Type 51 was, along with the Alfa P3, the great victim of the Teutonic monsters) with Dreyfus and Brivio. Then the German cars actually *deserted* the race at Spa in protest at the excessive duties imposed on their fuels. They then went to share the other four major Grands Prix (in those years numerous minor races were run as Grands Prix, including those at Tripoli, Rome, Avus and Eifel) in Switzerland (Auto Union 1-2), Italy (Mercedes), Spain (Mercedes 1-2) and Czechoslovakia (Auto Union). Caracciola returned to his spiritual home at Mercedes, while Nuvolari (with the Maserati) and Varzi were unable to compete on even terms with rivals that were more powerful, perfectly balanced and boasted avant-garde chassis designs. Thus began a period of

"manifest superiority" of the German models that lasted until the outbreak of the Second World War.

In reality Auto Union and Mercedes had already given advance warning of their potential. Auto Union, a company born out of the fusion of Horch, Audi, DkW and Wanderer, made its debut at the Avus GP but Stuck's crash favored Moll's victory. Mercedes was instead restored to greatness in the Eifel GP held at the Nürburgring. Apart from marking the comeback of the three-pointed star with a victory for von Brauchitsch, the event is worthy of mention for a curious expedient that earned a place in history, albeit one often cited as apocryphpa.

When the cars were weighed it was found that the Mercedes exceeded the permitted limit by a kilo. Amid the disappointment of the Mercedes pits, Neubauer had the brilliant idea of stripping the paint off the bodywork, thus allowing the car to scrape under the weight limit.

From then on the racing cars from Stuttgart were known as the Silver Arrows (*Silberpfeile*) and their racing livery became the metallic silver of that stripped bodywork.

The race was also notable for a rather unsavory incident. Fagioli, a great and passionate driver, was leading and was apparently unstoppable. However, the Fuhrer was in the grandstand and on the day of the great return of Germanic technology it was thought inappropriate for an Italian to win. Neubauer thus signalled Fagioli to allow von Brauchitsch to pass. The driver obeyed but after a violent argument with the team manager during a pit stop he returned to the track and commenced to hound his German colleague relentlessly. When Neubauer called him in Fagioli abandoned his car at the side of the track so as to deny Mercedes the satisfaction of a 1-2 triumph. In reality his gesture was an unwitting gift to Hitler as second place went to an Auto Union, thus amply justifying the strategy of the Reich.

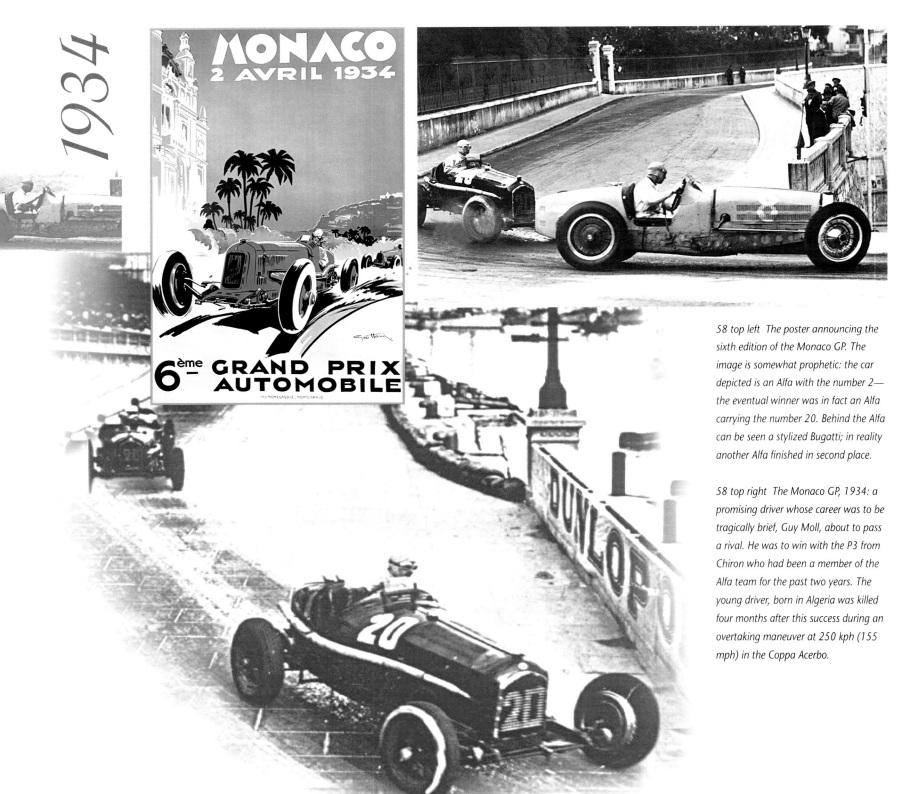

58 top left The poster announcing the sixth edition of the Monaco GP. The image is somewhat prophetic: the car depicted is an Alfa with the number 2—the eventual winner was in fact an Alfa carrying the number 20. Behind the Alfa can be seen a stylized Bugatti; in reality another Alfa finished in second place.

58 top right The Monaco GP, 1934: a promising driver whose career was to be tragically brief, Guy Moll, about to pass a rival. He was to win with the P3 from Chiron who had been a member of the Alfa team for the past two years. The young driver, born in Algeria was killed four months after this success during an overtaking maneuver at 250 kph (155 mph) in the Coppa Acerbo.

58 bottom The determination of Guy Moll, a driver who greatly impressed Enzo Ferrari, defeated all his rivals in the 1934 Monaco GP. He had already won a race at the Avus with the P3 Aerodinamica.

59 top left The official 1934 Alfa Romeo team photograph. The team managed by Enzo Ferrari entered three P3s (also known as the Tipo B) for the French GP and finished in the first three places. From left to right: Varzi, second at the finish, Chiron, the winner and Trossi, third, who shared his car with Guy Moll.

59 bottom left The jewel with which Alfa had the thankless task of attempting to challenge and beat the Mercedes W25. In the mid-Thirties there was also Bugatti to be taken into consideration, ever ready to profit from any Italian or German error. Moreover, there was ever-increasing talk about a new German model, Auto Union, whose strange cars were designed by Ferdinand Porsche. The driver of the Alfa in this 1934 photograph is Achille Varzi.

59 top right The hard work of the men in overalls: changing the gearbox on a P3. They had little time as this was the interval between practice and the race at the Dieppe GP of 1934.

59 center right The Alfa P3 had a strong presence in the collective imagination, perhaps due to the continuity with the celebrated and unforgettable P2. There were numerous illustrations and drawings immortalizing the red Italian car which dominated all the official races in which it took part between 1932 and 1934. This is the cover of an illustrated magazine.

59 bottom right He could have been a star; the meteoric Guy Moll at the wheel of a Scuderia Ferrari Alfa Romeo on the occasion of the 1934 Monaco GP in which he triumphed.

60 top left A photograph of the Monza overpass with (in the foreground) an Auto Union Type B and (behind) Nuvolari with an Alfa Romeo Type C. That year, 1935, Nuvolari had to settle for second place.

60 center left The Nürburgring, 1935: Nuvolari with the Alfa P3 streaking toward victory in the German GP at the height of German technical supremacy. Stuck's Auto Union finished second before Caracciola's Mercedes.

1935

In 1930 the new regulations had stated that GP fuel had to contain 30% benzole. With this requirement being dropped there was intensive research into ever more efficient fuels. Mercedes, for example, adopted a formula developed by Esso composed of 86% alcohol, 8.8% acetone, 4.4% nitrobenzole and 0.8% ether. There were notable differences as tests with the four-liter engine showed a power output of 370 hp when fuelled with benzole and 430 hp with methyl-alcohol (a fuel identified with the code WW).

60 center right Nuvolari in the prototype Alfa Bimotore. Alongside is Ferrari who had to accept Mussolini's order that he re-sign Nuvolari. It was fortunate that he did so as in the P3's last race Nuvolari beat the Mercedes and Auto Unions in Germany.

60 bottom The start of the 1935 Monaco GP. The front row of the grid is all Mercedes, from left to right: Caracciola, von Brauchitsch and Fagioli.

Unfortunately, however, the car consumed around a liter per kilometer, an unthinkable figure, although some years later the W125 was consuming 160 l/100 km.

In the end the team opted for a blend composed of 40% methyl-alcohol, 32% benzole, 24% ethyl-alcohol and an unidentified "super-fuel" (four parts per hundred) thanks to which consumption dropped to 75 l/100 km (20 gal./62 mi.). This blend, code-named XM, was tested under race conditions on the occasion of the 1935 Monaco GP won by the W25B.

In 1935 the unemployed Nuvolari attempted to get a drive with the awesome Auto Unions but Stuck and above all Varzi barred his way. Not even Ferrari wanted him back on his team after the parting of two years earlier, but affairs of state—or rather the wishes of Mussolini—suggested that it would not be appropriate to ignore the Grand Prix circus' most talented driver. Tazio thus returned behind the wheel of an Alfa Romeo.

At last a championship that rewarded the driver achieving the best results over the season was instituted. The idea was that of the German Automobile Club (ADAC) and was accepted by all the other European bodies with the exception of the ACF. The European Drivers' Championship thus

took in the Belgian, German, Italian, Spanish and Swiss GPs. Unfortunately it was again a handicap formula, with the least points being awarded to the winner: one point for first place, two for second, three for third, four for fourth and all those competitors who completed 75% of the race distance, five to those completing at least 50%, six for 25%, seven for less than 25% and eight for those not participating in the race. This confusing system aroused protests up to the championship's last edition held in 1939.

However, the first European title was deservedly won by Rudolf Caracciola at the wheel of the Mercedes-Benz W25B with victories in

Belgium, Switzerland and Spain as well as France (a non-championship GP). The racing calendar that year also featured the usual Czech race at Brno and a new Formula Libre event at Donington in which neither Mercedes-Benz nor Auto Union took part.

The two German firms, not content with the degree of superiority already demonstrated, presented "B" versions of their cars for the 1935 season, both with larger and more powerful engines producing 375 hp in the case of the Auto Union Type B and 430 hp for the Mercedes W25B. Bugatti and Alfa attempted to compete with the Germans with chassis and suspension modifications but they failed to make the progress they hoped for

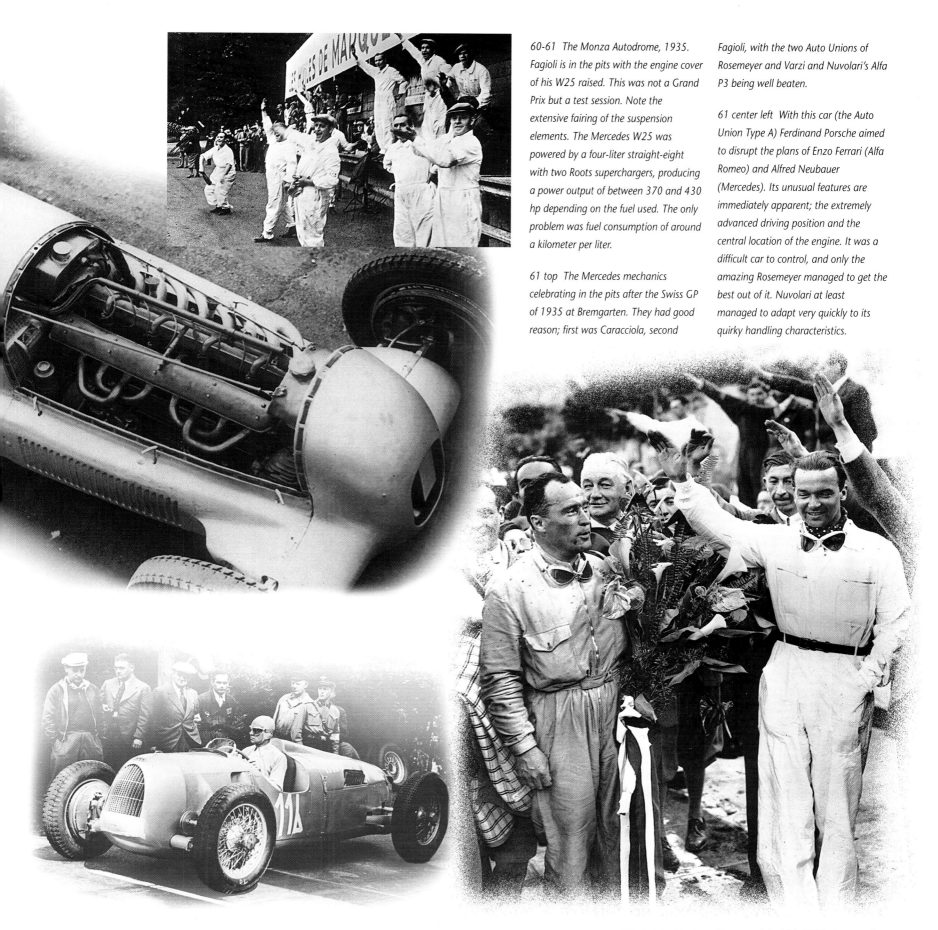

60-61 *The Monza Autodrome, 1935. Fagioli is in the pits with the engine cover of his W25 raised. This was not a Grand Prix but a test session. Note the extensive fairing of the suspension elements. The Mercedes W25 was powered by a four-liter straight-eight with two Roots superchargers, producing a power output of between 370 and 430 hp depending on the fuel used. The only problem was fuel consumption of around a kilometer per liter.*

61 top *The Mercedes mechanics celebrating in the pits after the Swiss GP of 1935 at Bremgarten. They had good reason; first was Caracciola, second* Fagioli, *with the two Auto Unions of Rosemeyer and Varzi and Nuvolari's Alfa P3 being well beaten.*

61 center left *With this car (the Auto Union Type A) Ferdinand Porsche aimed to disrupt the plans of Enzo Ferrari (Alfa Romeo) and Alfred Neubauer (Mercedes). Its unusual features are immediately apparent; the extremely advanced driving position and the central location of the engine. It was a difficult car to control, and only the amazing Rosemeyer managed to get the best out of it. Nuvolari at least managed to adapt very quickly to its quirky handling characteristics.*

despite Nuvolari's remarkable victory in Germany, of all places. Ironically, in a year of absolute domination, the Reich's teams were actually defeated in the Fatherland. This triumph was due entirely to Tazio's daring and the race was one of the greatest of his career.

While never in the lead, Nuvolari refused to give up and a series of retirements meant that he was eventually breathing down the neck of von Brauchitsch. Preoccupied by the Italian's tenacity, his rival decided not to stop to change his tires and went on to suffer two terminal punctures on the last lap. Three-hundred-thousand stunned spectators thus saw Nuvolari

cross the line first. This was the P3's last major race victory, and it would be hard to imagine a more fitting exit for one of the sport's all-time great machines.

If one believed in destiny, the defeat at the Nürburgring could be seen as punishment for Caracciola's irreverent behavior at Montlhéry. On that occasion the organizers decided to obstruct the powerful German cars by constructing a series of *chicanes*. The strategy had no effect due to the retirement of the potential adversaries and Caracciola and von Brauchitsch finished the race at a stroll, arousing no little anger amongst a crowd traditionally hostile to all things German.

61 center right *This 1935 photograph records the victory of the only Italian on the Mercedes team, Fagioli, at the Monaco GP. Alongside him Caracciola gives a decidedly half-hearted Nazi salute. Fagioli's character emerged during the Eifel GP in 1934, when the team manager wanted him to allow Rosemeyer to pass given that he was German and Hitler was in the stands. In protest Fagioli abandoned his car at the side of the track, denying Mercedes the pleasure of a certain 1-2.*

61 bottom *The triumph of Rudolf Caracciola in the Tripoli GP of 1935.*

The following year appeared to begin promisingly for Bugatti and Alfa Romeo. Following the traditional opening race of the season won by Caracciola with the third version of the W25, Nuvolari conquered the new Budapest circuit with the Tipo 8C-35, a development of the Tipo B/P3, tested successfully the previous year at Brno (second place). Bugatti in turn won on home soil with Wimille and Sommer (albeit with no German opposition) in a meaningless race reserved for sports cars (unfortunately the same thing happened the following year, disqualifying the most celebrated race of the whole GP season).

Bernd Rosemeyer, a young driver who the previous year had already taken five minutes from Nuvolari in becoming the first driver to win his debut Grand Prix, scored three consecutive victories at the wheel of the Auto Union Type C

his young rival with the consolation of the last race, the British Grand Prix at Donington being finally disputed by the German cars and drivers.

The French race, again reserved for sports cars, was meaningless and in Belgium the Auto Union Type Cs scored a 1-2 victory. However, fifteen days later the Mercedes revival got under way in Germany, team manager Rudolf Uhlenhaut having been replaced by Neubauer, with the W125 that finally overcame the fine-tuning difficulties experienced with the W25C. The team scored a 1-2 in Germany and 1-2-3s at Monte Carlo (von Brauchitsch winning), Switzerland, Italy (where the GP was held at Livorno rather than Monza) and Hungary. Mercedes was absolutely unbeatable while Nuvolari and the Alfa were always sadly distant from the podium despite the introduction of the 12-cylinder version of the Tipo C.

62 top left La Tribuna Illustrata *relates the accident that occurred during the San Paolo GP in 1936. Hellé Nice crashed into the grandstand, killing four people and injuring a further 38.*

62 top right *The poster announcing the 1936 Donington GP. The German teams were absent.*

and won the second European Championship. His Auto Union is still awe-inspiring given that the driver sat in such an advanced position aboard a car powered by a 16-cylinder engine developing 520 hp and weighing just 750 kg (1,653 lb.). Moreover, it was a particularly difficult car to drive and perhaps only Rosemeyer ever succeeded in exploiting its full competition potential.

Another effect of this perfect blend of man and machine was the secondary role that the older Nuvolari and Caracciola were forced to play. Neither of them was happy with the idea of being bullied by the youngster, particularly Caracciola, who in the past had been distinguished by his sporting attitude but who in the Swiss GP did all he could to obstruct Rosemeyer. In the end he was shown the blue flag by the race steward and obliged to give way and allow the much faster Auto Union driver to overtake.

Caracciola was by no means finished, however, and he was not slow in extracting his revenge. While in 1936 Rosemeyer won three consecutive races, in 1937 Caracciola triumphed in four, leaving

What was so special about the W125? Above all it boasted an enormous maximum power output of 646 hp per liter, a value not to be bettered until after the Second World War, and only then in limited applications. In the GP world, the overall output of the superlative Mercedes wasn't matched for 40+ years.

The W125, of which there were two versions, one with open wheels and the other with full-width bodywork, could easily reach 300 kph (186 mph). The chassis weighed just 52 kg (115 lb.) while the M125 engine tipped the scales at no more than 235 kg (518 lb.) in spite of its displacement of 5660 cc.

Auto Union rested on the laurels reaped by the

62 center left *The Scuderia Ferrari pits at the first edition of the Hungarian GP in 1936. Nuvolari won, with Tadini fourth.*

62 center right *Nuvolari competed in the 1936 Italian GP with a Tipo C. On that occasion he finished second behind Rosemeyer in an Auto Union. The Alfa Tipo C (below) won at Budapest and Donington in 1936.*

62 bottom *Nuvolari also enjoyed success with the revolutionary Auto Unions. Here he is seen tackling the extremely fast Pescara circuit in 1936.*

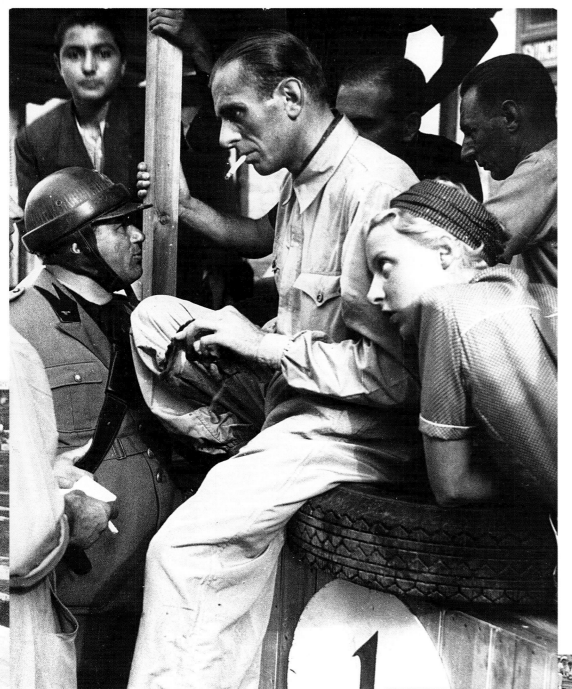

63 top left Achille Varzi is portrayed here during a pit stop at the Sanremo GP of 1937. As well as the international Grands Prix of the Twenties and Thirties, numerous other similar events were held, frequently to Formula Libre regulations.

63 top right The official poster for the 1936 Monaco GP has a different theme: no longer with Alfas dominating or duelling with Bugattis, but Auto Unions chased by Mercedes. The final result was to see these positions inverted.

63 center right The dashboard of the Mercedes W25. In the center the rev-counter, left the water temperature gauge and right the oil pressure gauge.

63 bottom Two Mercedes duelling in the 1937 Nürburgring GP driven by Manfred von Brauchitsch and Rudolf Caracciola, who was eventually to get the better of his aristocratic teammate. The car was a 125 version of the W-series, equipped with a still very powerful but even thirstier engine (160 l/100 km; 42 gal./62 mi.).

Type C which was not modified for the 1937 season; it was known that Grand Prix regulations would soon change and it was therefore not worth investing in new cars that would soon be obsolete.

It was nonetheless thrilling to watch the two streamlined German cars battling daggers-drawn at insane speeds on the straights and the banked curves not only for overall victory but also to beat the class speed records. It was in search of this record that the still very young Bernd Rosemeyer was pulverized together with his car in January of 1938 in a crash at over 400 kph (248 mph).

Thus was interrupted an era of great duels, those between Caracciola and Rosemeyer and Nuvolari and Varzi, the lattermost now but a shadow of his former self due to cocaine addiction.

Alfa was not content to take a back seat and took over the Scuderia Ferrari, devoting itself in the meantime to an ambitious and ultimately rewarding project, that of the 158 Alfetta. Ferrari remained as team manager but left the company in 1940 to found Auto Avio Costruzioni and subsequently the firm that carried his own name.

In 1938 the regulations were modified in favor of a weight limit of between 400 and 850 kg (882 and 1,875 lb.) in relation to the size of the engine (between 666 and 3,000 cc or 1,000 and 4,500 cc with or without a supercharger, respectively). The ratio between the weight of the car and its engine's power output thus became an envelope within which designers and engineers made their

ideological decisions in relation in part—in fact, above all—to their available chassis technology. A stiffer, lighter chassis and more sophisticated and reliable suspension allowed greater overall engine weights to be tolerated; in this respect the German teams were unrivaled, and thus continued to dominate.

The compact supercharged engines proved to be the more competitive thanks to the gulf between the specific power outputs achieved. Three-liter supercharged engines were adopted by Alfa Romeo, Auto Union, Bugatti, Mercedes-Benz and Maserati while only the French models Delahaye and Talbot opted for naturally aspirated 4.5-liter units.

The two year period 1938-39 was again dominated by Mercedes, with Caracciola taking the European title for the third time in 1938 (in practice it was German drivers and German cars that won every edition of the continental title). This time Rudolf was unable to fight for the title with Rosemeyer, as Bernd had been killed in a stubborn attempt to break the class speed record that stemmed from the two drivers' heated rivalry.

It was a mistake, in fact, to bring the Auto Union and Mercedes teams together for the record attempt. What happened was that Rosemeyer recorded a speed slightly lower than Caracciola's

(432.69 kph) and, in spite of the opinions to the contrary expressed by his technical staff, insisted on trying another run to beat Caracciola and the Mercedes. The attempt proved fatal.

As a consequence Auto Union required a talented and experienced driver capable of adjusting to the car's idiosyncrasies. The team was thus obliged to overcome its ostracism toward the indomitable Nuvolari and to sign the brilliant Italian in the middle of the season.

The historic change of models derived from Nuvolari's irritation at the fact that his Alfa Romeo team was severely lacking in organization and potential. During the Pau GP, the opening race of the season, his car's fuel tank ruptured, the car caught fire and Tazio was seriously burned. This was the last straw and the driver left Alfa and Ferrari (with whom he had never enjoyed a good relationship) and, after a long vacation, joined the German team. After having struggled to come to terms with the strange car (in the German GP he crashed full speed into the barriers on the first lap) the Italian won the last two races of the season with a Type D, distinguishable externally by the two rear projections resembling the tailplanes of aircraft.

Mercedes instead permitted Caracciola, Lang, Seaman and von Brauchitsch to dominate the season with the W154 equipped with a powerful 60° V-12 composed of four groups of three cylinders with 48 valves and two Roots-type superchargers. The unit produced a maximum power output of almost 470 hp and a specific output much greater than that of the W125: 158 hp/liter against 114. This car's limitation was its fuel consumption of 145 liters per 100 kilometers (38 gal./62 mi.), which meant frequent refuelling stops. This was partially solved by the adoption of supplementary tanks that allowed up to 390 liters (103 gal.) of fuel to be carried. Weight was also a problem as the car was 118 kg (260 lb.)

64 top left The Nuvolari/Auto Union combination aroused great surprise. Nuvolari was exasperated with Alfa's lack of competitiveness and in 1938 decided to move to Auto Union.

64 top center Farina at the wheel of an Alfa during the 1939 Belgian GP.

64 top right The 1939 French GP: Hermann Müller with an Auto Union D, the eventual winner; Rudolf Caracciola with the Mercedes W163, second on the grid; Hans Stuck with an Auto Union D, sixth at the finish, four laps down on the winner; Hermann Lang with a Mercedes-Benz, in pole position.

64 center right The 1938 Swiss GP; Rudolf Caracciola, the winner, discussing the race with another two drivers, Manfred von Brauchitsch on the left and Dick Seaman on the right.

64 bottom left The Mercedes W154 of 1938 was powered by a 60° V-12 engine developing 470 hp (with a specific output of 158 hp per liter).

64 bottom center The Eraria is an example of GP English cars at the end of the 1930s.

64 bottom right Tazio Nuvolari seen at the Monza Autodrome on the occasion of the 1938 Italian GP.

65 top left The Rio de Janeiro GP of 1938. Alfa produced an intermediate single-seater, the 308, in the late Thirties which Carlo Pintacuda drove to the only victory of his brief career. The context is important because Alfa had decided to return to competition and Enzo Ferrari was appointed as consultant to the team.

1938 1939

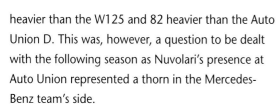

heavier than the W125 and 82 heavier than the Auto Union D. This was, however, a question to be dealt with the following season as Nuvolari's presence at Auto Union represented a thorn in the Mercedes-Benz team's side.

The problems were successfully overcome and in 1939, the last year of racing prior to the Second World War, Mercedes was able to field a competitive car, the W163, in which the maximum power output was increased to 485 hp at 8000 rpm thanks to a higher compression ratio.

Victories in the six Grands Prix were shared equally between Mercedes and Auto Union with the only driver to win two events being Hermann Lang. One could say that it was he who won the European title but the regulations did not allow the German ace to be officially recognized as champion because the young Hermann Müller with the uprated Auto Union D could also have achieved the necessary points total. Unfortunately definitive standings would depend on knowing the exact moment at which the pair retired in certain races. Lang and Müller were both outsiders: Lang, a humble mechanic, wrecked Caracciola's dream of conquering a fourth title while Müller was a virtual rookie.

However, far greater battles were on the horizon. In spite of the Munich Pact signed by Germany, Italy, France and Great Britain, in the July of 1939 Hitler moved his armored divisions to the Polish border and invaded in September after having strengthened his position in Central Europe. Motor racing like all other international sporting events was soon forgotten.

Another year marked by tragic accidents was 1939. It was the Mercedes driver Seaman, who crashed during the Belgian Grand Prix. His W163 caught fire and Seaman died shortly afterward in the hospital. Caracciola concluded his career with a surprise win in "his" German GP while Nuvolari's last GP victory came in Yugoslavia after the French and British ultimatum to Germany had already passed.

HONOR ROLL

Grands Prix from 1934 to 1939

Year	Grand Prix	Venue	Driver	Car	Av. Speed in KPH (MPH)
1934	Monaco	Monte Carlo	G. Moll	Alfa P3	90 (56)
1934	ACF	Montlhéry	A. Varzi	Alfa P3	136.8 (85)
1934	German	Nürburgring	H. Stuck	Auto Union A	122.9 (76)
1934	Belgian	Spa	R. Dreyfus	Bugatti T59	140.7 (87.4))
1934	Swiss	Bremgarten	H. Stuck	Auto Union A	140.3 (87.1)
1934	Italian	Monza	R. Caracciola/L. Fagioli	Mercedes W25A	105.4 (65)
1934	Spanish	Lasarte	R. Caracciola/L. Fagioli	Mercedes W25A	160 (99)
1934	Czech	Brno	H. Stuck	Auto Union A	127.3 (79)
1935	Monaco	Monte Carlo	L. Fagioli	Mercedes W25B	93.6 (58)
1935	ACF	Montlhéry	R. Caracciola	Mercedes W25B	124.5 (77)
1935	Belgian	Spa	R. Caracciola	Mercedes W25B	158.4 (98)
1935	German	Nürburgring	T. Nuvolari	Alfa P3	121.3 (75)
1935	Swiss	Bremgarten	R. Caracciola	Mercedes W25B	144.8 (89.9)
1935	Italian	Monza	H. Stuck	Auto Union B	138.3 (85.9)
1935	Spanish	Lasarte	R. Caracciola	Mercedes W25B	168.2 (104)
1935	Czech	Brno	B. Rosemeyer	Auto Union B	132.6 (82)
1935	Donington	Donington	R. Shuttleworth	Alfa P3	102.9 (63)
1936	Monaco	Monte Carlo	R. Caracciola	Mercedes W25B	83.2 (51.7)
1936	Hungarian	Budapest	T. Nuvolari	Alfa Tipo C	111.6 (69)
1936	ACF	Montlhéry	J. P. Wimille/R. Sommer	Bugatti T57G	125.3 (77.8)
1936	German	Nürburgring	B. Rosemeyer	Auto Union C	131.6 (81.7)
1936	Swiss	Bremgarten	B. Rosemeyer	Auto Union C	161.8 (100)
1936	Italian	Monza	B. Rosemeyer	Auto Union C	134.4 (83)
1936	Donington	Donington	H. Ruesch/D. Seaman	Alfa Tipo C	111.3 (69)
1937	ACF	Montlhéry	L. Chiron	Talbot T15OC	132.7 (82)
1937	Belgian	Spa	R. Hasse	Auto Union C	168 (104)
1937	German	Nürburgring	R. Caracciola	Mercedes W125	133.2 (82.8)
1937	Monaco	Monte Carlo	M. von Brauchitsch	Mercedes W125	101.8 (63)
1937	Swiss	Bremgarten	R. Caracciola	Mercedes W125	158.7 (98)
1937	Italian	Livorno	R. Caracciola	Mercedes W125	127 (78)
1937	Czech	Brno	R. Caracciola	Mercedes W125	138.5 (86)
1937	Donington	Donington	B. Rosemeyer	Auto Union C	133.3 (82.7)
1938	ACF	Reims	M. von Brauchitsch	Mercedes W154	162.8 (101)
1938	German	Nürburgring	D. Seaman/R. Caracciola	Mercedes W154	129.8 (80)
1938	Swiss	Bremgarten	R. Caracciola	Mercedes W154	143.6 (89)
1938	Italian	Monza	T. Nuvolari	Auto Union D	155.9 (96.8)
1938	Donington	Donington	T. Nuvolari	Auto Union D	129.5 (78.6)
1939	Belgian	Spa	H. Lang	Mercedes W163	148.5 (92.2)
1939	ACF	Reims	H. Müller	Auto Union D	169.7 (105.3)
1939	German	Nürburgring	R. Caracciola	Mercedes W163	121 (75)
1939	Swiss	Bremgarten	H. Lang	Mercedes W163	154.6 (96)
1939	Yugoslavian	Belgrade	T. Nuvolari	Auto Union D	130.7 (81)

THE WAR TERMINATES THE GOLDEN AGE

It could thus be said that with Nuvolari's last Grand Prix victory, an era drew to a close—an era in which he had been the undisputed king, and in which only in part was his glory temporarily obscured by the German and Italian drivers Caracciola, Rosemeyer, Campari and Ascari.

The war brought an end to the more noble (albeit politically influenced toward the end) automotive conflicts. But once peace had been declared, the number of races, the dedication of the manufacturers and the interest of the public revived rapidly. A number of early post-war events are worthy of particular mention including the formation of the FIA (Fédération Internationale de l'Automobile), still responsible for all international motor racing events of European origins. The FIA took it upon itself to reorganize the regulations for GP type racing within the context of a technological panorama in need of reconstruction and generally restricted economic resources. Thus was Formula 1

GRAND PRIX DE RHENANIE
27 Juillet 1947 NÜRBURGRING

66 top An advertisement for the Renania GP of 1947 held at the Nürburgring. This was not an international Grand Prix.

66 center Motor racing returned immediately after the end of the war, although it was not until 1947 that Grands Prix of international standing were held. This 1946 event is a city race organized in the Sempione Park in Milan. The cars date back to 1938 and Varzi can be recognized aboard an Alfa.

66 bottom The European Grands Prix returned in style in 1947. The event seen here is the Italian GP that was held on the streets of Milan rather than at Monza. The cars are two Alfetta 158s, the first driven by the winner Carlo Felice Trossi, the other by Achille Varzi, who finished second. The Tipo 158's success was completed by Consalvo Sanesi and Alessandro Gaboardi's third and fourth places.

born in 1947 with its initial format dictated by the availability of cars developed before the war. The 3-liter supercharged Mercedes and Auto Unions having disappeared (Mercedes was to make a triumphant comeback in 1954-55), this was the era of the 1.5-liter engines.

This meant that Alfa Romeo was immediately competitive. Just such a car had long been ready from Alfa's Modena branch, home of the racing team managed by Enzo Ferrari. In the late Thirties this car, the Tipo 158–a supercharged 1.5 that debuted in 1938 and was usually called the "Alfetta"– made impressive finishes in its class but a technological (and displacement) abyss clearly existed between the Italian voiturette and the larger German GP cars. After the war however, the Tipo 158 (and its Tipo 159 evolution) ruled Formula 1.

Before celebrating the Alfa triumphs a few more words need to be spent with regards to the automotive scene. Along with Alfa Romeo, Maserati also harbored grand post-war ambitions, having spent the conflict manufacturing machine tools, while another small Italian company, Cisitalia, approached the world of competition with the solid basis of a design acquired from Ferdinand Porsche, the supercharged, mid-engined type 360.

And Ferrari? Enzo was ready to take the great step of organizing a team under his own name capable above all of bringing technological benefits and fame to the Gran Turismo cars he had begun to construct in 1940 (albeit not yet carrying his own name). He retained Gioacchino Colombo, one of the fathers of the 158, at Modena and entrusted him with the development of a V12 even though Ferrari was well aware of the merits of the straight-Eight Colombo had placed at the heart of the Alfetta. The V12 engine remained a fixation with Ferrari for the rest of his life even when many years later it became clear that this architecture was inferior to other, more compact engine designs. Only with a certain reluctance would the Commendatore (a title conferred by Mussolini but actually taken from him following the collapse of Fascism) seriously consider alternative solutions.

At the beginning of the glorious history of the Prancing Horse, however, the new V12 proved to be

successful and can be considered as the forerunner of a long dynasty of enthusiastically received engines. With regards to Ferrari, while it is right to recognize his great talents as a manager and his understanding of men, we feel that much of the mythology surrounding him and his racing cars should be revised.

It is frequently easier to construct heroes and legends than it is to question them, and not everybody enjoys going against the flow. Nonetheless, we cannot ignore the fact that over the course of the first 40 years of Formula 1 history Ferrari came up against (not always emerging victorious) extremely acute rivals such as a host of British designers and team managers—Colin Chapman and Lotus above all—or extremely talented engineers such as those responsible for the Ford Cosworth engines. They and others like them were the true innovators, the true leaders. The statistics speak clearly and impartially: the Ford Cosworth engine has won many more races than that of any other company, Ferrari included, while the successful British teams gave to motor sport figures of great standing and highly successful cars. Should we draw up a table based on results achieved, Ferrari would by no means be in the top three, despite being considered by many as the quintessence of Formula 1. Take, for example, the modest results achieved in the Eighties and Nineties

in spite of the vast resources made available by Fiat to reinforce the prestige of the model and in spite of the team's considerable influence with the FIA.

Only toward the end of the century has the team, if not the car, managed to find a suitable blend of competence, talent and above all, modesty—a virtue that in the past has never been attributed to Maranello—and obtain results that lived up to the expectations of the model's countless fans. The only record on which Ferrari has a tenacious grip is that concerning the number of international Grands Prix in which it has participated, a record that of course penalizes the races/wins ratio.

After this obligatory digression that not by chance coincides with the recording of Ferrari's first victories (1949 Swiss GP, Alberto Ascari with the

125) we can return to the story of the races that preceded the constitution of the now celebrated World Championship title.

In 1947, of the four Formula 1 GPs, three were won by Alfettas driven by Wimille and Trossi. Apart from Wimille, considered the man to beat, and Trossi, Achille Varzi and Consalvo Sanesi were also members of the Alfa team. The team manager of the era was Giovan Battista Guidotti, himself a talented driver and famous for having navigated for Nuvolari on the 1930 Mille Miglia.

The Arese Reds deserted the last race of the year, which was won by the enduring Chiron with a Lago-Talbot. That year also saw the creation of a new racing car manufacturer later to enjoy great fame, BRM (British Racing Motors), as well as the death of Ettore Bugatti at 66 years of age.

1946 1947

67 left A side view of the Maserati 4CLT Supercharged, one of the protagonists in afterwar races.

67 right An evocative image of the front wheel of the Alfetta 158 and the leader board at the 1947 Italian GP.

The true protagonist of those years was thus the Alfetta. Alfa boasted a technical staff of undisputed prestige: Colombo, Nasi, Massimino, Giberti and Bazzi, Ferrari's right-hand man. In 1938 they prepared a car equipped with a 1.5-liter, eight-cylinder engine with an Alfa-made twin-lobe supercharger, twin overhead camshafts and a triple-barrel carb. The initial power output was 275 hp but this was subsequently raised to 350, thanks to which the car was capable of a maximum speed of 270 kph. The chassis was composed of tubular longerons. The Alfetta scored numerous victories, almost always accompanied by second and third placings. If its results are added to those of the 159—a developed 158—the model would probably be the most successful in the history of Formula 1. Apart from the World Championship conquered in 1950, the car's roll of honor includes four Italian GPs, two French and two Swiss GPs, as well as one Monaco and one Belgian GP. Then there were other important races of the era such as the two Nations

and three European GPs, two International Trophies, the Coppa Ciano, the Tripoli GP, those of Turin and Milan and the Coppa Acerbo.

At the wheel of this car could be admired the greatest drivers of the post-war age: Biondetti, Farina (the first World Champion), Fagioli, Trossi, Taruffi, Villoresi, Varzi (who was killed in 1948 during the Belgian GP), Wimille and above all Juan Manuel Fangio—probably the most talented driver of all time. It is curious to note that the Alfetta was also driven by Alberto Ascari, the son of the great Antonio, a man so closely associated with the Alfa colors. Alberto finished third in the French GP and then went on to win two World Championships with Ferrari.

The beautiful Alfetta can still be admired in the Museo Storico dell'Alfa Romeo at Arese where it represents one of the greatest historic treasures, especially considering that in 1951, shortly after winning the World Championship, Alfa withdrew from Formula 1, not to return until the

disappointing episodes of the late 1970s.

In 1948 too, the other teams, in particular Maserati and Lago-Talbot, were allowed opportunities to shine only when Alfa was absent. This was the case at the Monaco and British GPs (the latter notable for the debut of the former airfield circuit at Silverstone). In Switzerland, France and Italy the Alfetta shut the door firmly in the face of its opposition. The first race was won by Trossi from Wimille, while the others were conquered by Wimille from Consalvo Sanesi and Alberto Ascari in France and from Villoresi (a lap behind) in Italy. With regards to circuits, Monza (used as a military vehicle dump), Le Mans (occupied by the German air force and thus bombed by the British), and Montlhéry (destroyed by the Germans on their surrender), were unusable. All were later restored, but Montlhéry—the historic venue for the ACF Grand Prix—was abandoned by the World Championship.

Nineteen forty-eight is to be remembered as it saw the competition baptism of the first Formula 1

68 The first post-war Italian GP was held at Milan in 1947. Although it was organized by the local Automobile Club, the race had usually been staged at nearby Monza. The driver immortalized here is Pesci with a Maserati.

69 top left This very unusual photograph records a moment during the 1948 Grand Prix of Europe held at Bremgarten. The race was an Alfa Romeo triumph with Trossi and Wimille first and second, both at the wheel of Alfa Romeo 158s.

69 bottom left This 1949 photo portrays two racing cars, one with open wheels, the other fully enclosed. In 1939 Caracciola had driven experimental cars of a similar type to break speed records. Rosemeyer did the same for Auto Union with fatal results.

1947 1948 1949

Ferrari, an event that took place at the Turin GP, and the debut of the shadowy and hardly young Argentinean driver Juan Manuel Fangio, who between 1951 and 1957 won the World Championship title five times. Fangio was one of the few top drivers to pass away peacefully in his bed rather than amid the battered panels of a racing car. In this he was like another of the true greats, Nuvolari, who wracked by the death of his young children in 1947 and 1948, raced with such desperation at 55 years of age that the sporting literature of the era suggested that he was seeking, unsuccessfully, to anticipate death. Instead, death came to him in 1953 in a hospital bed.

Varzi in 1948 and Wimille in 1949 were instead killed while racing their Alfettas, and Alfa Romeo also lost Trossi through illness. The absence of leading drivers and the rising costs of racing persuaded the firm to desert the 1949 season, thus allowing the team's adversaries an open field. It was Ferrari above all that took advantage, scoring three

wins—Alberto Ascari in Switzerland and at Monza and Whitehead at Brno.

The three-year period 1947-49, punctuated by important events and debuts, was nonetheless a period of transition—a cushion between the two great epochs of modern motor racing, one which followed immediately after the pioneer phase and concluded with the outbreak of the Second World War, the other one beginning in 1950 with the advent of the Formula 1 World Championship.

69 top right The start of the 1949 Swiss GP. The Ferrari era began in the post-war period, albeit in conjunction with Alfa's two-year domination in which it won two World Championships with Farina (1950) and Fangio (1951). Here at Bremgarten the 125 driven by Alberto Ascari, son of Antonio, records

the first Grand Prix victory for a car bearing the Prancing Horse. The winner is aboard the car on the right, number 30.

69 bottom right This image shows the rolling chassis and engine of the Alfetta 159, the dominator of the 1948-1951 period.

HONOR ROLL

Grands Prix from 1947 to 1949

YEAR	GRAND PRIX	VENUE	DRIVER	CAR	AV. SPEED KPH (MPH)
1947	Swiss	Bremgarten	J.P. Wimille	Alfa R. 158	153.9 (95.6)
1947	Belgian	Spa	J.P. Wimille	Alfa R. 158	154.3 (95.8)
1947	Italian	Milan	C.F. Trossi	Alfa R. 158	113.2 (70.3)
1947	ACF	Lyons	L. Chiron	Lago-Talbot 126 C	124.5 (77.3)
1948	Monaco	Monte Carlo	G. Farina	Maserati 4CLT	96.1 (59.7)
1948	Swiss	Bremgarten	C.F. Trossi	Alfa R. 158	146.5 (90.9)
1948	ACF	Reims	J.P. Wimille	Alfa R. 158	165.7 (102.8)
1948	Italian	Turin	J.P. Wimille	Alfa R. 158	113.2 (70.3)
1948	British	Silverstone	L. Villoresi	Maserati 4CLT	116.3 (72.2)
1949	British	Silverstone	E. de Graffenried	Maserati 4CLT/48	124.4 (77.3)
1949	Belgian	Spa	L. Rosier	Lago-Talbot T26C	156.8 (97.4)
1949	Swiss	Bremgarten	A. Ascari	Ferrari 125	146.3 (90.8)
1949	French	Reims	L. Chiron	Lago-Talbot T26C	160.8 (99.8)
1949	Italian	Monza	A. Ascari	Ferrari 125	169 (104.9)
1949	Czech	Brno	P. Whitehead	Ferrari 125	123.4 (76.6)

70 top Villoresi was one of the great drivers who proved themselves at the wheel of the Maserati 4CLT Supercharged.

70-71 The similarity of the 1948 Maserati 4CLT Supercharged to a torpedo is immediately apparent. The Trident's season culminated in triumph at the last GP at Silverstone with Luigi Villoresi first and Alberto Ascari second (number 10). The Officine Maserati, which during the war had been converted to the production of machine tools, returned to the design and production of GT and single-seater cars.

70 bottom Luigi Villoresi tackling a
Grand Prix in 1948. The talented Italian
driver enjoyed great success with the
supercharged Maserati before moving to
Ferrari.

71 top Detail of the in-line engine of the
4CLT Supercharged; The great Fangio
drove this car to his first European
victory, at the Pau GP in 1948.

71 center left In 1947 the naturally
aspirated version of the Maserati 4CLT was
fourth in Switzerland behind three Alfas.
The car was driven by Raymond Sommer.

71 center right The rear of the Maserati
4CLT Supercharged also reveals stylistic
traits from the late Thirties that had been
mothballed during the war. In 1948
"Nino" Farina won the debut Grand Prix
with this version at Monaco in front of
Chiron aboard a Lago-Talbot.

FORMULA 1
THE CIRCUS OF SPEED

The birth of the Formula 1 World Championship splits the automotive century in two: the colorful saga, rich in characters and roles curiously similar to those of adventures stories, in fact began in 1950.

We have a "gray eminence," Bernie Ecclestone, who following the death of Enzo Ferrari—a charismatic figure not inclined to overt subjection—transformed from a Cardinal Mazzarino-type figure into the championship's absolute monarch. We have the baronies, the fiefdoms of ancient lineage or recent investiture, represented by the teams who submit to the decisions of the organizing bodies with heads bowed, despite frequently harboring dreams of rebellion. We also have the emergent economic potentates, the sponsors—initially the teams' financiers but later increasingly active and decisive in the selection of drivers and managers. Then of course we have the knights on horseback— the drivers themselves, who as in serial novels are

72 top This photograph reveals the absolute concentration of the modern racing driver awaiting the green light that signals the start of his high-speed challenge.

72 bottom This black and white picture shows two great Formula 1 protagonists, the Ferrari 158 F1 and John Surtees.

73 top At the very heart of Formula 1 is speed itself, as this photograph taken during the French GP of 1998 appears to emphasize.

73 bottom left Juan Manuel Fangio and Mercedes, an invincible combination in the Formula 1 of the 1950s. The Argentine driver conquered two of his five world titles at the wheel of the Silver Arrows, here seen without the streamlined bodywork covering the wheels.

73 bottom right Looking like astronauts invading Earth from some other planet, the mechanics in the pits can make the difference between winning and losing a Grand Prix. During split-second pit stops they load hundreds of liters of fuel into the tanks and change all four wheels.

75 top left A line-up of nose cones: this frontal element of the bodywork—in the picture can be seen those of the 1998 Sauber C17—is of fundamental importance to the car's aerodynamics and frequently the main difference between one model and another.

74 left Sitting in his car, elbow resting on the bodywork, Ayrton Senna appears more intent on a Sunday drive around the countryside rather than the last checks on his Lotus prior to the start.

74 top The drivers "parading" in front of the celebrities and enthusiastic admirers that have always accompanied the world of motor racing. This photograph shows the unmistakable lines of the celebrated Bugatti Type 35 driven by Tazio Nuvolari.

74 center Teamwork has its place in Formula 1, and not only when one of the two drivers administers or controls the race on behalf of his teammate: Pit-stops are perfectly choreographed with 40 hands moving around the car for just a few seconds.

74 bottom Prior to the birth of the World Championship, many Grands Prix, including the Italian GP seen here, were held on street circuits. This image shows the 1948 edition held on the Valentino circuit in Turin, won by Wimille in the Alfa Romeo Tipo 158, the first on the left in car number 52.

75 top right In-line fins, or rather the air intakes positioned above and immediately behind the driver to provide cool air for the engine. The photograph shows those of the 1990 McLaren powered by a Honda engine that was invincible in the early 1990s.

75 bottom Paired tires ready to be fitted in case of rain could almost be a work of automotive art: these are in fact wet weather covers with grooved treads.

apparently protagonists but in reality unwitting pawns in the hands of the powers that be. And then we have the cars, perfect transcriptions of the noble steeds of the past, with the mechanics their faithful handlers. As for beautiful maidens, Formula 1 has never been lacking in ideal candidates.

By 1950 motor racing had already long been subjected to the laws of big business. From this moment on there was however a slow but inexorable mutation from sporting events to spectacles, with many other sports following on behind as they adapted to suit the demands of television and entertainment in general. Take, for example, basketball, tennis, volleyball and even the Olympic Games.

The basic elements of the sport have apparently remained the same: cars and drivers. But in reality the true protagonist of modern racing is the

threshold to a new century. For the moment we shall continue to enjoy motor racing as a sport, a contest revisited in a mechanical key but nonetheless fed by courage, colored by passion and fired by emotions.

The story of these 50 years of single-seater racing is a fabric woven with threads of different kinds and colors: the "eras" of the great drivers, Fangio, Clark, Stewart, Lauda, Prost and Senna; the technological innovations comprising an infinite series of mechanical, structural and aerodynamic modifications that began with the momentary end of the supercharged era and includes the advent of telemetry (which extinguished like a light the value of the human factor); the changes in the regulations, frequently dictated by lobbyists or demagogic impositions; the historic races and the strategies of the various teams, some of which represent solid pillars of the establishment while others are of the second rank or merely bit players.

We would like to remain imprisoned within the logic of the plot and watch from above as this enthralling story fast-forwards before our eyes. The Formula 1 World Championship remains, albeit with its highs and lows, the world's greatest motor racing series—although to call it a "world" championship is perhaps stretching a point. Not only has Bernie Ecclestone, the true ringmaster, never succeeded in distracting the great American public from its Indy championship, but neither has he managed to establish a permanent bridgehead in the States by organizing attractive Grands Prix.

spectacle itself, stripped of its atmosphere and excitement and crudely channeled into television sets around the world. Thanks to the invasive presence of television, which changes the very nature of everything that passes in front of a camera, the interests revolving around the Formula 1 championship are such that it is legitimate to ask whether today the Grands Prix are anything but motor races.

We shall leave this question unanswered until the end of this chapter, which concludes at the

The Formula 1 story officially began on the 13th of June, 1950, at the former military airfield of Silverstone. With the pain and damage of the war slowly healing, motor racing had returned to thrill the public. There were endurance races, legendary road races, city-to-city raids and sporadic rallies. Above all the open-wheeled single-seaters began to roar again, even though their technological flywheel had yet to pick up speed: the cars were frequently those developed in the late 1930s and it was actually one of these, the Alfetta Tipo 158 and subsequently the Tipo 159 that was to dominate the first two editions of the World Championship, carrying Nino Farina and Juan Manuel

Fangio to consecutive titles. During the German occupation of Italy the 158s designed by Gioacchino Colombo had been hidden in a cheese factory.

The formula used to assign the new championship title was less abstruse than previous systems and was based on decreasing points from eight to two. At the end of the season the driver with the most points was crowned World Champion. A clause in the regulations rendered the races even more interesting: an extra point was assigned to the driver recording the fastest lap. This clause was eliminated in 1961, the point being added to those given to the winner of each race. The first championship was

of Fagioli, Chiron and Lang, and regrets that we would never again see on the starting grid aces of the caliber of Varzi, Rosemeyer and the debilitated Nuvolari. One of those new drivers, however—Juan Manuel Fangio—was to win no fewer than five World Championships, a record to this day.

Alfa Romeo's superiority was crushing thanks to the Alfetta 158 which won all 11 races for which it was entered in 1950. The first three places in the final championship table were filled by the *Alfisti*: Farina, Fangio and Fagioli. This domination was repeated in 1951, although the Ferrari was now competitive enough to challenge Fangio's leadership.

76 left Fangio and Farina are saluted by King George VI before the start of the 1950 British Grand Prix at Silverstone, the very first Formula 1 race.

76 right Fangio (top) arriving in the pits with the Alfa Tipo 158 Alfetta at the Italian GP, the last round of the 1950 championship. His race was curtailed by a broken gearbox on the 24th lap, thus putting an end to his championship hopes. The race was won by Farina who also became the first Formula 1 World Champion. In the photo below Farina is seen with the second Alfetta behind Ascari in the Ferrari. Ascari later took over Serafini's car (on the third lap after his own engine failed) and finished second.

composed of the British Grand Prix (that first race was attended by the Royal Family), and those of Monaco, Switzerland, Belgium, France and Italy. Up until 1960 the Indianapolis 500 was also valid for the World Championship, although in practice only local drivers competed in the American race.

The races were disputed by cars with 1.5-liter supercharged or 4.5-liter naturally aspirated engines. There were no restrictions on weight or power output.

Five main teams took part in that first championship season: Alfa Romeo, Ferrari, Maserati, Talbot and Gordini. Among the 19 drivers there were interesting newcomers such as the Italians, Farina and Alberto Ascari; two red-hot Argentines, Fangio and Gonzales; and two Britons, Parnell and Moss. Then there was the old guard composed of the likes

Certainly the 13-year-old Alfetta was by now aging, but it was still very reliable; the 158 had also evolved into the 159, the power output of which reached 470 hp with a specific output of 278 hp/liter (the engine had a total displacement of just 1479 cc).

In those years there was a custom that today appears curious but at the time added to the spectacle: the "stealing" of cars. It was in fact within the rules for the teams to move a driver from one car to another in the middle of a race. A classic example of this took place in the ACF Grand Prix of 1951. Ascari at the wheel of a Ferrari overtook Fangio but broke down on the 10th lap while the Argentine slowed with engine problems. Farina, the reigning champion, thus found himself in the lead. Fangio took over Fagioli's car while Ascari in turn took the place of Gonzales. Farina in the meantime lost a wheel but there were no more cars available. Victory went to Fangio, the Alfetta's 27th consecutive win.

In the following GP at Silverstone, Ascari broke with this tradition: he was let down by his own car but recognized that Gonzales had the opportunity not only to beat his fellow countryman Fangio but also to interrupt the Alfetta's winning streak. Ascari could have demanded Gonzales' car but refrained from doing so and the *simpatico* Gaucho Gonzales went on to win the race. It was a noble gesture but an error as far as the championship was concerned. By the last race held at Barcelona, Ascari was two points behind Fangio (he would have had a clear lead had he won at Silverstone) and was obliged to chase. The team got its tire strategy completely wrong and the dream was over: Fangio the *Chueco* (crooked-leg) won and was crowned champion.

Fangio was to be the undisputed king of 1950s Grand Prix racing, winning a further four championships from 1954 to 1957 when driving for Mercedes, Maserati and Ferrari. His last race was the 1958 French GP at the wheel of a Maserati, a race that

77 top On the extremely long (over 22 km/ 13.7 mi.) and difficult Nürburgring circuit, Fangio could only manage second place in the 1951 German GP. He was beaten by a Ferrari which thus scored its second Formula 1 win.

unfortunately will be remembered for the death of his great friend Luigi Musso: the Argentine's pain was so great he announced his definitive retirement.

His adieu was one of those that leave a vacuum. Apart from his five world titles, a feat yet to be equaled, he took with him a record of 51 Grands Prix disputed, nearly half of which he won (24), 28 pole positions and 23 fastest laps.

The Spanish GP of 1951 was the Alfetta's last great victory: at the height of its power Alfa Romeo realized that it could no longer squeeze anything more from its magnificent single-seater and decided to abandon GP racing. Forty-eight years later the firm returned to Formula 1 from 1979 to 1987, but with disappointing results.

77 center left Fangio with the Alfa Tipo 159 Alfetta dominated in Spain the last Grands Prix of 1951: he held pole position, got the fatest lap and, of course, won.

77 center Alfa Romeo against Ferrari, a duel that was to last two seasons and which was to see Alfa prevail. In this photograph Farina with the Tipo 159 is seen leading Taruffi with the Ferrari at the Italian GP of 1951: the two finished third and fifth, respectively.

77 center right Juan Manuel Fangio is applauded following his victory in the Swiss GP of 1951.

77 bottom Farina borne aloft in triumph following his victory in the Belgian GP held at the Spa-Francorchamps circuit.

FORMULA 2 CARS
WHILE AWAITING NEW REGULATIONS

78 top Alberto Ascari at the wheel of a Ferrari during the 1952 British Grand Prix.

78 center Two Ferrari drivers racing almost side by side during the 1952 Italian GP. The two, Ascari and Villoresi, were to cross the line in first and third places, respectively. With this win Ascari celebrated his sixth consecutive victory and his first World Championship title.

78 bottom The great absentee from the '52 championship was Fangio,

who only returned to the circus the following year. In the meantime he continued racing and taking risks: he crashed at the Monaco GP and suffered a concussion. Here he is seen on a stretcher while being loaded onto the ambulance.

79 top Farina, Ascari and Fangio during the 1953 Italian GP: the Argentine driver at the wheel of a Maserati took the race. Giuseppe "Nino" Farina was second, 1.4 seconds behind. Ascari was out of luck as he collided with slow-moving Fairman in the HWM coming out of the parabolica on the last lap.

Alfa's withdrawal was almost fatal for the World Championship. Lack of serious opposition meant that Ferrari's domination was so evident and absolute that it was hardly worth racing. The British teams were working hard and had some good ideas but were still well behind in terms of research and development. The most advanced of them was the youthful BRM (British Racing Motors), a concern born out of the collaboration between around a hundred different manufacturers. The team had presented the Formula 1 field's most powerful car in 1951, the Type 15 Mark 1 producing 525 hp. The Germans had the know-how and the experience, but did not yet have sufficient resources to enter the fray. Making up numbers on the grid were models such as Maserati, Simca-Gordini and Talbot.

There were many who believed that the FIA's attempt to run an organized championship was doomed, like its predecessors, to failure after just two editions. The solution that was found was valid and providential: in order to give the constructors time to design new Formula 1 cars, for two years the World Championship was reserved for Formula 2 cars, i.e., those with 2-liter naturally aspirated or 500-cc supercharged engines. (Supercharging was thus impractical, since it could not overcome such a severe disadvantage). Formula 1 was to return in 1954 with naturally aspirated engines of up to 2.5 liters or supercharged units of 750 cc.

The use of Formula 2 cars opened the Championship to new constructors that had previously been absent due to the exorbitant costs of developing Formula 1 cars. New and unknown models thus found themselves on the starting grids

for the Grands Prix: Cooper, Connaught, AFM, Veritas and OSCA to name some of them. The Cooper developed by Moss's mechanic Francis is worthy of particular mention as it was presented at the 1953 Italian GP with disc brakes, a novelty that was to be adopted on nearly all racing cars during the course of the 1950s, and fuel injection in place of carburetors.

The spectacle however was penalized by the new regulations: the earlier Formula 1 cars had boasted power outputs of well over 400 hp thanks to supercharging and reached extremely high maximum speeds on the order of 300 kph (186 mph). In acoustic terms, too, the roar of their engines was undoubtedly more thrilling. Nonetheless, the Formula 2 machines had the advantage of being lighter than the 1.5-liter supercharged cars and were thus themselves very fast (up to 260 kph/ 161 mph) despite power

outputs of under 200 hp. Moreover, the races were more straightforward as there were fewer refueling stops.

The two-year period was nonetheless dominated by Ferrari who won every round of the 1952 championship and six out of seven of the 1953 Grands Prix (excepting Indy in both cases, of course). Alberto Ascari, son of the great Antonio, who had died during the French GP in 1925, won all the 1952 championship races in which he participated (six out of seven, having missed the opening round in Switzerland because he was driving for Ferrari in the Indianapolis 500) and five of the seven rounds in 1953.

Fangio had moved to Maserati but missed the whole of the 1952 season. He crashed in the nonchampionship Monza GP, suffering the first and only serious injuries of his career. The

79 bottom left Ascari aboard a Ferrari
500 (number 10) and de Graffenried
(in a Maserati) passing the pits at Reims.
The race was the French GP of 1953:
the Englishman Hawthorn won, his
first victory for Ferrari.

79 bottom right The 1953 German GP
with Fangio at the wheel of a Maserati.
After 18 laps of the Nürburgring the
Argentine champion finished over
a minute behind the winner, Giuseppe
Farina in a Ferrari 500.

accident was due to the Argentine's state of fatigue as he had presented himself for the start of the Milanese race just an hour and a half beforehand, after having raced a BRM the day before in Ireland and undergoing an exhausting journey by plane to Paris and then by car to Italy. He started the race from the back of the grid, not having participated in the qualifying sessions, completed two laps and then crashed.

Even though he had completed only 6 km (3.8 mi.), they were sufficient to demonstrate the potential of the new A6CM from *Ingegnere* Colombo, who had recently joined Maserati after his success with Alfa Romeo and Ferrari.

Motor racing lost one of its all-time greats that year as Tazio Nuvolari died after a lengthy illness. He was buried with his leather helmet, yellow shirt and blue trousers.

1952 *1953*

79

The Return of Formula 1 Power

Maserati, Fangio (who won his second World Championship), and Mercedes (who poached the Argentine driver), were the protagonists of the 1954 season, an important year for the World Championship as it was the first to run to the new regulations specifying 2.5-liter naturally aspirated or 750-cc supercharged engines, a formula that remained unchanged until 1960. The reduced cylinder capacity for supercharged engines was a clear signal to the constructors from the FIA that they should concentrate their technical and economic resources on the development of naturally aspirated units.

Mercedes returned to the formula with the introduction of the new regulations and launched a series of mechanical and stylistic innovations that were to leave their mark not only on the world of competition but on automotive production in general. The German firm's participation in Formula

cars' aerodynamics allowed them to gain a second a lap over the agile Ferraris and the powerful Maseratis. The technological innovations were equally surprising: the W196 entranced both humble racing fans and enthusiasts of advanced mechanical engineering.

On its debut the Mercedes was the car to beat despite its weight: 680 kg (1,500 lb.) the streamlined version and 640 (1,411 lb.) for the open-wheeler. The W196 won straight out of the box in France with Fangio. The Argentine driver's remarkable results were due to the respect with which he treated his car as well as to his own undisputed talent: his was the Mercedes works car that suffered the least mechanical problems and wear over the season.

80 top and 81 center left Streamlined styling that would be the envy of the single-seaters of the 1990s, a full width body with covered wheels finished in the unmistakable silver unpolished metal livery. These are the characteristics of the Mercedes W196, the undisputed protagonist of the 1954 season. At the 1954 British GP (top) Fangio was obliged to chase the Ferraris and a Maserati that finished in the first three places. The Argentine finished fourth after a minor accident in which he struck a track marker, damaging the front part of his Mercedes W196's right-hand flank.

1 was to last only two seasons, however. At the end of 1955 the Silver Arrows (as the fearsome Mercedes race cars were known) were withdrawn. While it's generally assumed that this followed the tragic Levegh crash at Le Mans, in fact Mercedes-Benz was eager to concentrate its resources on its more profitable production models. This policy was also dear to Lancia, another debutante in the 1954 season but one which, like Mercedes, was to withdraw at the end of 1955.

When the Silver Arrows—the Mercedes W196s—took to the track at Reims, they catalyzed the attention of spectators and technicians alike with their streamlined full-width bodywork: the wheels were covered by flowing torpedo-like wings, lending the cars a degree of class and elegance that rendered the others obsolete. This was a lesson in design that Mercedes preached to the entire world, demonstrating that extreme performance and beauty could coexist. The streamlined bodywork worn by the W196s on fast circuits to improve the

80 center and 80-81 bottom After 15 years absence from the tracks, Mercedes returned with the W196 in 1954 when the championship was already under way: its first race was the French GP, in which it finished first and second. This photographs show the German car driven by Fangio: note the supplementary air intake integrated into the right-hand flank of the car to augment the flow of cooling air from the shark-like mouth at the front. The bodywork in this case left the wheels exposed and was used as an alternative to the full-width body on slow circuits such as that at Monaco in which handling was all-important. The weight

of the car in this form was 40 kg lighter at 640 kg, but it was still heavier than its rivals. The W196 nonetheless proved to be unbeatable. Fortunately for the other teams the German manufacturer's involvement in Formula 1 lasted for only two seasons, 1954-'55, during which it scored nine victories out of 12 Grands Prix disputed. The team's withdrawal came as a result of the manufacturer's decision to concentrate its resources on its production models. Mercedes returned to Formula 1 in 1994 as an engine supplier, firstly to Sauber and then to McLaren, with whom it won the championship in 1998.

81 top left The Mercedes were futuristic compared with the other cars seen here at the start of the 1954 Italian GP. They finished first and fourth in the race driven by Fangio and Hermann.

81 top right A Mercedes 1-2 at the French GP in 1954: the W196s lapped the rest of the field and finished first and second with just a tenth of a second separating Fangio from Kling, seen here with car number 20.

81 center right and bottom Posters are mementos of the races of the past. Like those of the 1954 French GP (center) held at Reims, or that of Pau (bottom), a French circuit, venue of a non-championship Grand Prix.

1954 1955

THE FIRST WORLD CHAMPIONSHIP VICTIMS

Nineteen fifty-four was unfortunately also the year of the Formula 1 World Championship's first fatality. The Argentine driver Marimon was killed at the wheel of a Maserati during practice for the German GP. The tragedies continued into 1955: the worst accident in motor racing history happened at Le Mans when Pierre Levegh's Mercedes collided with Lance Macklin's Austin-Healey and plunged into the crowd, killing its driver and 83 spectators. The obituary columns also recorded the deaths of Ascari and the two-time winner of the Indianapolis 500, Vukovich. As a mark of respect, the Swiss, German and French Grands Prix were canceled, while the AAA (American Automobile Association) withdrew as an organizer of motor racing in America.

"Ciccio" Ascari died like his father Antonio: a terrible premonitory sign had struck the Italian at the Monaco GP where he crashed at the chicane on the sea-front (at the same point where Bandini was to die 12 years later) but survived unscathed. Four days later while testing Castellotti's Ferrari 750 Ciccio failed to negotiate the Vialone curve at Monza, later

renamed the Ascari curve. His friend Villoresi was devastated and Gianni Lancia, patron of the team that had just signed Ascari, decided that enough was more than enough: he sold the company and ceded his racing cars, the D50s, to Ferrari.

The drivers' World Championship of 1955 was composed of just six races: Mercedes had signed the English driver Stirling Moss who, together with Fangio, formed an unbeatable duo. The car, the W196, presented a number of modifications to the chassis (shorter wheelbase) and the braking system (the front drums were moved outboard), while power had been increased to 290 hp, greater than that of the Ferraris and Maseratis. The new Silver Arrows won five of the six rounds that season, four of which were conquered by Fangio, the fifth by Moss.

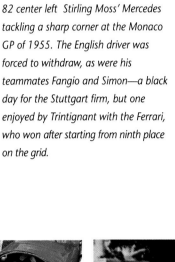

1955

82 top left The Italian GP of 1955 featured a modified circuit, including a high-speed section with 38° banked curves. The Mercedes of Fangio, in the foreground, and Taruffi, behind the Argentine ace, were in their element, reaching 260 kph (161 mph) and finishing first and second.

82 top right The heart of the Maserati 250 F was its longitudinal six-cylinder engine. The Trident's new single-seater made its debut in 1955 but it was in 1957 that it proved unbeatable when it carried Fangio to his fifth World Championship title and Stirling Moss to second place behind the Argentine.

82 center left Stirling Moss' Mercedes tackling a sharp corner at the Monaco GP of 1955. The English driver was forced to withdraw, as were his teammates Fangio and Simon—a black day for the Stuttgart firm, but one enjoyed by Trintignant with the Ferrari, who won after starting from ninth place on the grid.

82 center right At the start of the 1955 British GP held at Aintree, Jean Behra with the Maserati, first on the right, attempts to take the lead by out-sprinting the Mercedes of Fangio (center) and Moss (left). It was to be the latter who won the race.

82 bottom The remains of the Ferrari 750 driven by "Ciccio" Ascari at the Vialone Curve, later renamed after him, at Monza on the 26th of May, 1955. Thus passed one of the greats of the early days of Formula 1, the only Italian to have won two World Championships.

82-83 The 1957 Monaco GP on the Monte Carlo street circuit was the second race of the season and the first in Europe following the one in Argentina. It was won by Fangio with the Maserati 250F number 10; behind the Argentine were the Ferraris of Musso and Collins.

BRITISH ARRIVALS, MERCEDES FAREWELL

An English driver's victory in the British GP was a result of Mercedes' desire to improve its image on the other side of the Channel: an Englishman victorious at the wheel of a German car could only have had a positive effect on sales. Thus during the race Fangio was comfortably in the lead, his third World Championship title already in the bag, when he let Moss through and finished in second, two-tenths behind. In the meantime, the British Vanwall had made its debut for bearing magnate Tony Vandervell. The car's engine was built in collaboration with the engineers of the Norton motorcycle firm. That first season was not particularly successful but things picked up in 1956 with the cars designed by Frank Costin—brother of

83 top During the 1956 season Fangio raced for Ferrari after Mercedes had withdrawn from competition: in this photograph the Argentine is seen during the British GP which he won from the Ferrari of de Portago/Collins and Behra's Maserati.

83 center right Stirling Moss at the wheel of the Maserati 250F crosses the line first in the 1956 Italian GP, the last round of the Championship. Fangio finished behind him after taking over his team mate Collins' Ferrari on the 20th lap (his own car's engine had failed). The Argentinean's second-place finish earned him his fourth championship title.

83 bottom right Eternal runner-up Stirling Moss made his Formula 1 debut in 1951 at the Swiss GP. He finished second in the World Championships from 1955 to '58. A 1962 accident at Goodwood in

England brought an end to his career after disputing 66 Grands Prix, winning 16 overall and recording 16 pole positions. Here he is pushed to the pits at the 1957 Italian GP at the wheel of a British Vanwall.

Mike, who founded Cosworth in 1960 together with Keith Duckworth—and Colin Chapman, the father of Lotus. Jack Brabham also made his debut and in 1958 was to found his own famous team. He took part in the British GP with a Bristol-powered Cooper T40. This car, which retired with engine problems, was a forerunner of the cars of the 1960s with its lightweight construction and mid-mounted engine.

There were also innovations with regards to the circuits and at Monza the high speed oval with 38° banked curves was inaugurated—a project that was intended to provide spectacular racing but which actually proved to be an error. The uneven paving of the *parabolica* proved very hard on the cars, and over the years structural faults rendered the racing surface too dangerous to use.

Mercedes abandoned Formula 1 at the end of the 1955 season; Fangio, however, was still able to celebrate because his Mercedes had carried him to his third title. The fourth he was to conquer the following year with Ferrari after a close-fought season with Moss in the Maserati. To clinch it, Fangio again took advantage of the rule allowing him to take over a teammate's car: in Argentina his Ferrari-Lancia betrayed him on the 43rd lap and Musso gave way. At Monaco and Italy it was Collins who ceded his mount to the Argentine. (The Englishman himself, meanwhile, had been having a fine season and was currently leading the championship table—a third place in Italy would have been sufficient for him to win the title had he not been obliged to cede to his team leader.)

In the late 1950s, only Ferrari was left to defend the Italian colors that up until then had been so well represented. The Prancing Horse had insufficient resources, however, to contain the numerous ambitious British teams with their innovative cars for 1957. The new era of British motor racing—returning to greatness after over 30 years on the sidelines—dawned at the British GP which was won by the Vanwall of Moss, a driver destined to inherit the sceptre of the king of the track from his friend and former teammate Fangio.

COOPER AND VANWALL, NEW FORCES IN FORMULA 1

The Constructors' Championship came into being in 1958, and there was also a changing of the guard among the drivers and cars. The retirement of the champion of champions, Fangio was a tangible sign of this change and was unfortunately accompanied by the deaths of Musso, Collins, Lewis-Evans and Hawthorn. They were all killed in cars, whether it was on the track or on the road, in races or in practice. It was actually Musso's death that persuaded the 46-year-old Fangio to retire.

The British teams and drivers took it upon themselves to enliven the championship, overshadowing the Italian constructors. They were, however, pipped at the post by Ferrari thanks to the

84 top left Peter Collins during the 1958 British Grand Prix. Ferrari's English driver won at Silverstone despite starting from the last row of the grid, leading home Mike Hawthorn by 24 seconds.

84 bottom left The cars are still in the pits for the last checks prior to the start of the Italian GP of 1958, the penultimate round of the World Championship. In the foreground is the

Vanwall of Stirling Moss who was forced to retire during the race with a broken gearbox. The British team was the first to win the Constructors' Championship introduced in 1958.

84 top right The cover of La Domenica del Corriere recording the terrible accident at Monza during a non-points race in 1959. Tinazzo and Crivellari collided at 160 kph (99 mph).

1958 1959

points system: Stirling Moss at the wheel of the Vanwall lost the title to Mike Hawthorn and the Ferrari despite having won four races outright to his rival's single victory in France.

These bare statistics do not, however, have much to say about an episode that, especially when compared with the attitudes of drivers in the 1990s, is surprising if not literally incredible.

On the eve of the last World Championship round, the Casablanca GP in Morocco, Moss had won three races to Hawthorn's one but the latter had recorded five second-place finishes. In the race he was lying second behind Moss, a placing that would have been sufficient to give him the world title. However, he spun off in his Ferrari, got out of the car, pushed it back onto the track and restarted. He was later disqualified because according to the

officials he had pushed his car against the direction of traffic. Moss was thus the World Champion. Sporting to a fault, Moss testified that his rival had in fact acted within the regulations. This allowed Hawthorn and Ferrari to take the title and Moss to gain a reputation for absolute sporting integrity.

The British superiority was now manifest, and Vanwall deservedly won the first Constructors' Championship. The reasons behind this superiority were principally technical: the new had the legs on the old.

There was a veritable revolution in regards to engine location, the Cooper being powered by an engine mounted just ahead of the rear axle. Enzo Ferrari long held this to be a conceptual error: the "oxen should stay in front of the cart." He was later obliged to revise this opinion, but for the moment

the two whippings given to the Dino 246 in Argentina and Monaco were insufficient evidence. Anglo-Saxon supremacy ran deeper than the successes of the Championship-winning Vanwall and Cooper: in 1958 the surprising Lotus 16 designed by Colin Chapman made its debut in the hands of Allison and the then-unknown Graham Hill.

It appeared that success in the World Championship was a form of deadly disease: at the end of the season Vanwall too retired from Formula 1. Tony Vandervell's team nonetheless had the merit of kick-starting the British motor racing revival which was continued thanks to the feats of the Cooper.

In a curious coincidence, John Cooper's British team which won the Constructors' Championship in 1959 signed two unknown drivers, both from the southern hemisphere, the Australian Jack Brabham who immediately won the championship, and the New Zealander Bruce

84 right center Women were not immune to the appeal of motor racing and the most courageous of them joined in. In 1958 the Italian Maria Teresa de Filippis drove a Maserati in the Belgian, Portuguese and Italian Grands Prix. She finished 10th at Spa but was forced to retire at Oporto and Monza.

84 bottom right. Jack Brabham at the wheel of a Cooper-Climax passing the BRM driven by Harry Schell during the 1959 Italian GP. The Australian driver finished the race in third place, earning sufficient points to clinch the Formula 1 World Championship. The American finished the race in seventh place and the championship in tenth.

85 top The Englishman Hawthorn was the protagonist of 1958 season: he conquered his first World Championship

at the wheel of a Ferrari. He won only one Grand Prix, in France, but scored numerous placings that allowed Maranello to dominate the Constructors' Championship.

85 center left In 1958 Fangio competed in his last Grands Prix in Argentina and France. He finished both races in fourth place at the wheel of a Maserati 250F. "El chueco" withdrew from racing at 47 years of age after having won a record five World Championship titles, a feat yet to be matched.

85 center right The Lotus Mark 16 made its debut in 1958 driven by the unknown Graham Hill and by Cliff Allison. Here Hill is seen at the wheel of the Climax-powered Lotus as he attempts to make an impression in the British Grand Prix of 1959. He was to finish no better than ninth, nine laps down on the winner Jack Brabham in a Cooper-Climax.

85 bottom The Lotus Mark 16 was the genial Colin Chapman's first single-seater and made its debut at the Monaco GP in 1958.

McLaren who in winning the United states Grand Prix at just 22 years old became the youngest driver to win a Grand Prix. The coincidence lies not only in the fact that both came from distant former British colonies, but also in that they subsequently founded their own highly successful teams, Brabham in 1962 and McLaren four years later.

British celebrations were completed by the presence of competitive teams such as Lotus and BRM and by the somewhat uninspiring debut of Aston Martin, one of whose drivers, Carroll Shelby, was to become famous for his fabulous Shelby Cobra sports cars. In contrast, the British motor racing world was saddened by the loss of Mike Hawthorn, killed in a car accident in Surrey.

Another great champion also passed away, Rudolf Caracciola, finally defeated by liver disease.

THE CONSECRATION
OF THE MID-ENGINE LAYOUT

The early years of the new decade were marked by the ferocious criticism that for the first time was levelled at constructors regarding the fragility of their cars. At the center of this controversy was Colin Chapman (not for the last time) who was held responsible for the fatal accident involving Stacey in the Belgian GP; the bloody feathers found on the front of the car led to the accident being attributed to an unfortunate and unidentified bird. Shortly before at the same circuit Bristow had also lost his life when he crashed into a fence at the wheel of a Cooper. The Belgian GP took place immediately after a race in Holland that had also been marred by

Cooper leading the way. It was also the last year that the Indianapolis 500 was valid as a round of the Formula 1 World Championship.

In spite of the number of drivers who lost their lives, 1960 was notable for the debut of two other all-time greats, Jim Clark and John Surtees, the latter a World Champion motorcycle racer. Along with Brabham, McLaren and Moss (who changed teams all too frequently), Phil and Graham Hill were also challenging for the title. Although they were almost always off the pace, the Ferraris won at Monza in a race deserted by the British teams because the unevenness of the surface of the parabolica made it

Formula 2 engine designs while Ferrari—surprise, surprise—already had excellent engines up and running.

The Italian manufacturer had, in effect, been working for some years on a 1.5-liter V6, while a similar unit was dominating Formula 2. Ferrari found itself handed the 1961 World Championship on a silver platter, while the new formula also favored Porsche's participation in the series as the company already had an air-cooled four-cylinder boxer engine used successfully in sports car racing.

It goes without saying that there were many complaints of clear favoritism on the part of the CSI

tragedy when the brakes on Dan Gurney's BRM failed, causing him to plough into the crowd and kill a spectator.

The funereal 1960 was also the last season of the 2.5-liter formula (having lasted a record seven seasons), and the last with creditable front-engined cars. The central engine location represented the new technological frontier and was championed and perfected by the British teams, Lotus and

dangerous for their extremely lightweight cars.

The world titles remained firmly in the hands of Brabham and Cooper and the British run of successes extended into 1961. However, the Commission Sportive Internationale (CSI) took it upon itself to shuffle the cards, introducing the 1.5-liter formula. This was a body-blow for Cooper, Lotus and BRM as they had invested heavily in the preceding 2.5-liter formula and now had to dust off

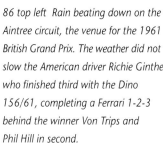

86 top left Rain beating down on the Aintree circuit, the venue for the 1961 British Grand Prix. The weather did not slow the American driver Richie Ginther who finished third with the Dino 156/61, completing a Ferrari 1-2-3 behind the winner Von Trips and Phil Hill in second.

86 top right The start of the 1961 Dutch Grand Prix saw the three Ferraris of Von Trips, Hill and Ginther on the front row of the grid. They were to finish first, second and fifth. The race earned its place in the record books because there were no retirements: fifteen drivers started, 15 finished.

toward the Italian and German teams, but the boycott attempted by the British teams came to nothing. As predicted, the championship season was a monotonous Ferrari cavalcade with five wins out of eight. The team conquered the Constructors' Championship for the first time while Phil Hill became the first American to win a Formula 1 championship title. The Ferrari's scarce international popularity was worsened by the Maranello team's attitude in refusing to withdraw from the Italian GP even though on the second lap Von Trips had collided with Clark's Lotus and his Ferrari had cartwheeled into the crowd killing 14 spectators as well as Von Trips himself.

In the light of the accidents of the previous year, the new regulations introduced by the CSI included new safety norms and minimum weight limits for the cars which also had to be fitted with an automatic starter that prevented push starts, an electrical cut-off switch for use in emergencies and a twin-circuit braking system. Among the innovations there was also the roll-bar—a tubular structure placed behind the driver's head designed to protect him should his car roll over. Unfortunately, there were no technical specifications regarding this feature and thus the constructors simply welded an ineffective semi-circular tube to the bodywork.

86 center left The indispensable work of the mechanics constantly searching for the optimal set up: the photograph shows the BRM (British Racing Motors) pits. Like Ferrari, the British team founded in 1947 built its own chassis and engines.

86 center right and 86 bottom Porsche cars participated in Formula 1 from 1957 to 1964, although mainly in the hands of privateers given that the Zuffenhausen company only officially participated in the World Championship in '61 and '62. In 1959 the Dutchman de Beaufort and the American Blanchard raced the RSK in the Dutch and United States Grands Prix: the first finished tenth at Zandvoort, the second seventh at Sebring.

86-87 and 87 center right Phil Hill waves to the crowd as he crosses the line at the 1961 Italian GP at the wheel of a Ferrari. The race had to be interrupted on the second lap when Von Trips' car (right) collided with Clark's Lotus and careened into the crowd, killing 14 before sliding to

a halt on the track. The German driver also lost his life, bringing a tragic conclusion to a Formula 1 career that had lasted just four years; he debuted at the 1957 Argentine GP with a Ferrari, won two out of the 27 Grands Prix he disputed and conquered one pole.

87 top right This poster publicized the 46th French Grand Prix held at Reims, a race dominated by the British contingent. In fact ten British cars filled the first ten places, mainly Coopers with Climax and Maserati engines. The race would be Vanwall's last.

87 bottom left The new regulations introduced by the FIA for 1961 specified maximum cylinder capacities of no more that 1500 cc, which favoured Porsche, officially returning to the championship in 1961 with a four-cylinder boxer engine and in 1962 with a flat-Eight. Jo Bonnier, seen here, was a Porsche works driver together with Gurney, Hermann and de Beaufort in the 1961 season.

87 bottom right An American in Italy: Phil Hill triumphed at Monza, winning the 32nd edition of the Italian GP in 1961 with a Ferrari.

THE INTRODUCTION OF MONOCOQUES

The British teams were determined to extract their revenge both in 1962 and 1963. The early favorite Ferrari reached the end of the season bloodied, battered and no higher than fifth out of six in the final Constructors' Championship table, while Phil Hill could manage no better than sixth in the Driver's Championship.

Formula 1 lost another of its leading lights in 1962, Stirling Moss, the eternal runner-up who was always so close to taking the championship title. He crashed in a nonchampionship race and the effects of the accident on his sight and reflexes persuaded him to retire from racing.

The British teams' successful innovations, with Chapman in the forefront as usual, were light monocoque chassis and super-smooth eight-cylinder engines of an efficiency that outclassed the Maranello V6. For the monocoque chassis the Lotus chief had drawn inspiration from aeronautical technology, creating a container in riveted light alloy that to some resembled the hull of a speedboat, to others a bathtub. The box sections of the lateral elements were occupied by rubber fuel tanks while steel bulkheads at the front and rear stiffened the structure. The main advantage of this new concept was increased torsional stiffness. The "bath-tub," equipped with wheels, suspension, brakes and an eight-cylinder engine, became the Lotus 25 and was entrusted to Jim Clark. He won the Belgian, British and United States Grands Prix but missed out on the World Championship, which went to another Briton, Graham Hill with the BRM.

The season's technical innovations were not restricted to the historically important integrated structure: the frontal sections of the cars were reduced by up to 30% in some cases, carburetors were replaced by fuel injection (which allowed more precise dosing of fuel and thus smoother power delivery at all engine speeds), wire wheels disappeared (replaced by those in light alloy), and steering wheels were reduced in diameter and trimmed in leather, not wood. The cars were, in fact, radically

transformed and had never been so different to the pioneering horseless carriages, being closer to four-wheeled horizontal rockets.

The Clark/Lotus pairing took a handsome revenge in 1963, winning seven of the ten World Championship rounds. The talent of the driver, the perfection of Chapman's monocoque Lotus 25 and the power of the fuel-injected Coventry-Climax V8 formed an explosive mixture that was capable only of winning.

Ferrari made its comeback in 1964. Where any other team would have crumbled in the face of the British onslaught, Ferrari held firm, ably dictating a season in which it was the only continental manufacturer in a field dominated by Lotus, BRM, Cooper and Brabham. The championship was up for grabs until the last three laps of the last round in Mexico: Clark with the Lotus, Graham Hill with the BRM and Surtees with the Ferrari had shared the victories during the season. In the final phase of the

race the British cars were obliged to retire (Hill being rammed by Bandini's Ferrari); Surtees finished second and Ferrari took both the Constructors' and Drivers' titles. This was the first time a former World Motorcycling Champion had repeated the feat in the automotive Formula 1 Championship.

88 top left The work of the mechanics in the pits is always frenetic and the space available always restricted. In the foreground Graham Hill's BRM is being prepared for the 1962 German GP. The labours were not in vain, as the Englishman went on to win the race.

88 top center The starting grid for the Belgian GP of 1962 saw Graham Hill in pole position at the wheel of a BRM; McLaren with a Cooper-Climax and Trevor Taylor with a Lotus completed the front row. Nineteen cars started the race while 11 finished.

88 top right Baghetti's Ferrari leads a quartet composed of de Beaufort, who is tackling this Nürburgring corner in his Porsche with plenty of opposite lock, Clark in a Lotus and Maggs in a Cooper-Climax hard on his heels. The race was the 1962 German GP.

88 center Jim Clark out on his own at Spa as he prepared to win the 1962 Belgian GP with the Lotus-Climax. The English cars proved to be unbeatable. BRM, Lotus, Cooper and Lola conquered the first four places in the Constructors' Championship.

88 bottom Graham Hill with a BRM passing Dan Gurney in a Porsche during the 1962 German GP held on the difficult but enthralling 22.722 km Nürburgring. Hill went on to win the race while Gurney finished third behind Surtees in a Lola-Climax.

89 top right This poster publicized the Dutch GP of 1962 which was also run as the Grand Prix of Europe. This was the first round of the championship season and was won by Hill in a BRM with Taylor in a Lotus-Climax 27 seconds behind. The fastest lap was recorded by Bruce McLaren in a Cooper-Climax.

89 center The crowded start of the 1962 British GP at Aintree saw the Lotus-Climax of Innes Ireland start from pole position. Victory went to another of Chapman's cars driven by Jim Clark.

89 bottom The podium at the Belgian GP at Spa-Francorchamps in 1962 was an all-star affair with Clark after his first victory with the Lotus 25 saluting the crowd together with the English and American Hills, Graham and Phil.

1962
1963

90 top left Tired after having covered 32 laps of the Zandvoort circuit for a total of 450 km, but happy to have won the race, Jim Clark celebrates with the trophy in hand following his victory in the 1963 Belgian GP, the second round in the World Championship.

90 top right The start of the 1963 French GP held at Reims. The starting grid, with four cars abreast rather than the two normal today, saw Clark (the eventual winner with the Lotus) fighting for the lead with Hill in a BRM, Gurney in a Brabham and Surtees in a Ferrari.

90 center left Jim Clark in his Lotus-Climax with the laurels, is acclaimed by his team: as well as having won the 1963 Italian GP and recorded the fastest lap, he was crowned as World Champion three races from the end of the season. He was to repeat the feat two years later, again with a Lotus-Climax.

90 center right The two Formula 1 greats who dominated the 1963 season: on the left Chapman, the man who revolutionized Formula 1 on a number of occasions with technological innovations, seen here using a stop-watch; on the right Clark, the British team's number one driver.

1963
1964

90 bottom left Surtees attempted to counter the domination of the Clark-Lotus pairing in 1963 with the Ferrari Dino 156. Clark won seven out of ten Grands Prix and Surtees had to submit to the British team's superiority as at Silverstone, where he finished second behind Clark.

90 bottom Open-face helmet with no sponsor's decals, plus goggles, gloves and a mini-windshield: this was racing in the 1960s. Only the determination and the will to win have remained over time. Surtees showed all these qualities as he raced to fourth place in the Monaco GP.

90-91 center left Jim Clark racing toward victory in the 1963 Dutch GP aboard his Lotus 25. Green was the British national racing color, red that of Italy, blue that of France and gray that of Germany.

91 top left Hill at the wheel of his BRM passing the grandstands erected against the buildings of the exclusive Monégasque capital. The 100 laps of the 1963 Monaco GP were completed on a fine spring afternoon. The British driver won the race from Ginther in the second BRM.

91 top right Hill loses his traditional British aplomb, spraying trophy and laurel wreath with champagne at the 1962 South African GP. He needed no justification as victory in the East London race gave him his first World Championship.

91 bottom Graham Hill concentrating in his BRM while Jim Clark has been distracted by something or someone. Both are waiting to start from the front row of the grid for the 1963 Dutch GP, which Clark went on to win with Hill finishing fourth.

HONDA, FORMULA 1'S FIRST JAPANESE CONSTRUCTOR

In a championship that had temporarily shifted its center of gravity to the continent, technical innovations were very conspicuous as they were provoked by changes in tire technology: tires had become wider and lower thanks to the use of nylon rather than cotton fibers in the carcass, and grip had been improved by the use of synthetic rubber for the tread.

The American manufacturer Firestone was the first company to introduce the new tires, supplying them to Honda. The highly successful Japanese motorcycle firm had decided to compete in Formula 1 as well, presenting a car powered by a 12-cylinder engine mounted transversely behind the driver.

BRM instead tested a four-wheel drive car with the engine rotated through 180° behind the driver. Drive was controlled via a special shaft mounted inside the cockpit to the left of the driver. Technical complexity meant that the first four-wheel drive Formula 1 car was never raced, and it remains an historical oddity.

Clark and Lotus had time to win the title again in 1965 before the 1.5-liter formula was abandoned. The great British driver, who captured the affection of racing enthusiasts as perhaps only Fangio had managed to do, won six of the ten championship races, took his second world title and brought the Constructors' Championship to Lotus. He was even able to desert Monaco in favor of traveling to the United States to become the first European in 48 years to win the Indianapolis 500. This was also the first time that a mid-engined car had taken the prestigious trophy.

While Jim Clark was simply unbeatable, his rivals were by no means also-rans. Graham Hill was joined by a young rookie, a certain Jackie Stewart, an extremely promising Scotsman who was to continue the fine tradition of drivers with names beginning with "J": Juan Manuel Fangio, Jack Brabham, John Surtees and Jim Clark. Evidently J is a lucky letter for Formula 1 drivers, and in the years to follow the Formula 1 honor roll was to be graced by others of the caliber of Jo Siffert, Jochen Rindt, Jacky Ickx, James Hunt, Jody Scheckter and Jacques Villeneuve.

1965 1966

92 top The Japanese proved to be hard workers in Formula 1: these mechanics are making Ginther's Honda ready for the 1966 Italian GP. The American driver was forced to retire on the 17th lap after an accident.

92 left Absent from the 1965 Monaco GP because he was in America winning the Indianapolis 500, Jim Clark, seen here in his Lotus with race number 17, returned to his Formula 1 day job in time for the Belgian GP which he won easily in the rain.

92 center Jim Clark chasing the leading group composed of Jack Brabham, Denny Hulme and Graham Hill in the 1966 British GP at Brands Hatch. He eventually finished in fourth place, a lap behind the winner Jack Brabham.

92-93 The 17 cars have just started the 1965 French GP, moved that year to the Clermont Ferrand circuit. The track was, however, poorly maintained, and the roughness of the surface caused 10 cars to retire. Clark won with the Lotus and also recorded the fastest lap.

92 bottom The starting grid for the 1966 German GP saw a front row composed of, from left to right, Scarfiotti with the Ferrari, Stewart with the BRM, Surtees with a Cooper-Maserati and Clark with the Lotus-Climax. Surtees recorded the fastest lap but the race was won by Jack Brabham, first right on the second row.

BRABHAM WINS
HIS THIRD TITLE

In the second half of the decade, with the advent of the three-liter engines that were to last until 1986, Formula 1 was transformed. A minimum weight limit of 500 kg (1,103 lb.; with oil and water but not fuel) was introduced while cylinder capacities were restricted to 3000 cc for naturally aspirated and 1500 cc for supercharged units.

These new engine sizes had been discussed since 1963, with the British constructors attempting to maintain the status quo—as with the old formula they had proved to be virtually unbeatable. The nascent American constructors were instead in favor, as they already had suitable three-liter engines available, while Ferrari could count on many years' experience with 12-cylinder units well suited to the new maximum displacement.

As in 1961, the new regulations appeared to have been introduced due to pressure from certain quarters rather than designed to prompt new technical developments. Coventry-Climax, which had in truth been in decline for the previous two years, announced that it was pulling out of Formula 1, leaving Lotus, Cooper and Brabham without engines. Of the 47 races disputed in those years with the 1.5-liter formula, no fewer than 34 had been won with Climax engines.

Only Brabham (with the Australian V8 Repco engine), Cooper (with a Maserati unit) and Ferrari (with its own V12) were ready for the new Formula 1 season. Lotus and BRM had to fall back on provisional solutions, boring out the old 1.5-liter engines to a full two liters. McLaren instead opted for the Indianapolis Ford V8. Honda started out with its old V12, postponing the presentation of a new engine with similar architecture until the end of the season. The 1966 World Championship also saw the debut of the Eagle team founded by Dan Gurney's new All-American Racers, a California-based firm that would go on to brilliant success in Indy- and sports-car racing.

However, during the course of the year the pre-season favorite Ferrari was unable to exploit its advantage due to Surtees' desertion in France (provoked by internal disputes) and the strike of Italian engineering workers which caused the firm to miss the British GP. (In effect, Maranello has frequently been an unsettled place: firstly the strong, despotic character of Enzo Ferrari and then the infighting amongst too many "prima donnas" for decades have had serious effects on the sporting side of the company.)

The list of competitors for that year's World Championship was one to gladden the heart of any racing enthusiast: Clark, Hill, Bandini, Scarfiotti, Surtees, McLaren, Rindt, Stewart... And the title? In the end it went to Brabham for the third time: Jack remains the only driver to win the title at the wheel of a car bearing his own name, his team also winning the Constructors' Championship.

93 The Australian Jack Brabham dominated the 1966 season. The image bottom right shows him close to the table full of bottles of champagne ready to be uncorked in his honor as winner of the British GP. Brabham was nicknamed Black Jack for his hardness and determination at the wheel. Driver and owner of the team carrying his name, he scored the four wins that gave his team the Drivers' Championship and, together with the points collected by Denny Hulme, the Constructors' title. The Australian's season, both as a driver and as a team manager, did not get off to the best of starts as he was forced to retire from the first race with mechanical problems. His desolate expression while gazing at his car as he sits on the pit wall in the photograph above says it all.

THE DAWN
OF THE FORD-COSWORTH ERA

94 top left The Silverstone circuit here is crowded—and not only with drivers—as preparations are completed for the start of the 1967 British GP. The Lotus-Ford in the foreground was driven by Clark who took both pole position and the race.

94 top right Hulme exploits all the power of his Brabham-Repco, the front wheels leaving the ground after a hump at the Nürburgring. The New Zealander won the race (the 1967 German GP) and the world title.

94-95 Clark at the wheel of the Lotus-Ford in the 1967 Italian GP. This was a difficult race for the Scot: starting from pole position, he was obliged to make a pit stop to change a tire. He restarted in 15th place but, one by one, he managed to pick off his rivals and regain the lead by the 59th lap. Exiting the parabolica on the last lap he ran out of fuel, but managed to coast home in third place.

94 bottom Jack Brabham in the Brabham pits talking to one of the Australian team's mechanics. This was the 1967 Italian GP won by Clark with the Lotus.

Chapman and his Lotus, deprived of a competitive engine, were overshadowed. BRM had no intention of ceding the V12 it was working on to its great rival and Coventry-Climax had ruled itself out of the picture. The old fox Colin Chapman then showed his true entrepreneurial colors and arranged an agreement between the giant Ford Motor Company and the tiny British engineering firm Cosworth for the production of Formula 1 engines: the £100,000 put up by the American carmaker allowed Cosworth to produce the first Cosworth V8, an engine that was to dominate the next 16 years from 1967 to 1983, winning no fewer than 155 Grands Prix, a record no other engine in the history of Formula 1 has ever matched.

The engine designers became obsessed with the figure 400—the power output asked of the new

three-liter engines, be they eight-cylinder, 12-cylinder or even 16-cylinder units (as in the case of the BRM). Ferrari won the horsepower race, achieving 408 hp with its 48-valve V12 which was initially available as a 36-valve variant developing 390 hp. The Honda V12 and the new Ford-Cosworth V8 fitted to the Lotus followed with 405 hp while the Eagle's Weslake V12, the BRM H-16 and the 36-valve Maserati V12 managed a round 400 hp. The BRM V12 and the 36-valve Maserati V12 trailed with 375 and 365 hp, respectively.

The world of motor racing lost one of its leading figures that year in Tony Vandervell, the founder of the Vanwall team that had given Ferrari and Maserati so much trouble in the early 1950s, thus stimulating the United Kingdom's prolific small specialist manufacturers. As for Maserati, the firm took its final bow after having ceased supplying engines to Cooper.

One young driver decided that his future lay in team management and branched out on his own. His name was Frank Williams.

The tragic death of Lorenzo Bandini was the key event of the 1967 championship and led to the adoption of stricter safety norms. The tragedy occurred at the Monaco GP. The Italian driver started the race from the front row of the grid with his Ferrari 312 and was confident he could score only his second Formula 1 victory (his first had come in the 1964 Austrian GP, again at the wheel of a *Rossa*). On the 82nd lap, at the entrance to the chicane after the tunnel, his car hit a barrier, overturned and caught fire. Bandini was extracted from the wreck with severe burns and died in agony the following Wednesday.

The causes of that accident were never fully explained. Fatigue due to the 100 laps traditionally covered in the Monaco GP was blamed, as was the inadequacy of the rescue services provided by the organizers. From the following year, the Monaco GP was run over 80 laps, while firefighters and extinguishers were installed in the pits and around the tracks immediately after Bandini's accident. Shortly afterward, the drivers began wearing fireproof overalls made of Nomex, a fabric made by DuPont.

In spite of Clark's four victories and Brabham's pair, it was Hulme who took the championship thanks to his numerous placings.

95 top Jim Clark triumphed in the Dutch Grand Prix of 1967, a race that entered the history books as the debut of the Ford-Cosworth eight-cylinder engine that was to dominate the Formula 1 circus until 1983, collecting 155 victories along the way.

95 center and bottom This mass of scorched wreckage can be recognized as the remains of Lorenzo Bandini's Ferrari 312 that crashed into the barriers coming out of the chicane during the 1967 Monaco Grand Prix and burst into flames. Nothing could be done for the driver who died of his burns three days later.

It's time for spoilers, wings and sponsors

At the 1967 Belgian GP Clark was the center of attention when he took to the track in a Lotus 49 fitted with an unusual appendage at the front designed to generate negative lift—a.k.a. "downforce"—that would press the car to the ground. Similar devices were quickly tested and adopted by the other teams but, once again, it was Colin Chapman who led the way.

By the following year's Belgian GP, virtually all contenders tried spoilers or wings in order to keep the car—for better or worse—more firmly on the ground. These aerodynamic appendages often resembled nothing so much as ironing boards above the cars, and they flexed dangerously with the risk of breakage at every corner. Another innovation was the full-face helmet, first popularized by Dan Gurney.

However, the key feature of the 1968 season was not technical. From that year on the teams began to carry advertising on their cars, which thus became multicolored high-speed billboards. Sponsors were essential to the survival of the World Championship in the light of the delicate economic situation that arose at the end of 1967, wherein suppliers such as Firestone, BP, and Esso asked to be paid for their products, rather than providing them *gratis*.

In that season AAR-Eagle, Honda and Cooper abandoned Formula 1 and the sport lost the great Jim Clark, Schlesser, Spence and Scarfiotti.

The season concluded with Hill taking the title with the Ford-Cosworth powered Lotus 49. This engine was also fitted to the new Matra and the McLaren and won 11 of the 12 rounds, an exceptional performance given that this was only its second year of competition.

Formula 1 ended the 1960s with the success of Matra International and Jackie Stewart who won six of the 11 championship races. Matra's debut in Formula 1 had been a result of Ken Tyrrell's need to find a chassis suitable for the Ford-Cosworth engine that he had purchased—and one worthy of Jackie Stewart's talent. Matra, an aeronautical engineering firm supported by the French government and Elf-Aquitaine, was designing its own engine (the introduction of which was to be a fiasco) and was

96 top Grace Kelly and Prince Ranier alongside Graham Hill, who had just won the Monaco GP for the fifth time in his career. This was in 1969 and the record number of wins on the Monte Carlo circuit set by the Englishman remained until 1993 when Ayrton Senna won his sixth.

96 bottom left The Lotus-Fords in the pits. The Dutch GP of 1968 was not a happy one for Colin Chapman's team as its cars could do no better than Graham Hill's ninth place. Siffert with the Rob Walker Lotus was obliged to retire with gearbox problems.

1968 1969

The Clark tragedy occurred in a Formula 2 race at Hockenheim after he had begun the new World Championship season with a win in the first Grand Prix in South Africa, thus breaking Fangio's record with his 25th victory. Schlesser lost his life during the French GP, the first F1 race of his career (this was actually the first time the French race had been run under that name, the glorious ACF GP having finally been abandoned). Scarfiotti and Spence, on the other hand, were the victims of fatal accidents in a hillclimb event with a Porsche and during practice at Indianapolis, respectively. Ironically, Spence had taken Jim Clark's place at Lotus and died exactly a month after the great British champion.

more than happy to co-operate with Tyrrell and lend its name to the enterprise. The company was delighted to win the title only a year after its debut.

The Ford-Cosworth V8 engine that in the 1969 season powered the Lotus, Brabham and McLaren cars as well as the French cars, won every World Championship round and conquered all three places on the podium in every race with the exception of the Dutch and United States Grands Prix (third place for Amon with the Ferrari and third for Surtees with the BRM, respectively). The supremacy of the British V8 was thus undisputed: the Ferrari and BRM V12s appeared lightyears away from the performance provided by their rival.

Another statistic may help to comprehend the efficiency, versatility and longevity of the Ford-Cosworth DFV. From 1968 to 1982, with the exception of 1975, 1977, and 1979, it powered the car driven by every World Champion driver.

In 1969 new wing regulations were introduced, as too many accidents had been caused by spoilers breaking; under these conditions the cars became uncontrollable and thus extremely dangerous for both drivers and spectators. Another question resolved at the end of the 1960s was four-wheel drive: such chassis were all built by Lotus, McLaren, Matra and Cosworth, but each proved too heavy, complex and expensive in the end.

96 bottom center *Siffert's Lotus attempting to keep Surtees' Honda at bay. Neither driver was to finish the 1968 Monaco GP, Siffert retiring on the 11th lap with a broken transmission, the Englishman lasting another six laps before he too was forced out with gearbox problems.*

96 bottom right and 97 bottom *The Brabham-Repco stripped down by the mechanics of the Australian team: note the eight-cylinder engine, the small spoiler and the grooved tires.*

97 top *Matra International made its debut in 1968. The team was managed by Ken Tyrrell with cars powered by the Ford-Cosworth V8 and driven by Jackie Stewart. The MS10 single-seater is seen here in the pits at the British GP, in which Stewart finished sixth.*

97 center *In the late 1960s the constructors tackled the problem of aerodynamics by fitting towering wings such as those of the Lola T102, which were very similar to ironing boards.*

97 bottom left *The Lotus touching down with its rear wheels on the Nürburgring asphalt. The demanding 1968 German GP with its apparently modest 14 laps (totalling 320 km) saw Hill finish second behind Stewart in the Matra-Ford. This was the French team's second F1 victory.*

97 bottom right *Graham Hill is extracted from his Lotus-Ford after the frightening accident caused by the loss of the car's wings in the 1969 Spanish GP. Fortunately the English driver escaped with his life. This was not the only accident caused by wings: Rindt's Lotus also crashed after losing its spoilers.*

ENZO FERRARI GOES HALVES

June, 1969 was an important month for Ferrari, albeit not in terms of results. As his Formula 1 cars continued to be dominated by their British Cosworth-powered rivals, 50% of the Modenese firm, forever in financial difficulties, was sold to Fiat. The Fiat buyout was the final movement in a dance which had actually begun between Ferrari and Ford at the dawn of the decade. This dance had ended in acrimony on both sides, and in Ford's intense commitment to racing—or at least to beating Ferrari.

Thus, Formula 1 celebrated its first 20 years—a period in which the changes and revolutions had been such that it would have been difficult for similar mutations to have taken place in the 20 years that followed. Much had, of course, changed since 1950. For the manufacturers, it had been Italy (with Alfa Romeo and then Ferrari), then Germany with Mercedes-Benz, then Italy again. Later the Union Jack reigned supreme. As for the drivers, between 1958 and 1969 the World Champion's flag was British on no fewer than seven occasions.

Would someone, or something, be able to dent the supremacy of British drivers, technicians and teams in the years ahead?

RINDT, THE POSTHUMOUSLY CROWNED CHAMPION

The answer to the question at the end of the last paragraph has to be yes, because Ferrari staged a magnificent comeback—at least in terms of the Constructors' Championship, which was won by Maranello four times (Lotus also won four titles, Tyrrell and McLaren one each). The team enjoyed less success in the Drivers' Championship as on seven occasions the champion's car was powered by the Ford-Cosworth engine and on each occasion the team was British. It was a decade of doubles for the drivers: Stewart won two titles (his second and third, thus equaling Brabham's record), as did the Brazilian, Fittipaldi (the first South American champion after Fangio), and Lauda, the Ferrari team's number one.

Although his grip on his company may have been weakened, Enzo Ferrari stubbornly resisted the British domination and never despaired. He retained Ickx and signed Regazzoni. The moustachioed Swiss driver, much later confined to a wheelchair after a serious accident, was to be remembered for his audacity and the good luck that, up until that final

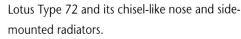

98 top The start of the 1970 British GP with Rindt in the Lotus (left), Brabham in a Brabham (center) and Ickx in a Ferrari (right) immediately in the thick of things. Rindt went on to win with Brabham second; Ickx retired on the seventh lap.

98 bottom left Enzo Ferrari on the pit wall at Monza timing one of his drivers. They were to give him partial satisfaction in that in 1970 the Italian Grand Prix was won by Regazzoni but Ickx and Giunti both retired.

98 bottom right Ferrari managed to record four victories in the 1970 championship, all coming in the last part of the season. Three went to Ickx, one (the Italian GP) to Regazzoni, seen here.

98-99 and 99 bottom right Tyrrell and Jackie Stewart were the protagonists of the 1971 season: the driver and the car formed an unbeatable pairing, as had happened the previous decade with Lotus and Jim Clark. After his experience with March and Matra late in 1970 Ken Tyrrell presented his own Ford-powered car that proved unbeatable the following season. Jackie scored no fewer than seven wins including the British (left) and Monaco (right) Grands Prix.

crash, had always seen him emerge unscathed from wrecked Formula 1 and sports cars. Regazzoni was joined by other names new to the highest level of the sport: Emerson Fittipaldi, Ronnie Peterson, Rolf Stommelen and Henri Pescarolo.

Ferrari finally enjoyed some long-overdue success in the Austrian GP and this was to be repeated in Italy, Canada and Mexico, which was sufficient for the team to finish second in both the Constructors' and the Drivers' Championships with Ickx. The title, however, again went to Lotus, and it was once more Chapman who was in the forefront of technological innovation with the wedge-shaped structure of his

Lotus Type 72 and its chisel-like nose and side-mounted radiators.

There was unfortunately a macabre note to this season as the champion was crowned posthumously, Jochen Rindt having been killed during practice for the Italian GP. Death also came to Bruce McLaren who, like Jack Brabham, John Surtees and Dan Gurney (team Eagle), raced in Formula 1 with cars belonging to his own team. McLaren was killed while testing a McLaren-Chevrolet M8D Can-Am: the car's engine cover opened suddenly and the driver crashed into a wall. Piers Courage, at the wheel of a de Tomaso—a new team competing in the colors of Frank

Williams' British effort with Ford power and a chassis by Dallara (a young but very talented engineer with experience at Ferrari, Lamborghini and Maserati)—fell in Holland. On the other hand, François Szisz, the winner of the very first French Grand Prix in 1906, died in his own bed at the age of 97.

Monocoques, aerodynamic appendages, fireproof overalls, sponsors: the World Championship circus was gradually being modernized. Another element first appeared in the Grand Prix in 1971, although it had already become common in the US: slick tires for maximum grip on dry tracks. (Grooved tires were still required in the wet, of course).

The second World Championship won by Stewart and Tyrrell could hardly have been predicted at the start of the year. Ferrari won the opening race in South Africa with its new driver Mario Andretti. Maranello had not, however, taken into account the Ford Cosworth engine and the Stewart-Tyrrell pairing which won six of the season's 11 Grands Prix. And to think that the V8 engine layout—which was used by all teams but BRM, Ferrari and Matra—was considered by many to have reached the end of its lifespan, about to be eclipsed by more powerful V12s! Nothing could in fact be further from the truth: the latest version of the DFV produced 440 hp, equaling the outputs of the BRM and Matra units and only slightly trailing the Ferrari's 480. Alfa continued its attempts to regain respect in Formula 1, in 1971 its V8 engines powering the March, not the McLaren. The results were again unsatisfactory, as were those of the curious gas-turbine Lotus.

Giunti was killed at Buenos Aires in January at the wheel of a Ferrari 312P. Pedro Rodriguez, the Mexican idol, also competed in his last race at the wheel of a Ferrari, in this case an Interseries event at Nuremberg in Germany.

As a result of the 31-year-old driver's death, the Mexican GP was canceled. The CSI's justification for this was that the circuit was unsafe, as it allowed the crowd to line the track as if it were a road race. In reality, however, it was a purely commercial decision: in the absence of Mexico's local hero there would be less interest in the event, and it would thus be less profitable. In the end fate intervened, playing a cruel trick on poor Jo Siffert. The Mexican GP was in fact replaced by a "Race of Champions" at Brands Hatch, a nonpoints contest in which Siffert lost his life due to the delay of the rescue services (he was trapped in his blazing car after having struck an earth bank and overturned).

1970 1971

99 top left Jochen Rindt scored his second victory of the season in the 1970 Dutch GP at the wheel of the Lotus-Ford. The Lotus 72, with its unusual wedge shape, was very fast and the German finished 30 seconds ahead of Stewart.

99 top right The remains of Rindt's Lotus after his crash at the parabolica during the 1970 Italian GP. Jochen was killed, and thus became the sport's first and only posthumous World Champion.

99 center right In 1971 the Italo-American Mario Andretti met his dream of driving for Ferrari. This was not a good season for Maranello and after his first victory in South Africa, Mario's best result was fourth place in Germany.

SINGLE-SEATS AND ADVERTISING: BRINGING FORMULA 1 BACK TO LIFE

The world of Formula 1 revealed its total economic dependency on its sponsors in 1972 when the name of the company or relative products to be promoted was adopted as an integral or even principal part of the name of the team (Marlboro-BRM, for example). In the extreme case of Lotus, the name of the team became that of a brand of cigarettes, John Player Special, and the cars were finished in black with gold pin-striping like the cigarette packaging.

Depailler, Lauda, Pace, Scheckter, de Adamich, Bell and Reutemann were the new generation of drivers of whom much was to be heard in the future. In the meantime the Brazilian Emerson Fittipaldi, in his third Formula 1 season, conquered the World Championship with the Lotus-Ford, alias John Player Special, winning five of the 12 Grands Prix.

100 top right Beltoise took the BRM to victory at Monaco. This was the British team's sole win in the 1972 championship. Its next best placing was Ganley's fourth in Germany.

100 center right Emerson Fittipaldi spraying the crowd below the podium with champagne as he celebrates victory in the 1972 British GP. This was the Brazilian's third win of the season at the wheel of the Lotus, and he went on to take the title.

Every time that a great driver, a leading team or a previously unbeatable car has left the stage after a period of domination a cycle draws to a close. A vacuum is created, and there is increasing anxiety that the roughly blended cocktail of potent emotions, intense fears and unforgettable joy—or at least its former intensity—has been lost forever. These fears are stilled in front of the podium on which a new laurel wreath is placed around the neck of a new champion.

The vacuum created in 1973 was a result of the departure of Jackie Stewart, fortunately not in tragic circumstances. The Scottish driver retired at the top as reigning champion after winning his third title and with a record of 99 Grands Prix disputed, 17 pole positions and 27 victories, thus overtaking Fangio (24) and Clark (25).

Lotus continued to play a leading role, winning its sixth Constructors' Championship (Ferrari and Brabham were well behind with two each). During the season Chapman's designers continued working on the aerodynamic appendages and the shape and

position of the air intakes, above all the one for the engine intake air that was located above and behind the driver and resembled some kind of rocket launcher ready to blast away all rivals.

In terms of accidents, the most confused was the one provoked by the impulsive South African Jody Scheckter at the start of the British GP that involved the entire field. Over an hour was needed to clean up the track and de Adamich spent interminable minutes trapped in his car with his legs fractured. As a result of his injuries the Italian driver was forced to retire from the sport prematurely. At Zandvoort in Holland, Roger Williamson burned to death in his car, the trackside rescue services criminally slow in responding to the emergency. The tragic and frightening spectacle was witnessed by helpless millions as the television images were transmitted throughout the world.

Racing fans everywhere were anxiously awaiting the renaissance of the Prancing Horse. The miracle took place in 1974, thanks to the 312B3 12-cylinder, the fulcrum around which rotated Maranello's hopes

100 bottom Emerson Fittipaldi sewed up the Championship title with two races to go: in the 1972 Italian GP he won easily with the black and gold Lotus 72, more properly known as the John Player Special.

and plans. Regazzoni and Lauda, fresh from a season with BRM, were the new drivers.

The team was now under the wing of Fiat with the solid backing of the Agnelli family which led to a significant injection of capital and a complete revision of the organizational side: there were new chief race technicians, while Luca Cordero di Montezemolo, Giovanni Agnelli's protégé, was appointed as team manager. A dual team of mechanics was also assembled, one for each car.

Such attention to detail paid off, even though the Italian team had to settle for second place in both the Drivers' (52 points for Regazzoni against

Fittipaldi's 55, the Brazilian now at McLaren) and the Constructors' Championships (65 points, seven behind McLaren). The reasons for this partial success are to be found in the psychological collapse of the team and the heated rivalry between the two drivers.

McLaren and Fittipaldi earned respect as an unbeatable pairing. The M23 proved to be reliable and competitive, the World Champion's car having a widened lower cockpit and an offset steering wheel to accommodate Fittipaldi and his Brazilian hips. This was also a year of glory for the American rubber giant Goodyear, whose tires equipped all the year's Grand Prix winners.

101 top left Ronnie Peterson going straight into the lead at the start of the 1973 British GP. However, a massive pile-up provoked by Scheckter led to a restart at Silverstone.

101 top right Chris Amon with the Matra-Simca made a very good start at the 1972 French GP but the ill-luck that dogged him struck again at Clermont-Ferrand when a stone damaged his car and he dropped back to finish third.

101 center right Clay Regazzoni's BRM caught fire after crashing into the barriers during the 1973 South African GP. Hailwood stopped to lend assistance and dragged Clay out of the car, burning his hands in the process.

101 bottom McLaren won the Constructors' Championship in 1974 thanks to the points accumulated by Hulme, Hailwood and Fittipaldi. The latter is seen here at the French GP, where he was forced to retire on Lap 26.

NIKI LAUDA, THE PERFECTIONIST

After the first two races of the 1975 season, the Argentine and Brazilian GPs, in which the 312 B3s could manage no better than a fourth place with Regazzoni, Ferrari seemed to have sunk back into oblivion. For the following race in South Africa the Maranello team decided to introduce the new 312T. The T stood for "trasversale," referring to the transverse location of the gearbox—a feature that allowed for better weight distribution and consequently better handling.

The new car came good on its third outing at the Monaco GP where Lauda led home Fittipaldi in the McLaren-Ford by almost three seconds. The meticulous Austrian driver, capable of painstakingly testing until he had found an optimum set-up, reaped further reward by winning in Belgium, Sweden, France and the United States, thus conquering his first World Championship. Regazzoni won in Italy, Ferrari's total of six wins bringing the Constructors' Championship home to Maranello.

A tragic destiny awaited Graham Hill, a hero of the 1960s who had recently retired from racing to

found his own team. He was killed in a plane crash, along with his driver Brise and five colleagues. The moustachioed driver earned his place in the record books with two World Championships, 176 Grands Prix disputed, 14 victories and 13 pole positions.

Hill's death was not the only tragedy that season. The Spanish GP started badly and finished worse. At Barcelona's Montjuich circuit the drivers, led by Fittipaldi, were unwilling to race because they claimed that the armco barriers had been erected incorrectly. The organizers threatened to confiscate all the teams' equipment in a partial compensation for the lost revenue should the race be canceled. The drivers were thus obliged by their teams to take part in practice and to race: Fittipaldi protested by completing just two deliberately slow practice laps that were sufficient for McLaren to reclaim its expenses. Clearly the Brazilian did not make the grid and did not take part in a race that lasted just 29 laps. Immediately after the start there was an accident involving the two Ferraris and

Andretti's Parnelli. Then, on the 26th lap Stommelen with the Hill-Ford lost his rear wing while holding a clear lead. His car went out of control and crashed into the barriers, causing the deaths of a track marshal, two fire fighters and a journalist. On the 29th lap the race was abandoned with victory being assigned to Jochen Mass in the McLaren. Lella Lombardi became the first, and so far only, woman to score points in a World Championship race.

102 top Carlos Reutemann raced at the wheel of a Brabham-Ford in 1975. He scored his first and only win of the season in Germany in a race in which tire problems caused the retirement of no fewer than 12 cars.

102 left and bottom Lauda won the 1975 World Championship at the wheel of a Ferrari 312T. The photo on the left shows him in mid-corner during the Italian GP, a race in which the Austrian had to settle for third place behind Regazzoni and Fittipaldi. Things went better in France (bottom): Niki dominated at the Paul Ricard circuit where he started from pole and was first across the line.

102-103 and 103 top left Concentration and tension can be seen in the gaze of Niki Lauda who, before his frightening accident in the 1976 German GP (right), had collected five wins and had the championship all but won.
Forty days after the crash Niki was back fighting for the title. However, he retired from the last race in Japan after just three laps due to a rainstorm that was beating down on the Fujiyama circuit.

103 bottom left The English aristocrat, the moustache of Formula 1, Graham Hill was killed in a plane crash in 1975. The great driver left a record of 14 victories from 176 Grands Prix and two World Championship titles.

THE DEBUT OF THE TYRRELL SIX-WHEELER

103 top right A car that all Formula 1 enthusiasts will remember: the Tyrrell P34 six-wheeler; with four small wheels at the front and two standard wheels at the back.

103 bottom right James Hunt was forced to retire from the 1976 Monaco GP after the engine of his McLaren broke. The Englishman made up for this disappointment by winning six of the season's 16 Grands Prix and snatching the World Championship title.

A six-wheeled car, the Argentine GP canceled because of the coup d'état, victories canceled and then reinstated...the 1976 championship was really a controversial affair!

While the no-holds-barred duels between Lauda, Regazzoni and Hunt were spectacular, an equally fascinating moment came at the Spanish GP when the Tyrrell P34 six-wheeler took to the track with four 10-inch wheels on two front axles. The narrow front track and largely faired tires were meant to reduce drag, but this aerodynamic advantage was compromised by the standard-width rear axle. In its first season the P34 scored a 1-2 victory in Sweden, but in the end the benefits of six wheels did not compensate for their added cost and complexity.

The struggle for the 1976 title eventually became a private affair between Lauda and Hunt, with Lauda dominating the early part of the season, Hunt in the second. New safety norms were introduced at the Spanish GP that specified that the cars should be fitted with a supplementary rollbar

for the cockpit and deformable structures in front of the driver to protect his lower limbs. A tangible result was the moving of the air intakes, which were now almost concealed beneath the rollbar rather than towering above the driver.

In accordance with the new regulations, checks made at the end of the Spanish GP revealed that Hunt's winning McLaren was wider than permitted. The victory thus passed to Lauda, but McLaren appealed and Hunt's win was later reinstated.

At the start of the British GP, on the other hand, Regazzoni collided with Lauda, who had not given way to his teammate. The Swiss driver spun and collided with a series of cars including Hunt's. The race was stopped, and when it restarted Hunt was back on the track. Under way Lauda kept a firm grip on the lead until gearbox problems obliged him to let Hunt past, and the Englishman went on to win. Then Ferrari appealed, claiming that Hunt had used his spare car rather than the repaired race chassis. The CSI accepted this claim, largely on the evidence of two Italian journalists who had photographed the

English driver running toward the pits. With this surprise verdict the CSI probably intended to right the wrong suffered by Ferrari in Spain, but to many this decision only cast further doubts on the impartiality of the authorities.

The German GP was marred by a dramatic accident. On the second lap, Lauda crashed into the barriers and his car burst into flames. He was rescued by Merzario, Ertl and Lunger who stopped at the side of the track to pull him from his blazing Ferrari before the rescue services arrived. The Austrian driver suffered severe burns to his head, hands and arms and his life was in danger for days because he had inhaled toxic fumes during the fire.

The team signed Carlos Reutemann, who the following season would replace Regazzoni. Forty days after his accident, however, Lauda was back on for the Italian GP. The bandaging on his face and hands did not prevent him from finishing fourth and retaining his lead in the championship, although Hunt was just a few points behind.

The finale to the season seemed to hold the promise of a titanic struggle between Hunt and the revitalized Lauda. Hunt pulled off a scorching start and shot into the lead, and on the second lap the unthinkable happened: Lauda pulled out of the race. The Ferrari organization at first tried to cover up this embarrassing situation by attributing Lauda's retirement to mechanical problems, but the Austrian soon released a brief but firm statement to the press: "My life is my own, and it is more important than the World Championship."

The Championship was won by James Hunt. Enzo Ferrari never forgave Niki Lauda.

TURBOS AND GROUND EFFECTS WIN THE DAY

After a season poisoned by disputes, it was the genial Lotus chief who revitalized Formula 1 by launching the era of the first "wing," or ground effects, cars, the Lotus 78-79, featuring an innovative technical package that glued the cars to the track and thus improved overall performance and handling.

The Lotus 78 scored its first victory at the United States West GP, although the spectators and the technicians attributed the success to the presence of a new Getrag differential rather than to ground effects. The 1977 World Championship was nonetheless dominated by Lauda at the wheel of the Ferrari with wins in South Africa, Germany and Holland as well as a series of top three and points-scoring placings.

The Maranello team denied the Austrian driver total commitment, no longer trusting him after his dramatic retirement in the Japanese GP the previous season. In Brazil, in fact, a new rear wing was fitted to Reutemann's car but not to Lauda's. The relationship between Lauda and Ferrari deteriorated to such an extent over the course of the season that the day after Niki won in Holland and consolidated his lead in the Drivers' Championship, Ferrari announced that the young Austrian driver's contract would not be renewed at the end of the season. Lauda gained the point he required to make sure of the World Championship title at the United States West GP and took his revenge on Ferrari by deserting the last two races in Canada and Japan.

104 top right Niki Lauda had to settle for second place in the 1977 British Grand Prix. The Austrian was forced to follow in James Hunt's dust but gained handsome revenge elsewhere and won the championship that year.

104 center right Gilles Villeneuve made his Formula 1 debut in 1977 at the wheel of a McLaren. His performance so impressed Enzo Ferrari that he was signed to drive for Maranello by the Canadian GP.

104 bottom right On paper and in the metal, entrusted to the care of its mechanics, the engine that represented at the 1977 British GP the introduction of turbocharging to Formula 1: the 1500 cc Renault V6 that powered Jabouille's car. The same race also saw the debuts of Gilles Villeneuve with the McLaren-Ford and the return of Michelin tires.

1977 *1978*

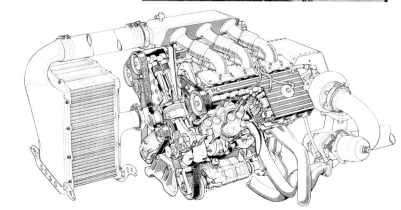

104 top left Andretti scored consecutive wins in Belgium and Spain in 1978. The two victories were added to the one he scored in the first race in South Africa and another three he scored in France, Germany and Holland as he went on to win the title.

104 bottom left The yellow Renault RS01 Turbo of Jean Pierre Jabouille struggling for a decent result in the 1978 British GP. The Frenchman was forced to retire on the 46th lap with a broken engine.

104-105 The 1977 Ford-powered McLaren M23 that the team prepared for James Hunt, winner of the 1976 World Championship. The square-cut air intake in the center of the nose characterized a car that carried the reigning champion to a meagre total of eight points, a third place in the French GP being his best placing. The team also underwent a financial crisis in 1978 that was only resolved in 1980, when McLaren passed into the hands of Ron Dennis. The new organization brought renewed stability and success (eight Drivers' and seven Constructors' Championships) to a team that had struggled to achieve equilibrium in the '70s despite winning championships in 1974 and '76.

105 top right James Hunt tackling one of the straights at Brands Hatch, venue for the 1978 British Grand Prix. The driver had to retire on the seventh lap, after a very short race.

105 bottom right The large rear fan designed to improve ground effects earned the 1978 Brabham BT46B the nickname of "Hoover." This efficient solution gave Lauda victory in the Swedish GP.

During this edition of the World Championship the legendary Ford-Cosworth V8 engine recorded its 100th GP win at Monaco. The season was also marked by the return in revolutionary form of the Renault team which had been missing from the Grand Prix circus since 1908 and which ushered in the turbo era. The RS01 was powered by a mighty 1.5-liter V6 that developed 500 hp but was dogged by the delayed throttle response typical of turbocharged engines. Another return was that of Michelin, which supplied tires for the RS01 and thus interrupted the rule of Goodyear and Firestone. Gilles Villeneuve made such a convincing debut at Silverstone that he was signed by Ferrari the following week.

Tragically, Carlos Pace was killed in a plane accident and Tom Pryce ran into and killed a track marshal who had unthinkingly strayed into the middle of the track with a fire extinguisher to lend assistance to Zorzi in the Shadow. The extinguisher struck Pryce who was killed instantly. The glorious BRM model took its leave of the Grand Prix scene due to severe financial problems.

The year spent fine-tuning the ground effects Lotus paid off in 1978. The type 78 was replaced by the 79, which in terms of negative lift was very similar to its predecessor but offered 15% less drag. The creativity of Chapman and his team appeared to be inexhaustible in the late 1970s, light years ahead of their rivals. While in 1978 the other constructors were only just beginning to comprehend the advantages of the wing cars and hurriedly preparing similar models (the exceptions to the rule were the flat 12-cylinder Ferraris and Alfa-powered Brabhams; the packaging difficulties with this type of engine architecture restricted the area of low pressure below the car), Lotus was already tackling the first experiments into aerodynamic aids that were soon to become ubiquitous: side-skirts or lateral seals between the bodywork and the asphalt.

In the meantime, the Lotuses triumphed in eight of the 16 Grands Prix in 1978: six won by Andretti and two by Petersen. Chapman's team scored 1-2s in the Belgian, Spanish, French and Dutch Grands Prix.

Another team in the late 1970s technological avant-garde was Brabham. At the Swedish GP the team presented the BT46-Alfa Romeo equipped with a large fan in the tail that generated a low pressure zone beneath the car (the underbody was sealed with side skirts), thus allowing higher cornering speeds. Despite its "Hoover" nickname, the BT46 proved to be extremely quick and Lauda, who had moved to the Australian team from Ferrari, drove the car to victory on its debut. This was a historic win both for Brabham—its first in three years—and for Alfa Romeo, who tasted Grand Prix success again after 27 years, albeit only as an engine supplier. However, the fan car was immediately outlawed because the extractor fan sucked up gravel and other particles and spat them into the path of the following cars. Moreover, the regulations had clearly stated since 1969 that moveable aerodynamic aids were prohibited, and the fan was classified as such.

"GILLES," HEIR TO CLARK IN THE ENTHUSIASTS' HEARTS

106 top left An extremely rapid Jean Pierre Jabouille conquered pole position at the 1979 German GP, relegating Alan Jones in the Williams to second place on the grid. The Australian driver gained revenge in the race by taking the lead at the first corner and retaining it to the finish.

106 top right The 1979 Austrian GP saw the same Franco-Australian front row as the previous race in Germany: Arnoux took pole at the wheel of the Renault bi-turbo, while Jones was René's closest rival. It was Alan who went on to win the race, his second successive triumph of the season.

106 left The 1979 Spanish GP was one to remember for the Ligier team: the French équipe placed two cars on the front row and Patrick Depailler went on to win the race. Lafitte was instead obliged to retire on the 18th lap with a broken engine.

106-107 The Ford-powered McLarens suffered at the 1979 Monaco GP. The Englishman John Watson conquered an honorable fourth place after starting from the seventh row with the 14th fastest time. Patrick Tambay, in the image, did not even manage to qualify.

106 bottom left In spite of recording the fastest lap and starting from the second row, Gilles Villeneuve in the Ferrari finished only seventh in the 1979 Spanish GP—a disappointing result after two consecutive victories.

106 bottom right An historic 1-2 for the Ferraris in the 1979 Italian Grand Prix: Jody Scheckter and Gilles Villeneuve finished first and second. The following 1-2 for the "Reds" at Monza will be achieved only 9 years later.

1979

The 1970s were left behind but the wing cars and the ground effects technology introduced by Lotus remained. Renault, who in previous years had invested heavily and believed firmly in the turbo, successfully reintroduced boosted engines as the way forward, much in the same way as happened in the 1950s, when supercharged engines—the Alfas above all—enjoyed their heyday. The Renault RS01, powered by a twin-turbo, 1.5-liter V6 won in France with Jean Pierre Jabouille at the wheel, thus earning the company its first turbocharged Grand Prix victory.

The championship title returned to Maranello in 1979 thanks to the 312 T4 and Jody Scheckter, the South African replacement for Reutemann (who had moved to Lotus and who, like Andretti, failed to score a single victory that season). Williams (with Jones and Regazzoni) and Ligier (Laffite, Depailler and Ickx) scored five and three wins respectively, thus taking their places among the circus' leading teams. Similar ambitions were harbored by Alfa Romeo, who had decided to build its own car. The Tipo 177 was, however, conceptually dated and proved to be uncompetitive. The Tipo 179 wing car was instead introduced for the Italian GP powered by a 60° narrow-angle V12 that was also successfully fitted to the Brabham BT48 and allowed modern aerodynamics to be employed.

Ferrari conquered the world title thanks to the reliability of its 12-cylinder engines rather than its chassis, which did not benefit from ground effects. Scheckter scored points in no fewer than 12 of the 15 scheduled Grands Prix, collecting three wins; Villeneuve won another three races.

The audacity of the Canadian driver endeared him to the Italian fans: his duel with René Arnoux in the Renault is the stuff of legends. The pair were fighting for second place, given that Jabouille in the other Renault could not be caught. The last few laps were heart-stopping, an unforgettable show for the millions of people in Dijon and glued to their television screens (it was in these years that the television audience expanded exponentially and became Formula 1's major player). The Ferrari and the Renault touched at every corner as the drivers attempted to barge their way through, the wheels of one scraping the flanks of the other. In the end Villeneuve had the last word, but the duel was to remain one of the greatest episodes of modern Formula 1, a sport that generally lacks the battles, the overtaking and the explosive laps the Grands Prix of the 1930s and 1950s had offered.

Thirty years had passed since the days of the Alfetta 158 and Giuseppe Farina—30 years alternately marked by on-track rivalries, political infighting, technological innovations and the rising economic influence of firstly sponsors and then television. In spite of moments of intense drama such as those recounted above, it can be said that the cars and drivers have passed gradually, inexorably and perhaps unwittingly into the background.

In the 1980s the actual racing, already corrupted by outside interests, came up against another powerful enemy in the form of electronics. The new technology began to be applied throughout the cars and tended to unify performance levels, making the figure of the driver increasingly less important.

The situation that arose was somewhat akin to Enzo Ferrari's position, so jealous was he of the glory earned by the drivers at the wheel of his cars. In spite of the commercial vicissitudes, in spite of the fact that his team never succeeded in anticipating the technological innovations introduced by his Anglo-Saxon rivals, the great Enzo was alone in battling on for three decades against the domination of the small but fearsome British teams.

107 left In the 1979 German GP, Emerson Fittipaldi at the wheel of a Type F6/A completed just five laps after which he was betrayed by his Ford engine. He conquered third place— among the retirees!

107 top right Arrows, backed by the Warsteiner Brewery for 1979, employed a chassis design very similar to the French Renault's. No surprise: Renault, achieved all its objectives at that year French GP, earning pole position, fastest lap, and overall victory in the race. Jabouille started from the pole and went on for the win; Arnoux scored fastest lap.

107 bottom right The Ferrari team ready to give their all in their home GP. In 1979 Villeneuve performed well early in the season, collecting three important victories for Maranello. He failed to repeat that feat in Italy, however, yielding first to teammate Scheckter.

A CROWD OF TEAMS IN FORMULA 1

The 1980s opened to violent arguments between the FISA and the FOCA regarding the adoption or banning of side-skirts.

The Fédération Internationale du Sport Automobile (FISA) had been founded at the end of 1978 within the CSI and was supposedly subordinate to the FIA. In reality, it had succeeded in acquiring increasing autonomy and campaigned against the adoption of side-skirts. The Formula One Constructors' Association (FOCA), on the other hand, defended side-skirts at all costs and its members—with the exception of Ferrari, Alfa Romeo

and Renault—threatened to organize their own championship. This and other political struggles, plots and boycotts had the effect of alienating the public, keeping people away from the circuits and their television screens. This was enough to set the sponsors' alarm bells ringing and the teams, for whom the future looked bleak without sufficient funds to plan for a full season, saved face by pretending to engage in serious and constructive attempts to reach a mutually satisfactory solution.

Why did side-skirts cause so much stubborn controversy? The answer is that without the skirts

the British teams could not hope to compete against the turbo-charged units that had already broken the 600 hp barrier. Side-skirts, the fruit of Anglo-Saxon invention, were partially able to compensate for the power differential. The presence of the skirts allowed lap times to be reduced a lot, though in some cases the drivers were subjected to dangerous lateral *g* forces.

108 top Nineteen-eighty was a season to forget for Jody Scheckter: after winning the championship the previous year, the South-African's best result was a fifth place in the United States. In Canada he even failed to qualify.

The nose is slightly protruding, the wheels are set forward and there are no spoilers: the 1981 Ligier-Matra driven by our French drivers, Lafitte, seen here, Jarier, Jabouille and Tambay.

108 center left The first of the two Formula 1 GPs held in the USA in 1980 was the United States West at Long Beach, which proved to be a disaster for Regazzoni: his Ensign's brakes failed and he crashed into a retaining wall. The accident has confined him to a wheelchair ever since.

Nonetheless, racing continued for better or for worse, with Jones in the Williams and Piquet with the Brabham dominating the 1980 season in which no fewer than 20 teams took part. Jones took the title with five victories and a total of 67 points: the Brazilian finished 13 points behind.

Ferrari and Lotus had indifferent seasons in spite of new engines, and absent from the circus was Niki Lauda, who at the end of the '79 season had announced he was retiring to devote himself to his new airline. Clay Regazzoni started the season with Ensign but he too was forced to withdraw after just four Grands Prix—an accident at the United States West GP would confine him to a wheelchair for life. Depailler was even less fortunate, perishing while testing at Hockenheim.

The Italian GP was held at Imola rather than Monza, on the circuit dedicated by Enzo Ferrari to his son Dino who had died at age 24. The following year the race returned to Monza, Imola becoming the San Marino GP.

The most up-to-date engines were turbocharged, with Renault, the technology's chief advocate, scoring three wins in 1980: two with Arnoux (in Brazil and South Africa) and one with Jabouille, in Austria. However, in spite of its prodigious power output the Renault engine was fragile, failures conditioning the outcome of a number of races.

Key players in the 1981 season were the watch manufacturer Longines and Olivetti computers—not as might be imagined in the role of sponsors or racing teams, but involved in the timing of the races. Ten cars were fitted with a micro-transmitter that communicated with a receiver composed of an aluminum strip located on the finishing line. Each car transmitted a different signal that was picked up by the receiver and then decoded by an Olivetti computer which provided lap times to the nearest thousandth of a second, the gaps between cars and the race positions, information which could be superimposed over the television images and which added to the event's interest.

In 1981 FISA banned sliding side-skirts but the designers were cleverly able to overcome the obstacle. The regulations stated that the cars should have a minimum ground clearance of 60 mm. This ground clearance could, however, only be verified with the car stationary, and so hydropneumatic systems were successfully employed that slowly lowered the car until the skirts were grazing the asphalt. Grip was guaranteed, but very rigid suspension had to be used to avoid even the slightest bump nullifying the ground effects for even a fraction of a second. The driver thus had to put up with extremely violent blows to his spine and neck as well as g-forces similar to those experienced by a fighter pilot in a tight turn. Some adopted orthopedic supports. The hydraulic trickery was firstly contested and then adopted by the majority of the teams, tolerated by the FISA and subsequently legalized for the San Marino GP, the fourth race of the season.

Nineteen eighty-one saw the debut of another of the sport's greats, the only driver to threaten Fangio's record of five World Championship titles: Alain Prost, who that season drove for Renault. During his career he took the title four times and was second in the final table on a further three occasions. Fittipaldi instead retired to devote himself to his own team.

The 1981 champion was Nelson Piquet who won the Argentine, San Marino and German GPs at the wheel of a Brabham.

108 bottom right Jean Pierre Jabouille partnered with René Arnoux at Renault in 1980, scoring a single victory in the Austrian GP at the Osterreichring and finishing in eighth place in the championship.

109 top Nelson Piquet with the Brabham-Ford was one of the protagonists of the 1980 season: three wins, two second places, a third and a fastest lap. These results placed him second in the championship behind Australia's Alan Jones.

109 center Jacques Lafitte and Didier Pironi took Ligier to second place in the 1980 Constructors' Championship, a result better than their respective fourth and fifth places in the Drivers' Championship.

109 bottom right By 1980 Gilles Villeneuve was into his fourth season with Ferrari: he scored the last two victories of his career at Monaco and in Spain as well as the highest number of accidents, four.

108 center right The 1980 Monaco GP provided thrills at the start when Derek Daly in the Tyrrell took off, involving his team mate Jarier, Prost in the McLaren and Giacomelli in the Alfa Romeo in a multiple pile-up without serious consequences.

108 bottom left and 109 bottom left These photographs show the Renault (left) and Ferrari (right) pits at the 1980 United States West GP held at Long Beach. The race was an indifferent one for both Maranello, with a fifth place and a retirement, and for the French team, with a ninth and a DNQ.

1980 1981

THE LOSS OF COLIN CHAPMAN AND VILLENEUVE

Following the polemics between the FISA and the FOCA that had been suppressed so as not to preoccupy the sponsors, it was thought that Formula 1 might finally be able to put on a show composed solely of competition and speed. This was not to be the case, however, as 1982 was also marred by disputes and, just for a change, cheating. This was the verdict passed on measures adopted by certain teams to overcome the new FISA ruling

whereby the minimum weight of the cars, without fuel but including oil and water, was set at 580 kg (1,279 lb.).

With this system the FISA attempted to favor the smaller teams that did not yet have access to turbocharged engines, encouraging technological research. On the other hand, the turbocharged cars were much lighter than the prescribed minimum, and in order to get round this problem Williams, Brabham, Lotus, Arrows and McLaren invented a fake liquid-cooling circuit for the braking system. The reservoirs were filled prior to the weighing of the car so as to reach the 580 kg (1,279 lb.) minimum and then emptied during the race. The trick was discovered as early as the Brazilian GP, the second race of the '82 season, with a protest being presented by Ferrari and Renault. Piquet in the Brabham and Rosberg with the Williams were disqualified. The situation went critical again two races later at San Marino: the British teams within the FOCA decided not to race unless the Brazilian disqualifications were revoked. The entertainment value of the racing undoubtedly suffered with only 14 drivers taking part. Dispute led to dispute.

Next it was the two Ferrari drivers who were involved as Pironi had failed to respect team orders and allow Villeneuve to win the race. The two refused to speak even on the podium and unfortunately they never had time to make their peace. During the second qualifying session for the successive Belgian Grand Prix, Villeneuve was

pressing hard to snatch pole position from his team-mate/rival when he collided violently with the March that Jochen Mass was driving slowly toward the pits after having completed his qualifying laps. Gilles died that evening and Ferrari withdrew Pironi from the race as a mark of respect.

Fate seemed determined to persecute the Ferrari driver who was involved in an accident similar to that of his former teammate. Pironi started from pole position in Canada but his engine

1982

110

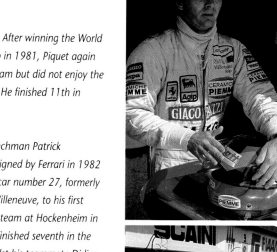

110 top right After winning the World Championship in 1981, Piquet again drove a Brabham but did not enjoy the same success. He finished 11th in the final table.

110-111 Frenchman Patrick Tambay was signed by Ferrari in 1982 and he drove car number 27, formerly belonging to Villeneuve, to his first victory for the team at Hockenheim in Germany. He finished seventh in the final table whilst his teammate Didier Pironi was second: Ferrari took the Constructors' title.

110 center right At the first of the three GPs held in the United States in 1982—the first time that this had happened in Formula 1, which generally held only one race per country— Bruno Giacomelli with the Alfa Romeo started well from the third row but crashed out on the fifth lap.

110 bottom right Alain Prost with the Renault seen overtaking Riccardo Patrese in the Brabham-Ford. The French driver had the better of the Italian also in the final table as they finished fourth and tenth respectively.

died as the lights changed. All the other drivers managed to avoid him but Paletti, at the wheel of the Osella-Alfa Romeo and starting from the last row of the grid. He never saw the stationary Ferrari: there were no signs of braking, no attempt to avoid the obstacle; the young Italian driver was killed instantly. Pironi instead climbed from his burning car miraculously unscathed.

Formula 1 was about to lose another of its leading figures: in the close of the season, while working on his team's cars for 1983, Colin Bruce Chapman died of a heart attack on the 16th of December. One of the greats had been taken from us—the Fangio of the constructors, a genial, astute and daring man who on a number of occasions changed the face of the sport.

The death of the Lotus chief, together with those of the two drivers and the polemics and subterfuge with regards to the fake water tanks, made 1982 a rather depressing year. The tragedies overshadowed innovations in the field of chassis

technology involving the use of composite materials in the construction of monocoques rather than the sheet aluminum that had characterized the cars of the previous 20 years. A Nomex and aluminum honeycomb sandwich was bonded on both sides to rigid sheets of aluminum and composite materials (Kevlar, carbon-fiber). This type of monocoque was 40% lighter than aluminum equivalents but was exorbitantly expensive to produce. Carbon-fiber and Kevlar were subsequently also used for other components such as wings and brake discs.

Another innovation was that of the "fast tank": the car started the race with soft tires and sufficient fuel to complete half the race, then made a pit-stop during which the tires were changed and fuel for the remainder was provided.

The 1982 World Championship was won by the Finnish driver Keke Rosberg: despite winning only one Grand Prix (the Swiss) he nonetheless finished in the points on numerous occasions.

111 Gilles Villeneuve competed in Formula 1 for just six seasons (1977-1982), almost always at the wheel of a Ferrari: following his debut with the McLaren-Ford at the British GP in 1977 he was signed by the Italian manufacturer and was driving a Ferrari by the Canadian GP. Gilles' brief career at the very top was sufficient to earn him a place in the hearts of the tifosi. His boldness and tenacity and above all his generosity captured the public, but during practice for the Belgian GP in 1982 he ran full tilt into the March being driven slowly back to the pits by Jochen Mass. The Ferrari was launched into the air and when it came crashing back to earth Gilles was thrown out still strapped into his seat. He hit the back of his head against one of the safety fence uprights and died of his injuries.

THE RETIREMENT OF ANOTHER GREAT

112 top left In 1983 Nelson Piquet conquered his second world title. His BMW-powered Brabham was triumphant in Brazil, Italy and in the Grand Prix of Europe held at Brands Hatch.

112 center left Alain Prost, seen here during the 1983 French GP, missed out on the '83 championship by two points, while Renault finished runner-up to Ferrari in the Constructors' Championship. This scenario was repeated in 1984 when Alain, who had in the meantime moved to McLaren-Porsche, was second to Lauda by just half a point.

The year 1983 marked the end of an era, of a period in the history of Formula 1 that had lasted no less than 16 years. In this case it was not a driver, a team or a manager that left the stage but an engine. The Ford-Cosworth V8, mounted in a Tyrrell, scored its 155th and last Formula 1 win since its debut in 1967.

In little more than six months Grand Prix racing had lost both Chapman and the Ford-Cosworth engine that Colin himself had helped make great. Another quirk of fate had it that the year of the turbocharged engine's definitive consecration was also marked by Renault's last Formula 1 win, at the Austrian GP: the French team abandoned the F1 circus at the end of 1985 without having managed to repeat this feat, and instead concentrated on supplying its V6 engines to Lotus, Ligier and Tyrrell.

The turbo's success also coincided with the abandonment of the ground effects sidepods and the rigid suspension that had been so hard on the drivers. The wing cars were replaced by those with flat underbodies while sufficient downforce was provided by aerodynamic appendages regulated in size by the FISA.

The widespread use of carbon-fiber and composite materials in chassis as well as brake discs allowed closed monocoques to be constructed that required no external bodywork. While these tubs were excellent in terms of torsional stiffness and lightness (the one produced by ATS weighed just 18 kg! [40 lb.]), they were prohibitively expensive. Moreover, the integral monocoque did not allow the suspension geometry to be modified, as the various elements could not be bolted directly to the panel-work but

rather to aluminum plates buried deep in the carbon-fiber.

The McLaren-TAG-Porsche made its debut at the Dutch GP driven by Niki Lauda, who had returned to racing in 1982 to resolve his airline's severe financial difficulties. TAG (Techniques d'Avant Garde) was a company owned by the Arab financier Mansour Ojjeh that presented a turbocharged 80° V6 engine designed and built by Porsche. Another debut toward the end of the season was that of the new Honda V6 powering the Williams.

The 1983 title went to Piquet with the Brabham-BMW: this was his second since 1981 and was again conquered by a handful of points from Alain Prost.

112 bottom and center right Prost, seen below during the Belgian GP, thought he was going to win the 1984 Championship at the wheel of the McLaren but had to settle for second place in spite of scoring seven wins, two more than his teammate and eventual champion Niki Lauda.

FROZEN FUEL

In order to curb the escalating power outputs of the turbo engines (which were approaching the 1000 hp threshold), the FISA fell back on the old system of restricting the amount of fuel that could be carried. In 1984 cars were thus allowed to take on board no more than 220 liters (58 gal.). The teams worked on legal and quasi-legal systems of getting round the new regulations including super-chilling the fuel. A tank that held just 220 liters of standard fuel held roughly 235 liters (62 gal.) of fuel at -50°—enough for five extra laps.

Serious problems would arise, however, in the

1983
1984

case of a delayed or repeated start as the fuel would return to its normal liquid state and burst the tanks. Fortunately this situation never occurred.

The 220-liter (58 gal.) limit modified the way the drivers approached the races, as they would ease off the pace toward the end to the detriment of the spectacle. Late charges, desperate overtaking and chases were abandoned in favor of conserving fuel. Some races were more akin to regularity trials.

Nineteen eighty-four was the year of the McLaren-TAG-Porsches. Lauda and Prost formed an unbeatable pair, taking the Constructors' title and the first two places in the Drivers' Championship. It was Lauda who took the title—the third of his career—despite the fact that his teammate won more races.

The record books show that an Italian, in this case Michele Alboreto, drove a Formula 1 Ferrari for the first time in years, but the most important event of the year was the step up from the ranks of the British Formula 3 championship of the young Brazilian driver Ayrton Senna, a phenomenal wet-weather performer.

113 center Ayrton Senna made his Formula 1 debut in 1984. Leap-frogging F2, he reached the F1 circus via the British Formula 3 series with Toleman (top photograph) being the first team to offer him an F1 drive for the Brazilian GP. It was a difficult debut with Senna starting from 16th place on the grid and retiring on the 8th lap with a broken turbo. In the 1984 German GP (center photograph) held at Hockenheim, Ayrton was involved in an accident that had no serious consequences but put him out of the race on the 4th lap. The photograph below, again from the 1984 German GP, shows Tambay's Renault, fifth despite these flames.

112-113 Piquet was the first champion of the turbo era and brought success to BMW. The three-time champion of the world is closely associated with Brabham: for 15 seasons he drove for the Australian team using three different engines (Alfa, Ford and turbo BMW). He also drove for Ensign, McLaren,

Williams, Lotus and Benetton in a career that concluded in 1991.

113 top left Rain curtailed the entertainment at the 1984 Monaco GP: only 31 of the scheduled 77 laps were completed. Prost won, but Ayrton Senna was breathing down his neck when the race was interrupted.

113 top right An Italian car and driver excited the Ferrari tifosi in 1984, but Michele Alboreto managed only one win (Belgian GP) and finished fourth in the final table.

113 bottom left The podium at the 1983 San Marino GP was all French: from the left, René Arnoux, third with the Ferrari; Patrick Tambay, the winner with the other Ferrari; and Alain Prost, second with the Renault.

113 bottom center and right Lauda (in the photograph on the right with Frank Williams) won his third title in 1984 at the wheel of the McLaren-Porsche that also won the Constructors' Championship.

113

LAUDA, FAREWELL AND PROST JOINS THE GREATS

The 1985 season saw the confirmation of the 220-liter (58 gal.) limit on fuel, but this was to be reduced to 195 in 1986/87 and again to 185 liters (49 gal.) in '88/89, while frozen fuel was outlawed. FISA thus confirmed its wish to control power outputs while the constructors were faced with the conundrum of combining high power outputs with low fuel consumption. The engineers concentrated on ever more sophisticated injection systems and introduced a wastegate control to the cockpit, which the driver could use to temporarily increase turbo boost and therefore horsepower.

The season revealed the talent and daring of Ayrton Senna, with the Brazilian driver scoring his first Formula 1 victory in the Portuguese GP in torrential rain. On the eve of the Austrian GP, Niki Lauda again announced his retirement from racing in spite of the lavish offer of 6.5 million dollars from Bernie Ecclestone, boss of Brabham, to compete in the 1986 season.

Renault and Alfa Romeo also withdrew at the end of the year, due to financial problems. The 1985 title went to Alain Prost, the first Frenchman to win a Formula championship, after two successive seasons in which he had finished second.

Fourteen-hundred hp: this was the awe-inspiring new power output record achieved by a number of cars during practice for the 1986 races. Given that there were no fuel consumption problems during qualifying as the fuel limits did not apply, the teams used special qualifying engines and extremely soft tire compounds in order to pare away fractions of a second per lap—fractions that were vital to the conquest of pole position.

Nineteen eighty-six was a close-fought season and by the last race, the Australian GP at the Adelaide circuit, Mansell, Piquet and Prost were all well placed to win the title. Rosberg took the lead at the start of the race and held it until the 57th lap, when he was forced to retire. Piquet then took up the running, followed by Mansell. That second place would have been enough to guarantee the British driver the championship, but six laps later he was forced to retire when a tire blew. The World Championship thus appeared to be Piquet's,

114 first photograph top Niki Lauda scored his last Formula 1 victory in 1985 with the McLaren-Porsche number 7. This was the Dutch GP won by two-tenths of a second from his teammate Prost.

114 second photograph The Brazilian Nelson Piquet, at the wheel of car number 6, finished third in the final table in 1986, behind his teammate Nigel

Mansell by a single point (69 against 70) and with a single win less (four against five, with two successive victories in Germany and Hungary).

114 third photograph Ayrton Senna talking with Elio de Angelis: the two Lotus drivers finished the 1985 season fourth and fifth, respectively, separated by just five points.

114 fourth photograph Senna's first Formula 1 victory came in the rain-drenched 1985 Portuguese GP. In such conditions Ayrton was truly unbeatable.

114 fifth photograph Alain Prost keeping things under control as he goes on to win the 1985 Monaco GP. This was an unforgettable season for Alain as he won the first of his four titles.

114-115 Victories in Canada and Germany and numerous points-scoring placings were not enough to allow Michele Alboreto to take the championship title in 1985. The Italian driver nonetheless finished runner-up.

until he was passed by Prost while in the pits. The Frenchman retained the lead to win both the race and the title, thus joining that select band of drivers to have won at least two consecutive titles: Alberto Ascari (1952-53), Juan Manuel Fangio (1954-57) and Jack Brabham (1959-60). He also broke Fangio's record and matched that of Jim Clark with 25 Grand Prix victories. The following year he was to overtake even Stewart, and would to record a remarkable career total of 51 victories.

Meanwhile, the floundering Toleman team was bought by Italian clothing manufacturer Benetton— with results that would surprise everyone....

1985 1986

115 top Riccardo Patrese had a poor season at the wheel of the Benetton-sponsored Alfa Romeo in 1985: ninth place was his best result, achieved in the British GP and the GP of Europe held at Brands Hatch. Ill-luck persecuted the Italian driver: in this photograph his car is seen as it catches fire in the dramatic accident at the Monaco GP that also involved Nelson Piquet, fortunately without further consequences.

115 center The Englishman Nigel Mansell (left) heading for victory in the Williams-Honda, lapping all his rivals still in the race with the exception of Piquet. This was the 1986 British GP. Nicknamed "Lionheart", Mansell raced for Williams from 1985 to 1988, in 1991-1992 and four Grand Prix in 1994, winning 13 Grands Prix and conquering 11 pole positions. In the picture in the middle Piquet (left) jokes with Mansell (right) while an amused Prost looks on. The three drivers were the protagonists of the 1986 season which finished with Prost champion, Mansell second and Piquet third. This was the fourth season in which Williams used V6 turbocharged Honda engines.

115 bottom Thanks to the Pirellis that allowed him to complete the race without a single pit stop, Gerhard Berger scored his first Formula 1 victory in Mexico in 1986.

THE END OF THE ROAD FOR THE TURBOS

1986 1987

The rush to exploit the power of turbocharging had been expensive, and in 1987 the FISA introduced regulations designed to penalize their use: naturally aspirated 12-cylinder engines with total displacements of 3.5 liters (0.9 gal.) fitted to cars with a minimum weight of 500 kg (1,103 lb.) were allowed to compete against turbocharged cars weighing at least 540 kg (1,191 lb.) and with maximum boost pressures of four bar.

In 1988 the restriction on the total amount of fuel that the naturally aspirated cars could carry was to be removed, while the turbo cars would be

The season's anti-hero was instead the Paul Ricard circuit at Le Castellet, used for testing before and during the championship as well as for the French GP. While returning from a test session in March, Frank Williams had a serious road accident that has confined him to a wheelchair ever since. Two months later the Italian driver de Angelis crashed at the Verriere corner after his car lost its rear wing. He died as a result of the delayed arrival of the rescue services. After the organizers came in for heavy criticism the circuit was halved in length and the Verriere esses were eliminated.

Silverstone in Great Britain and the Nürburgring and Hockenheim in Germany) the rotation was to be on a five-year basis.

The great novelty of 1987 was telemetry: an on-board computer transmitted data during the race regarding the engine, suspension, chassis, bodywork and tires, allowing appropriate strategies to be devised and adopted. Telemetry equipment was very expensive and thus only Honda, Brabham and Ferrari were able to take immediate advantage of the system.

The Williams-Honda proved to be extremely rapid. The turbocharged Japanese 80° V6 was peerless, and at the British GP it demonstrated crushing superiority with the two Williams and the two Honda-powered Lotuses finishing in the first four places. It was a memorable race. Although Mansell and Piquet were teammates, there was no love lost between them and they battled tooth and claw from the very first corner. Mansell was forced into the pits with a vibrating wheel but then stormed back in a seemingly impossible chase given that 17 laps from the end Piquet had a lead of 16.8

restricted to 150 liters (40 gal.) and boost pressure would be restricted to 2.5 bar. In 1989 turbocharging would be definitively outlawed.

In short, at every turn the regulations were modified without the slightest respect for technological progress, while innovations were a result not of logical development but of the FIA's desire to manipulate the World Championship as it saw fit. Officially, the Federation was attempting to lighten the teams' financial burden, but in reality it was favoring Ferrari (which that year celebrated its 400th Grand Prix): the admission of 12-cylinder naturally aspirated engines clearly favored Maranello—the firm had always favored this architecture—but it killed stone-dead the new V8s under development by Ford and Honda. Honda was nonetheless the protagonist of the 1987 season with its 80° V6 powering the mighty Williams.

With the reintroduction of naturally aspirated engines in 1987 the Colin Chapman Cup and the Jim Clark Cup were awarded to constructors and drivers respectively. Even though Lotus had been orphaned it demonstrated that it had not lost its ability to be innovative with the presentation of self-levelling hydraulic suspension allowing the car's ride height to remain constant, to the benefit of grip.

Before the season got under way, new regulations were defined that would be valid for the next five years: the television revenue was divided between the FIA (30%), the FOCA (24%) and the teams (46%); the technical specifications of the cars (engines, gearbox, weight) were to remain unchanged until 1991; the number of races was fixed at 16; in those countries where the Grand Prix was held alternately at two different tracks (Le Castellet and Dijon in France, Brands Hatch and

116 top left and top center The daring, exuberant Mansell collected six wins in 1987, three fastest laps and eight pole positions. This last achievement was particularly impressive given the presence of the pole position king Ayrton Senna. Here Mansell is seen at the start of the Brazilian GP (left) and engaged in a duel with his team mate Piquet (right).

seconds. With two laps to go Mansell had narrowed that gap to 1.6 seconds and, with his fuel running dangerously low and the race all but over, he caught his teammate at Stowe Corner, overtook in a bold thrust, and won by two seconds. During his lap of honor he stopped at the point where he had overtaken, got out of the car and kissed the asphalt.

Piquet nonetheless won the World Championship laurels, with Williams of course taking the Constructors' title. Meanwhile the Lotus 99T introduced another significant novelty: an electronically controlled suspension that, via fast-acting solenoids, continually optimized the suspension settings. The season was also marked by a violent argument that broke out between Mansell and Senna, eventually leading the furious Englishman to be escorted from the Brazilian's pits.

116 bottom Satoru Nakajima made his Formula 1 debut in 1987 at the wheel of a Lotus-Honda. His presence was determined by Honda's habit of imposing its own drivers on the teams using its engines.

116 top right Nigel Mansell enjoyed a fine season in 1987 with the Williams-Honda, even though he was unable to crown it with the Championship title that went to his teammate Nelson Piquet. Here the Englishman celebrates his victory in the French GP.

116 center In 1987 Mansell had to settle for second overall in the championship, just as the previous season when he was beaten by Alain Prost. His first championship title was only postponed, however, until 1992, when he triumphed with the unbeatable Renault-powered Williams.

117 left and top right Nigel Mansell retired again from Formula 1 after 1995, but rather than abandon motor sport he moved to CART and the British Touring Car Championship (BTCC). He left his mark on the Grand Prix circus with a total of 31 victories placing him

fourth in the list of the most successful drivers, behind Prost, Senna and Schumacher.

117 bottom Nigel Mansell's face reveals the pain caused by the crash during the warm-up lap for the 1987 Japanese GP.

Two greats for McLaren

The McLaren-Honda was in a league of its own in 1988, and never in the history of modern Formula 1 had a team so convincingly dominated the Championship. The results were 15 wins out of 16 Grands Prix disputed, eight going to Senna and seven to Prost; ten 1-2s; 13 pole positions; the Drivers' Championship won by Senna, with Prost runner-up for the third time; and the Constructors'

more say in Ferrari following the death of the 90-year-old Enzo on the 14th of August. According to the agreement drawn up between the Agnelli family and Ferrari in 1969 that saw 50% of the Modena company sold to Fiat, on the death of the Drake the Turin group's share would increase to 90%, Piero Lardi Ferrari retaining the remaining 10%. Ferrari's death, the corporate changes and the new

Championship won with 199 points—no fewer than 134 ahead of the second-place team, Ferrari. Ayrton Senna confirmed the talent of the Brazilian drivers, the latest South American champion joining his fellow countrymen Piquet and Fittipaldi.

The McLaren-Honda combination was thus one of the most successful of all time. While McLaren proved capable of exploiting its turbocharged performance advantage over the naturally aspirated units to the full, the other teams were hurriedly turning to new engines. Williams, Ligier and March opted for the Judd units, Benetton chose Ford and Arrows Megatron (in effect, revised BMW units). Brabham had instead dropped out of the championship, Ecclestone selling out to Italy's Fiat concern.

The Italian mass manufacturer also had even

organizational structure conditioned the team's performance that season—Maranello won only a single race, but at least this came at the Italian GP, where Berger and Alboreto finished 1-2.

The 1988 World Championship was also characterized by the introduction of pre-qualifying on the previous Friday, together with untimed practice. The 18 teams participating in the championship had entered 31 drivers but the FISA provided only 26 places on the grid and thus a number of hopefuls had to be eliminated before each race. For the first half of the season the drivers recording the slowest times were eliminated while in the second half the results achieved in the first part of the championship were used to decide who would be allowed to start.

118 top and bottom Alain Prost salutes the crowd at "his" French GP of 1988 (bottom). The Professor started from the pole (top) and finished the race over 30 seconds ahead of teammate Ayrton Senna with the two Ferraris of Alboreto and Berger in third and fourth. Alain's victory interrupted Senna's winning streak: two successive wins prior to this race and four in a row afterward.

118 center A line-up of drivers of this calibre would be the envy of any team. In 1988 McLaren had both Ayrton Senna and Alain Prost on its books, the pair finishing first and second in the championship.

118-119 and 119 top left The two aces Alain Prost and Ayrton Senna between them won all the 1988 Grands Prix with the exception of the Italian GP at Monza, which went to Gerhard Berger in the Ferrari. On that occasion

Prost (bottom) was forced to retire with mechanical problems (the first of the season for McLaren) while Senna (top, in the pits) could finish no better than tenth after problems with fuel.

119 top right Ayrton Senna, Alain Prost and Nelson Piquet on the podium, a scene repeated twice during the course of the 1988 season at San Marino (in the photograph) and in Australia. Down Under it was Prost who won with Senna second.

1988

The late Eighties and early 1990s were characterized by the monopoly enjoyed by McLaren-Honda and its drivers Ayrton Senna and Alain Prost. As had occurred at Williams between Mansell and Piquet, the rivalry at McLaren between Senna and Prost was fierce and at times extremely personal. Ayrton's talent was now undisputed, as was his exceptional bravura in wet conditions—an authentic champion in continual conflict with his teammate, another of Formula 1's undisputed greats. On a number of occasions Prost accused the

1989

120 top and center left Nineteen eighty-nine was a year to forget for Gerhard Berger: the start to the season was disastrous with an accident in the opening round in Brazil involving Senna immediately after the start. In the next race at San Marino things went from bad to worse because on the third lap Berger lost a front wing and his Ferrari crashed into a retaining wall; the car caught fire but the rapid response of the rescue services avoided a tragedy. Gerhard escaped with burns to his hands and arms.

McLaren team of favoring the Brazilian by providing him with better equipment and manipulating the telemetry data. An end was in sight to the arguments, however, as at the Italian GP Prost announced that he would be driving for Ferrari the following season.

McLaren started the 1989 season as the clear favorite but a surprise was sprung in the first race as Nigel Mansell won with the Ferrari. The Italians, however, were not among the teams tipped for the title because the innovative seven-speed semiautomatic gearbox had not proved its reliability during winter testing. The new transmission system featured two paddles, mounted on either side of the steering wheel, with which the driver engaged gears without having to use the clutch pedal, which only came into play at the start. The Tipo 640 was the first and only Ferrari to be developed and built in England at Ferrari's Guildford premises set up at the behest of John Barnard; final assembly and the building of the mechanical components were still carried out at Maranello.

The 1989 Drivers' and Constructors' Championship tables were in effect photocopies of those of the previous year with the exception of the order of the drivers: first was Alain Prost, taking his third title, with Senna second. Prost left McLaren as champion and helped the team to win its second successive Constructors' Championship. Senna,

even though he actually won more races, had to settle for second place. It is curious that the Brazilian covered no fewer than 2295 km in the lead during the 16 races, almost twice Prost's total of 1217 km.

The 1989 season, the 40th since the birth of Formula 1, saw the banning of the turbocharger and the return of 3.5-liter naturally aspirated engines. The problem faced by all the teams was that of deciding on the optimum engine layout, a decision complicated by the FISA's praiseworthy decision to oblige the constructors to place the pedal-box behind the front axle, thus ensuring greater safety for the drivers.

This measure created packaging difficulties, as with the cockpit set further back the space available for the engine and fuel tanks had to be revised. Would an eight-, ten-, or 12-cylinder engine be better? From the point of view of compactness the former was undoubtedly the best, especially with the cylinders in V-formation. However, an Eight would struggle to match the piston speed of a Twelve. On the other hand, a 12-cylinder engine was bulky, and with the cylinders in V-formation subtracted space from the fuel tanks (that with this type of unit had to be capacious). The solution, as ever, was a compromise: a V10 layout solved all the problems of space.

This type of engine was adopted by Renault (Williams) and Honda (McLaren); Ford (Benetton), Cosworth (AGS, Arrows, Coloni, Dallara, Ligier, Minardi, Onyx, Osella, Rial and Tyrrell), Judd (Brabham, Euro-Brun, Lotus, March), whereas Yamaha (Zakspeed) preferred the V8 while Ferrari and Lamborghini (Lola) stuck with the V12.

120 bottom and 121 top Turbo engines were outlawed in 1989 and the teams returned to naturally aspirated units. Their dilemma was whether to go for 8 or 12 cylinders. Honda found the ideal compromise and fitted a V10 to the McLarens that proved to be powerful, fast and reliable, allowing Prost to win the Drivers' Championship (Senna with the second McLaren was runner-up) and McLaren the Constructors' title.

121 center left Alain Prost started the 1990 season as reigning champion at the wheel of the Ferrari. The duel with Senna was repeated this season, too: the Brazilian took the title by five points.

121 center right In 1989 Nigel Mansell temporarily abandoned Williams (he returned in 1991) to drive for Ferrari. He got off to a fantastic start by winning the first race of the season in Brazil.

121 bottom Jean Alesi made his debut with the Tyrrell-Ford in 1989 and was unfortunate not to achieve better than fourth place. He had to wait until 1995 for his first Formula 1 victory, at the wheel of a Ferrari in the Canadian GP.

120 center right Rain ruined the last race of the 1989 season in Australia: no fewer than 18 drivers retired whilst the champion Prost did not even start after completing a warm-up lap. Boutsen won at the wheel of a Williams.

120-121 Alain Prost won his third title in 1989, and his third for McLaren. The Professor still had time to win his fourth in 1993, this time with Williams, at the venerable age of 38.

UNDER THE SIGN OF SENNA AND THE JAPANESE TEAM

1990 1991

Formula 1 was powered toward the end of the century by the Japanese, who proved to be major players in the sport, at least in the early 1990s, from both the technological and economic points of view. The pride of the Land of the Rising Sun was Honda, a company that thanks to its powerful technological and financial resources seemed ready to dominate the decade.

From 1986 the Japanese firm, having found a niche as an engine supplier rather than as a constructor of complete cars, entered a cycle of remarkable success that concluded in 1991 with a record of six consecutive Constructors' titles. The firm's absence from the GP circus from 1992 has proved to be unsupportable for the powers-that-be,

podium, and faith in his own abilities, following the Frenchman's three successive wins in Mexico, France and Great Britain. Senna finished the season with six wins to Prost's five and made sure of the title with one race still to be run. He was in fact crowned as champion at the Japanese Grand Prix, a race that revealed the intensity of his rivalry with Prost: the two had both made claims of favoritism on the part of the FISA and their teams in previous championships. The situation seemed to have been defused at the 1990 Italian GP, when the pair shook hands at a press conference. This was merely a cease-fire, however, not lasting peace. At Suzuka, with both drivers in the running for the title, the Brazilian needed just seven seconds to settle the

and thus in 1998 it was announced that it would be returning to the sport in the year 2000 with the help of *Ingegnere* Dallara, a fount of motor racing expertise in general who has never fully embraced Formula 1, preferring to consolidate his reputation in the United States. Dallara will work on the production of the new car and will lend his know-how to the firm as it attempts to regain a leading role in Grand Prix racing. It is not only Honda that has revealed nostalgia for Formula 1 either: the comeback of BMW is also planned for the new millennium, as is the debut of Toyota.

The wave of Japanese success and its inebriating, beneficial effects involved the Williams and McLaren teams and drivers such as Alain Prost, who won two of his four titles with Honda engines, Nelson Piquet and above all Ayrton Senna. In the Honda-McLaren combination Senna found the ideal conditions in which to express his talent to the full, to confirm his reputation as the undisputed Rain King and to conquer his second and third World Championships in 1990 and '91. He won 13 of the 32 Grands Prix staged in the period.

The conquest of those two titles was by no means easy for Senna: in 1990 Alain Prost was the thorn in his side. Early in the season the Professor led the Championship table with four wins to the Brazilian's three. In the second half, at the German GP, the ninth round, Senna finally regained the

122 top left Jean Alesi joined Ferrari in 1991, the Maranello firm thus finding itself with prevalently French drivers (there was also Prost) apart from the Italian Morbidelli. Jean's best result was third in Germany, Monaco and Portugal.

122 center left bottom and bottom right Prost and Senna continued their ongoing duel in 1990. The Frenchman, having joined Ferrari, challenged the Brazilian for the title

up to the penultimate round in Japan (right). Here the duel lasted just seven seconds, as Senna rammed the Professor on the first lap, preventing him from continuing and thus conquering the title with a race still to run. With this move Ayrton settled a score with Alain: the previous year Prost had done the same to Senna, again at Suzuka.

matter and re-ignite the polemics: he rammed Prost at the first corner, thus gaining revenge for the incident at Suzuka the previous year in which it had been the Professor who sent Senna crashing out and took the World Championship title.

In 1991 the threat posed by Alain Prost diminished in that the Ferrari he was now driving was inconsistent: he failed to score a single win, obtaining just three second-place finishes in the

122-123 and 123 top left Nigel Mansell's Williams-Renault took pole position at the 1991 British Grand Prix. Here shortly before the start the car is on the grid with covers still on the tires. The British Lion won the race and set fastest lap: this was the second of three consecutive wins together with those in France and Germany.

123 center Two titles, 174 World Championship points, 23 pole positions, 13 victories, four fastest laps: the statistics whereby Ayrton Senna with highs and lows allowed McLaren to conquer two Constructors' Championships in the 1990 and '91 seasons.

123 bottom left At the start of the 1991 Belgian GP Alain Prost in the Ferrari (in the foreground turning into the corner) is second behind Ayrton Senna. He was to retire on the second lap with a broken fuel pump.

123 bottom right Michael Schumacher in the 1991 Italian GP, his second Formula 1 race. The German driver finished fifth at the wheel of a Benetton-Ford (on his debut he drove a Jordan).

122 top right and 123 top right The first part of the 1991 season was totally dominated by Ayrton Senna. The Championship became almost monotonous as he won the first four races and started from the pole in all four, including his national GP in

Brazil. At the Sao Paolo Interlagos circuit Ayrton won for the first time in front of his home crowd. Although this brought Senna immense joy he was exhausted at the finish and struggled to hold the trophy due to pains in his shoulders caused by over-tight safety belts.

USA, France and Spain. Senna's chief rival was instead Nigel Mansell, who had moved from Ferrari to Williams. Following a start to the season which had seen Senna register four consecutive victories in the first four Grands Prix, including the one held in his home city of Sao Paolo—where he reached the podium so exhausted he was unable to hold the trophy and with his shoulders bruised by over-tight safety belts—Mansell began his fight back. After a win in France where he succeeded in overtaking Prost after a duel lasting 53 laps, the Englishman arrived at his national Grand Prix in dominant form, taking pole position, setting the fastest lap and winning the race. He repeated the exploit in Germany with the exception of the fastest lap which fell to his teammate Riccardo Patrese. As was becoming customary, the rivalry between Senna and Mansell was settled at the penultimate race in Japan: the Englishman attempted to slip past Senna into second place (Berger was leading in the McLaren and went on to win the race), but on the ninth lap finished in the sand and had to abandon the race and all hopes of the title. However, the impulsive Mansell's first World Championship triumph was only postponed by a year. In 1992, thanks in part to the superb chassis developed by the Williams technicians and a Renault engine in sparkling form, Mansell achieved the most important objective of his career, scoring nine Grand Prix wins along the way. Senna and Berger had to settle for the crumbs, winning three and two GPs respectively. Patrese finished in second place in the World Championship thanks to his consistency and excellent series of placings (one victory, six seconds).

ALAIN PROST, SECOND ONLY TO FANGIO

Even though the Professor had had to give way to the Brazilian in the early 1990s, he was by no means a spent force. Not satisfied with the three World Championship titles he had conquered with McLaren in 1985, '86 and '89, Prost wanted to match Juan Manuel Fangio's record of five championship victories. The Frenchman eventually finished up with four titles, a remarkable haul nonetheless—and an honorable second place that he is unlikely to have to share for some time. His fourth came in 1993 at the venerable age (for a Formula 1 driver) of 38. He had spent 1992 away from the tracks following his divorce from Ferrari at the last race of the 1991 season in Australia. The Professor returned at the wheel of a Williams-Renault, taking the place of reigning champion Mansell, who had decided to race in America's CART/Indy series. Prost's teammate would instead be Damon Hill, son of the late, great Graham.

The Williams once again proved to be the car to beat and allowed Hill to record three victories.

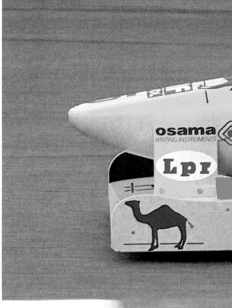

Combined with the talent of Alain Prost it formed an exceptional cocktail that Senna and his McLaren-Ford was able to oppose on only four occasions. The only other Grand Prix not to fall to Williams was won by Michael Schumacher, who thus scored his second Formula 1 victory. Prost was crowned World Champion two races from the end of the season at Estoril in Portugal. Twenty-four hours later he announced his retirement (once again) from racing.

As with Honda, however, Formula 1 was Alain Prost's drug of choice, and he returned to the circus in 1997 with his own team. The Professor's fourth title confirmed the French *grandeur* in the sport, with Honda being replaced by Renault as the leading engine supplier. Between 1992 and 1997 the firm powered to six consecutive Constructors' Championships. This success was the French company's return on the massive investment it had made in the sport since 1977, during which time it had competed with its own cars up until 1985 and had had the merit of introducing turbocharging. The firm's wisest decision was that of devoting itself to engines: success followed success from when it began supplying its power units to Williams and Benetton. Renault thus proved to be a worthy successor to Honda and confirmed its position as a major player in the Formula 1 of the 1990s.

1992 1993

125 top Shortly after the start of the 1992 French GP Senna and Schumacher found themselves in trouble. The race was won by Nigel Mansell.

125 center Michael Schumacher was the most promising young Formula 1 driver in 1993. After his first victory in the Belgian GP the previous year he repeated the feat in the Portuguese GP after having started sixth on the grid and conquered six second-place finishes over the course of the season. He came to the fore in 1994, winning his first World Championship title.

125 bottom left Prost won his fourth World Championship in 1993 with the Williams. That season the Professor yet again had to battle against Ayrton Senna who finished runner-up: the Frenchman won seven GPs, of which four came in succession, while the Brazilian won five, all concentrated in the second half of the season.

125 bottom right The last 1992 podium with Gerhard Berger preparing to spray Michael Schumacher with champagne: in the Australian GP the Austrian driver crossed the line just seven-tenths of a second ahead of the German.

124 top left Ayrton Senna, portrayed here in his McLaren-Ford, was, with Alain Prost and Michael Schumacher, one of the key figures in the Formula 1 of the Nineties.

124 top center Ayrton Senna (seen here in the pits) went through a transitional period in 1992, not shining with his McLaren as in previous seasons. However, he still managed three wins and interrupted the domination of Nigel Mansell, heading toward the title with the Williams-Renault. Senna concluded the season in fourth place, bettering teammate Berger by a single point.

124 top right Eddie Irvine joined the F1 circus in 1993 at the Japanese GP. At the wheel of a Jordan-Hart, the driver finished sixth—a good start that kept him at Jordan for three seasons before he moved to Ferrari.

124 center Prost leaving the pits and preparing to join battle. His last Grand Prix came in Australia in 1993: having won his fourth World Championship with two races to go, he retired from competition.

124 bottom Riccardo Patrese enjoyed a fine season in 1992 at the wheel of the Williams-Renault, with which he finished runner-up in the championship to teammate Nigel Mansell.

1994

Ayrton Senna

126 Tragedy struck at the 1994 San Marino Grand Prix at Imola. Ayrton Senna started from pole position but never completed the first lap, the last of his life: at the Tamburello Corner his Williams crashed into the retaining wall (bottom left) and a suspension arm perforated his helmet's visor and his skull. Worse still, Senna's was not the only death that May weekend. At the start of the race itself Lahmy's Lotus and Lehto's Benetton collided (bottom center) causing a number of injuries among the spectators. During practice Ratzenberger crashed his Simtek at the Villeneuve Corner at 314 kph (195 mph), and was killed instantly (bottom right).

127 top The 1994 season was also to be the last for another of the sport's greats, albeit in this case not as a result of an accident: Nigel Mansell announced he would be retiring from motor racing at the end of the season (although he was to be seen in a McLaren in 1995).

127 center The 1994 Monaco GP was the first race after Senna's death and his colleagues commemorated him at a circuit where he had triumphed no fewer than six times with a banner bearing his portrait. The Monte Carlo race was itself not without incident: in practice Wendlinger (left) exited the tunnel and

crashed into the barriers. The Austrian driver was left in a coma but gradually recovered. Mika Hakkinen with the McLaren and Damon Hill in a Williams collided at the Sainte Dévote corner; the Finnish driver spun (right) out of the race together with the Englishman.

ADIEU AYRTON

While Renault took over the reins from Honda in the field of engines, Michael Schumacher became the sport's new star driver, filling the vacuum left by Ayrton Senna, whose brilliant career was cut short at the 1994 San Marino Grand Prix. At 2:17 on Sunday, the first of March, at the Dino and Enzo Ferrari Circuit of Imola, Senna was killed in an accident shortly after the start when he crashed into the retaining wall at the Tamburello Curve. In the massive impact a suspension arm perforated his visor. A cruel destiny: had the suspension arm struck a few millimeters higher he would have survived—and he would have won the 1994 and '95 titles; of this Frank Williams was convinced after having managed to woo Senna away from McLaren. The Brazilian had won three titles and brought three

Constructors' titles to the team. Ayrton passed away, and still today the responsibilities for his death have yet to be ascertained. His thrilling Formula 1 career lasted ten years, from his debut with the Toleman at the Brazilian GP in 1984 after having arrived directly from Formula 3—leap-frogging the intermediate categories like his fiercest rival, Professor Alain Prost—through to his last GP victory in Australia in 1993. In that period he won three championships and 41 Grands Prix, claiming 65 pole positions in the bargain. Senna was the latest driver to die in his car, perhaps—as was death on the battlefield for a warrior—the most honorable fate for a racing driver, although in this case it was particularly brutal and premature.

Schumacher gives nothing away to Senna in terms of driving ability in the wet, courage, daring

or technique.

Benetton, the team owned by the well known Italian clothing concern and born out of the ashes of Toleman in the Eighties, was ably managed by Flavio Briatore and had the merit of bringing Michael Schumacher's talent to the fore. On his Formula 1 debut in 1991 Schumacher had immediately impressed and moved directly from Jordan to the Italian team, which managed to retain his services until 1995.

Schumy's first World Championship title came in 1994, snatched by a single point from Damon Hill. Of the year's 16 races, eight were won by the German (four in succession at the start of the season) and six by the Englishman, the crumbs being picked up by Gerhard Berger and Nigel Mansell. Michael's talent was shown by

127 bottom Eleven cars were involved in two different accidents immediately after the start and seven retired during the race at the 1994 German GP: this was not the brightest of starts to the Hock-enheim race, in which only eight cars managed to finish. Gerhard Berger won for Ferrari, a triumph for the Prancing Horse which thus returned to the winner's enclosure after an absence of four years.

the fact that he won the title in a car that was competitive but not dominant like the Williams, and with a Ford V8 engine that was not on the same level as its highly successful Ford-Cosworth predecessors—and no real match for the Renault unit.

In spite of the abolition of turbos, the French manufacturer still in fact retained its leadership in the field, a position unaffected by the shift to naturally aspirated 3.5- (and subsequently three-) liter engines. The naturally aspirated power units fitted to the Formula 1 cars of the early 1990s were developing in the order of 700 hp in qualifying and 670-680 hp in race tune. The precise power outputs, like the other technical specifications of the cars, were not released by the constructors—a policy adopted by Honda and subsequently by all the other teams.

INCREASED DRIVER SAFETY

The FISA introduced new regulations for the new decade that further addressed driver safety: the cars were now to be subjected to frontal crash tests and had to be fitted with cockpit structures that allowed the driver to climb out of the car unaided in five seconds.

From a stylistic point of view, the Tyrrells caught the eye with their raised noses resembling that of Concorde. There was finally a degree of

him at the wheel of the McLaren, which from 1995 was powered by a Mercedes engine. The first German World Champion at the wheel of a car powered by an engine bearing the three-pointed star would have been a very popular combination in his homeland.

originality to the lines of the cars, rather than anonymous tubes dressed up in wings, spoilers and side-skirts. The British car boasted exceptional aerodynamics: drag had been considerably reduced while the ground effects were optimal, the result of hundreds of hours in the wind tunnel.

In 1995 Schumacher revealed all his driving talent and took his second Championship title, again at the wheel of a Benetton but this time powered by Renault. The Italian team could thus count on the best driver in the field and the best engine, and used these advantages to best effect in taking the Constructors' Championship. The conquest of the title seemed to repeat the previous season's script with Damon Hill again second, albeit further behind, and Jean Alesi again finishing fifth in the Ferrari. David Coulthard and Johnny Herbert finished in well-earned third and fourth places, respectively.

With two titles to his name Schumy was red hot and assiduously courted by all the leading teams, who made multimillion-dollar offers for his services. Many of his fellow Germans hoped to see

128 top The British Lion returned to Formula 1 in 1995, but results were very disappointing. At the San Marino GP Nigel could manage no better than tenth with his McLaren-Mercedes.

128 center The 1995 German Grand Prix was held at Hockenheim and was won by Michael Schumacher with the Benetton-Ford, his fifth victory of the season.

129 top right Dramatic moments in the pits at the 1995 Belgian GP as the fuel filler leaks petrol over Irvine's car, which bursts into flames. Fortunately there were no consequences for the mechanics or driver.

129 center right David Coulthard in the pits to change tires and refuel. After his F1 debut in 1994 the Scot was into his second season with Williams and finished third in the Championship behind Schumacher and Hill.

1995

128 bottom Hill finished in the gravel together with Schumacher on the 23rd lap of the Italian GP. Damon had rammed Schumy's Benetton and the furious German demanded an explanation. He was held back by the marshals, allowing the Englishman to get out of his car.

128-129 There was the usual crowding at the Sainte Dévote corner immediately after the start of the 1995 Monaco GP and the two Ferraris, together with Coulthard's Williams, provoked a multiple pile-up. The race had to be restarted.

129 bottom right Michael Schumacher and Flavio Briatore, the Benetton chief, celebrating the conquest of the Drivers' and Constructors' titles. This was in 1995 and the German had won nine of the 17 scheduled Grands Prix.

1996

130

SCHUMY ATTEMPTS TO REVIVE FERRARI'S FORTUNES

The Prancing Horse has an undeniable appeal, however, even for a cold, calculating champion like Schumacher: the opportunity to race with the only team to be an ever-present in the Formula 1 circus and the only team to have retained its national racing color in spite of the best efforts of wealthy

sponsors persuaded Michael to move to Maranello in 1996. The Italian constructor was looking to Schumacher to restore it to what it saw as its rightful position; its last Drivers' World Championship title dated back to 1979 with Jody Scheckter, the last Constructors' Championship to 1983.

It was love at first sight between Schumacher and the Ferrari team. The German conquered everyone at Maranello, and not only through his driving: Giorgio Ascanelli, Ferrari pits chief, who has seen plenty of fine drivers pass within range of his spanners and screwdrivers, happily recounts that Schumy is one of the very few drivers able to describe exactly how a racing gearbox is put together. An ace driver, therefore, with the technical knowledge to back up his talent, who is so meticulous, conscientious and precise as to remind one of Lauda.

131 top left Four wins, three pole positions, six fastest laps and second place overall in the 1996 Championship for the young Jacques Villeneuve, seen here at the wheel of his Williams-Renault duelling with Schumacher's Ferrari.

131 center Berger hitches a lift with Alesi: this was the 1996 German GP held at Hockenheim where the Austrian was betrayed by his Benetton's engine two laps from the finish. Jean instead came second to Hill in the Williams.

131 bottom left Making his debut in 1996, the son of the impetuous but shy Gilles (who had been killed 14 years earlier), drove like an authentic veteran. This photo shows the celebrations for his victory at the Hungarian GP.

131 bottom right Damon Hill was World Champion in 1996 with eight victories, nine pole positions and five fastest laps. Williams was thus repaid for the faith it had shown in the Englishman signed to flank Prost in 1993. In this photograph the driver is celebrating victory in the Argentine GP.

130-131 Signed by Ferrari to win the team's first championship since 1979, Michael Schumacher, seen here during the German GP at Hockenheim, was beaten into third place overall by Damon Hill and Jacques Villeneuve.

130 bottom Eddie Irvine joined Ferrari in 1996. The Irishman appeared to settle in well as Schumacher's number two. He collected 11 points with a best placing of third in Australia.

Since 1996 the spotlights have been trained on Maranello and its long awaited revival and on Schumacher, a driver who had inherited the mantle of Ayrton Senna and appeared destined to match the number of championships won by Prost or even Fangio.

However, as is frequently the case when expectations are allowed a free rein, the results were disappointing. Ferrari undoubtedly made progress with Schumacher, but in 1996 came up against the Williams-Renault and Damon Hill (the son of Graham, the 1962 and 1968 World Champion) who finished in the top three in 12 of the 16 Grands Prix, with eight victories, three second places and a third. In 1997 it was the turn of Jacques Villeneuve, son of the dashing Gilles who was killed in 1982 before he had the chance to translate his great natural talent into trophies and titles.

In 1996 Schumacher could finish no better than third and Damon Hill gained revenge for having twice finished second to the German when he won his World Championships with Benetton. In second place was Jacques Villeneuve, a fine performance given that he was finishing in front of the driver of the moment.

The following year Schumy improved, but the title was lost during the last race when the German attempted to run Villeneuve off the track as the Canadian tried to overtake in a corner. The German came off the worse in the fight, as following the collision he was forced to retire, thus losing any hope of taking the title.

When in 1998 it appeared that Schumacher would have a clear run at the championship, McLaren-Mercedes arrived from nowhere with an innovative car that appeared to corner as if on rails. Schumy's excellent form and a well prepared car nonetheless allowed him to challenge for the title up to the last race in Japan. At Suzuka, however, the 29-year-old from Hürth-Hermühlheim had to start from the back of the grid after stalling on the starting line, and after staging a thrilling comeback that saw him reach as high as third place, had to retire with a blown tire on the 32nd lap.

The talented Mika Hakkinen of Finland thus won his first World Championship after a fantastic season in which he won eight Grands Prix and collected 100 points—14 more than Schumacher—and dominated the World Championship scene from the first race to the last.

132 top Alexander Würz in the Benetton started from the fifth row of the grid and finished in fifth place in the 1998 French GP. His teammate Fisichella started alongside Würz but could only manage ninth place at the finish.

132 bottom They can win or lose a Grand Prix, are fundamental elements in race strategy, determinant in pit-stops and are prepared for the race by being heated in electric covers: The importance of tires is thus evident.

132-133 The Ferrari faithful celebrate a 1-2 triumph in the 1998 Italian GP, something that had not happened for ten years. Schumacher thus joined Hakkinen at the top of the championship table, something that until then had seemed impossible.

133 top Eighth place for "Fisico" Fisichella and the retirement of Würz on the 24th lap with a broken gearbox was all the Benetton B198s could manage at the 1998 Italian GP. This was nonetheless better than the previous GP in Belgium, where both drivers failed to finish.

133 center right The Argentine GP was Michael Schumacher and Ferrari's first win of the 1998 season. The rain and Hakkinen's errors after two consecutive victories took the German to the highest step of the podium.

133 bottom left The Finnish driver Mika Hakkinen started from pole position in the 1998 Brazilian GP with his extremely rapid McLaren-Mercedes: this was the first of a total of nine poles during the season.

133 bottom right Hakkinen, Coulthard and Schumacher made up the podium at the Brazilian GP, a lineup repeated in Spain and Austria. At the Luxembourg GP the order of first and second place was inverted.

HONOR ROLL

Year	Champion Driver	Nationality	Car	Champion Constructor
1950	Giuseppe Farina	Italian	Alfa Romeo 158/159	-
1951	Juan Manuel Fangio	Argentine	Alfa Romeo 159	-
1952	Alberto Ascari	Italian	Ferrari 500	-
1953	Alberto Ascari	Italian	Ferrari 500	-
1954	Juan Manuel Fangio	Argentine	Merc.-Benz W196/Maserati 250F	
1955	Juan Manuel Fangio	Argentine	Mercedes-Benz W196	-
1956	Juan Manuel Fangio	Argentine	Lancia-Ferrari D50	-
1957	Juan Manuel Fangio	Argentine	Maserati 250F	-
1958	Mike Hawthorn	British	Ferrari Dino 246	Vanwall
1959	Jack Brabham	Australian	Cooper T51-Climax	Cooper-Climax
1960	Jack Brabham	Australian	Cooper T53-Climax	Cooper-Climax
1961	Phil Hill	USA	Ferrari Dino 156	Ferrari
1962	Graham Hill	British	BRM P57	BRM
1963	Jim Clark	British	Lotus 25-Climax	Lotus-Climax
1964	John Surtees	British	Ferrari 158	Ferrari
1965	Jim Clark	British	Lotus 33-Climax	Lotus-Climax
1966	Jack Brabham	Australian	Brabham-Repco Bt19/Bt20	Brabham-Repco
1967	Denny Hulme	New Zealand	Brabham-Repco Bt20/Bt24	Brabham-Repco
1968	Graham Hill	British	Lotus-Ford 49/49B	Lotus-Ford
1969	Jackie Stewart	British	Matra-Ford MS10/MS80	Matra-Ford
1970	Jochen Rindt	Austrian	Lotus-Ford 49C/72	Lotus-Ford
1971	Jackie Stewart	British	Tyrrell-Ford 001/003	Tyrrell-Ford
1972	Emerson Fittipaldi	Brazilian	Lotus 72-Ford	Lotus-Ford
1973	Jackie Stewart	British	Tyrrell-Ford 005/006	Lotus-Ford
1974	Emerson Fittipaldi	Brazilian	McLaren M23-Ford	McLaren-Ford
1975	Niki Lauda	Austrian	Ferrari 312T	Ferrari
1976	James Hunt	British	McLaren M23-Ford	Ferrari
1977	Niki Lauda	Austrian	Ferrari 312T2	Ferrari
1978	Mario Andretti	USA	Lotus-Ford 78/79	Lotus-Ford
1979	Jody Scheckter	South African	Ferrari 312T3/T4	Ferrari
1980	Alan Jones	Australian	Williams FW07B-Ford	Williams-Ford
1981	Nelson Piquet	Brazilian	Brabham BT49C-Ford	Williams-Ford
1982	Keke Rosberg	Finnish	Williams-Ford FW07C/FW08	Ferrari
1983	Nelson Piquet	Brazilian	Brabham-BMW BT52/52B	Ferrari
1984	Niki Lauda	Austrian	McLaren MP4/2-TAG Porsche	McLaren-TAG
1985	Alain Prost	French	McLaren MP4/2B-TAG Porsche	McLaren-TAG
1986	Alain Prost	French	McLaren MP4/2C-TAG Porsche	Williams-Honda
1987	Nelson Piquet	Brazilian	Williams Fw11B-Honda	Williams-Honda
1988	Ayrton Senna	Brazilian	McLaren MP4/4-Honda	McLaren-Honda
1989	Alain Prost	French	McLaren MP4/5-Honda	McLaren-Honda
1990	Ayrton Senna	Brazilian	McLaren MP4/5B-Honda	McLaren-Honda
1991	Ayrton Senna	Brazilian	McLaren MP4/6-Honda	McLaren-Honda
1992	Nigel Mansell	British	Williams FW14B-Renault	Williams-Renault
1993	Alain Prost	French	Williams FW15C-Renault	Williams-Renault
1994	Michael Schumacher	German	Benetton B194-Ford	Williams-Renault
1995	Michael Schumacher	German	Benetton B195-Renault	Benetton-Renault
1996	Damon Hill	British	Williams FW18-Renault	Williams-Renault
1997	Jacques Villeneuve	Canadian	Williams FW19-Renault	Williams-Renault
1998	Mika Hakkinen	Finnish	McLaren MP4/13-Mercedes	McLaren-Mercedes

134 Jacques Villeneuve prepares to restart after a pit stop at Interlagos (San Paulo). The 1997 World Champion started from the fifth row of the grid in 1998's Brazilian GP and eventually finished in seventh place.

135 top 1998 was a truly fantastic season for Mika Hakkinen; the Finnish driver at the wheel of the silvery McLaren-Mercedes conquered the World Championship title by winning no fewer than eight Grands Prix and accumulating 100 points.

135 bottom Ferrari and Williams were, apart from the McLaren-Mercedes of course, the protagonists of the 1998 season. The red cars had the unenviable task of chasing the silver McLarens. This photograph from the Brazilian GP shows Michael Schumacher trailing a Williams. The German driver finished the race third behind the McLaren-Mercedes of Hakkinen and Coulthard.

Drivers to Have Won the Most Championship Titles

DRIVER	TITLES	YEARS
Juan Manuel Fangio	5	1951, 54-5-6-7
Alain Prost	4	1985-6, 89, 93
Jack Brabham	3	1959-60, 66
Niki Lauda	3	1975, 77, 84
Nelson Piquet	3	1981, 83, 87
Ayrton Senna	3	1988, 90-1
Jackie Stewart	3	1969, 71, 73
Alberto Ascari	2	1952-3
Jim Clark	2	1963, 65
Emerson Fittipaldi	2	1972, 74
Graham Hill	2	1962, 68
Michael Schumacher	2	1994-5

Drivers to Have Won the Most Grands Prix

DRIVER	VICTORIES
Alain Prost	51
Ayrton Senna	41
Michael Schumacher	33
Nigel Mansell	31
Jackie Stewart	27
Jim Clark	25
Niki Lauda	25
Juan Manuel Fangio	24
Nelson Piquet	23
Damon Hill	22
Graham Hill	14

Manufacturers to Have Won the Most Titles

TEAM	TITLES	YEARS
Williams	9	1980-1, 86-7, 92-3-4, 96-7
Ferrari	8	1961, 64, 75-6-7, 79, 82-3
McLaren	8	1974, 1984-85, 1988-9-90-91, 1998
Lotus	7	1963, 65, 68, 70, 72-3, 78
Brabham	2	1966-7
Cooper	2	1959-60

Teams to Have Won the Most Grands Prix

TEAM	VICTORIES
Ferrari	119
McLaren	115
Williams	104
Lotus	79
Brabham	35
Benetton	26
Tyrrell	23
BRM	17
Renault	15
Cooper	14
Alfa Romeo	10

Engine Suppliers to Have Won the Most Championship Titles

MAKER	TITLES	YEARS
Ford	10	1968-9-70, 1971-2-3-4, 1978, 1980-1
Ferrari	8	1961, 64, 1975-6-7, 1979, 1982-3
Honda	6	1986-7-8-9, 1990-1
Renault	6	1992-3-4-5-6-7
Climax	4	1959-60, 63, 65

136 and 137 top Pit stops are the most delicate moments of a Grand Prix, together with the start: in just a few seconds a well-prepared crew of mechanics is capable of changing all four tires and loading hundreds of liters of fuel. The race is thus fought out in the pits, too, and the FIA should perhaps award, as once was the case for the fastest lap, an extra point for the fastest pit stop—the point valid for the Constructors' Championship! These photographs show pit stops during the 1998 season: Ferrari at the San Marino GP (large photographs), Williams at the Brazilian GP (top left) and Benetton in Australia (top right).

137 bottom An almost antiseptic atmosphere reigns in the comfortably appointed Benetton pits in Germany. The pits are more akin to exclusive clinics than workshops. The mechanics even have armchairs from which to follow the progress of the race on television screens.

THE GREAT EVENTS

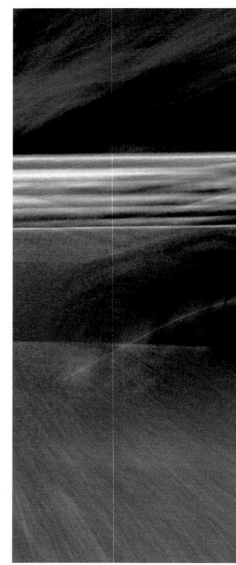

Chicanes, checkered flags, warm-up laps, pits, pit lanes, pit stops, pole position, grids, paddock, telemetry, laps: the terminology of Formula 1, but more precisely the terminology of its pulsing heart, the circuits, the autodromes, the places in which the races are physically staged. Those kilometers of asphalt laid out in the most diverse shapes that are pampered, patched, cleaned and lined with protective barriers before every race so as to allow cars of now undeclared—but undoubtedly stratospheric—power outputs to give their all and to be prepared for even the most tragic of events.

Grand Prix: two words that express the essence of motor racing, that is to say running faster than the other competitors for 50, 60, 80 or 100 laps, striving to cross the finishing line first to conquer that all-important trophy.

The French, German, British, Italian and Monaco Grands Prix are Formula 1's hard core, and not only because they are the veterans of the world's greatest series or because they have the fortune of being staged at the great temples of speed. The heart of Europe in fact stages the events that attract the greatest number of spectators and keep millions of viewers glued to their television screens throughout the world.

In the pages that follow we shall recount the spirit of these Grands Prix, the circuits at which they are staged and their peculiarities. We shall describe the tracks and the great protagonists and present a list of the winners of each. The last chapter is instead devoted to the Formula 1 season's other most important appointments, those races special in terms of their position within the racing calendar, the Japanese GP for example, or for their particular characteristics (United States) or because they have been marked by particular episodes or events (San Marino, Belgium). Our attempts to document these events appropriately have inevitably obliged us to omit others. For this, and for the inevitable errors and inaccuracies that may derive from the sheer quantity of facts and figures presented, we ask our readers' forgiveness.

138-139 Jean Alesi's Ferrari 412 T1 seems to be flying, even though the Italian manufacturer has been starved of World Championship titles for many years.

139 top The 1986 Brazilian GP: two Brazilians on the podium at their home Grand Prix, Nelson Piquet the winner on the right and Ayrton Senna in second place on the left.

139 bottom Michael Schumacher was too hot to handle with the Benetton in 1994. That year the German conquered his first World Championship title and the team finished as runner-up in the Constructors' Championship.

Grand Prix

THE FRENCH GRAND PRIX

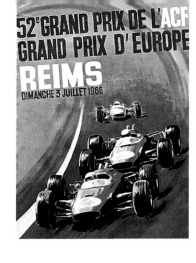

When the Formula 1 World Championship took its first steps to legitimacy in 1950, among the six races in the calendar was the Grand Prix de l'ACF (Automobile Club de France), the veteran of the Grand Prix circus given that the first edition dated back to 1906.

Renamed the French Grand Prix in 1967, the race has been a part of every World Championship season with the exception of 1955 and has been staged at an impressive number of different circuits.

The inaugural edition in 1950 was held at Reims, on a spectacular and fast circuit used for motor racing until 1970 when it was closed due to a combination of economic and political motives. Up until the 1960s the Grand Prix alternated between Reims and Rouen-les-Essarts, a very fast and dangerous circuit in operation since 1950. Clermont-Ferrand, located 170 km from Lyons, has hosted four editions, while Le Mans-Bugatti staged a single GP in 1967, on the new Bugatti track rather than the historic endurance race circuit. The venue failed to find favor with the public.

The Paul Ricard circuit, replaced for four editions of the Grand Prix by Dijon-Prenois, brought the French GP up to the 1990s: this autodrome, located at Le Castellet in the South of the country, was the scene of the tragic accident involving Elio de Angelis who died while testing in 1986.

The home of French Formula 1 racing up to 1990, the Paul Ricard circuit was to become another victim of political influence. The then–President of the Republic, Mitterrand, a Ligier supporter, wanted to transfer the French GP to Magny-Cours in the Nevers region, a circuit well known as being the Martini Racing test base.

The French Grand Prix has been characterized by numerous debuts over the years: in 1954, for example, it was the setting for the return of Mercedes and its Silver Arrows, and in 1956 for that of Bugatti. (The glorious French model's comeback lasted just 18 laps, however: a broken accelerator linkage forced Trintignant out of the race, a retirement the team experienced as a disgrace to the extent that it never again participated in

Formula 1). The 1961 edition of the race saw the Italian driver Giancarlo Baghetti make his F1 debut at the wheel of a Ferrari, while at Rouen-les-Essarts in 1964 the Brabham team scored its first Grand Prix victory. In 1985 the Paul Ricard circuit hosted Pirelli's return to the Formula 1 circus, the Italians running for the first time since 1957.

The driver who has won the French GP most frequently is a national hero: Alain Prost triumphed six times, three of these wins consecutive between 1988 and 1990. Michael Schumacher has instead won the race on five consecutive occasions between 1994 and 1998.

140 top This poster publicized the Grand Prix held at Reims in 1966. Reims was a fast and spectacular triangular circuit located in the west of the city and was used between 1925 and 1970, the year in which it was closed due to economic and political motives.

140 center Feverish preparations in the Alfa pits for the 159 that, driven magnificently by Juan Manuel Fangio and Luigi Fagioli, won the ACF GP in 1951 at Reims, relegating the Ferraris to second, third and fourth places. The fifth car home was another Alfa, driven by Farina.

140 bottom This poster also publicized a race held at Reims. The length of the circuit was reduced from the original 7.8 km in 1952 to 7.2 on the occasion of the modification of the southern link; the following year, it was increased to 8.3 km with the introduction of the Virage de Muizon and modifications to the northern section. Reims has staged 15 GPs, the first of which was held in 1932.

140-141 The silvery shape of a Porsche flashes past the checkered flag after having completed 54 laps of the Rouen circuit with Dan Gurney at the wheel. This was the American's only Grand Prix victory in 1962. He finished fifth overall in the World Championship.

141 bottom left The 1963 edition was held at Reims and on the front row of the grid were Jim Clark (in the foreground) with the Lotus, Graham Hill in the center with the BRM and, with a slight advantage, Dan Gurney in the Brabham. Clark won and also recorded the fastest lap. Hill was third and Gurney fifth.

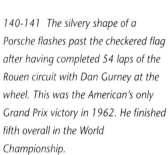

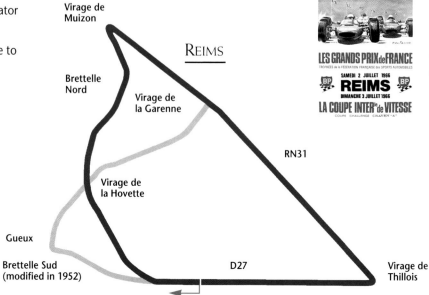

Virage de
Muizon

REIMS

Brettelle
Nord

Virage de
la Garenne

RN31

Virage de
la Hovette

Gueux

Brettelle Sud
(modified in 1952)

D27

Virage de
Thillois

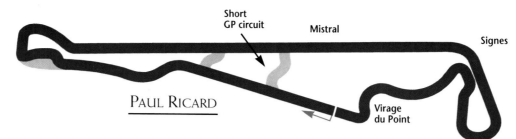

PAUL RICARD

Short
GP circuit

Mistral

Signes

Virage
du Point

*141 top right A great driver gains his
first GP win while another will never win
again: this too, unfortunately, is part of
the history of Formula 1. Jacky Ickx won
his first GP in France in 1968, but Jo
Schlesser was killed on the third lap
when his Honda rolled and caught fire.*

*141 bottom right The 1968 French GP
starts in torrential rain with Jochen
Rindt in the Brabham-Repco, Jackie
Stewart in the Matra-Ford and Jacky
Ickx in the Ferrari on the front row. The
fourth protagonist of this race was,
however, the charging Mexican Pedro
Rodriguez who recorded the fastest lap.*

MONTLHÉRY

La Forêt
Corner

Gendarme
Corner

Epingle
du Faye

Ascari
Curve

Virage
de la
Ferme

Banking

Les Bruyeres
Hairpin

Les Biscornes

MAGNY-COURS

Estoril

180°

Grande
Courbe

Golf

Nürburgring

Chicane

Imola

Lycée

Adelaide

Château
d'Eau

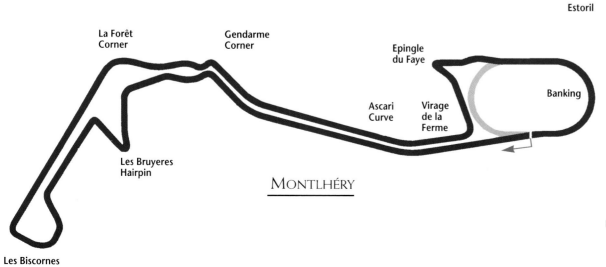

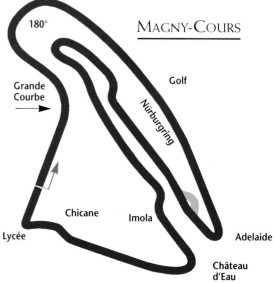

HONOR ROLL

Winners of the French GP

YEAR	CIRCUIT	DRIVER	NATIONALITY	CAR
1950	Reims	Juan Manuel Fangio	Argentine	Alfa Romeo 158
1951	Reims	Luigi Fagioli -	Italian	
		Juan Manuel Fangio	Argentine	Alfa Romeo 159
1952	Rouen-les-Essarts	Alberto Ascari	Italian	Ferrari 500
1953	Reims	Mike Hawthorn	British	Ferrari 500
1954	Reims	Juan Manuel Fangio	Argentine	Lancia-Ferrari D50
1956	Reims	Peter Collins	British	Maserati 250F
1957	Rouen-les-Essarts	Juan Manuel Fangio	Argentine	Lancia-Ferrari D50
1958	Reims	Mike Hawthorn	British	Ferrari Dino 246
1959	Reims	Tony Brooks	British	Ferrari Dino 246
1960	Reims	Jack Brabham	Australian	Cooper T53-Climax
1961	Reims	Giancarlo Baghetti	Italian	Ferrari Dino 156
1962	Rouen-les-Essarts	Dan Gurney	USA	Porsche 804
1963	Reims	Jim Clark	British	Lotus 25-Climax
1964	Rouen-les-Essarts	Dan Gurney	USA	Brabham BT7-Climax
1965	Clermont-Ferrand	Jim Clark	British	Lotus 25-Climax
1966	Reims	Jack Brabham	Australian	Brabham BT19-Repco
1967	Le Mans-Bugatti	Jack Brabham	Australian	Brabham BT24-Repco
1968	Rouen-les-Essarts	Jacky Ickx	Belgian	Ferrari 312
1969	Clermont-Ferrand	Jackie Stewart	British	Matra MS80-Ford
1970	Clermont-Ferrand	Jochen Rindt	Austrian	Lotus 72-Ford
1971	Paul Ricard	Jackie Stewart	British	Tyrrell 003-Ford
1972	Clermont-Ferrand	Jackie Stewart	British	Tyrrell 003-Ford
1973	Paul Ricard	Ronnie Peterson	Swedish	Lotus 72D-Ford
1974	Dijon-Prenois	Ronnie Peterson	Swedish	Lotus 72E-Ford
1975	Paul Ricard	Niki Lauda	Austrian	Ferrari 312T
1976	Paul Ricard	James Hunt	British	McLaren M23-Ford
1977	Dijon-Prenois	Mario Andretti	USA	Lotus 78-Ford
1978	Paul Ricard	Mario Andretti	USA	Lotus 79-Ford
1979	Dijon-Prenois	Jean-Pierre Jabouille	French	Renault Re10
1980	Paul Ricard	Alan Jones	Australian	Williams FW07B-Ford
1981	Dijon-Prenois	Alain Prost	French	Renault Re30
1982	Paul Ricard	René Arnoux	French	Renault Re30B
1983	Paul Ricard	Alain Prost	French	Renault Re40
1984	Dijon-Prenois	Niki Lauda	Austrian	McLaren MP4/2-TAG Porsche
1985	Paul Ricard	Nelson Piquet	Brazilian	Brabham BT54-BMW
1986	Paul Ricard	Nigel Mansell	British	Williams FW11-Honda
1987	Paul Ricard	Nigel Mansell	British	Williams FW11B-Honda
1988	Paul Ricard	Alain Prost	French	McLaren MP4/4-Honda
1989	Paul Ricard	Alain Prost	French	McLaren MP4/5-Honda
1990	Paul Ricard	Alain Prost	French	Ferrari 641/2
1991	Magny-Cours	Nigel Mansell	British	Williams FW14- Renault
1992	Magny-Cours	Nigel Mansell	British	Williams FW14B- Renault
1993	Magny-Cours	Alain Prost	French	Williams FW15C-Renault
1994	Magny-Cours	Michael Schumacher	German	Benetton B194-Ford
1995	Magny-Cours	Michael Schumacher	German	Benetton B195-Renault
1996	Magny-Cours	Michael Schumacher	German	Ferrari F310
1997	Magny-Cours	Michael Schumacher	German	Ferrari F310B
1998	Magny-Cours	Michael Schumacher	German	Ferrari F300

142 top At Dijon-Prenois, the red Ferraris could manage no better than fifth in 1981: Didier Pironi finished behind the two Renaults, a McLaren and a Brabham, while the second Ferrari, driven by Villeneuve, retired on the 41st lap with fuel delivery problems.

142-143, 143 top right and 143 bottom left The start of the 1989 French GP at the Paul Ricard Circuit was breathtaking: the tragic memory of three years earlier, when the Italian Elio de Angelis died during practice, was still vivid and led to a two-km reduction in the length of the track. At the first corner Mauricio Gugelmin in the Leyton House-Judd took off in the middle of the pack, the incident resulting in a restart. Ayrton Senna, one of the favorites, had a poor day: he ran strongly from the restart but was betrayed by his differential, allowing his teammate (and bitter rival) Alain Prost, in the other McLaren-Honda, to take the lead, which he retained until the finish. The French GP was the Professor's last win of the season as he was forced to bow to the superiority of teammate Ayrton. He nonetheless won the championship thanks to his numerous points-scoring finishes.

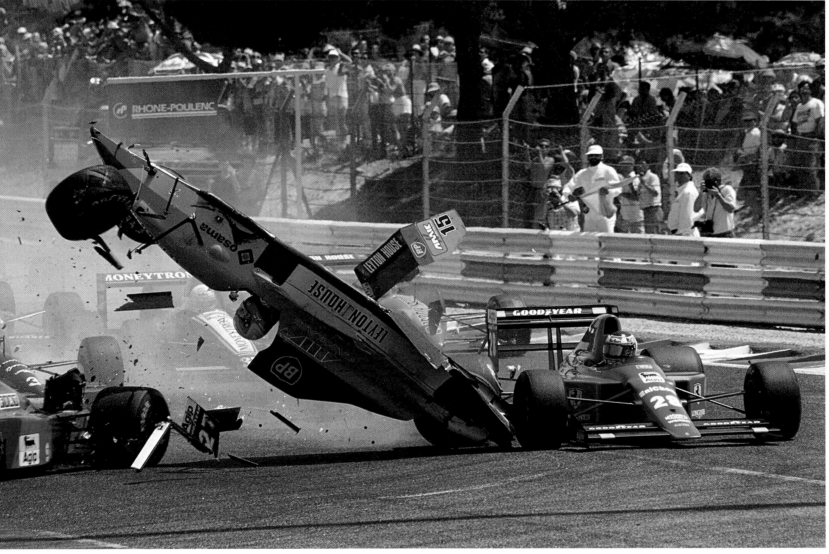

143 bottom right The Frenchman Jean Alesi never managed to win his home Grand Prix during his five-year spell at Ferrari: between 1991 and 1995 his best finish was fifth (in 1995) at Magny-Cours after having started from the second row of the grid.

142 bottom Three red overalls brighten up the podium of the 1988 French GP: from the left, Ayrton Senna (second), the winner Alain Prost (his second victory of the season) and Michele Alboreto, who brought smiles back to Ferrari after a poor start to the season.

143 top left Nigel Mansell scored his fourth win of the season at the Paul Ricard Circuit, which hosted the 1987 French GP. He won from Nelson Piquet, who had started from pole position and set the fastest lap.

THE GERMAN GRAND PRIX

Avus, Hockenheim, Nürburgring: three historic German venues close the hearts of motor racing enthusiasts, as they have hosted Formula 1 races from the outset. The Nürburgring is of course one of the great temples of speed—one of the longest and most attractive circuits in the world, at least in its original 22-km (13.7 mi.) form, snaking through the Eifel mountains and past the castle of the village of Nürburg, located some 70 km (43 mi.) south of Bonn.

Drivers who have won on this long and challenging circuit have emerged with enhanced reputations as true racers. In the history of the German GP many have struggled to complete the race: in 1963 only 10 of the 23 cars to start managed to cross the finishing line. Rebuilt in 1970, the Nürburgring was declared unsafe for Formula 1 following the near-fatal accident involving Niki Lauda in 1976. The German government decided to build a new track—one laid out with the aid of a computer and thus with little of the romance and appeal of the old circuit that had attracted drivers and spectators alike.

Hockenheim hosted the Formula 1 circus in 1970 and has done so uninterruptedly from 1977 with the exception of 1985. Located near the renowned university city of Heidelberg, this circuit is unfortunately famous for being the scene of the death of Jim Clark, the celebrated Scottish driver and Formula 1 aristocrat who was killed while competing in a Formula 2 event in April, 1968. The

144 top right Fourth win of the 1954 season for Juan Manuel Fangio at the wheel of the open-wheeled Mercedes W196 Silver Arrow, which in this configuration was better suited to the Nürburgring. He won the German GP from the Ferraris of Gonzales-Hawthorn and Trintignant.

144 top left The fifth of the seven rounds of the second Formula 1 World Championship held in 1951. As ever, Fangio was at home on the German circuit with the Alfa Romeo 159, but despite starting from the first row of the grid he could only finish second to Ascari in the Ferrari.

144-145 and 145 top left For Jim Clark, victory at the Nürburgring in the German GP was his fifth win in succession in the 1965 season and the sixth out of the first seven Championship rounds. The Scotsman in the Lotus-Climax conquered the highest step on the podium (here he is seen with the laurel wreath and trophy prior to the celebrations) after also having claimed pole position and set the fastest lap. Behind were Graham Hill in the BRM, who finished second, and Dan Gurney in the Brabham-Climax, third.

144 bottom left Graham Hill with a satisfied smile as he is crowned as victor of the 1962 German GP, his second victory in a season that was to see him win the World Championship. The 1962 win was the Englishman's only victory on German soil.

145 top right Seventeen drivers started the 1967 German GP, including the rookie Jacky Ickx, who was spotted by Enzo Ferrari and signed the following season. The favorite Jim Clark was obliged to retire with suspension problems, thus opening the way for Hulme's victory in the Brabham.

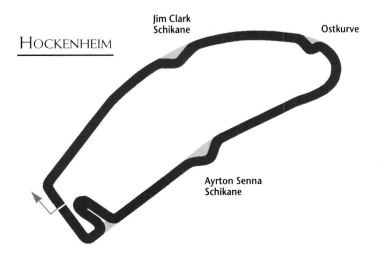

HOCKENHEIM

Jim Clark Schikane

Ostkurve

Ayrton Senna Schikane

French hero Patrick Depailler was also killed here during practice for the 1980 GP, while Didier Pironi's serious accident in 1982 resulted in his retirement from the sport.

Honda and the Belgian driver Jacky Ickx have particularly close ties with the German GP as both the team and the driver made their F1 debuts in the event, in 1964 and 1967, respectively. On a bleaker note, the race also resulted in the Formula 1 World Championship's first racing fatality: Onofre Marimon was killed during practice for the 1954 event.

British drivers dominate the roll of honor with 15 wins in the first 50 years of Formula 1 history, John Surtees, Tony Brooks and Nigel Mansell all scoring two victories each. While no single driver has managed four wins, four undisputed aces have scored three: Fangio, Stewart and Senna.

145 bottom left Dreadful weather conditions meant that the 1968 German GP risked being canceled. The extremely long (over 22 km) and difficult Nürburgring crowned Jackie Stewart as its undisputed king that season: the Scotsman proved unbeatable at the wheel of his Ford-powered Matra.

145 bottom right Going so fast that all four wheels left the ground was not enough for Graham Hill at the 1968 German Grand Prix: the Englishman in fact finished second, four minutes behind winner Stewart in the Matra-Ford. Hill lost the battle but not the war, as the Championship title was his that year.

NÜRBURGRING

width:1652 height:2286

146 top left The 1996 German GP was staged at Hockenheim, while the historic Nürburgring—now reduced to a fifth of its original length—hosted the Grand Prix of Europe. Hill and Coulthard were the protagonists of the two races, Damon winning at Hockenheim and finishing second at the 'Ring, David vice versa.

146 top right Teo Fabi started the 1985 German GP from pole position but his Toleman-Hart let him down after 29 laps when he was forced to retire with a blown engine. Victory went to Alboreto with the Ferrari, his second win of the season. He finished the season in second place in the championship table behind Prost with the McLaren-TAG-Porsche.

146-147 Ferrari suffered numerous retirements during 1987, as on this occasion at the German GP when both Alboreto and Berger abandoned the race with broken turbos, the Italian on the 10th lap and the Austrian on the 19th.

146 bottom The Hockenheim circuit is sadly famous for the death of Jim Clark in April of 1968 while he was competing in a Formula 2 event. Following the first edition in 1970, since 1977 the auto-drome near Heidelberg has regularly hosted the GP circus, the only exception being the 1985 season. This photograph shows the last-minute preparations on the starting grid in 1990.

HONOR ROLL

Winners of the German GP

YEAR	CIRCUIT	DRIVER	NATIONALITY	CAR
1951	Nürburgring	Alberto Ascari	Italian	Ferrari 375
1952	Nürburgring	Alberto Ascari	Italian	Ferrari 500
1953	Nürburgring	Giuseppe Farina	Italian	Ferrari 500
1954	Nürburgring	Juan Manuel Fangio	Argentine	Mercedes-Benz W196
1956	Nürburgring	Juan Manuel Fangio	Argentine	Mercedes-Benz W196
1957	Nürburgring	Juan Manuel Fangio	Argentine	Maserati 250F
1958	Nürburgring	Tony Brooks	British	Vanwall VW4
1959	Avus	Tony Brooks	British	Ferrari Dino 246
1960	Nürburgring	Jo Bonnier	Swedish	Porsche 718
1961	Nürburgring	Stirling Moss	British	Lotus 18/21-Climax
1962	Nürburgring	Graham Hill	British	BRM P57
1963	Nürburgring	John Surtees	British	Ferrari Dino 156
1964	Nürburgring	John Surtees	British	Ferrari 158
1965	Nürburgring	Jim Clark	British	Lotus 33-Climax
1966	Nürburgring	Jack Brabham	Australian	Brabham BT19-Repco
1967	Nürburgring	Denny Hulme	New Zealander	Brabham BT24-Repco
1968	Nürburgring	Jackie Stewart	British	Matra MS10-Ford
1969	Nürburgring	Jacky Ickx	Belgian	Brabham BT26-Ford
1970	Hockenheim	Jochen Rindt	Austrian	Lotus 72-Ford
1971	Nürburgring	Jackie Stewart	British	Tyrrell 003-Ford
1972	Nürburgring	Jacky Ickx	Belgian	Ferrari 312B2
1973	Nürburgring	Jackie Stewart	British	Tyrrell 006-Ford
1974	Nürburgring	Clay Regazzoni	Swiss	Ferrari 312B3
1975	Nürburgring	Carlos Reutemann	Argentine	Brabham BT44-Ford
1976	Nürburgring	James Hunt	British	McLaren M23-Ford
1977	Hockenheim	Niki Lauda	Austrian	Ferrari 312T2
1978	Hockenheim	Mario Andretti	USA	Lotus 79-Ford
1979	Hockenheim	Alan Jones	Australian	Williams FW07-Ford
1980	Hockenheim	Jacques Lafitte	French	Ligier JS11/15-Ford
1981	Hockenheim	Nelson Piquet	Brazilian	Brabham BT49C-Ford
1982	Hockenheim	Patrick Tambay	French	Ferrari C126C2
1983	Hockenheim	René Arnoux	French	Ferrari C126C3
1984	Hockenheim	Alain Prost	French	McLaren MP4/2-TAG Porsche
1985	Nürburgring	Michele Alboreto	Italian	Ferrari 156/85
1986	Hockenheim	Nelson Piquet	Brazilian	Williams FW11-Honda
1987	Hockenheim	Nelson Piquet	Brazilian	Williams FW11B-Honda
1988	Hockenheim	Ayrton Senna	Brazilian	McLaren MP4/4-Honda
1989	Hockenheim	Ayrton Senna	Brazilian	McLaren MP4/5-Honda
1990	Hockenheim	Ayrton Senna	Brazilian	McLaren MP4/5B-Honda
1991	Hockenheim	Nigel Mansell	British	Williams FW14-Renault
1992	Hockenheim	Nigel Mansell	British	Williams FW14B-Renault
1993	Hockenheim	Alain Prost	French	Williams FW15C-Renault
1994	Hockenheim	Gerhard Berger	Austrian	Ferrari 412T1B
1995	Hockenheim	Michael Schumacher	German	Benetton B195-Renault
1996	Hockenheim	Damon Hill	British	Williams FW18-Renault
1997	Hockenheim	Gerhard Berger	Austrian	Benetton B197-Renault
1998	Hockenheim	Mika Hakkinen	Finnish	McLaren MP4/13-Mercedes

147 top The podium moved to a samba rhythm at the 1985 German GP, at least as far as the first two places were concerned: the Brazilians Nelson Piquet in the Williams (photograph) and Ayrton Senna in the Lotus finished first and second, respectively, while the bronze medal went to Nigel Mansell in the second Williams.

147 center A German winning in Germany and catapulted head-long toward his first Championship title: in 1995 Michael Schumacher dedicated victory to his home crowd after bringing his Benetton-Renault across the line first, thanks in part to making only two pit stops to the hard-charging, second-placed Coulthard's three.

147 bottom Senna wins and thanks the huge crowd that gathered to watch the 1988 German GP. Prost, who finished second, attempts to distance himself so as not to give his teammate and great rival the satisfaction of celebrating victory. The exhausted Berger returned to the podium after a series of indifferent races.

THE BRITISH GRAND PRIX

Welcome to tradition, passion, or as the signs at the entrances to Silverstone have it, the home of motor racing. The British have motor racing in their blood and it was no coincidence that the Formula 1 World Championship got under way in England, attracting a huge crowd that has remained faithful over the years. As ever, ranks of enthusiasts still fill every available space, the most dedicated arriving the Thursday afternoon before the race and leaving on Sunday evening, having spent three nights sleeping in their cars.

All of the country's leading drivers have made their mark on this World Championship race: Clark, Moss, Collins, Stewart, Hunt, Herbert, Watson,

Scheckter provoked a serious pile-up at Woodcote that involved seven cars.

Brands Hatch, 30 km from London, was inaugurated in the same year as the World Championship, and between 1964 and 1986 it alternated with Silverstone as the venue for the British GP. The original Indy-style circuit was just 1.6 km long and was one of the most difficult in the world, with the Paddock Hill Bend—the first corner after the start—being particularly dangerous and heavily criticized on a number of occasions in relation to safety.

The Aintree circuit was instead located eight km to the north of Liverpool and was characterized by

Mansell and Hill, father and son, are the most prestigious names that the British Isles have offered to Formula 1. Jim Clark dominated the event in the 1960s, winning five editions (four of which came consecutively, 1962-65). The feat was repeated by Alain Prost in the 1980s and 1990s.

The Silverstone circuit was built on a former military airfield that was very active during the Second World War. Located 50 km to the northeast of Oxford, the track has been heavily modified over the years so as to slow the cars and increase safety. This last theme was very topical in 1973 after Jody

a layout with very slow corners. It played host to the British GP on five occasions, alternating with Silverstone between 1955 and 1962.

The British GP has, of course, been the backdrop to drama, debuts and tragedy: in 1954 no fewer than seven drivers recorded the fastest lap, a feat unique in the history of Formula 1 and motor racing in general and undoubtedly favored by the use of timing instruments that were less precise than those of today. Three years later a British team, Vanwall, won its national Grand Prix for the first time. Nineteen seventy-three was instead the year in which the Italian driver Andrea de Adamich was obliged to abandon the sport: he was involved in an accident and the delayed arrival of the rescue team meant that he was trapped in his car with fractured legs and was never to race again. Nineteen seventy-seven was a year of debuts: Gilles Villeneuve, the Michelin GP tire, and Renault's turbocharged engine were all introduced to the Formula 1 circus.

SILVERSTONE

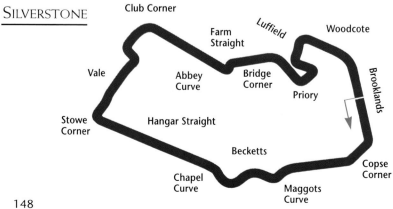

Club Corner

Farm Straight

Luffield

Woodcote

Vale

Abbey Curve

Bridge Corner

Priory

Brooklands

Stowe Corner

Hangar Straight

Becketts

Copse Corner

Chapel Curve

Maggots Curve

148 center right Moss wins the 1955 British GP thanks to his teammate Fangio who, with the title in his pocket, let the Englishman past to take the checkered flag in front of his home crowd. The other two Mercedes (of Kling and Taruffi) finished third and fourth.

148 bottom and 148-149 A Lotus 24 in front of a Porsche 804, Brabham versus Gurney: despite the latter starting from higher on the grid, the Australian driving for Colin Chapman's team had the better of the duel with the German car in the 1962 British GP,

finishing fifth—no less than four places higher. Lotus had a highly satisfactory day with Jim Clark (photo, right) starting from pole position and winning the race by almost a minute from Surtees in the Lola-Climax.

149 top right The Swedish colors faded at the 1966 British GP that returned to Brands Hatch after the previous edition held at Silverstone. Jo Siffert, at the wheel of a Brabham-Climax, retired just 13 laps from the end of the race due to gearbox problems.

149 center right In spite of the height of its wing, Denny Hulme's McLaren could manage no better than fourth in the 1968 British GP,

a decent result nonetheless for the New Zealander who had started from 11th place on the grid.

BRANDS HATCH

Derek Minter

Westfield Bend

Hawthorn Bend

Dingle Dell

Hawthorn Hill

Druids

Pilgrims Drop

Dingle Dell Corner

Stirlings Bend

Hailwood Hill

Graham Hill

Cooper Straight

Clearways

Graham Hill Bend

McLaren

Paddock Hill Bend

Surtees

Brabham Straight

Clark Curve

149 bottom left Starting from the second row with the fifth fastest time, Jochen Rindt was aiming to finish in the points at Brands Hatch after being obliged to retire from the preceding races with his Brabham-Repco due to mechanical problems. The 1968 British GP was, however, another unlucky race for the Austrian, who retired on the 56th lap with fuel feed problems.

149 bottom right A Frenchman at Brands Hatch: Jean-Pierre Beltoise at the wheel of a Team Matra car (Matras were also run by Ken Tyrrell) during the 1968 British Grand Prix. Beltoise's race was over by the 12th lap.

HONOR ROLL

Winners of the British GP

Year	Circuit	Driver	Nationality	Car
1950	Silverstone	Giuseppe Farina	Italy	Alfa Romeo 158
1951	Silverstone	José Froilan Gonzalez	Argentina	Ferrari 375
1952	Silverstone	Alberto Ascari	Italian	Ferrari 500
1953	Silverstone	Alberto Ascari	Italian	Ferrari 500
1954	Silverstone	José Froilan Gonzalez	Argentine	Ferrari 625
1955	Aintree	Stirling Moss	British	Mercedes-Benz W196
1956	Silverstone	Juan Manuel Fangio	Argentine	Lancia-Ferrari D50
1957	Aintree	Tony Brooks - Stirling Moss	British	Vanwall VW4
1958	Silverstone	Peter Collins	British	Ferrari Dino 246
1959	Aintree	Jack Brabham	Australian	Cooper T51-Climax
1960	Silverstone	Jack Brabham	Australian	Cooper T53-Climax
1961	Aintree	Wolfgang von Trips	German	Ferrari Dino 156
1962	Aintree	Jim Clark	British	Lotus 25-Climax
1963	Silverstone	Jim Clark	British	Lotus 25-Climax
1964	Brands Hatch	Jim Clark	British	Lotus 25-Climax
1965	Silverstone	Jim Clark	British	Lotus 33-Climax
1966	Brands Hatch	Jack Brabham	Australian	Brabham BT19-Repco
1967	Silverstone	Jim Clark	British	Lotus 49-Ford
1968	Brands Hatch	Jo Siffert	Swiss	Lotus 49B-Ford

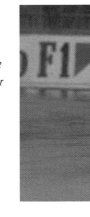

150 Alain Prost in the McLaren-TAG-Porsche (left) crossed the line first while Stefan Johansson in a Ferrari (right) was the first to retire after an accident immediately after the start. The French and Swedish drivers were thus protagonists in the 1985 British GP held at Silverstone.

1969	Silverstone	Jackie Stewart	British	Matra MS80-Ford
1970	Brands Hatch	Jochen Rindt	Austrian	Lotus 72-Ford
1971	Silverstone	Jackie Stewart	British	Tyrrell 003-Ford
1972	Brands Hatch	Emerson Fittipaldi	Brazilian	Lotus 72D-Ford
1973	Silverstone	Peter Revson	USA	McLaren M23-Ford
1974	Brands Hatch	Jody Scheckter	South African	Tyrrell 007-Ford
1975	Silverstone	Emerson Fittipaldi	Brazilian	McLaren M23-Ford
1976	Brands Hatch	Niki Lauda	Austrian	Ferrari 312T2
1977	Silverstone	James Hunt	British	McLaren M26-Ford
1978	Brands Hatch	Carlos Reutemann	Argentine	Ferrari 312T3
1979	Silverstone	Clay Regazzoni	Swiss	Williams FW07-Ford
1980	Brands Hatch	Alan Jones	Australian	Williams FW07B-Ford
1981	Silverstone	John Watson	British	McLaren MP4/1-Ford
1982	Brands Hatch	Niki Lauda	Austrian	McLaren MP4/1B-Ford
1983	Silverstone	Alain Prost	French	Renault Re40
1984	Brands Hatch	Niki Lauda	Austrian	McLaren MP4/2-TAG Porsche
1985	Silverstone	Alain Prost	French	McLaren MP4/2B-TAG Porsche
1986	Brands Hatch	Nigel Mansell	British	Williams FW11-Honda
1987	Silverstone	Nigel Mansell	British	Williams FW11B-Honda
1988	Silverstone	Ayrton Senna	Brazilian	McLaren MP4/4-Honda
1989	Silverstone	Alain Prost	French	McLaren MP4/5-Honda
1990	Silverstone	Alain Prost	French	Ferrari 641/2
1991	Silverstone	Nigel Mansell	British	Williams FW14-Renault
1992	Silverstone	Nigel Mansell	British	Williams FW14B-Renault
1993	Silverstone	Alain Prost	French	Williams FW15C-Renault
1994	Silverstone	Damon Hill	British	Williams FW16-Renault
1995	Silverstone	Johnny Herbert	British	Benetton B195-Renault
1996	Silverstone	Jacques Villeneuve	Canada	Williams FW18-Renault
1997	Silverstone	Jacques Villeneuve	Canada	Williams FW19-Renault
1998	Silverstone	Michael Schumacher	German	Ferrari F300

150-151 and 151 top right The 1986 British GP—the last Grand Prix of Jacques Lafitte's career. Just 200 meters after the start Boutsen's Arrows provoked an accident that involved a number of cars including Lafitte's Ligier. It was Jacquot, as he was known, who came off worst and was never again able to drive a Formula 1 car. Lafitte retired with a record of 176 Grands Prix disputed and seven victories.

151 top left A fast circuit and a race held in torrential rain: in these conditions there could be only one winner, Senna the Rain King. Senna lived up to his reputation in the 1988 British GP which he won in the McLaren-Honda 23 seconds ahead of Lionheart Mansell.

151 bottom left After a scorching start from the third row, Jean Alesi, on the left in the Ferrari, tucked in behind Damon Hill who had started from pole. Neither the Frenchman nor the Englishman were to win the 1995 British GP, which went to Johnny Herbert in the Benetton.

151 bottom right At the 1986 British GP Nigel Mansell, at the wheel of the Williams powered by a fantastic Renault engine, took pole position, recorded the fastest lap and won the race, thus scoring the second of three consecutive victories that season.

THE ITALIAN GRAND PRIX

152 top left Nino Farina at the wheel of the Lancia-Ferrari D50 during the 1955 Italian GP: the Turin-built cars had been ceded to the Maranello team complete with spare parts after having competed in two Formula 1 seasons (1954 and 1955), disputing four Grands Prix without a single victory.

The Italian round of the Formula 1 World Championship is intimately associated with the Monza Autodrome. The Lombard circuit, located just outside Milan, is one of the most famous and attractive in the world, a temple of speed ranking alongside Silverstone, Indianapolis, Le Mans, the Nürburgring, and Daytona. There are few other circuits where average speeds of 240 kph (149 mph) can be maintained with peaks of 360 kph (224 mph) at the end of the main straight. Therefore, Monza has always hosted the Italian GP except in 1980, when the event was held at Imola on the circuit named after Enzo and Dino Ferrari.

Monza has been modified on a number of occasions in order to control the speed of the cars.

There are numerous corners, one of them dedicated to Ascari who was killed here during private testing in 1954. Similarly there are numerous chicanes and a high speed oval with 38° banked curves, constructed in 1955 but soon abandoned due to the uneven surface that was so hard on suspensions that it made the cars undriveable. With these modifications the original track length of 10 km (6.2 mi.) was reduced over the years, being practically halved to the current length of 5.8 km (3.6 mi.). While Monza has been the setting for thrilling battles it has also seen more than its fair share of tragedy. Jochen Rindt was killed here in 1970, becoming Formula 1's first (and thankfully so far only) posthumous

champion, while in 1978 it was the turn of the popular Swede Ronnie Peterson.

As with the German GP, no single driver has dominated the Italian race, but a number have won twice while Juan Manuel Fangio, Stirling Moss, Ronnie Peterson, Nelson Piquet and Alain Prost have all won three times here. The situation is rather different though with regards to the cars, as the undisputed master of Italian Formula 1 is of course a team as famous and celebrated as the Monza circuit itself: up to 1998 Ferrari has won the Italian Grand Prix no fewer than 12 times, with Michael Schumacher (1996 and 1998), Clay Regazzoni ('70 and '75), Phil Hill ('60 and '61) and Alberto Ascari ('51 and '52) all winning twice.

152 center left Three seconds and 400 meters divided the winner Jackie Stewart in the BRM from Graham Hill in the British team's second car in the 1965 Italian GP. Formula 1's fastest moustache had victory in his grasp up to the parabolica but a poor line allowed Jackie to pass and go on to take the race.

152 bottom left Time for a brief exchange before the start between Jim Clark (foreground) in the Lotus and John Surtees in the Ferrari: the third driver hidden on the front row was Jackie Stewart, who won the 1965 Italian GP in the BRM.

152 top right Juan Manuel Fangio at the wheel of the streamlined Mercedes W196 crossed the line first in the 1954 Italian GP, the penultimate race of the season. The pounding race left just 11 finishers at the end.

153 top Skillful application of opposite lock to control the car coming out of a corner by Jim Clark during the 1967 Italian GP. After leading for 13 laps Clark was forced to stop to change a tire. He restarted a breathtaking drive.

153 center Brabham is pushed to the pits by his mechanics at the 1968 Italian GP. The importance of spoilers and wings having been discovered, they were mounted precariously at first and frequently collapsed during the race, rendering the car undriveable and greatly compromising driver safety.

153 bottom Ready to start at the 1968 Italian GP: on the front row, left, recognizable by its high rear wing is the McLaren of Bruce McLaren. Denny Hulme won the race for the McLaren team.

152 right center Stirling Moss straightens up his Maserati as he exits a corner, hustled by Harry Schell in a Vanwall. The British driver stayed ahead of the American and won the race, the 1956 Italian GP. The driver of the Vanwall was less fortunate and was forced to retire on the 32nd lap with a broken suspension.

152 bottom right One of the 68 laps of the 1967 Italian GP: John Surtees in the Honda won by just two tenths of a second ahead of Jack Brabham in his Brabham-Repco. Clark was third after a spectacular charge: a stop to change tires meant he had to restart the race in 15th place.

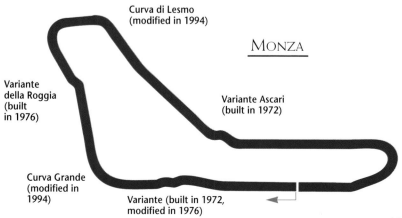

MONZA

Curva di Lesmo
(modified in 1994)

Variante
della Roggia
(built
in 1976)

Variante Ascari
(built in 1972)

Curva Grande
(modified in
1994)

Variante (built in 1972,
modified in 1976)

154 top left Ill luck frequently dogged Riccardo Patrese, as at the 1983 Italian GP. The Italian driver started from pole position at Monza but was forced to retire after just two laps when the turbo on his Brabham-BMW failed.

154 top right Ayrton Senna, right in the Lotus-Renault, and Keke Rosberg, left in the Williams-Honda, on the front row of the grid for the 1985 Italian GP. The winner of the race, however, was two rows back: Alain Prost in the McLaren-TAG-Porsche. The French driver started with the fifth fastest time, took the lead and streaked away from the pack, leading home the second-placed Piquet by 51 seconds.

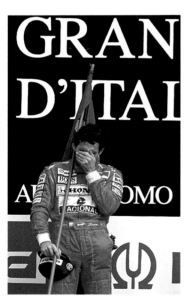

154 bottom left Ayrton Senna with the Brazilian flag in his hand overcome by emotion after having won the 1992 Italian GP. He started from the front row of the grid and won in part thanks to the problems suffered by Mansell and Patrese.

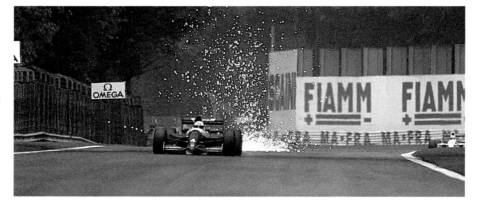

154-155 Ayrton Senna attempts to overtake on two wheels to the detriment of Damon Hill in the 1993 Italian GP while Alain Prost (foreground) in a Williams and Jean Alesi in a Ferrari proceed calmly on their way. The Brazilian failed to finish while Graham's son won easily by 40 seconds from the second-placed driver.

154 bottom right Partial disappointment for Alain Prost at the 1993 Italian GP: having started from pole position, he retained the lead until five laps from the end, when his engine failed and he fell back to 12th. He nonetheless retained his championship lead and his fourth title was not far off.

HONOR ROLL

Winners of the Italian GP

YEAR	CIRCUIT	DRIVER	NATIONALITY	CAR
1950	Monza	Giuseppe Farina	Italian	Alfa Romeo 159
1951	Monza	Alberto Ascari	Italian	Ferrari 375
1952	Monza	Alberto Ascari	Italian	Ferrari 500
1953	Monza	Juan Manuel Fangio	Argentine	Maserati A6GCM
1954	Monza	Juan Manuel Fangio	Argentine	Mercedes-Benz W196
1955	Monza	Juan Manuel Fangio	Argentine	Mercedes-Benz W196
1956	Monza	Stirling Moss	British	Maserati 250F
1957	Monza	Stirling Moss	British	Vanwall VW5
1958	Monza	Tony Brooks	British	Vanwall VW5
1959	Monza	Stirling Moss	British	Cooper T51-Climax
1960	Monza	Phil Hill	USA	Ferrari Dino 246
1961	Monza	Phil Hill	USA	Ferrari Dino 156
1962	Monza	Graham Hill	British	BRM P57
1963	Monza	Jim Clark	British	Lotus 25-Climax
1964	Monza	John Surtees	British	Ferrari 158
1965	Monza	Jackie Stewart	British	BRM P261
1966	Monza	Ludovico Scarfiotti	Italian	Ferrari 312
1967	Monza	John Surtees	British	Honda Ra300
1968	Monza	Denny Hulme	New Zealander	McLaren M7A-Ford
1969	Monza	Jackie Stewart	British	Matra Ms80-Ford
1970	Monza	Clay Regazzoni	Swiss	Ferrari 312B
1971	Monza	Peter Gethin	British	BRM P160
1972	Monza	Emerson Fittipaldi	Brazilian	Lotus 72D-Ford
1973	Monza	Ronnie Peterson	Swedish	Lotus 72D-Ford
1974	Monza	Ronnie Peterson	Swedish	Lotus 72E-Ford
1975	Monza	Clay Regazzoni	Swiss	Ferrari 312T
1976	Monza	Ronnie Peterson	Swedish	March 761-Ford
1977	Monza	Mario Andretti	USA	Lotus 78-Ford
1978	Monza	Niki Lauda	Austrian	Brabham BT46-Alfa Romeo
1979	Monza	Jody Scheckter	South African	Ferrari 312T4
1980	Imola	Nelson Piquet	Brazilian	Brabham BT49-Ford
1981	Monza	Alain Prost	French	Renault Re30
1982	Monza	René Arnoux	French	Renault Re30B
1983	Monza	Nelson Piquet	Brazilian	Brabham BT52B-BMW
1984	Monza	Niki Lauda	Austrian	McLaren MP4/2-TAG Porsche
1985	Monza	Alain Prost	French	McLaren MP4/2B-TAG Porsche
1986	Monza	Nelson Piquet	Brazilian	Williams FW11-Honda
1987	Monza	Nelson Piquet	Brazilian	Williams FW11B-Honda
1988	Monza	Gerhard Berger	Austrian	Ferrari F187/88C
1989	Monza	Alain Prost	French	McLaren MP4/5-Honda
1990	Monza	Ayrton Senna	Brazilian	McLaren MP4/5B-Honda
1991	Monza	Nigel Mansell	British	Williams FW14-Renault
1992	Monza	Ayrton Senna	Brazilian	McLaren MP4/7A-Honda
1993	Monza	Damon Hill	British	Williams FW15C-Renault
1994	Monza	Damon Hill	British	Williams FW16B-Renault
1995	Monza	Johnny Herbert	British	Benetton B195-Renault
1996	Monza	Michael Schumacher	German	Ferrari F310
1997	Monza	David Coulthard	British	McLaren MP4/12-Mercedes
1998	Monza	Michael Schumacher	German	Ferrari F300

155 top Damon Hill celebrates with an upraised fist as he wins the 1993 Italian GP, but he was well aware that there was a large element of luck in his triumph: Alain Prost had been leading until five laps from the end before his Williams' engine failed.

155 center The two Ferraris lapped together in their home Grand Prix in 1995: at Monza Gerhard Berger and Jean Alesi started with the third and fifth fastest times but neither made it to the finish. The Austrian broke his suspension on the 32nd lap while the Frenchman's driveshaft failed just 13 laps later.

155 bottom A pit stop and then away on to victory. The Ferraris scored an historic one-two in the 1998 Italian GP. Two cars from Maranello had not crossed the line first and second at Monza for ten years. Schumacher and Irvine were the protagonists of the day, the German also conquering pole position.

THE MONACO GRAND PRIX

It was a cigarette manufacturer, Antony Nogues, who had the idea of staging a Grand Prix on the streets of the small but exclusive Principality of Monaco. The Race of the Hundred Corners, as the event is known, snakes around Monte Carlo and represents the most sophisticated event of the Formula 1 calendar—the race that attracts VIPs and celebrities, that has spectators crowding apartment balconies and that sweetens the usually acrid smells of burnt oil, special fuels and scorched rubber laid down on the track surface as if an eraser had passed over sandpaper.

The length of the race was reduced in 1968 from the original 100 laps to 80 following the death of Lorenzo Bandini: among the causes of his death, fatigue has always been considered one of the most important due to the incessant, grueling rhythms the Monegasque circuit imposes. Monaco certainly separates the men from the boys and to win here a driver needs innate talent rather than raw speed, and frequently an ability to drive in the wet given the number of times it has rained during the race. This explains why the Master of Monaco was Ayrton

Senna, unbeatable on slippery surfaces, who won no fewer than six editions of the Grand Prix, five of them consecutively between 1989 and 1993. Neither is it any coincidence that another great wet weather driver, Graham Hill, collected the winner's laurels on five occasions in Europe's most prestigious and exclusive salon.

The circuit laid out around the city streets was increased in length over the years from the original 3.180 km (1.95 mi.) to the current 3.3 km (2.1 mi.). Located 20 km (12.4 mi.) from Nice, on the

magnificent Cote d'Azur, the Monaco circuit saw the construction of a new tunnel under the Loews Hotel in 1973, the addition of the Rascasse Corner (modified in 1976 together with Ste. Devote in the southern section) and a chicane in 1986.

There has been no lack of accidents such as the spectacular crashes of Ascari in 1955 and Hawkins ten years later, while John Surtees in 1960 and Riccardo Patrese, 17 years later, both made their Formula 1 debuts here. This was also the magnificent setting for Lotus' first Grand Prix victory.

156 top left and right An everyday Formula 1 occurrence: the photograph on the left shows three battered cars after an accident in the 1959 Monaco GP: the Porsche of von Trips (car number 6), Halford's Lotus-Climax (44) and Allison's Ferrari (52). Brooks in the second Ferrari (right photograph) finished second behind Brabham in a Cooper-Climax.

156 bottom left Helmet, goggles, gloves, overalls and an immense will to win: Jim Clark at the wheel of the Lotus-Climax number 9. The driver's 1963 Monaco GP finished on the 78th lap after he had led from the start. Jim was left with the consolation of having recorded the fastest lap.

157 top Having started from pole position, Jim Clark appeared destined to win the 1964 Monaco GP, but continual problems with his gearbox forced the Scotsman to settle for fourth place behind the two BRMs driven by Hill and Ginther and Arundell in the second Lotus.

157 center right Jack Brabham started from the front row in the 1965 Monaco GP, but the driver and owner of the Australian team failed to complete the 100 laps: he retired on the 43rd lap, leaving victory to Graham Hill in the BRM, who as well as having claimed pole position recorded the fastest lap at an average of 123.469 kph (76.7 mhp).

157 bottom left A circuit composed of city streets with the crowd massed behind the barriers and perching on the balconies overlooking the track; this is the appeal of the Formula 1 circus' most exclusive city race, the Monaco GP, seen here in its 1965 edition.

MONACO

La Rascasse (modified in 1976)
Virage Antony Nogues
Tunnel
New Chicane
Swimming Pool
Gasworks Hairpin (1929-1972)
Station Hairpin (Loews)
Old Chicane
Casino
Massenet
Tabac
Portier
Beau Rivage
Start (from 1973)
Mirabeau
Sainte Dévote (modified in 1976)

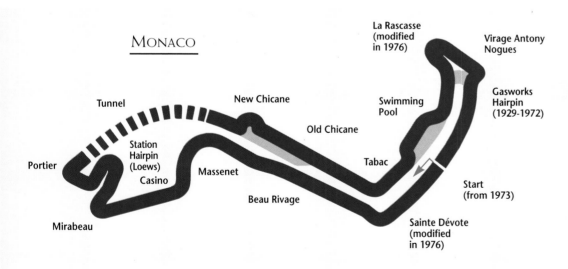

157 bottom right Prior to the race mechanics and onlookers roam amongst the cars. This is the 1965 Monaco GP. The figure 7 of Lorenzo Bandini's Ferrari number 17 can be seen. The Italian finished second while John Surtees with the other Ferrari was fourth.

158 top A magnificent view for Formula 1's most sophisticated and exclusive setting: the Race of One Hundred Corners, as the city-center race was nicknamed. The circuit snakes through the streets of Monte Carlo and the race was first held in 1929, the idea of the cigarette manufacturer Antony Nogues.

158 center left Starting from the front row of the grid, Damon Hill shot into the lead ahead of Schumacher who had claimed pole position. The German Ferrari driver's race ended a few hundred meters further on when he crashed into the armco. Damon did not enjoy better fortune in this, the 1996 Monaco GP: his Williams' Renault engine blew up on the 40th lap.

158 center right The McLarens running one-two in the 1988 Monaco GP: Ayrton Senna leads from Alain Prost but the Professor went on to win the race, relegating Gerhard Berger in the Ferrari and Thierry Boutsen in the Williams to second and third places.

158 bottom left The 1976 World Champion, James Hunt, seen here at the wheel of a Wolf, completed just five laps of the 1979 Monaco GP before stopping and deciding to retire from Formula 1.

158 bottom right The rain that accompanied the drivers from the start of the 1984 edition of the Monaco GP intensified to the point where the race was abandoned on the 31st lap. Many considered the suspension of the race at this point to be designed to allow Alain Prost (photograph) to win in the McLaren-TAG-Porsche. The race steward Jacky Ickx had close ties with Porsche and had the race continued for a few more laps the Rain King Senna would have undoubtedly passed the Frenchman.

HONOR ROLL

Winners of the Monaco GP

YEAR	DRIVER	NATIONALITY	CAR
1950	Juan Manuel Fangio	Argentine	Alfa Romeo 158
1955	Maurice Trintignant	French	Ferrari 625
1956	Stirling Moss	British	Maserati 250F
1957	Juan Manuel Fangio	Argentine	Maserati 250F
1958	Maurice Trintignant	French	Cooper T45-Climax
1959	Jack Brabham	Australian	Cooper T51-Climax
1960	Stirling Moss	British	Lotus 18-Climax
1961	Stirling Moss	British	Lotus 18-Climax
1962	Bruce McLaren	New Zealander	Cooper T60-Climax
1963	Graham Hill	British	BRM P57
1964	Graham Hill	British	BRM P261
1965	Graham Hill	British	BRM P261
1966	Jackie Stewart	British	BRM P261
1967	Denny Hulme	New Zealander	Brabham BT20-Repco
1968	Graham Hill	British	Lotus 49B-Ford
1969	Graham Hill	British	Lotus 49B-Ford
1970	Jochen Rindt	Austrian	Lotus 49C-Ford
1971	Jackie Stewart	British	Tyrrell 003-Ford
1972	Jean-Pierre Beltoise	French	BRM P160B
1973	Jackie Stewart	British	Tyrrell 006-Ford
1974	Ronnie Peterson	Swedish	Lotus 72E-Ford
1975	Niki Lauda	Austrian	Ferrari 312T
1976	Niki Lauda	Austrian	Ferrari 312T2
1977	Jody Scheckter	South African	Wolf WR1-Ford
1978	Patrick Depailler	French	Tyrrell 008-Ford
1979	Jody Scheckter	South African	Ferrari 312T4
1980	Carlos Reutemann	Argentine	Williams FW07B-Ford
1981	Gilles Villeneuve	Canadian	Ferrari 126CK
1982	Riccardo Patrese	Italian	Brabham BT49D-Ford
1983	Keke Rosberg	Finnish	Williams FW08C-Ford
1984	Alain Prost	French	McLaren MP4/2-TAG Porsche
1985	Alain Prost	French	McLaren MP4/2B-TAG Porsche
1986	Alain Prost	French	McLaren MP4/2C-TAG Porsche
1987	Ayrton Senna	Brazilian	Lotus 99T-Honda
1988	Alain Prost	French	McLaren MP4/4-Honda
1989	Ayrton Senna	Brazilian	McLaren MP4/5-Honda
1990	Ayrton Senna	Brazilian	McLaren MP4/5B-Honda
1991	Ayrton Senna	Brazilian	McLaren MP4/6-Honda
1992	Ayrton Senna	Brazilian	McLaren MP4/7A-Honda
1993	Ayrton Senna	Brazilian	McLaren MP4/8-Honda
1994	Michael Schumacher	German	Benetton B194-Ford
1995	Michael Schumacher	German	Benetton B195-Renault
1996	Olivier Panis	French	Ligier-Mugen
1997	Michael Schumacher	German	Ferrari F310B
1998	Mika Hakkinen	Finnish	McLaren MP4/13-Mercedes

159 top The 1994 Monaco GP was the first race after the death of Senna: Hill (photograph) failed to complete the first lap after touching Hakkinen's McLaren-Peugeot at the Ste. Devote corner. Both drivers were eliminated and Damon had to postpone his appointment with the winner's laurels until the next race.

159 bottom left The Ferraris at Monte Carlo: in 1991 the two Ferraris of Prost and Alesi started from the fourth and fifth rows respectively. Jean finished third but the Professor had to settle for fifth place.

159 bottom right Alesi's 1995 Monaco GP finished thus: at the Tabac corner he crashed violently into the armco with his Ferrari as he tried to avoid Martin Brundle in his spinning Ligier. Jean was briefly trapped in his car but was not seriously injured.

THE AUSTRALIAN GRAND PRIX

The Australian GP could be considered as a "novice" event in Formula 1 terms, as it has only been held since 1985. Despite its relative youth, however, the Australian race has led a double life, the first period marked by the impetuosity of adolescence, the second by a more temperate, tranquil maturity. For the first 11 years, in fact, the race was held on the Adelaide street circuit located just 8 km (5 mi.) from the city center, a layout that, in contrast with most other Grand Prix street circuits, was very fast. The race then moved to the city of Melbourne.

During the Adelaide period the Australian GP was always the last race in the Formula 1 calendar. From 1996 onward, when the circus moved to Melbourne, the kangaroo Grand Prix opened the season, losing something of the atmosphere, tension and emotions that were created at the end of the championship when the drivers' and constructors' titles were at stake over those last laps of the season, or when they represented the last race for a driver before moving to a new team or retiring from the sport.

The history of the Australian GP is, in fact, rich in "first" and "last" times, from the very first edition in 1985 when the Finnish driver Keke Rosberg scored his last victory as World Champion and the young Alain Prost suffered his first and only retirement after a fantastic season. The following year was one of farewells, as Rosberg and Australia's Alan Jones—understandably the local hero—took their leave of Formula 1. In 1987 Ferrari celebrated its 90th World Championship victory with Gerhard Berger.

Four years later the powers that be at Ferrari (and thus Fiat) decided to sack Prost on the occasion of the Australian GP. That race lasted just 14 laps

but, in terms of driver safety, it should never have even been started—a tropical downpour flooded the track and made racing impossible.

Although nobody could possibly have imagined it at the time, the 1993 Australian Grand Prix marked the very last occasion Ayrton Senna was seen on a Formula 1 podium as he celebrated his 41st victory. Early the following season Imola's Tamburello Curve took him from us forever during the San Marino GP. Apart from the death of Senna in 1994 the Formula 1 world also had to accept the retirement of the British Lion, Nigel Mansell.

The last edition of the Australian GP at Adelaide in 1995 was hardly one of the most memorable:

Mika Hakkinen crashed into the Malthouse corner barriers at 200 kph (124 mph) in his McLaren-Mercedes. He lost consciousness and suffered a dangerous fracture at the base of the cranium, his life hanging by a thread for some time. The Finnish driver pulled through, however, and thanks to the help of his wife recovered so well that three years later he won his first World Championship title, scoring an important victory in Australia that helped him sweep away the horrific images of 1995.

The start of the Melbourne race in 1996 was blighted by a spectacular accident involving numerous cars. Brundle's Jordan was broken in two, but fortunately the driver emerged virtually unhurt.

160 top Eddie Irvine celebrates the first win of 1999 in the World Championship's opening Grand Prix. His Ferrari covered the 302.3 kilometres of the Melbourne race at an average speed of 190.852 kph. Frentzen finished second in the Jordan Mugen-Honda.

160 center The 1991 Australian GP, held in at Adelaide in torrential rain, lasted just 14 laps before being abandoned. In the foreground on the right is Piquet's Benetton B191; young Schumacher is driving the second Benetton. The race was won by Senna's McLaren-Honda.

160 bottom A difficult, ambitious challenge awaited Michael Schumacher at the start of the 1999 season: bring the World Championship back to Ferrari after a 20-year absence. The year began badly for the German, however: after starting from the second row in Australia he could finish no higher than eighth, one lap down on the winner.

HONOR ROLL

Year	Circuit	Driver	Nationality	Car
1985	Adelaide	Keke Rosberg	Finnish	Williams FW10-Honda
1986	Adelaide	Alain Prost	French	McLaren MP4/2C-TAG Porsche
1987	Adelaide	Gerhard Berger	Austrian	Ferrari F187
1988	Adelaide	Alain Prost	French	McLaren MP4/4-Honda
1989	Adelaide	Thierry Boutsen	French	Williams FW13-Renault
1990	Adelaide	Nelson Piquet	Brazilian	Benetton B190-Ford
1991	Adelaide	Ayrton Senna	Brazilian	McLaren MP4/6-Honda
1992	Adelaide	Gerhard Berger	Austrian	McLaren MP4/7A-Honda
1993	Adelaide	Ayrton Senna	Brazilian	McLaren MP4/8-Honda
1994	Adelaide	Nigel Mansell	British	Williams FW16B-Renault
1995	Adelaide	Damon Hill	British	Williams FW17-Renault
1996	Melbourne	Damon Hill	British	Williams FW18-Renault
1997	Melbourne	David Coulthard	British	McLaren MP4/12-Mercedes
1998	Melbourne	Mika Hakkinen	Finnish	McLaren MP4/13-Mercedes

ALBERT PARK

161 bottom Celebrations in Ferrari's pits: Michael Schumacher crosses the line second in the '97 Australian GP, the first round of the championship. This was encouraging for the German driver, but he wasn't to win outright until four races later at Monte Carlo.

160-161 In 1996 Jacques Villeneuve, at the wheel of a Williams-Renault, started from pole position in the Australian GP at Melbourne but finished second to his teammate Damon Hill, who also won the World Championship title.

THE BELGIAN GRAND PRIX

The Belgian Grand Prix is one of the Formula 1 World Championship's historic events given that, with exceptions in 1957, '59, '69 and '71, it has been an ever-present in the calendar. The Spa-Francorchamps circuit has hosted the greatest number of Grands Prix, as well as the Spa 24-Hour event, the celebrated endurance race for sports prototypes. In use since the 1920s, the circuit is located near Liege and was rebuilt in 1979. It was shortened (from the original 15 km [9.3 mi.] to the present seven) but remains extremely fast, with a long start-finish straight terminating with the insidious La Source curve. Apart from Spa, the Belgian GP has also been held at Nivelles and Zolder in the 1970s and 1980s. The Zolder circuit near Brussels is sadly famous for the tragic death of Gilles Villeneuve in 1982. The chicane constructed in 1986 was named after the Canadian driver, even

162 top The Silver Arrow driven to victory by the greatest GP pilot of all time: Juan Manuel Fangio at the wheel of the open-wheeled Mercedes W196 at the 1955 Belgian GP, the third round of the World Championship and the Argentine's second win.

162 center left The starting grid of the 1962 Belgian GP saw, from the right, Graham Hill in the BRM, Bruce McLaren in a Cooper-Climax and Trevor Taylor in a Lotus-Climax. None of the three was to win the race, however, which went to Jim Clark—who started all the way back on the fifth row.

162 center right This photograph shows a section of the Spa-Francorchamps circuit that hosted the 1962 Formula 1 Grand Prix. The leading car is the Lotus-Climax driven by eventual winner Jim Clark, followed by Graham Hill in the BRM that finished second some 43.9" behind.

162 bottom Some great drivers were also experts in the mechanical side of the cars they launched toward victory: as well as a driver, Jack Brabham was the owner of the team that carried his name. Here he's seen working on his car prior to the Spa race of 1968.

though the Formula 1 GP had returned to Spa two years earlier.

In the past the Belgian GP has been dominated by Ayrton Senna who won five editions, no fewer than four of them consecutively (from 1988 to 1991). The Brazilian driver was particularly at home at Spa which, apart from being very fast, has also staged a number of editions in torrential rain, conditions in which he was truly unbeatable. It is no coincidence that other multiple winners here are wet weather masters of the caliber of Michael Schumacher and Jim Clark.

The Belgian GP can also boast that it was the first Formula 1 event to welcome a woman driver: in 1958 the Italian Maria Teresa de Filippis started the race at the wheel of a Maserati. The "fairer sex" was showing its muscles in a traditionally masculine sector—*muscles* truly being the operative word, as they were indispensable to keep the bucking cars of the day on the track at speeds of close to 300 kph

(186 mph). De Filippis finished that race in tenth place and was to appear at another two Grands Prix—a fleeting presence to be sure, but one that earned her an honorable place in the history of Formula 1.

Other significant debuts that occurred in Belgium included those of the six-wheeled Tyrrell P34 in 1976 and Michael Schumacher (in a Jordan) in 1991. A curious episode instead took place in 1973, when the race was moved from Spa to Zolder for the first time: the drivers were reluctant to take part in the Grand Prix as the asphalt was so fresh that it compromised the handling of their cars. Their protests were in vain, however. The organizers threatened to sequester the teams' equipment in recompense for the cancelation of the race, at which point the team managers obliged their drivers to take to the track. Team orders are team orders....

163 top A tangle of cars following the start of the 1986 Belgian GP. The Spa circuit has hosted the race since the first edition in 1925, save during wartime and a period during the 1970s. The original track length of 15 km (9.3 mi.) was reduced to just 6.9 (4.3 mi.) in 1979, then slightly pared again in 1986 before being extended to a full seven in '94.

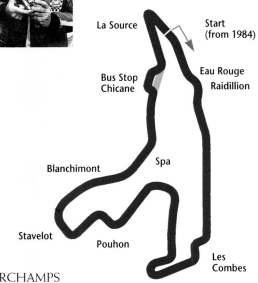

La Source
Start (from 1984)
Bus Stop Chicane
Eau Rouge Raidillion
Spa
Blanchimont
Stavelot
Pouhon
Les Combes
Malmédy

HONOR ROLL

Winners of the Belgian Grand Prix

YEAR	CIRCUIT	DRIVER	NATIONALITY	CAR
1950	Spa-Francorchamps	Juan Manuel Fangio	Argentine	Alfa Romeo 158
1951	Spa-Francorchamps	Giuseppe Farina	Italian	Alfa Romeo 159
1952	Spa-Francorchamps	Alberto Ascari	Italian	Ferrari 500
1953	Spa-Francorchamps	Alberto Ascari	Italian	Ferrari 500
1954	Spa-Francorchamps	Juan Manuel Fangio	Argentine	Maserati 250F
1955	Spa-Francorchamps	Juan Manuel Fangio	Argentine	Mercedes-Benz W196
1956	Spa-Francorchamps	Peter Collins	British	Lancia-Ferrari D50
1958	Spa-Francorchamps	Tony Brooks	British	Vanwall V W5
1960	Spa-Francorchamps	Jack Brabham	Australian	Cooper T53-Climax
1961	Spa-Francorchamps	Phil Hill	USA	Ferrari Dino 156
1962	Spa-Francorchamps	Jim Clark	British	Lotus 25-Climax
1963	Spa-Francorchamps	Jim Clark	British	Lotus 25-Climax
1964	Spa-Francorchamps	Jim Clark	British	Lotus 25-Climax
1965	Spa-Francorchamps	Jim Clark	British	Lotus 33-Climax
1966	Spa-Francorchamps	John Surtees	British	Ferrari 312
1967	Spa-Francorchamps	Dan Gurney	USA	Eagle AAR 104-Weslake
1968	Spa-Francorchamps	Bruce McLaren	New Zealander	McLaren M7A-Ford
1970	Spa-Francorchamps	Pedro Rodriguez	Mexican	BRM P153
1972	Nivelles	Emerson Fittipaldi	Brazilian	Lotus 72D-Ford
1973	Zolder	Jackie Stewart	British	Tyrrell 006-Ford
1974	Nivelles	Emerson Fittipaldi	Brazilian	McLaren M23-Ford
1975	Zolder	Niki Lauda	Austrian	Ferrari 312T
1976	Zolder	Niki Lauda	Austrian	Ferrari 312T2
1977	Zolder	Gunnar Nilsson	Swedish	Lotus 78-Ford
1978	Zolder	Mario Andretti	USA	Lotus 79-Ford
1979	Zolder	Jody Scheckter	South African	Ferrari 312T4
1980	Zolder	Didier Pironi	French	Ligier JS11/15-Ford
1981	Zolder	Carlos Reutemann	Argentine	Williams FW07C-Ford
1982	Zolder	John Watson	British	McLaren MP4/1B-Ford
1983	Spa-Francorchamps	Alain Prost	French	Renault RE40
1984	Zolder	Michele Alboreto	Italian	Ferrari 126C4
1985	Spa-Francorchamps	Ayrton Senna	Brazilian	Lotus 97T/Renault
1986	Spa-Francorchamps	Nigel Mansell	British	Williams FW11-Honda
1987	Spa-Francorchamps	Alain Prost	French	McLaren MP4/3-TAG Porsche
1988	Spa-Francorchamps	Ayrton Senna	Brazilian	McLaren MP4/4-Honda
1989	Spa-Francorchamps	Ayrton Senna	Brazilian	McLaren MP4/5-Honda
1990	Spa-Francorchamps	Ayrton Senna	Brazilian	McLaren MP4/5B-Honda
1991	Spa-Francorchamps	Ayrton Senna	Brazilian	McLaren MP4/6-Honda
1992	Spa-Francorchamps	Michael Schumacher	German	Benetton B192-Ford
1993	Spa-Francorchamps	Damon Hill	British	Williams FW15C-Renault
1994	Spa-Francorchamps	Damon Hill	British	Williams FW16B-Renault
1995	Spa-Francorchamps	Michael Schumacher	German	Benetton B195-Renault
1996	Spa-Francorchamps	Michael Schumacher	German	Ferrari F310
1997	Spa-Francorchamps	Michael Schumacher	German	Ferrari F310B
1998	Spa-Francorchamps	Damon Hill	British	Jordan 198-Peugeot

163 center Senna, the winner on the highest step of the podium, Mansell in the foreground and Prost in the background, spray the crowd with champagne. As if all the water that had fallen on Spa-Francorchamps on the 27th of August, 1989, during the Belgian GP had not been enough.

163 bottom right Third victory of the season for Damon Hill in the 1994 Belgian GP, a race that entered Formula 1 history for the disqualification of Michael Schumacher due to the irregularity of his Benetton-Ford's underbody. This exclusion did not, however, prevent the German from winning the title.

163 bottom left Johnny Herbert spins but Gerhard Berger manages to pass unscathed. The Austrian nonetheless retired from the race, stopping on the 22nd lap with electronic problems. The 1995 Belgian GP was thus won by Michael Schumacher at the wheel of a Benetton-Ford.

THE BRAZILIAN GRAND PRIX

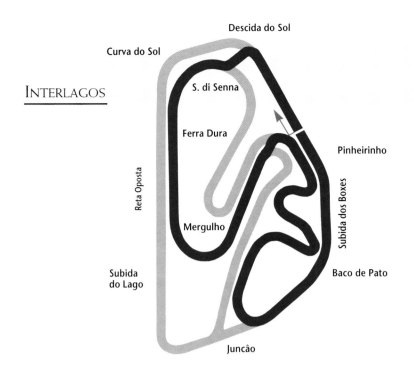

Descida do Sol
Curva do Sol
S. di Senna
Ferra Dura
Pinheirinho
Reta Oposta
Subida dos Boxes
Mergulho
Baco de Pato
Subida do Lago
Juncâo

Brazil joined the Grand Prix circus in 1973, representing South America along with Argentina. The merit for the Brazilian GP's inclusion in the Formula 1 calendar is largely due to Emerson Fittipaldi, who brought the World Championship title to his homeland for the first time in 1972. It was Fittipaldi himself who won the first edition of the race at Interlagos, just outside Sao Paolo, a victory that he went on to repeat the following year. Located 850 meters above sea level, Interlagos was one of the circuits favored by turbo engines, which give their best at high altitudes. Another Brazilian was crowned with the winner's laurels in 1975, Carlos Pace scoring his only Formula 1 victory.

Alain Prost, however, was the true master of the Brazilian GP given that he won no fewer than six editions of the race (1982, '84, '85, '87, '88 and '90). The Frenchmen Lafitte and Arnoux also won in Brazil in '79 and '80 in a decade in which the Old Continent dominated the South American event.

The Interlagos circuit was completely rebuilt in 1990 after 50 years of staging motor racing and, like many other temples of speed, it was reduced in length. The first S-bend was named after another of the Brazilian automotive greats, Ayrton Senna, who won the race in 1991 in front of his home crowd, in the city in which he was born. That victory at Interlagos has remained impressed in the memory of racing fans: Senna climbed onto the podium with shooting pains in his shoulders caused by over-tight safety belts. He was so exhausted that he was unable to lift the trophy, and struggled to toast and spray the crowd with the customary champagne.

In 1978 and throughout the 1980s (with the exception of 1981), the Brazilian GP was held at the Jacarepagua circuit dedicated to another great Brazilian driver, Nelson Piquet, winner of three World Championship titles. Jacarepagua is located some 30 km (18.6 mi.) from Rio de Janeiro.

164 top Ayrton Senna's car is on fire in front of his home crowd. In 1986 at the first race of the season in Brazil, Senna claimed the pole in the Lotus but could only finish second to Piquet's Williams.

164 bottom left From the left, Gerhard Berger in the Ferrari, Ayrton Senna in the McLaren-Honda and Riccardo Patrese in the Williams-Renault shortly after the start of the 1989 Brazilian GP. All three were beaten in the race by Nigel Mansell, who drove his Ferrari to victory.

164 bottom right Despite an excursion onto the grass, Ayrton Senna nonetheless managed to win the Brazilian GP for the

first time in 1991. Ayrton was thus finally able to celebrate with his home crowd thronging the Sao Paolo circuit. Credit for the victory was also due to the McLaren-Honda in sparkling form.

165 top left Ayrton Senna managed just eight laps of the 1984 Brazilian GP at the Jacarepagua circuit: he was forced to retire with a broken turbo on his Toleman-Hart. Prost won with his Williams-Honda.

165 bottom left Interlagos, 1992, saw the third round of the Formula 1 World Championship, and Williams (with Mansell and Patrese) and Benetton (with Schumacher) dominated on the 4.325-km (2.7-mi.) circuit. The British team emerged triumphant, taking the first two places.

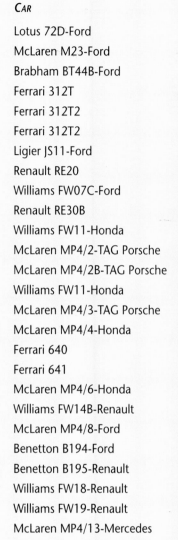

HONOR ROLL

Winners of the Brazilian Grand Prix

YEAR	CIRCUIT	DRIVER	NATIONALITY	CAR
1973	Interlagos	Emerson Fittipaldi	Brazilian	Lotus 72D-Ford
1974	Interlagos	Emerson Fittipaldi	Brazilian	McLaren M23-Ford
1975	Interlagos	Carlos Pace	Brazilian	Brabham BT44B-Ford
1976	Interlagos	Niki Lauda	Austrian	Ferrari 312T
1977	Interlagos	Carlos Reutemann	Argentine	Ferrari 312T2
1978	Rio de Janeiro	Carlos Reutemann	Argentine	Ferrari 312T2
1979	Interlagos	Jacques Lafitte	French	Ligier JS11-Ford
1980	Interlagos	René Arnoux	French	Renault RE20
1981	Rio de Janeiro	Carlos Reutemann	Argentine	Williams FW07C-Ford
1982	Rio de Janeiro	Alain Prost	French	Renault RE30B
1983	Rio de Janeiro	Nelson Piquet	Brazilian	Williams FW11-Honda
1984	Rio de Janeiro	Alain Prost	French	McLaren MP4/2-TAG Porsche
1985	Rio de Janeiro	Alain Prost	French	McLaren MP4/2B-TAG Porsche
1986	Rio de Janeiro	Nelson Piquet	Brazilian	Williams FW11-Honda
1987	Rio de Janeiro	Alain Prost	French	McLaren MP4/3-TAG Porsche
1988	Rio de Janeiro	Alain Prost	French	McLaren MP4/4-Honda
1989	Rio de Janeiro	Nigel Mansell	British	Ferrari 640
1990	Interlagos	Alain Prost	French	Ferrari 641
1991	Interlagos	Ayrton Senna	Brazilian	McLaren MP4/6-Honda
1992	Interlagos	Nigel Mansell	British	Williams FW14B-Renault
1993	Interlagos	Ayrton Senna	Brazilian	McLaren MP4/8-Ford
1994	Interlagos	Michael Schumacher	German	Benetton B194-Ford
1995	Interlagos	Michael Schumacher	German	Benetton B195-Renault
1996	Interlagos	Damon Hill	British	Williams FW18-Renault
1997	Interlagos	Jacques Villeneuve	Canadian	Williams FW19-Renault
1998	Interlagos	Mika Hakkinen	Finnish	McLaren MP4/13-Mercedes

165 right top, bottom and center Moments of joy and desperation for the Ferrari drivers at the '90 Brazilian GP: Alain Prost (top) celebrates victory, conquered in part thanks to the unwitting help offered by Nakajima who rammed Senna, obliging the Brazilian to make a stop and settle for third place overall. Nigel Mansell (bottom), instead, could manage no better than fourth and was the last of the unlapped drivers. The center photograph shows an embrace between perhaps the two greatest drivers in Formula 1 history: Ayrton Senna celebrates his victory in the '93 Brazilian GP with Juan Manuel Fangio—a great moment that will, unfortunately, never be repeated.

165 bottom right Red at the 1998 Brazilian GP: the car from Maranello is in the pits for a rapid, split-second tire change and refuelling. Michael Schumacher finished the race in third place behind the two McLaren-Mercedes of Hakkinen and Coulthard.

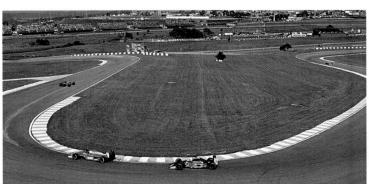

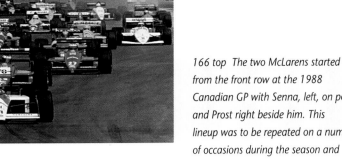

THE CANADIAN GRAND PRIX

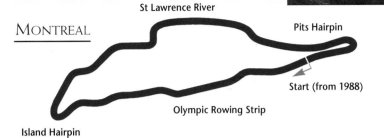

MONTREAL

St Lawrence River
Pits Hairpin
Start (from 1988)
Olympic Rowing Strip
Island Hairpin

166 top *The two McLarens started from the front row at the 1988 Canadian GP with Senna, left, on pole and Prost right beside him. This lineup was to be repeated on a number of occasions during the season and was also frequently the finishing order, as it proved in Canada that year.*

When the Canadian Grand Prix is mentioned thoughts immediately turn to Gilles Villeneuve. The circuit at Montreal that has hosted Formula 1 racing since 1978 is named after him and its construction actually owed much to the daring and brilliance of the little driver from Chambly. Following his 1977 debut, the organizer of the Grand Prix managed to exploit the success then being enjoyed by the new Canadian hero to build (in record-breaking time) a new circuit near Montreal to replace Mosport Park, which is located about 100 km (62 mi.) from Toronto and considered relatively unsafe. Mosport held its last "Canadian Grand Prix" in 1977 after 14 editions, eight of which being true Formula 1 events.

The first Formula 1 Canadian Grand Prix was held in 1967 and the event has been ever-present since then, with the exceptions of 1975 and '87. The North American race is often scheduled for the first half of the season when cars and drivers are still fine-tuning. In contrast with many other circuits, there has been no one specialist in particular: Michael Schumacher has won three editions (two of which with Ferrari), while Ayrton Senna, Alan Jones, Jackie Stewart and Jacky Ickx have each won two.

HONOR ROLL

YEAR	CIRCUIT	DRIVER	NATIONALITY	CAR
1967	Mosport Park	Jack Brabham	Australian	Brabham BT24-Repco
1968	St. Jovite	Denny Hulme	New Zealander	McLaren M7A-Ford
1969	Mosport Park	Jacky Ickx	Belgian	Brabham BT26-Ford
1970	St. Jovite	Jacky Ickx	Belgian	Ferrari 312B
1971	Mosport Park	Jackie Stewart	British	Tyrrell 003-Ford
1972	Mosport Park	Jackie Stewart	British	Tyrrell 005-Ford
1973	Mosport Park	Peter Revson	USA	McLaren M23-Ford
1974	Mosport Park	Emerson Fittipaldi	Brazilian	McLaren M23-Ford
1976	Mosport Park	James Hunt	British	McLaren M23-Ford
1977	Mosport Park	Jody Scheckter	South African	Wolf WR1-Ford
1978	Montreal	Gilles Villeneuve	Canadian	Ferrari 312T3
1979	Montreal	Alan Jones	Australian	Williams FW07-Ford
1980	Montreal	Alan Jones	Australian	Williams FW07B-Ford
1981	Montreal	Jacques Lafitte	French	Ligier JS17-Matra
1982	Montreal	Nelson Piquet	Brazilian	Brabham BT50-BMW
1983	Montreal	René Arnoux	French	Ferrari 126C2B
1984	Montreal	Nelson Piquet	Brazilian	Brabham BT53-BMW
1985	Montreal	Michele Alboreto	Italian	Ferrari 156/85
1986	Montreal	Nigel Mansell	British	Williams FW11-Honda
1988	Montreal	Ayrton Senna	Brazilian	McLaren MP4/4-Honda
1989	Montreal	Thierry Boutsen	Belgian	Williams FW12C-Renault
1990	Montreal	Ayrton Senna	Brazilian	McLaren MP4/5B-Honda
1991	Montreal	Nelson Piquet	Brazilian	Benetton B191-Ford
1992	Montreal	Gerhard Berger	Austrian	McLaren MP4/7A-Honda
1993	Montreal	Alain Prost	French	Williams FW15C-Renault
1994	Montreal	Michael Schumacher	German	Benetton B194-Ford
1995	Montreal	Jean Alesi	French	Ferrari 412T2
1996	Montreal	Damon Hill	British	Williams FW18-Renault
1997	Montreal	Michael Schumacher	German	Ferrari F310B
1998	Montreal	Michael Schumacher	German	Ferrari F300

166 center *Schumacher had a torrid time in the 1996 Canadian GP. Left standing when the cars started their warmup lap, he was obliged to start from the back of the grid. Pulling away from a pit stop on the 42nd lap he accelerated hard to avoid problems with the clutch but the driveshaft broke and shot away dangerously, fortunately without further consequences.*

166-167 *Senna was firmly in control of the rainy 1989 Canadian GP when, three laps from the end, his engine began to play up, obliging him to settle for seventh place.*

166 bottom *The image shows the 1985 Canadian GP podium: from left to right are Stephan Johansson, Michele Alboreto (who won), and Alain Prost.*

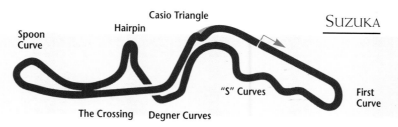

THE JAPANESE GRAND PRIX

Spoon Curve

Casio Triangle

Hairpin

SUZUKA

The Crossing   Degner Curves

"S" Curves

First Curve

167 top right, 167 center right and 167 bottom left Schumacher ran hard in the '94 Japanese GP, favored by the rain—an irresistible temptation for the German to press on, as he is in his element on slippery surfaces. Things are rather different for other drivers, caught out by locked wheels and spins

sending them off the track. Similar antics entertain the crowd, including the little girl wearing the overalls with the name of the unforgettable Senna. However, poor race strategy with a pit stop ten laps from the end to change tires and refuel (center right) cost Michael victory. He finished second to Hill.

167 top left Two starts at the 1996 Japanese GP: David Coulthard had a problem on the grid and the start was repeated, including the warmup lap. The race was thus reduced by a lap with Damon Hill taking the checkered flag in front of Schumacher and Hakkinen in second and third.

167 bottom right Just seven seconds behind the wheel, the rest of the race spent trackside: Senna and Prost heading back to the pits on foot at the 1990 Japanese GP after the Brazilian World Champion had gained his revenge over his French teammate who the year before had driven him off the track, again in Japan.

Scheduled among the last races of the season, the Japanese Grand Prix has frequently been decisive in determining the outcome of the championship and has thus been the scene of epic duels that have entered the championship's folklore. The first edition was held in 1976 in torrential rain at Fuji, some 60 km (37 mi.) from Yokohama. This circuit was an American-style layout with very long straights on which the drivers could exploit the power of the cars.

That inaugural race was won by Mario Andretti, while James Hunt's third place was sufficient for him to win the World Championship title. After 1977 the race was dropped following a dramatic accident caused by Gilles Villeneuve who, in an improbable and hazardous manoeuvre, rammed Ronnie Peterson in the Tyrrell with his Ferrari. The incident finished in tragedy as the Canadian's car went out of control and flew into two hapless spectators who were standing on the wrong side of the barriers.

The Japanese GP was not revived until ten years later at Suzuka, a figure-eight track which is principally a Honda testing site. (Since 1994 a second World Championship round has also been held in Japan, the Pacific Grand Prix staged at the Aida circuit outside Kobe.) There are no undisputed masters of the Japanese Grand Prix—not surprising, in light of its youthful nature: Berger, Hill, Schumacher, and Senna have all earned two wins, but none consecutively.

HONOR ROLL

YEAR	CIRCUIT	DRIVER	NATIONALITY	CAR
1976	Fuji	Mario Andretti	USA	Lotus 77-Ford
1977	Fuji	James Hunt	British	McLaren M26-Ford
1987	Suzuka	Gerhard Berger	Austrian	Ferrari F187
1988	Suzuka	Ayrton Senna	Brazilian	McLaren MP4/4-Honda
1989	Suzuka	Alessandro Nannini	Italian	Benetton B189-Ford
1990	Suzuka	Nelson Piquet	Brazilian	Benetton B190-Ford
1991	Suzuka	Gerhard Berger	Austrian	McLaren MP4/6-Honda
1992	Suzuka	Riccardo Patrese	Italian	Williams FW14B-Renault
1993	Suzuka	Ayrton Senna	Brazilian	McLaren MP4/8-Ford
1994	Suzuka	Damon Hill	British	Williams FW16B-Renault
1995	Suzuka	Michael Schumacher	German	Benetton B195-Renault
1996	Suzuka	Damon Hill	British	Williams FW18-Renault
1997	Suzuka	Michael Schumacher	German	Ferrari F310B
1998	Suzuka	Mika Hakkinen	Finnish	McLaren MP4/13-Mercedes

The Portuguese Grand Prix

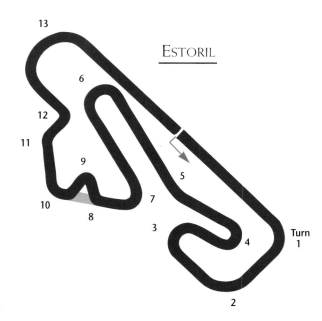

168 top Alain Prost conquered his third title in 1989 at the wheel of the McLaren-Honda. He is seen here at the Portuguese GP where he finished second behind Gerhard Berger in the Ferrari.

168 bottom A close-up of Ayrton Senna in his Lotus-Renault at the 1985 Portuguese GP. Ayrton started from pole position, recorded the fastest lap at an average speed of 150.401 kph (93.399 mph) and won his first Grand Prix.

168-169 The two Williams, with Nigel Mansell on pole and Riccardo Patrese alongside him, started from the front row of the grid in the last race of the 1992 season. Senna instead started from the back of the grid as his McLaren-Honda stalled during the warm-up lap. The Brazilian eventually finished third.

The Portuguese Grand Prix has been something of a British preserve, given that of the 16 editions that have been staged off and on since 1958, no fewer than eight have been won by British drivers, with Stirling and Damon both triumphing twice. The Frenchman, Alain Prost, is however the master of Estoril, the circuit which has hosted the Formula 1 Grand Prix from 1984—when the race returned to Portugal after an absence of 24 years—until 1996.

The first edition of the Portuguese GP dates back to 1958 and was held at Oporto: Stirling Moss won that first race, a feat he repeated the following year when the event moved to Monsanto, another center for sports car racing up until the end of the 1950s. This was a road circuit laid out in a park in the Lisbon hills and incorporating part of the road leading to Estoril. This last circuit, built in 1972, was not used for a World Championship race until 1984 when it was able to offer suitable facilities. (With maintenance having been neglected, by the late 1970s the track had in fact become unusable.) Inserted as the last race of the season, Estoril proved decisive in a contest between two teammates, Prost (who absolutely had to win) and Lauda (who only needed to finish second to be sure of his third championship). The Austrian put on a spectacular show, recording the fastest lap and picking off all the adversaries separating him from Prost. Lauda, with the determination that had always characterized his racing, achieved his objective and Prost, despite crossing the line first, was obliged to settle for second in the championship.

Still, it was at Estoril that Prost later went on to clinch his fourth World Championship title. The race also provided Ayrton Senna's first Formula 1 win, in 1985 with a Lotus-Renault. (Between Ayrton's genius and the evocative JPS livery, some fans thus dreamed that Lotus might still grasp glory after Chapman.)

ESTORIL

169 top left A car out of control crashes into the armco: this was one of the five accidents that occurred during the 1989 Portuguese GP at the renowned Estoril circuit. Caffi, Piquet, Warwick, Mansell and Senna were involved in one wreck or another.

169 top right During the 1995 Portuguese GP, Katayama in the Tyrrell is launched up into the air after colliding with Badoer's Minardi and heads toward the Pacific driven by Montermini, who in order to avoid him crashed into the pit wall. This breathtaking incident at Estoril meant that the race had to be restarted.

169 center right Threatening clouds build up over Estoril but fortunately there was to be no rain at the 1993 Portuguese GP. Jean Alesi started from the third row of the grid with the Ferrari and finished fourth behind the winner Schumacher in the Benetton and Prost and Hill in Williams.

169 bottom The stuff of champions is there but has yet to be fully revealed: in 1991 Michael Schumacher drove the Benetton-Ford in the Portuguese GP, finishing fifth and scoring two points. He finished the season in 12th place with a total of four points in front of Mika Hakkinen, an order that was to be reversed years later.

HONOR ROLL

Winners of the Portuguese Grand Prix

Year	Circuit	Driver	Nationality	Car
1958	Oporto	Stirling Moss	British	Vanwall VW10
1959	Monsanto	Stirling Moss	British	Cooper T51-Climax
1960	Oporto	Jack Brabham	Australian	Cooper T53-Climax
1984	Estoril	Alain Prost	French	McLaren MP4/2-TAG Porsche
1985	Estoril	Ayrton Senna	Brazilian	Lotus 97T-Renault
1986	Estoril	Nigel Mansell	British	Williams FW11-Honda
1987	Estoril	Alain Prost	French	McLaren MP4/3-TAG Porsche
1988	Estoril	Alain Prost	French	McLaren MP4/4-Honda
1989	Estoril	Gerhard Berger	Austrian	Ferrari 640
1990	Estoril	Nigel Mansell	British	Ferrari 641/2
1991	Estoril	Riccardo Patrese	Italian	Williams FW14-Renault
1992	Estoril	Nigel Mansell	British	Williams FW14B-Renault
1993	Estoril	Michael Schumacher	German	Benetton B193B-Renault
1994	Estoril	Damon Hill	British	Williams FW16B-Renault
1995	Estoril	David Coulthard	British	Williams FW17B-Renault
1996	Estoril	Damon Hill	British	Williams FW18-Renault

THE SAN MARINO GRAND PRIX

Relegated until the early 1980s to a supporting role behind the most famous of Italian motor racing circuits Monza, the Enzo and Dino Ferrari Autodrome at Imola returned to the spotlight in 1980 when it hosted the Italian Grand Prix for the first time. With the exception of a number of editions held on street circuits in the 1920s and 1940s, this World Championship event had always been staged at the Lombard track. The change had been dictated by the death of Ronnie Peterson in the 1978 Italian GP which led to accusing fingers being pointed at the Monza safety precautions.

The transfer of the Grand Prix to Imola lasted just a single season, however, but a circuit named after one of Formula 1's most famous figures and his son, who had died young, could hardly continue to host minor races only (Formula 3 and 3000, sports prototypes, national championship races).

From 1981 onward Imola thus found a permanent place within the Formula 1 circus as the venue for the San Marino GP.

Even though Ferrari can be said to be at home at Imola, the team from Maranello has only managed to win the San Marino GP on two occasions, in 1982 and '83 with Pironi and Tambay. The 1982 edition was, however, characterized by the absence of the British teams—the adversaries to beat for the cars from Maranello—due to the violent arguments that had broken out between the FIA and the FOCA regarding the legality of the false water tanks supposedly mounted on the cars to supply the brake cooling circuits but in reality to bring the weight of the cars above the minimum limit. Pironi's victory triggered the profound personal dislike between the Frenchman and Gilles Villeneuve: Didier was leading during the race and refused to accept the team orders and allow the Canadian pass to win.

The Imola circuit is tragically famous for the death of Ayrton Senna in 1994. Shortly after the start the Brazilian failed to negotiate the Tamburello curve, crashed into the retaining wall and was killed. Moreover, the circuit had already witnessed a terrible accident the previous day when Ratzenberger crashed and was killed at the Villeneuve curve during practice.

170 top and bottom right Twenty-four cars lined up on the starting grid for the 1986 San Marino GP at Imola. The front row was all Brazilian with Ayrton Senna in the Lotus-Renault and Nelson Piquet in the Williams-Honda. Victory however went to the Frenchman Alain Prost, seen in the bottom photograph on the podium together with Piquet (left) in Williams Honda and Benetton-BMW driver Gerhard Berger (right). Prost crossed the line first after the scheduled 60 laps in the McLaren-TAG-Porsche.

170-171 center The weekend from the 29th of April through to the 1st of May was the blackest and most tragic in the history of Formula 1, the dates being branded in the hearts of all the sport's enthusiasts. Tragedy followed tragedy during practice and culminated on the Sunday during the race. On Saturday April 30th, during the last qualifying session, Austrian Roland Ratzenberger crashed his Simtek at the Villeneuve curve at 314 kph (195 mph) and died. The crowd and the organizers were incredulous: on Friday the 29th

tragedy had barely been averted at the Dino and Enzo Ferrari circuit when Rubens Barrichello crashed his Jordan (images in sequence page 170 and 171), fortunately without serious consequences. The atmosphere on race day was bleak, but the worst was still to come: Immediately after the start

Lamy's Lotus and Lehto's Benetton collided and pieces of wreckage flew into the crowd injuring a dozen spectators. On the fifth lap the nadir was reached: at 2:17 p.m. Ayrton Senna (page 170 top center) crashed into the retaining wall at the Tamburello Corner and was killed.

IMOLA

(Circuit map labels: Rivazza, Variante Alta, Variante Bassa, Arrival, Piratella, Acque Minerali, Tamburello, Villeneuve, Tosa)

HONOR ROLL

Winners of the San Marino Grand Prix

YEAR	CIRCUIT	DRIVER	NATIONALITY	CAR
1981	Imola	Nelson Piquet	Brazilian	Brabham BT49C-Ford
1982	Imola	Didier Pironi	French	Ferrari 126C2
1983	Imola	Patrick Tambay	French	Ferrari 126C2B
1984	Imola	Alain Prost	French	McLaren MP4/2-TAG Porsche
1985	Imola	Elio De Angelis	Brazilian	Lotus 97T-Renault
1986	Imola	Alain Prost	French	McLaren MP4/2C-TAG Porsche
1987	Imola	Nigel Mansell	British	Williams FW11B-Honda
1988	Imola	Ayrton Senna	Brazilian	McLaren MP4/4-Honda
1989	Imola	Ayrton Senna	Brazilian	McLaren MP4/5-Honda
1990	Imola	Riccardo Patrese	Italian	Williams FW13B-Renault
1991	Imola	Ayrton Senna	Brazilian	McLaren MP4/6-Honda
1992	Imola	Nigel Mansell	British	Williams FW14B-Renault
1993	Imola	Alain Prost	French	Williams FW15C-Renault
1994	Imola	Michael Schumacher	German	Benetton B194-Ford
1995	Imola	Damon Hill	British	Williams FW17-Renault
1996	Imola	Damon Hill	British	Williams FW18-Renault
1997	Imola	Heinz-Harald Frentzen	German	Williams FW19-Renault
1998	Imola	David Coulthard	British	McLaren MP4/13-Mercedes

170 bottom left Fisichella is Italy's most promising young F1 driver: he debuted in 1996 at the wheel of the Ford-powered Minardi in the San Marino GP. The Roman driver started from the penultimate row on the grid and was forced to retire after 30 laps with a broken engine.

171 top right One of the last portraits of Ayrton Senna, a driver who lives on in the memories of motor racing enthusiasts everywhere.

171 bottom The 1996 Grand Prix: David Coulthard in the McLaren-Mercedes is hounded by Michael Schumacher in the Ferrari (left photograph). The Scot was

forced to retire on the 44th lap with gearbox problems while the German finished second behind Damon Hill, chasing his first championship title. Jacques Villeneuve (right photograph) started from the second row but finished only eleventh: his Williams was rammed by Alesi as he rejoined the circuit after an excursion onto the grass.

THE SPANISH GRAND PRIX

Should each Grand Prix be identified with a number, an ideal candidate for the figure five would be the Spanish GP: five is in fact the number of circuits that have hosted this World Championship race and Juan Manuel Fangio won the first of his five titles (a record still unbroken today) by taking the Spanish GP in 1951. After the *Chueco's* first title, Formula 1 in Spain made a brief reappearance in 1954 before resuming an annual cadence in 1968.

The Pedralbes circuit, built on the outskirts of Barcelona, was inaugurated immediately after the Second World War and hosted the first two editions of the Grand Prix in 1951 and 1954. Characterized by an original slipper layout, it featured very fast curves and a straight named after General Franco.

The event was staged twice during the 1960s

and more frequently in the 1970s and late 1980s at Jarama. This circuit, built in 1967, 30 km (18.6 mi.) north of Madrid on what had been one of the principal battlefields of the Spanish Civil War, owed its existence to John Hugenholts, the "father" of the Dutch circuit of Zandvoort and Suzuka in Japan. In its last Formula 1 season Jarama saluted the Formula 1 circus with an unusual episode: Villeneuve, Lafitte, Watson, Reutemann and de Angelis all crossed the line within a second of each other.

Until the move to Jerez de la Frontera in 1986 the alternative to Jarama had been Montjuich Park, a circuit that in 1975 was the scene of a tragic accident in which four spectators were killed when Stommelen's car left the track. The

incident led to the circuit being closed.

The autodromes of Jerez de la Frontera and Catalunya were constructed recently (in 1986 and 1991 respectively): the first is located 100 km (62 mi.) to the south of Seville and presents no particular problems for the drivers. Its distance from major cities makes it difficult to attract large crowds, however. The second circuit has hosted the Formula 1 circus since 1991, the year after the accident in which Donnelly was nearly killed at Jerez during practice for the Grand Prix. The fourth track to be built in the Barcelona region achieved maximum exposure in its debut year when Senna and Mansell battled wheel-to-wheel for the conquest of the title.

172 top left The 1979 Spanish GP held at Jarama was not a particularly happy race for Renault: the two Frenchmen Arnoux and Jabouille could manage no better than ninth place and a retirement after just 21 laps. The race was won by Dépailler who went straight into the lead and crossed the line ahead of the two Lotuses of Reutemann and Andretti.

172 center left A victorious Gilles Villeneuve at the 1980 Spanish GP. The race did not count toward the Formula 1 World Championship because the FIA was in open conflict with the FOCA over the adoption or banning of side-skirts, and at Jarama the drivers had boycotted the obligatory pre-race meeting.

172 bottom left With flames coming from its exhaust pipes, Ayrton Senna's McLaren at the 1991 Spanish GP was not in the best of health, thus preventing the Brazilian from fighting for the lead in spite of the torrential rain, conditions in

which he usually excelled. After starting from the second row of the grid Senna (seen here walking in the rain) completed the race but could finish no higher than fifth behind the Williams of Mansell and Patrese—the Italian recorded the fastest lap—and the Ferraris of Prost and Alesi.

172 top right All set for the start of the 1968 Spanish GP held at Jarama: fourteen cars lined up on the grid but

only five of them crossed the finishing line. Graham Hill in the Lotus-Ford won from Hulme in the McLaren-Ford and Redman in the Cooper-BRM.

172 bottom right The Dutchman Lammers did not pass unobserved in the 1979 Spanish GP: his Ford-powered Shadow was very colorful. In this photograph Lammers is being chased by Emmo in the Copersucar–Fittipaldi. The Shadow finished in 12th place.

HONOR ROLL

Winners of the Spanish Grand Prix

YEAR	CIRCUIT	DRIVER	NATIONALITY	CAR
1951	Pedralbes	Juan Manuel Fangio	Argentine	Alfa Romeo 159
1954	Pedralbes	Mike Hawthorn	British	Ferrari 553 Squalo
1968	Jarama	Graham Hill	British	Lotus 49-Ford
1969	Montjuich	Jackie Stewart	British	Matra MS80-Ford
1970	Jarama	Jackie Stewart	British	March 701-Ford
1971	Montjuich	Jackie Stewart	British	Tyrrell 003-Ford
1972	Jarama	Emerson Fittipaldi	Argentine	Lotus 72D-Ford
1973	Montjuich	Emerson Fittipaldi	Argentine	Lotus 72D-Ford
1974	Jarama	Niki Lauda	Austrian	Ferrari 312B3
1975	Montjuich	Jochen Mass	German	McLaren M23-Ford
1976	Jarama	James Hunt	British	McLaren M23-Ford
1977	Jarama	Mario Andretti	USA	Lotus 78-Ford
1978	Jarama	Mario Andretti	USA	Lotus 79-Ford
1979	Jarama	Patrick Depailler	French	Ligier JS11-Ford
1980	Jarama	Alan Jones	Australian	Williams FW07B-Ford
1981	Jarama	Gilles Villeneuve	Canadian	Ferrari C126CK
1986	Jerez	Ayrton Senna	Brazilian	Lotus 98T-Renault
1987	Jerez	Nigel Mansell	British	Williams FW11B-Honda
1988	Jerez	Alain Prost	French	McLaren MP4/4-Honda
1989	Jerez	Ayrton Senna	Brazilian	McLaren MP4/5-Honda
1990	Jerez	Alain Prost	French	Ferrari 641/2
1991	Catalunya	Nigel Mansell	British	Williams FW14-Renault
1992	Catalunya	Nigel Mansell	British	Williams FW14B-Renault
1993	Catalunya	Alain Prost	French	Williams FW15C-Renault
1994	Catalunya	Damon Hill	British	Williams FW16-Renault
1995	Catalunya	Michael Schumacher	German	Benetton B195-Renault
1996	Catalunya	Michael Schumacher	German	Ferrari F310
1997	Catalunya	Jacques Villeneuve	Canadian	Williams FW19-Renault
1998	Catalunya	David Coulthard	British	McLaren MP4/13-Mercedes

173 right In the wet Michael Schumacher (top photograph) displays all his driving talent and brings to mind earlier Rain Kings such as Ayrton Senna and Graham Hill. The rain worked to Ferrari's advantage in the 1996

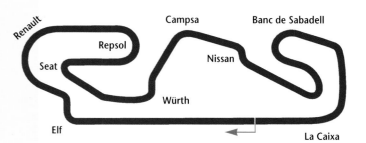

CATALUNYA

Spanish GP with Schumacher's machine first across the line and also setting the fastest lap. His victory was in part due to record-breaking pitstop times (bottom photograph). Schumacher was joined on the podium by Alesi and Villeneuve (center photograph). The second Ferrari driven by Eddie Irvine crashed out just after the start, one of a number of accidents that occurred before the end of the first lap that involved and eliminated Coulthard, Fisichella, Panis, Rosset, Lamy and Brundle.

173 bottom left Pit stops are always timed to the hundredths of a second: this picture shows the reigning World Champion Jacques Villeneuve in the Williams pits during the 1998 Spanish GP. Jacques finished only 12th in this race after starting from the fifth row.

THE UNITED STATES GRAND PRIX

174 top left and bottom Patrick Tambay, as can be seen in the photograph at bottom, was launched into the air and landed on the Brabham-Alfa Romeo of Niki Lauda immediately after the start of the 1979 USA West GP. Victory at Long Beach went to the Ferrari driven by Gilles Villeneuve, followed by the second Ferrari of Jody Scheckter. Reutemann's black and gold Lotus-Ford (top photograph) started from pole position but was forced out on the 22nd lap with a broken driveshaft.

174 top right The drivers are ready to start their warm-up lap at Watkins Glen, venue of the 1962 United States GP. Joakim Bonnier, in Porsche number 11, almost cuts in front of the Cooper number 21 of Bruce McLaren. Carol de Beaufort in the Porsche number 12 is instead behind.

174 bottom right   The Long Beach circuit hosted (in 1980) the United States West GP (the calendar also featured the United States East GP held at Watkins Glen). The edition that ushered in the new decade was unfortunately marred by an accident

that robbed the Grand Prix circus of one of its protagonists: Clay Regazzoni crashed into a retaining wall when his brakes failed and suffered serious fractures to his legs. The Swiss driver has been confined to a wheelchair ever since.

The New World has played an active part in the Formula 1 circus since the series' inauguration: up until 1961 the Indianapolis 500 was considered a valid round of the World Championship, even though in practice only local drivers tended to compete in the American race.

From 1959 the most celebrated American endurance race gave way to the annual Grands Prix which were held up to 1991. The United States of America is, furthermore, the only country in which three Formula 1 World Championship races have been held in a single season; exceptional circumstances that occurred in 1982 when Grands Prix were held on the Long Beach, Detroit and Las Vegas circuits.

The merit for this enterprise is due to Chris Pook, the organizer of the Long Beach and Las Vegas races: in the case of the gambling town *par excellence*, Pook even managed to have the cars run on a track less than two miles long laid out within the parking lot of Caesar's Palace Hotel. Calling it a circuit would be an insult to the temples of speed such as Le Mans, Silverstone, the Nürburgring or Italy's Monza.

While that triple-bill in the same season was a one-off occurrence, for nine years—between 1976 and 1984—two Grands Prix held in the United States in the same season was the norm. In order to differentiate the two events the organizers named them the United States East for the one held at

Watkins Glen (up to 1980) and then at Detroit (from 1982 to '84) and United States West for the races held at Long Beach (until 1983) and the Dallas street circuit (1984). Sebring, Riverside and Phoenix complete the line-up of circuits that have played host to the F1 circus, many of them well known to European enthusiasts who readily associated them with the famous sports-prototype endurance races or the American NASCAR, CART, Indy and IRL championships.

The American Grands Prix were dominated by the Brazilian Ayrton Senna who won five editions, becoming the man to beat at Detroit and Phoenix. Colin Chapman's Lotus was the leading team, the British cars crossing the line first in 9 editions.

175 top left In this image of the 1982 USA West Grand Prix note the compact "tail" of the group tackling a corner shortly after the start. The records show that Niki Lauda started from pole position and went on to win the race comfortably at the wheel of the McLaren-Ford.

HONOR ROLL

Winners of the United States Grand Prix

YEAR	CIRCUIT	DRIVER	NATIONALITY	CAR
1959	Sebring	Bruce McLaren	New Zealander	Cooper T45-Climax
1960	Riverside	Stirling Moss	British	Lotus 18-Climax
1961	Watkins Glen	Innes Ireland	British	Lotus 21-Climax
1962	Watkins Glen	Jim Clark	British	Lotus 25-Climax
1963	Watkins Glen	Graham Hill	British	BRM P57
1964	Watkins Glen	Graham Hill	British	BRM P261
1965	Watkins Glen	Graham Hill	British	BRM P261
1966	Watkins Glen	Jim Clark	British	Lotus 43-BRM
1967	Watkins Glen	Jim Clark	British	Lotus 49-Ford
1968	Watkins Glen	Jackie Stewart	British	Matra MS10-Ford
1969	Watkins Glen	Jochen Rindt	German	Lotus 49B-Ford
1970	Watkins Glen	Emerson Fittipaldi	Brazilian	Lotus 72-Ford
1971	Watkins Glen	François Cevert	French	Tyrrell 002-Ford
1972	Watkins Glen	Jackie Stewart	British	Tyrrell 005-Ford
1973	Watkins Glen	Ronnie Peterson	Swedish	Lotus 72D-Ford
1974	Watkins Glen	Carlos Reutemann	Argentine	Brabham BT44-Ford
1975	Watkins Glen	Niki Lauda	Austria	Ferrari 312T
1976	Watkins Glen	James Hunt	British	McLaren M23-Ford
1976	Long Beach	Clay Regazzoni	Swiss	Ferrari 312T
1977	Watkins Glen	James Hunt	British	McLaren M23-Ford
1977	Long Beach	Mario Andretti	USA	Lotus 78-Ford
1978	Watkins Glen	Carlos Reutemann	Argentine	Ferrari 312T3
1978	Long Beach	Carlos Reutemann	Argentine	Ferrari 312T3
1979	Watkins Glen	Gilles Villeneuve	Canadian	Ferrari 312T4
1979	Long Beach	Gilles Villeneuve	Canadian	Ferrari 312T4
1980	Watkins Glen	Alan Jones	Australian	Williams FW07B-Ford
1980	Long Beach	Nelson Piquet	Brazilian	Brabham BT49-Ford
1981	Long Beach	Alan Jones	Australian	Williams FW07C-Ford
1981	Las Vegas	Alan Jones	Australian	Williams FW07C-Ford
1982	Long Beach	Niki Lauda	Austrian	McLaren MP4/1B-Ford
1982	Detroit	John Watson	British	McLaren MP4/1B-Ford
1982	Las Vegas	Michele Alboreto	Italian	Tyrrell 011-Ford
1983	Long Beach	John Watson	British	McLaren MP4/1C-Ford
1983	Detroit	Michele Alboreto	Italian	Tyrrell 011-Ford
1984	Dallas	Keke Rosberg	Finnish	Williams FW09-Honda
1984	Detroit	Nelson Piquet	Brazilian	Brabham BT53-BMW
1985	Detroit	Keke Rosberg	Finnish	Williams FW10-Honda
1986	Detroit	Ayrton Senna	Brazilian	Lotus 98T-Renault
1987	Detroit	Ayrton Senna	Brazilian	Lotus 99T-Renault
1988	Detroit	Ayrton Senna	Brazilian	McLaren MP4/4-Honda
1989	Phoenix	Alain Prost	French	McLaren MP4/5-Honda
1990	Phoenix	Ayrton Senna	Brazilian	McLaren MP4/5B-Honda
1991	Phoenix	Ayrton Senna	Brazilian	McLaren MP4/6-Honda

175 right The McLaren-Honda monopoly of the front row of the grid in 1988 was finally broken at the United States GP by Gerhard Berger in the Ferrari. Michele Alboreto (bottom photograph) in the second Ferrari started from the second row but retired on the 45th lap following an accident. Ayrton Senna won the race (in the top photograph he is pictured in the pits), followed by his teammate Alain Prost, frequently seen as his greatest rival.

THE WORLD RALLY CHAMPIONSHIP

Two worlds: one in which absolute speed reigns, generated by four-wheeled rockets lapping pampered asphalt tracks always in the same direction and on the same line; the other dominated by a different, furious driving style and a breed of machine outwardly similar to everyday road cars. The habitat of the latter is composed of improbable by-ways, rough tracks, sheets of ice and desert sands. Each event, each special stage and every kilometer covered is unique.

Enthusiasts of that first world of circuit racing are unlikely to demonstrate the same passion for the second—that of the rallies—and vice-versa. As for

176 bottom This picture from 1906 refers to the dawn of motor racing; the car is a Fiat 60 hp, the driver behind the wheel Salmson, the winner of two Winter Cups.

177 top Carlos Sainz tackling one of the special stages on the 1998 Monte Carlo Rally he went on to win. The car is a works Corolla WRC. In spite of Sainz's contribution to the Japanese firm's cause, Toyota failed to win its first title since 1994.

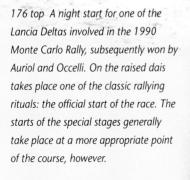

176 top A night start for one of the Lancia Deltas involved in the 1990 Monte Carlo Rally, subsequently won by Auriol and Occelli. On the raised dais takes place one of the classic rallying rituals: the official start of the race. The starts of the special stages generally take place at a more appropriate point of the course, however.

the drivers, rally fans will swear that any half-decent driver competing in the World Rally Championship would beat the socks off the best of his Formula 1 colleagues. This is an area of interminable (and ultimately pointless) arguments, and we would thus prefer to devote ourselves to describing the rally atmosphere itself.

Rallies effectively evolved out of the early 20th century city-to-city raids and represent a valid alternative to those endurance road races in which speed has always been limited due to inherent perils. It is no coincidence that one of the oldest and most famous road races, the Targa Florio—the theatre of bitter Porsche-Ferrari rivalry up to the

1960s—subsequently became a rally.

Independently of the Championship to which it belongs (World, European or National), a rally is an agglomeration of short races known as special stages that each crew (driver and navigator) completes against the clock. The sum of the special stage times is used to compile the standings for each *leg* (for example, those concentrated in a day or night session). Eventually the *overall*, *group* (cars meeting the same regulatory criteria) and *class* (cars with the same cylinder capacities) standings are determined by combining special-stage performance with the least negative points scored in transit between stages.

Rally

and navigators lie behind every corner and they constantly have to bear in mind that within every crowd there is always the occasional irresponsible.

But had these spectators the privilege of completing a special stage at full speed alongside a rally ace they would soon realize just what it takes to launch these machines towards a blind corner placing absolute faith in the voice of the navigator: *"right two, thirty... left two and crest fifty hairpin left thirty..."* . These are moments experienced with a racing pulse in which the smallest error might compromise the outcome of the race, not to mention the safety of the crew and spectators.

In the World Rally Championship these dangers are, theoretically, reduced by more scrupulous organization: night stages are increasingly rare, and special stages are frequently held in inaccessible areas. But the rallying faithful are willing to put up with freezing cold, violent blizzards or baking heat accompanied by clouds of dust and sand.

Another important aspect of the rallying world is the commitment of those manufacturers with suitable platforms on which to build durable, competitive cars that demonstrate the robustness and reliability of their mass-produced brethren in this extreme context. Frequently there are periods of varying duration in which one model or model dominates the sport.

In terms of spectacular entertainment there are few more enthralling sports than rallying, as the images published here testify.

It is possible that during the course of a sequence of special stages the starting order will be revised on the basis of the provisional standings so that slower cars do not delay those that are performing better, but perhaps started a few tens of seconds later.

Rallies are held on ordinary roads, except for those stages in which unsurfaced tracks are used, and herein lies an embarrassing contradiction: the fact that the road is closed to the public does not mean that the cars are authorized to break the normal speed limits. This is why at times the average speeds recorded over the stage are not revealed. Further perplexity is aroused by the behaviour of the

spectators, who insanely insist on watching the action from the most dangerous vantage points imaginable, running grave risks. The marshals may shout themselves hoarse, but no sooner has the control car (the counterpart of which is the "sweeper" bringing up the tail of the caravan), covered the section at full throttle, paving the way for the rest of the competitors, than the spectators converge on the cars' ideal trajectories, ignoring all markers and tapes: there are those who lie on the asphalt, those who dangle their legs over a retaining wall, those who lean out to take a daredevil photograph. Potential and utterly unpredictable dangers for the drivers

UNDILUTED ADVENTURE, BUT MORE ORGANIZATION

The birth of motor rallies is generally recognized as coinciding with the first edition of the Monte Carlo Rally held in 1911. The 1950s nonetheless laid the foundations of modern rallying with the consolidation of the special stage concept, the class subdivisions, the constant presence of navigators and the organized back-up provided by service crews and tire suppliers. A European Drivers' Championship was also instituted in 1953 and up until 1977 was to remain the most prestigious title for rally crews.

The first edition was won by Polenski at the wheel of a Porsche while the fabulous Mercedes 300 SL carried Engel in 1955 and Schock the following year to the continental title. Coltelloni was the only driver to win the title (in 1959) driving cars of two different models, Citroën and Alfa Romeo, in the same season. He drove the celebrated Citroën DS to victory in the Monte Carlo Rally.

Interest in rallying continued to increase in the following decade, although the epic quality and atmosphere of the events remained unchanged. Each rally was a story that unfolded over days and nights of frenetic, grueling activity and sacrifice. The spectators felt obliged to participate in the discomfort suffered by the crews and spent whole nights in the open for the privilege of a glimpse of a pair of rapidly approaching headlamps, trying to

178 top The 96 can be considered as the most important Saab ever to be used in competition. It was driven to victory in the Monte Carlo Rally by the giant Erik Carlsson in 1962 and 1963. The car also won three consecutive editions of the RAC rally between 1960 and 1962 as well as various events in Sweden (as seen in the picture).

guess the car's make on the basis of the cones of light projected into the darkness or to identify the driver on the basis of the engine note alone.

In 1960 the European title returned to Schock, the only driver to have won the European Championship twice before it was transformed into the FIA Cup. Rally drivers became ever more famous, some achieving star status. The Scandinavian contingent was already unbeatable with Timo Mäkinen, Rauno Aaltonen, Pauli Toivonen and above all the likeable Swedish giant Erik Carlsson whose success, including wins in the Monte Carlo, was intimately bound up with that of Saab, a firm that apart from rallying in this period has never displayed any great interest in competition. Carlsson was responsible for the tradition of washing the cars prior to crossing the finishing line; the Swedish company remained close to the blond giant, who was subsequently employed as chief test driver and head of the experimentation department and adopted as the firm's ambassador and figurehead. The car that carried Carlsson to so many victories was the Saab

178 center right Identified by its classic front grille, the 1969 Ford Escort was a rally great, especially during the Seventies. This long-lived model successfully defended the Ford colors up to the late Nineties prior to being replaced by a new European mid-range model, the Focus.

178 center left Bulky but blessed with unexpected agility, a four-door Mercedes 190 saloon tackles the insidious Col de Turini, the focal point of the Monte Carlo Rally. This photograph refers to the 1963 edition, the second in succession won by Sweden's Carlsson in a Saab.

96, a compact, solid saloon powered by an 850 cc engine.

A number of cars became increasingly familiar in this period, an unequivocal sign of the end of improvisation and the establishment of organized teams with cars designed and prepared to tackle at least two competitive seasons at the highest levels. Rallying became a business, and as in other sporting disciplines, technical evolution and success went arm-in-arm with professionalism and strategic planning, factors that themselves demanded resources dedicated to logistics, research and testing. Nonetheless, rallying retained significant elements of self-sacrifice, passion and inspiration.

The cars that dominated the 1960s rallying scene are famous independently of their competition success. This is particularly true of the Mini, which in Morris and Cooper form won three Monte Carlo Rallies and three 1000 Lakes as well as the Swedish, Safari and RAC events to name but the most important; the Porsche 911 and the Citroën DS. Cars that perhaps enjoy a slightly lower profile but which were no less successful are the Ford Cortina and Escort, the Volvo PV544, the Peugeot 404, the Renault Dauphine and R8 Gordini and the Mercedes 200/300SE.

Late in the decade a veritable tornado struck this thoroughbred field, the Lancia Fulvia, which made its debut in 1966 and soon imposed itself on the

178 bottom and 179 left These photographs show the attractive profile of the Porsche berlinetta. In the right photograph the car is tackling a bleak, snow-covered section of the 1965 Monte Carlo Rally (won by Mäkinen in a Mini-Cooper). This car was probably crewed by Böhringer and Wütherich.

179 top right This picture immortalizes the winner of the 1959 Algiers-Cape Town Rally, an event with a particularly arduous route from the Algerian Mediterranean coast to the extreme tip of South Africa, making it more akin to a raid than a true rally. The winner, to the right of the Mercedes 190 D, was Karl Kling, the famous Mercedes driver. His co-driver, to the left in tennis shoes, was Rainer Günzler.

179 center right Porsche had long remained one of the leading and most competitive marques in the Monte Carlo Rally. This photograph shows the Carrera 2 driven by Klauss. In the 1964 edition victory went to another equally historic car, Paddy Hopkirk's Mini-Cooper.

179 bottom right In 1968 the principality's rally marked a brief but intense period of domination by the Porsche 911. One of the marque's leading drivers (in the sports prototype category too) was Vic Elford.

sport in contrast with the relatively modest showings of the Flavia and Flaminia.

The Fulvia was the first element in a trio completed by the Stratos and the Delta that allowed Lancia to became the world's premier rally model up until its late-millennium decline. Attractive in its unique, square-cut bluffness, the Fulvia HF was the first model built specifically as a rally car. The first version was powered by a 1200 cc engine providing the driver with around 90 hp; successive versions featured a 1600 cc power unit developing up to 155 hp. Lancia won its first international title with the Fulvia in 1972 and the pretty coupé's glorious career lasted over 10 years. However, before the Fulvia had had time to demonstrate its full potential, the Ford Escort TC took center stage by winning the two editions of the International Championship for Makes instituted between 1968 and 1969. There was no equivalent for drivers, but the European titles in those years were won by Toivonen in a Porsche 911S and Kallstrom in a Lancia Fulvia HF 1.6.

This takes us into another decade, the 1970s, an era which in our opinion was marked by a fine balance between mechanical features and electronics, inspiration and reasoning, science and empiricism, amateurism and professionalism, the human factor and technology, sport and business, improvisation and calculation. In short, technology was making rapid progress but had yet to disturb man's prerogative over machinery.

With regard to rallies, 1970 saw the institution of the first International Championship for Makes. The Monte Carlo, Swedish, Sanremo-Sestrière, Safari, Austrian Alps, Acropolis and RAC rallies made up the championship season. The first title went to Porsche, with the 911 of course, closely followed by Alpine–Renault, which had given birth to a new star of the first magnitude, the A110. The pattern was repeated the following year and again in 1973. Taking into account the events mentioned above, the most successful driver was the Porsche number one, Waldegård; instead, the title went to the

equally talented French driver Andruet. The gentleman driver Jean-Luc Thérier also enjoyed great success while another of the rallying greats, Stig Blomqvist, was not to win the title until 1984.

In the 1970s and 80s, the battle amongst the drivers was made all the more thrilling by the intense yet thoroughly sporting rivalry between these aces and the rising stars such as Munari, Mikkola, Rörhl, Vatanen and Alén, to mention just a few of the madcap aces who inflamed the world championship in the two decades.

The Alpine reign was interrupted in 1972 by an Italian manufacturer that over the two previous seasons had assumed a rightful place among the giants of international rallying with a series of well deserved placings. Despite coming close on a number of occasions, Lancia had yet to win a major rally. The company founded by a great racing driver Vincenzo Lancia placed the talented Sandro Munari and the navigator Mannucci in a Fulvia HF 1.6, and this proved to be the winning combination as the crew took the opening rally of the season, the Monte Carlo. This was an event that Munari, nicknamed the Drago, was to win on a further two occasions. He had made his debut in the 1000 Lakes in 1965 and always remained faithful to Lancia, both parties enjoying great benefits from the relationship: the European Drivers' Championship in 1973, the International Championship in 1977, and as number one driver on the team that brought four Championship titles back to Turin between 1972 and 1977 (the World Drivers' Championship was not instituted until 1979).

The Fulvia won the championship by a comfortable margin, but this does not mean that it had no rivals. Among its adversaries was the Fiat 124 Spider SS that carried Pinto to the European Drivers' Championship, while others included the tried and trusted Saab 96, the Porsche 911, the Citroën DS and the Ford Escort.

The World Championship for Makes, subdivided into groups, was finally instituted in 1973. Groups 1 and 2 were reserved for saloons while Groups 3 and 4 were for sports cars.

180 top left *Thanks to the performance of the Stratos, Lancia won the International Constructors' title in 1974. Among the drivers of this remarkable car mention must be made of Sandro Munari (a winner at Sanremo and in Canada) and Andruet (winner of the Tour de Corse).*

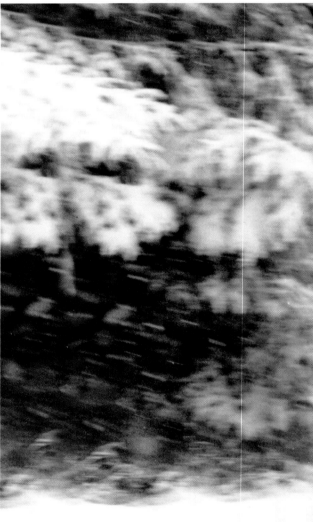

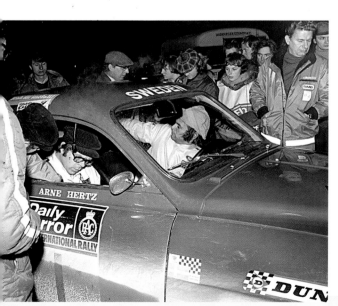

The first manufacturer to inscribe its name on the trophy was Alpine, which entered its A110 with an engine bored out to 1800 cc. As well as a revised car, the team competing under Renault's wing could also count on leading crews that won six of the 13 rounds and also allowed the manufacturer to score no less than two 1-2-3 triumphs (the most spectacular in the Monte Carlo with Mikkola's Ford almost a minute down on the third placed Alpine) and a 1-2 in Portugal. In the midst of this collective Alpine domination mention should be made of the success of Warmbold and Todt's Fiat 124 Spider in the Polish Rally, an extremely arduous event completed by only three of the 62 crews that entered.

Nineteen seventy-four saw another Lancia exploit, this one even more comprehensive, with the World Championship being dominated by the futuristic lines of perhaps the most thrilling car in the history of rallying, the Bertone-bodied, Ferrari Dino-powered Stratos.

The revolutionary wedge-shaped Stratos won the World Championship in 1974, '75 (in combination with the Beta Coupé) and '76. The first prototype, the basis for all future versions, was presented by Bertone, who had already helped revolutionize some of the classic automotive themes with the production of the glorious Miura GT in 1967. In reality, the subsequent versions of the Stratos were themselves mere prototypes

constructed in relatively large numbers for the sole purpose of rallying. It is clear, therefore, that significant investments lay behind the project, the returns from which were to be seen in terms of image-building and marketing potential as well as sporting success.

Experience with GT cars led the Stratos to be equipped with a mid-mounted engine that favored weight distribution and roadholding. It was initially powered by the 1584 cc V4 engine from the Fulvia developing 130 hp, but it was soon decided to adopt a new unit—that of the Ferrari Dino, a 24-valve V6 of 2418 cc developing 270 hp. Reduced weight and a short wheelbase proved to be the Stratos' trump cards.

180 top right Andruet's Alpine–Renault speeding through the night during the 1973 Monte Carlo Rally. The driver won the event in his A110 1800.

180-181 The only Japanese car to make a significant impression in the early Seventies was the Datsun 240Z that won the Safari in 1971. This photograph portrays a climate very different from the heat of Africa, but the Datsun is still doing itself justice.

181 top right The Porsche 911S won the Swedish and Austrian events (with Waldegård at the wheel on both occasions) on its way to clinching the first international Constructors' Championship in 1970.

181 bottom right One of the leading rally cars of the 1970s was Fiat's twincam 124 Spider (note the roof), the international WRC runnerup in 1972 and 1973.

180 center left The RAC Rally, 1971: Waldegård's Porsche 911S tackling a tricky road surface. At the end of the rally Waldegård was sandwiched between Blomqvist (first) and Orrenius (third) in Saab 96s. Porsche was unable to repeat its championship victory of the previous season, finishing third behind Alpine and Saab.

180 bottom left This photograph immortalizes one of the great iron rally pairings. In the foreground is Hertz, the navigator, in the background the driver Blomqvist. The picture was taken on the 1972 RAC Rally and the car is their Saab 96 V4, which finished second. The event was won by an Escort RS 1600.

180 bottom right Toyota mechanics at work during the 1972 RAC Rally. During the 70s the most active Japanese firm was Datsun (now Nissan), but Toyota also participated, albeit with poor results. In the 1990s Toyota, Subaru and Mitsubishi took a stranglehold on the championship, overwhelming the European marques.

1974

Nineteen seventy-four was a bleak year for motor sport due to the oil crisis; three of the most important rallies, the Monte Carlo, the Swedish and the Acropolis were canceled, but the state of grace of the Italian teams was underlined with Fiat's second place in the championship. A Canadian event was included in the calendar for the first time, the Rideau Lakes Rally (the first US event, the Press On Regardless, had featured the previous year).

The final championship table for that year showed a Japanese name, Toyota, in fifth place with a best placing of third in Canada. The car, as is traditional with Japanese models, carried a name that was set to run and run, becoming a veritable

obsession for its rivals towards the end of the century: the Celica.

The same pattern was repeated in 1975 with Lancia winning the championship and Fiat finishing as runner-up. The internecine rivalry between the two Italian models served as a stimulus rather than dispersing energy and created a kind of cushion between them and their adversaries. Despite never winning a rally outright, the Beta Coupé accumulated points that, while not indispensable for the conquest of the championship title, served to distance Lancia from Fiat which was still running the 124 Spider, now aggressively prepared by Abarth.

Despite having 25 crews in the Tour de Corse,

Alpine could manage no better than second place in any event that season and eventually finished third in the championship behind Fiat.

Lancia's supremacy in 1976 reached embarrassing proportions: four wins out of 10 events with two 1-2-3s (Monte Carlo and Sanremo) and a 1-2 (Tour de Corse). Another Japanese firm now began to make a name for itself with Mitsubishi managing to place three Colt Lancers on the podium in the grueling Safari Rally. Fiat withdrew temporarily but Opel began to mount a challenge, its Asconas and Kadetts fighting it out with the Ford Escort RS and the Saab 96-99 for the minor placings. In spite of having secured the services of local expert

182 top right The first International Constructors' Championship rose from the ashes of the European Championship in 1970. The series immediately saw a classic battle between the Porsches and the Alpine Renaults. Originally designed for hillclimbs, the A110 was immediately competitive even on very demanding routes. Runner-up in 1970, Alpine won the title the following year and again in 1973. The A110 was powered by a highly tuned 1600 cc production engine.

182 bottom right An evocative image of the 1975 edition of the Sanremo Rally. The car portrayed is an Alpine– Renault A110 with an engine enlarged to 1800 cc. The rally taking its name from the resort on the Ligurian Riviera, in reality snakes also through the central Italian regions of Tuscany and Umbria. There are many opportunities to admire the area's famous medieval towns.

182 top left A night shot of the Lancia Stratos of Munari and Mannucci. The photograph was taken during the 1974 Sanremo Rally won by a Stratos—as was the championship title.

182 center left Anything goes, as long as you reach the finish. Here the Stratos HF has abandoned its engine cover so as to stay in the race. The event is the RAC Rally of 1975—not one to remember for Lancia, given that none of its crews finished in the top five.

182 bottom left The King of the Safari, Shekker Metha, is seen here tackling a watercourse during the 1975 edition. Note the spotlights mounted high on the body—in other words, as far from the water as possible.

Mikkola, Toyota's best result was third place in the Finnish 1000 Lakes.

Nineteen seventy-seven was marked by two significant events: the institution of the FIA Drivers' Cup, predecessor of the World Championship title, and the abdication of the Stratos in favor of the Fiat 131 Abarth. At the end of the year the points scored by the former queen were worth a disappointing fifth place overall. Munari was, however, consoled by winning the FIA title that took into account points obtained in the World Championship events and the European Drivers' Championship.

The Fiat 131 made an immediate impact with five victories out of 11 rallies and four second places,

finishing equal at the end of the season. This represented Opel's swan-song as the following season it failed to make the podium and had to wait until 1982 before it could make a significant challenge again.

Although it remained competitive, the Fiat 131's crown was to be snatched by the Ford Escort RS which carried its number one driver, Björn Waldegård, to the first World Drivers' Championship just a single point ahead of his Finnish teammate, Hannu Mikkola. Fiat's Alén was third. From a technological point of view mention must also be made of the Saab 99's victory in the Swedish Rally— the first major rally victory for a turbocharged car.

The hugely successful Fiat 131 still had plenty in reserve and the following season it brought the Italian manufacturer another title, outstripping Datsun/Nissan and Ford. This time it was Rörhl and Alén who, in spite of their personal rivalry, took their revenge as a team, Rörhl winning the Drivers' Championship from Mikkola, who drove first the Escort and then the Mercedes 500SLC before concluding the season again behind the wheel of the Ford. The reigning champion Waldegård was third. Rörhl was by now considered by many to be the most efficient rally driver of all time, inclined to exaggerate in word but never (or hardly ever) in deed at the wheel.

a one-two-three and a one-two. The team could count on a trio of outstanding drivers, Alén, Andruet (highly successful with Alpine–Renault and Lancia) and Bacchelli.

An era drew to a close in which the competitiveness of the cars and their reliability had grown enormously as a corollary of the massive investments made by the European car manufacturers.

In 1978 Marku Alén, the winner of the FIA Drivers' Cup, was flanked by another great driver (and future World Champion in 1980 and '82), Walter Rörhl. Together they took the Fiat 131 to the World Championship, thus extending the list of titles won by Italian models. Behind Fiat there was a passionate struggle between Ford and Opel, the two

183 top The 1979 Monte Carlo Rally. The snow has finally cleared but the surface is still wet and slippery, obliging the driver of this Porsche 911 Carrera to apply lavish opposite lock.

183 center The winner of the 1979 Sanremo Rally competed simply as "Tony" but was actually Fassana, later to become a successful entrepreneur and one of the largest auto dealers in Europe. The car is a Stratos HF.

183 bottom The backbreaking Acropolis Rally in Greece. Immortalized here are the 1979 winners, Waldegård and Thorszelius with their Escort RS (the pair had already won the event two years earlier). In the rally championship cars and drivers must be prepared to tackle extremely varied surfaces, from snow to beaten earth, from mud to shale. The drivers change their style of driving while the suspension set-up, tires and shielding of the cars are modified even during the event itself.

A number of former stars were eclipsed in the 1981 season as along with Fiat, Ford too failed to make an impression and Opel was even further behind, with Mercedes well out of the picture. New forces arose to take their place, among them the ephemeral Lotus-powered Talbot-Sunbeam (that to everyone's surprise won the World Championship title), and Renault, which took the Monte Carlo Rally with the R5 Turbo. Datsun prepared and entered the Violet which earned the Japanese manufacturer a fine second place overall. The most significant event of the season, however, was the debut of the Audi Quattro. The first four-wheel-

drive car to win a World Championship event, the Swedish Rally with Mikkola (who was also the first non-Swedish driver to win the event), the Audi was also triumphant at Sanremo, where Michelle Mouton became the first woman to win a World Championship rally.

The Audi Quattro was a four-wheel-drive car powered by a 2.1-liter, five-cylinder engine developing no less than 300 hp and in 1982 it destroyed its adversaries (only the Opel Ascona 400 put up any serious resistance). The Drivers' Championship went not to one of the Audi crews (Blomqvist, Mikkola and Mouton) however, but to Rörhl, who thus brought some reflected glory to the Opel Ascona and just managed to prevent Mouton's becoming the first female World Champion.

From this season the regulations were radically revised with the championship subdivided into three Groups distinguished by letters rather than numbers: Group N was for unmodified four-seater production cars built and sold in at least 5000 units,

184 top left The second World Champion driver, Walter Rörhl, one of the all-time greats, is portrayed here in an almost aerial shot during the 1980 Acropolis Rally. On this occasion he finished fifth in his Fiat Abarth 131. He was preceded by three other great names, Vatanen,

Salonen, and Alén. That year Waldegård and Mikkola were also challenging for the title. The early Eighties saw what was probably the greatest ever concentration of rallying talent, a situation similar to that which developed in Grand Prix racing in the Thirties and Fifties.

184 bottom left This photograph shows Markku Alén aboard his Fiat 131. The Fiat Group followed up the success of the Lancia Stratos era with a hat-trick of championship wins for the robust 131 in Abarth form. The world titles came in 1977, 1978 and 1980; Alén also won the 1978 FIA Drivers' Cup.

Group A was for four-seater touring cars built in 5000 examples in 12 months with modifications to the engine and other mechanical parts but no changes to the bodywork; and Group B was reserved for sports cars built in at least 200 units with modifications to the engine and coachwork being permitted. Subsequent events, some of them tragic, led to the banning of the over-1600 cc class Group B machines, considered to be ungovernable instruments of death.

This brings us to the thrilling 1983 season that promised to be as profitable for Audi as the previous one had been. Instead, the predictions were immediately overturned by Lancia, whose 037 scored a 1-2 victory in the Monte Carlo Rally, Rörhl winning from Alén with the Audi Quattros of Blomqvist and Mikkola only third and fourth. The Ingolstadt firm was not prepared to give up without a fight, however, and in the successive Swedish Rally Mikkola, Blomqvist, Lampi and Mouton came home first, second, third and fourth. Outright war had been declared between the Audis and Lancias.

In the third round of the championship season

Metha taking the place of Lampi, staged a fight-back and recorded another 1-2-3-4 triumph in what was fast becoming the most enthralling season ever.

Audi were on form in Finland with Mikkola and Blomqvist scoring a one-two victory, while on home turf in the Sanremo Rally Lancia came up trumps, colonizing the podium with Alén, Rörhl and another promising young Italian, Attilio Bettega (yet another Italian—one soon to join the élite—finished fifth with another 037: Miki Biasion). Both Audi and Lancia continued to suffer from *mal d'Africa* and avoided the Ivory Coast, leaving the way clear for Waldegård to drive the Toyota Celica Turbo to victory. Audi's 1-2 in the RAC Rally was in vain as Lancia interrupted the German model's domination by winning the championship with 128 points, 118 of which were valid, to Audi's 122, 116 of which were valid—a margin of just two points.

Audi nonetheless obtained considerable satisfaction from the Drivers' title won by Hannu Mikkola, a tireless member of the awesome group of "Flying Finns" who managed to defeat probably the greatest concentration of rallying talent ever

seen: Walter Rörhl and Markku Alén tied for second followed by Stig Blomqvist, Michelle Mouton, Vatanen, Bettega, Lampi, Metha and Eklund. The World Rally Championship was enjoying one of its greatest periods with technologically exceptional cars and a group of well-matched drivers among whom it was truly difficult to identify a clear leader.

From a technical point of view, the Lancia victory showed that a good two-wheel-drive car (the 037) could still get the better of a 4x4 (the Quattro), even in a loose-surface rally such as the Sanremo. Power outputs grew in the meantime to well beyond 400 horsepower.

in Portugal, Audi floored Lancia once again with a 1-2 victory, Mikkola and Mouton leading home three 037s (Rörhl, Alén and the Italian Adartico Vudafieri). The two sworn enemies then called a cease-fire with Audi well ahead in the championship standings. The Safari Rally this time went to Vatanen in the Opel Ascona, the driver as ever reluctant to play a mere supporting role. Immediately afterwards the scene shifted to Corsica, the setting for the 037's first great epic with four crews filling the first four places. While in Monte Carlo Alén and Rörhl had finished first and second respectively; in Corsica the placings were reversed, and the dance continued in Greece, too, in the Acropolis Rally.

At this point the championship situation was as follows: Lancia, three victories, three seconds and two thirds; Audi, two victories, three seconds and four thirds. The rally circus then crossed the globe to race in New Zealand where Lancia again emerged victorious, and in Argentina where Audi's three musketeers (plus Madame Mouton), with

184 right New Zealand, 1980: despite this off with his Mercedes SLC, Waldegård did not lose heart; the officials managed to get the car back on the road and the driver went on to finish the event in fifth place.

185 left Monte Carlo, 1981: the Porsche 911s were no longer the cars to beat but were still worth watching, especially out of the hairpins.

185 top right Should rallies serve to demonstrate the robustness of the cars? If this is true, there's no reason why this battered Triumph should not continue on its way, especially as it was competing in its home event, the 1980 RAC Rally.

185 center right, top photograph The 1981 World Rally Champion, Ari Vatanen, at the wheel of his Escort RS. Ford actually won the title during the transitional 1979 season when Vatanen was competing with a Japanese Datsun.

185 center right, bottom photograph Walter Rörhl powers through a tight descending hairpin with a gravel surface. This was on one of the special stages that from Sanremo head into the Tuscan and Umbrian hills in central Italy. The photograph shows an Opel Ascona competing in the 1982 edition won by Blomqvist with an Audi Quattro.

185 bottom A historic picture portraying the 1982 RAC Rally, the last championship round. The event was won by Mikkola and Hertz in an Audi but the most important fact was that the German marque conquered its first World Championship title. The drivers' title went to Rörhl with the attractive and talented Michelle Mouton becoming the first woman to finish runnerup in the WRC.

186 left Audi went into the 1984 edition of the Rally New Zealand with four wins under its belt and the championship there for the taking. Stig Blomqvist came home five minutes ahead of Alén's Lancia and won the driver's title from the reigning champion Mikkola by 21 points. The Lancia Rally 037 was vastly powerful and constructed as an out-and-out competition machine. The Audi Quattro instead had close ties with the production coupé of the same name and the less exotic but very popular GT.

186-187 center right The 1000 Lakes, 1985: Timo Salonen drove the Peugeot 205 T16 E2 to victory in the year the marque won the Constructors' Championship. The small Peugeot intervened in the epic struggle between Lancia and Audi, demonstrating that a compact car could compete at the highest levels. Observing the works 205 (a car very different from the production model and recognizable by its rear intakes) in action one could see the fluidity and naturalness with which it tackled the tightest bends with a degree of balance that the Delta, for example, lacked, its driver being forced to juggle the throttle to control the enormous output.

186 bottom A night drive for Walter Röhrl in the Quattro. Note the triangular disposition of the supplementary lights set between the fixed headlamps. Only by spectating at a special stage illuminated by the cars' powerful lights alone can one gain a true impression of the innate danger and appeal of on-the-limits night driving.

187 top left A difficult section for the Peugeot 205 T16 E2 that with victory in the 1986 RAC managed to keep its championship rival the Lancia Delta at bay. On this occasion the RAC event was not the last rally of the season, an honor that went to the Olympus Rally in the United States.

The Audi-Lancia duel was repeated in 1984 with Röhrl joining Blomqvist and Mikkola in Germany. In his first event in a four-wheel-drive car, Röhrl scored his fourth win in the Monte Carlo Rally (three of which were consecutive). Lancia compensated for the loss of Röhrl by promoting Miki Biasion who thus flanked Bettega and Alén. Audi went into the championship with all guns blazing, winning the first three rounds. In spite of Lancia's best efforts with the 037, the team was 12 points adrift of its rival at the end of the season. Blomqvist took the drivers' title.

Another car joined the leading pair, the Peugeot 205 T16, which was soon to bring considerable success to a French model that had previously concentrated on extreme events such as the Safari Rally. Peugeot's excellent debut—the 205 won three of the last four events in 1984—promised a more

186 top right Attilio Bettega posing alongside his Lancia Rally 037 in 1984. The talented Italian driver was killed at the age of 32 when he crashed into a tree around a kilometer after the start of the fourth special stage of the 1985 Tour de Corse. Maurizio Perissinot, his navigator, was unhurt. Bettega was the best and most experienced of the Italian drivers and like the other members of the Lancia team was waiting for the debut of the heir to the 037, the Delta Integrale S4 that arrived in time for the last event of the season, the RAC Rally. It was ironic that he should die marking time in a transitional season.

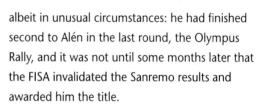

187 top right The 1986 Monte was as usual the opening round of the championship season. The driver portrayed is Kankkunen who finished only fifth but was champion at the end of the season with Peugeot, the marque repeating its success of the previous year.

187 bottom right The reigning World Champion, Timo Salonen during the 1986 Monte Carlo Rally: at the wheel of his Peugeot 205 he is staging a thrilling but ultimately futile attempt to catch Toivonen's Lancia Delta S4 on virtually its official debut after its outing in the RAC in 1985. At the end of the year, however, the Constructors' title remained with Peugeot.

open championship for '85 following the Lancia-Audi domination of recent years.

The promise was immediately maintained with the conquest of the championship title. The 205 was a compact, agile and very well balanced car that could be effortlessly drifted through the special stages with ample safety margins. In 1985 the Peugeot works cars were entrusted to Salonen and Vatanen. By the end of the season the former was streets ahead of all his rivals while the latter set the remarkable record of being the first driver to win five consecutive rallies (between 1984 and '85) valid for the Constructors' Championship.

Toyota also put up a serious challenge, Kankunnen driving the Celica to two victories and fifth place overall in the championship, signalling his arrival among the group of championship contenders. Peugeot were regular winners, especially in the first half of the season, and this relegated Rörhl, Blomqvist or Biasion to second place, the latter unable to take the aging 037 to a last victory. Lancia only got its breath back in the final round in Great Britain, the RAC Rally being won by Toivonen with Alén second in a brand new car of some promise. This was the S4 version of the Delta, the car that was to star in the third Lancia era, the longest and most profitable.

Lancia had little to cheer about in 1985, however, as Bettega was killed when his car went off the road during the Tour de Corse. The 037 burst into flames and burnt out completely in just a few seconds. Vatanen was also involved in a terrible accident in Argentina and spent a number of days in critical condition before making a recovery. It was no coincidence that these tragic events coincided with escalating power outputs that went beyond the 500 hp threshold (in the same period Formula 1 cars were producing in the region of 700-800 hp).

The time was not yet ripe for the Delta, and the extremely agile 205 won the title again in 1986. This time, however, Kankunnen was driving for the French model and took the drivers' championship,

albeit in unusual circumstances: he had finished second to Alén in the last round, the Olympus Rally, and it was not until some months later that the FISA invalidated the Sanremo results and awarded him the title.

Looking at the results obtained by the highly talented Markku Alén, it is both sad and surprising that he never won a World Championship title, apart from the second edition of the FIA International Cup. He was dogged by ill-fortune, twice finishing runner-up and three times third.

Returning to the 1986 championship, the theme was again the Peugeot-Lancia rivalry even though the build-up to the season had promised much more: Citroën, Ford, MG and Audi were apparently preparing technologically advanced cars designed to take Group B (the most important) by storm; this time, however, the promises were not maintained. The 205 and the Delta fought it out for the title, but once again the championship was marred by tragedy. In Portugal, Santos in a Ford Escort RS200 ploughed into the crowd, killing three spectators, while Corsica was again disastrous for the Lancia drivers: Toivonen and Cresto were killed after their Delta crashed and exploded. The time had come to restrict excessive performance because rallying, as spectacular as it may have been, should never have had to pay such a high price.

It was thus decided that from 1987 Group B cars with cylinder capacities of over 1600 cc would be outlawed. This meant the end for the incredible Lancia Delta S4, whose vast power output was difficult to harness effectively but which was unbeatable where outright performance counted over agility.

1984 1986

POWER OUTPUTS ARE TONED DOWN

188 top right The Costa Smeralda Rally in Sardinia is a non-championship but extremely well known event (the driver portrayed is Kankkunen) which is prevented from representing Italy in the championship calendar by the Sanremo Rally. The neighbouring island of Corsica hosts perhaps the most dangerous rally, the Tour de Corse, famed for the sheer drops lining the high-speed special stages.

188 top left Biasion tackling a demanding section on the 1988 Olympus Rally which he won at the wheel of a Lancia Delta Integrale. That year the pairing was to win the World Championship. The Olympus Rally was held in the northern state of Washington, but in North America the sport has never attracted much attention. The 1988 edition of the Olympus Rally was in fact the last of three.

188-189 Carlos Sainz at the wheel of the Toyota Celica GT4 during the 1990 Safari Rally which he finished in fourth place. In spite of missing out on victory here, the Spaniard succeeded in ruining Lancia's party by depriving it of the Drivers' Championship, even though the firm won the constructors' title. Sainz got the better of drivers of the caliber of Auriol, Biasion and Kankkunen.

The 1987 season thus opened with new or modified cars, or rather re-modified to bring them closer to the original production models, and was anything but boring. Kankunnen set a record as the first driver to conquer the Drivers' Championship twice. This time he was at the wheel of a Lancia Delta HF Integrale. His teammates were Biasion and Alén and both were in the running for the title up to the last round, the RAC Rally. Lancia's adversaries could put up little resistance although Mazda did win its first rally with Salonen in the 323 and a BMW won in Corsica. Mikkola, then still at Audi, became the first driver to take part in 100 championship rallies and attempted to contain the all-conquering Lancias at the wheel of the Audi 200.

The Italians were able to celebrate Lancia's success but were anxious to see one of their fellow countrymen take the Drivers' Championship for the first time after Munari's international title. They did not have to wait long, Miki Biasion winning the Championship in 1988 with no fewer than five victories, leaving his veteran teammate Alén 31 points adrift. Beyond the Lancia camp there was little of interest with the Ford Sierra Cosworth that had overtaken the aging Audis never managing better than third place.

Lancia continued to dominate and the Delta's third Constructors' and third Drivers' Champion–ships arrived the following season with Biasion again

The Delta was still in fine fettle and gave no signs of loosening its grip on the championship in 1991 or 1992. The team thus notched up its fifth and sixth constructors' titles and Kankkunen once again topped the table of drivers with the most world titles to his name. After his championship win in 1990, Sainz for his part proved his worth with a second place in 1991 and a second title in 1992, as ever at the wheel of his trusty Celica, which became the first Japanese car to win the Monte Carlo Rally. Biasion finished fourth overall in both the '91 and '92 seasons but failed to score a single victory.

The Delta, first in HF 4WD and then Integrale form, filled its trophy cabinet to the bursting point. Its six golden years can be summed up as follows: 47 victories out of 79 World Championship rallies (including those in which it did not take part), 16 one-twos, 12 one-two-threes and a record-breaking 10 wins in 11 events in 1988. This record is unique in the history of rallying and one that is unlikely to be broken.

189 top In this evocative shot from 1991 one can barely recognize the car being driven by Kankkunen, a Delta Integrale. That year the Finnish driver conquered the third of the four drivers' titles that make him the "Fangio" of rallying. Kankkunen has also finished second overall once and third three times in his fantastic career. Sainz has won more rallies, but has "only" two titles to his credit.

189 center The 1990 Sanremo Rally, an exciting edition for Sainz seen in this photograph. The rally was won by his rival Auriol, but third place and victory in the RAC Rally was sufficient for the Spaniard to take the world title.

189 bottom Despite the incisiveness of Carlos Sainz, seen here at the wheel of his Toyota Celica in Argentina in 1992, Lancia retained the Constructors' Championship. The driver's title none-theless went to Sainz with the Lancia driver Kankkunen second, a trick he had already pulled off in 1990.

first, thus joining Kankkunen in the rallying Hall of Fame. Alex Florio's second place completed the Italian triumph over the "Flying Finns".

Lancia triumphed yet again in 1990, but this time the team had to settle for the constructors' title only. The Drivers' Championship was instead won by Carlos Sainz in the Toyota Celica, beating out Lancia's new driver Didier Auriol. However, as Cesare Florio, the deus ex machina of the Lancia team, had prophesied, this was to be the era of the Mediterranean drivers.

1987 1992

Who could possibly defeat the compact Italian saloon? The answer was to be seen in the final results of the championships between 1989 and 1992, with Toyota an ever-present second and Mitsubishi and Subaru hard on its heels.

The new rallying panorama featured a heavy and highly successful Japanese presence that brought the first championship title back to Tokyo in 1993. It was Toyota, who "poached" Kankkunen and Auriol from Lancia, who finally deposed the Delta, forcing it back into an ignominious final fourth place. A degree of opposition to the Toyota Celica Turbo 4WD was provided by the Ford Escort RS Cosworth, while the drivers' title was won relatively easily by Juha Kankkunen (his fourth). The following year, however, Kankkunen was displaced by his Toyota teammate Auriol, while the revived Sainz finished as runner-up at the wheel of the highly competitive Subaru Impreza. Ford had an excellent team with Biasion and Delecour but failed to win the title.

In 1995 a reduced edition of eight championship rounds went to Subaru with the Impreza 555 WRX, the Scot Colin McRae becoming the first Briton to win the World Rally Championship title. Mitsubishi also put up a fine showing with the third version of the Lancer Evolution. While always competitive, the Escort was again to miss out on the title in the seasons that followed.

The Celica disappeared from the rankings after Toyota took an enforced 12-month sabbatical from rallying. The disqualification was due to serious irregularities that had been discovered with the team's engines, a humiliation for Toyota Team Europe which had hitherto been one of the Championship's leading players.

Nineteen ninety-six saw the emergence of another great driver, Tommi Mäkinen, who finally restored the reputation of the once unbeatable Scandinavian drivers. Mitsubishi had entrusted a works car to Mäkinen the previous year and the young driver had not disappointed. The constructors' title again went to Subaru whose

three wins in nine rallies were sufficient to maintain its grip on the trophy, something it again managed in 1997 with the continually modified Impreza. Mäkinen won the drivers' title in both '96 and '97, putting himself forward as the Kankkunen (still competing in 1997 with Ford) of the new Millennium. This impression was confirmed in 1998 when he completed a hat-trick of championship victories, his Mitsubishi team this time taking the Constructors' Championship with the Lancer Evolution IV.

The epic struggles between Audi and Lancia, the Minis, Alpine, Porsche and Peugeot are now long gone, with the Italian, English, German and French cars resting after decades of grueling effort in snow, ice, sand and dust. The World Rally Championship had thus become a primarily Japanese affair, and only Ford (with the Focus) and Peugeot (with the 206) look as if they might once again challenge the Asian models' supremacy.

191 top Franco Cunico, a talented Italian driver who has never managed to establish himself among the World Rally Championship élite, gained great satisfaction from winning the Sanremo Rally: he is seen here celebrating victory in 1993 together with his navigator Evangelisti. The car is an Escort RS Cosworth.

191 center The Safari offers continual surprises for cars and drivers. What is hidden beneath the water and mud can never be known. It is a form of blind race in which good fortune is indispensable even for the most talented. The photograph shows a Toyota Celica GT4 whose crew was formed by Duncan and Mumro during the Safari Rally of 1993.

1993 1998

191 bottom Mäkinen, the three-time World Champion (as at late 1998) in Australia in 1996. Rather than a ford this would seem to be more of a navigable river. The car is a Mitsubishi Lancer Evo III. The first edition of the Rally Australia was held in 1989 while that of neighbouring New Zealand had long figured in the calendar. Considering the vastness of the Australian territory, the rally can be said to be staged in a fairly restricted area, to the south of Perth, the capital of Western Australia, one of the most desolate and difficult parts of the country. The coastal region is one of a rare beauty, with a spring-like climate all year long. The rally is generally held in September (that is, the region's early spring).

HONOR ROLL

The Constructors' World Rally Championship

Year	Car	Crews*	Constructor
1968**	Escort TC	Clark-Porter, Mikkola-Järvi	Ford
1969**	20M, Escort TC	Hilliard-Aird, Mikkola-Järvi	Ford
1970***	911, 911S	Waldegård-Helmer, Waldegård-Thorszelius	Porsche
1971***	A110	Andersson-Hertz, Andersson-Nash	Alpine-Renault
		Andersson-Stone, Nicolas-Todt	
1972**	Fulvia HF	Ballestrieri- Bernacchini, Munari-Mannucci	Lancia
1973	A110	Andruet-"Biche", Nicolas-Vial	Alpine-Renault
		Therier-Jaubert, Therier-Delferrier	
1974	Stratos	Andruet-"Biche", Munari-Mannucci	Lancia
1975	Stratos	Munari-Mannucci, Darniche-Mahè	Lancia
		Waldegård-Thorszelius	
1976	Stratos	Munari-Maiga, Waldegård-Thorszelius	Lancia
1977	131 Abarth	Alén-Kivimäki, Andruet-Delferrier	Fiat
		Bacchelli-Rossetti	
1978	131 Abarth	Alén-Kivimäki, Rörhl-Geistdörfer	Fiat
1979	Escort RS	Mikkola-Hertz, Waldegård-Thorszelius	Ford
1980	131 Abarth	Alén-Kivimäki, Rörhl-Geistdörfer	Fiat
1981	Lotus 2.2 Gr. 2	Frequelin-Todt	Talbot
1982	Quattro Gr. 4	Blomqvist-Cederberg, Mikkola-Hertz	Audi
		Mouton-Pons	
1983	Rally Gr. B	Alén-Kivimäki, Rörhl-Geistdörfer	Lancia
1984	Quattro Gr. B	Blomqvist-Cederberg, Rörhl-Geistdörfer	Audi
1985	205 Turbo 16 Gr. B	Salonen-Harjanne, Vatanen-Harryman	Peugeot
1986	205 Turbo 16 Gr. B	Kankkunen-Piironen, Saby-Fauchille	Peugeot
		Salonen-Harjanne	
1987	Delta 4WD	Alén -Kivimäki, Biasion-Siviero	Lancia
		Kankkunen-Piironen, Witmann-Pattermann	
1988	Delta Integrale	Alén -Kivimäki, Biasion-Cassina	Lancia
		Biasion-Siviero, Recalde-Del Buono	
		Saby-Fauchille	
1989	Delta Integrale	Auriol-Occelli, Biasion-Siviero	Lancia
		Recalde-Del Buono	
1990	Delta Integrale 16V	Auriol-Occelli, Biasion-Siviero	Lancia
1991	Delta 16V	Auriol-Occelli, Kankkunen-Piironen	Lancia
1992	HF Integrale	Aghini-Farnocchia, Auriol-Occelli	Lancia
		Kankkunen-Piironen	
1993	Celica 4WD	Auriol-Occelli, Jonsson-Backman	Toyota
		Kankkunen-Giraudet, Kankkunen-Grist	
		Kankkunen-Piironen	
1994	Celica 4WD	Auriol-Occelli, Duncan-Williamson	Toyota
		Kankkunen-Grist, Radstrom-Backman	
1995	Impreza WRX	Fujimoto-Hertz, Liatti-Alessandrini	Subaru
		McRae-Ringer, Sainz-Moya	
1996	Impreza WRX	McRae-Ringer	Subaru
1997	Impreza WRC	Eriksson-Parmander, Liatti-Pons	Subaru
		McRae-Grist	
1998	Lancer Evo IV	Mäkinen-Mannisenmäki, Burns-Reid	Mitsubishi
			Carisma GT

* Crews who won at least one Championship rally
** European Championship for Makes
*** International Championship for Makes

192 top The works Mitsubishi Lancer entrusted to Mäkinen and Burns tackles a difficult section. The team won the 1998 WRC Constructors' Championship, with Mäkinen additionally securing the drivers' title.

192 center Mäkinen and Manninsmäki celebrate victory in the 1998 Sanremo Rally with the Mitsubishi Lancer Evo that broke the Subaru stranglehold on the title lasting from 1995.

192 bottom The Toyota Corolla WRC of Sainz and Moya failed 500 meters from the finish of the 1998 RAC Rally.

Makes That Have Won The Most Championship Rallies

Lancia	72
Toyota	39
Ford	32
Mitsubishi	24
Subaru	22
Fiat	21
Audi, Peugeot	18
Datsun/Nissan	9
Alpine-Renault	6

Drivers Who Have Won The Most Championship Rallies

Sainz	22
Kankkunen	21
Alén	19
Auriol, Mikkola	18
Biasion	17
Mäkinen, McRae, Waldegård	16
Rörhl	14

Navigators Who Have Won Most Championship Rallies

Moya	22
Harjanne	21
Kivimaki	19
Hertz	17
Occelli, Siviero	16
Piironen	14
Geistdörfer, Thorszelius	13
Cederberg	10

193 top Auriol crossing a ford during the 1998 Safari Rally in which he was to finish fourth, 14 minutes down on the winner Burns with the Mitsubishi. The event is remembered for the performance of Vatanen who would have finished second had he not intentionally incurred a penalty to allow his teammate Kankkunen to pass him.

193 bottom Bruno Thiry, on Ford Escort WRC, Ford's lead driver replacing Sainz, tackling a classic Monte Carlo stage in 1998. He was to finish sixth overall.

HONOR ROLL

The World Drivers' Championship

YEAR	DRIVER	NAVIGATOR	CAR
1977	S. Munari (ITA)*	Maiga, Sodano	Lancia Stratos
1978	M. Alén (FIN)*	Kivimäki	Fiat 131 Abarth
1979	B. Waldegaard (SWE)	Billstam, Thorszelius	Ford Escort RS
1980	W. Rörhl (GER)	Geistdörfer	Fiat 131 Abarth
1981	A. Vatanen (FIN)	Richards	Ford Escort RS
1982	W. Rörhl (GER)	Geistdörfer	Opel Ascona 400
1983	H. Mikkola (FIN)	Hertz	Audi Quattro
1984	S. Blomqvist (SWE)	Cederberg	Audi Quattro
1985	T. Salonen (FIN)	Harjanne	Peugeot 205 T16
1986	J. Kankkunen (FIN)	Piironen	Peugeot 205 T16
1987	J. Kankkunen (FIN)	Piironen	Lancia Delta 4WD
1988	M. Biasion (ITA)	Cassina, Siviero	Lancia Delta Integrale
1989	M. Biasion (ITA)	Siviero	Lancia Delta Integrale 16V
1990	C. Sainz (ESP)	Moya	Toyota Celica 4WD
1991	J. Kankkunen (FIN)	Piironen	Lancia Delta Integrale 16V
1992	C. Sainz (ESP)	Moya	Toyota Celica 4WD
1993	J. Kankkunen (FIN)	Giraudet, Grist, Piironen	Toyota Celica 4WD
1994	D. Auriol (FRA)	Occelli	Toyota Celica 4WD
1995	C. McRae (UK)	Ringer	Subaru Impreza WRX
1996	T. Mäkinen (FIN)	Harjanne	Mitsubishi Lancer Evo III
1997	T. Mäkinen (FIN)	Harjanne	Mitsubishi Lancer Evo IV
1998	T. Mäkinen (FIN)	Mannisenmäki	Mitsubishi Lancer Evo IV/V

* *FIA Pilots Cup*

THE MONTE CARLO RALLY

Leaving aside any discussion on the meaning of the term "rally" and its modern interpretation, the Monte Carlo Rally can be considered the oldest example of this type of event in the world. The first edition was held in 1911 and was born out of an idea from a leading lawyer, Gabriel Vialon, that was taken up by the British specialist periodical *The Motor*. It would appear that behind the rally was the desire to create an élite automobile club in Monaco capable of organizing automotive events on dry land that could compete with the then-famous "Monte Carlo Week," a competitive regatta devoted to motorboats.

Originally any kind of car could compete in the Monte Carlo Rally, irrespective of its cylinder capacity. The event had the added complication that there was no common starting point; the competitors instead converged on Monaco from all over Europe. The final results took into account the distances covered, presupposing that the average speed should be 30 kph (18.6 mph) and that the event should last a week. The state of the vehicle at the finish also contributed to the number of points scored, as did the number of passengers carried.

Twenty-three crews took part in the first edition, which was won by Henry Rougier, who covered 900 km in 28 hours and 10 minutes aboard a 25-hp Turcat-Méry. The last edition before the First World War was held in 1914 and was marked by the introduction of the concept of the *special stage;* in this case a timed climb of the Col du Braus. Since

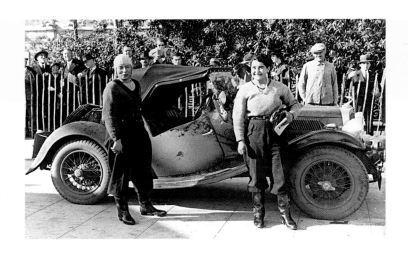

194 top In the 1920s women began to experience motor racing firsthand. The Monte Carlo Rally accepted the entries of women drivers, this photograph showing Madame Siko and Mademoiselle Des Forest alongside their small Triumph at the 14th edition of the event.

194 center At the start of the '92 season Carlos Sainz commenced his assault on the title with a second place in Monte Carlo behind Auriol.

194 bottom left The Monte Carlo Rally of 1995 saw this Toyota literally sliding on the icy asphalt. In spite of the best efforts of the other participating teams, the event was won by Sainz and Moya in a Subaru Impreza WRX.

then (and up to the late 1950s) the Monte Carlo Rally existed as an autonomous event thanks to its very special appeal that went well beyond its sporting characteristics. As with other more or less important races it was dominated by that sophisticated worldliness that was indigenous to the realm of gamblers.

Still, we do not wish to suggest that the rally should therefore be seen in the same light as the principality's rather anachronistic Formula 1 Grand Prix. Apart from those not-infrequent displays of nationalism that have in the past penalized non-

French cars and crews, the Monte Carlo Rally has long remained one of the most prestigious events in the sport's calendar, thanks in large part to the frequent presence of snow and ice on the route, especially on the Col de Turini. This special stage has earned a place in the history of motor racing alongside Monza's Lesmo curve, the Scillato descents in the Targa Florio, the Avus straight in Germany, the start of the Le Mans 24 Hours and the Rascasse in Monaco itself.

The Turini—the last special stage of the Monte Carlo Rally—was in the past generally held at night, frequently in prohibitive weather conditions at an altitude of 1600 meters.

At the dawn of the new Millennium, however, "the Monte" is in danger of letting its history usurp its future. The Monte Carlo Rally was the only truly international event of its kind up until the late 1950s, and the 1953 event saw a record number of entries: 440. During the early 1960s the queen of the event was the little Mini, which won in 1964, '65 and '67 editions. The following three years it was Porsche's 911.

In 1973, the first year of the Constructors' World Rally Championship, French motoring celebrated in style with a 1-2-3 victory for the Alpine-Renault A110s, which opened the way for the model's conquest of the title. French fans then had to wait until 1981 to see another French win, in this instance that of the Renault 5 Turbo crewed by Ragnotti-Andriè.

The only drivers to have won four editions of the Monte are Walter Röhrl and Sandro Munari, three of those consecutive in both cases. Nineteen ninety-one instead saw the first victory for a Japanese car, the Toyota Celica of Sainz and Moya.

The Monte Carlo Rally is now one of the very few rallies to be staged on asphalt, albeit generally snow-covered on the Turini; the other WRC rounds are staged largely on ice or forest tracks, surfaces that represent an insurmountable barrier in terms of difficulty and costs for non-professional or non-works teams.

194 bottom center This photograph immortalizes the feats of the Swedish ace Stig Blomqvist in the year in which he conquered the World Championship, 1984. The car is an Audi Quattro and Blomqvist finished second to his teammate Walter Röhrl.

194 bottom right Colin McRae, the 1995 World Champion, at the wheel of his Subaru Impreza 555. Victory in the opening rally of the season went to his teammate (and the reigning champ) Spaniard Carlos Sainz.

195 left A traditional presence at the Monte Carlo Rally is Porsche's 911. This picture dates from 1979: a 911 had won the previous year with Nicolas.

195 right A photograph immortalizing Munari and his Lancia Fulvia 1.6 HF, first overall in the 1972 edition of the Monte Carlo Rally. Munari repeated his win in this, the world's oldest rally, in 1975, this time at the wheel of a Lancia Stratos—the winning car in 1976 and 1977, too.

HONOR ROLL

The Winners of the Monte Carlo Rally

YEAR	CAR	CREW	YEAR	CAR	CREW
1911	Turcat-Méry	Rougier	1965	Mini-Cooper	Mäkinen-Easter
1912	Berliet	Beutler	1966	Citroën	Toivonen-Mikkander
1914	Bignan	Ledure	1967	Mini-Cooper	Aaltonen-Liddon
1925	Renault	Repusseau	1968	Porsche 911S	Elford-Stone
1926	AC	Bruce	1969	Porsche 911T/E	Waldegård-Helmer
1927	Amilcar	Lefevre-Despaux	1970	Porsche 911S	Waldegård-Helmer
1928	Fiat	Bignam	1971	Alpine Renault A110	Andersson-Stone
1929	Graham-Paige	Sprenger Van Eijk	1972	Lancia Fulvia HF	Munari-Mannucci
1930	Licorne	Petit	1973	Alpine Renault A110	Andruet-"Biche"
1931	Invicta	Healey	1975	Lancia Stratos	Munari-Mannucci
1932	Hotchkiss-Peugeot	Vasselle ex-aequo De Lavallette-De Cortanze	1976	Lancia Stratos	Munari-Maiga
1933	Hotchkiss	Vasselle	1977	Lancia Stratos	Munari-Maiga
1934	Hotchkiss	Gas-Trevoux	1978	Porsche 911 Carrera	Nicolas-Laverne
1935	Renault	Lahye-Quatresous	1979	Lancia Stratos	Darniche-Mahè
1936	Ford	Zafirescu-Cristea	1980	Fiat Abarth 131	Röhrl-Geistorfer
1937	Delahaye	Le Begue-Quinlin	1981	Renault 5 Turbo	Ragnotti-Andriè
1938	Ford	Bakkeschut-Karelton	1982	Opel Ascona 400	Röhrl-Geistorfer
1939	Hotchkiss-Delahaye	Trevoux-Lesurque ex-aequo Paul-Contet	1983	Lancia 037	Röhrl-Geistorfer
1949	Hotchkiss	Trevoux	1984	Audi Quattro	Röhrl-Geistorfer
1950	Hotchkiss	Becquart-Secret	1985	Peugeot 205 T16	Vatanen-Harryman
1951	Delahaye	Trevoux-Corvetto	1986	Lancia Delta S4	Toivonen-Cresto
1952	Allard	Allard-Warburton	1987	Lancia Delta HF 4WD	Biasion-Siviero
1953	Ford Zephyr	Gastonides-Worledge	1988	Lancia Delta HF 4WD	Saby-Fauchille
1954	Lancia Aurelia	Chiron-Basadonna	1989	Lancia Delta Integrale	Biasion-Siviero
1955	Sunbeam-Talbot	Malling-Fadum	1990	Lancia Delta Integrale	Auriol-Occelli
1956	Jaguar	Adams-Bigger	1991	Toyota Celica GT4	Sainz-Moya
1958	Renault	Feret-Monraisse	1992	Lancia HF Integrale	Auriol-Occelli
1959	Citroën DS	Coltelloni-Alexandre	1993	Toyota Celica Turbo 4WD	Auriol-Occelli
1960	Mercedes	Schock-Moll	1994	Ford Escort RS Cosworth	Delecour-Grataloup
1961	Panhard	Martin-Bateau	1995	Subaru Impreza WRX	Sainz-Moya
1962	Saab	Carlsson-Haggbom	1996	Mitsubishi Lancer Evo III	Mäkinen-Harjanne
1963	Saab	Carlsson-Palm	1997	Subaru Impreza WRC 97	Liatti-Pons
1964	Mini-Cooper	Hopkirk-Liddon	1998	Toyota Corolla WRC	Sainz-Moya

THE SAFARI RALLY

If rallies are by definition automotive adventures the outcome of which is always uncertain, the Safari is undoubtedly the rally *par excellence*. Simply finishing is a victory in itself, given the grueling nature of the event and the innumerable logistical difficulties that face both crews and service teams. The setting for the Safari Rally is today Kenya, while in the past it has also been staged in other East African countries. The first edition was held in 1953 to mark the coronation of Queen Elizabeth II.

Instead of special stages, the event is divided into competitive sectors which account for around 1,500 km (931 mi.) of the total length of over 2,500 km (1,552 mi.). The rally is subdivided into three legs and, as with other rallies, the route may differ from one edition to the next. The whole rally is staged on unsurfaced tracks, both special and transit stages.

Thanks to its unique nature, victory in the Safari has a dual significance: not only does it testify to the competitiveness of the team, it can also be seen as a guarantee of the robustness of the car—a reputation that is carried over to the production versions. For this reason the Safari has frequently been dominated by cars that have not figured highly in other rallies worldwide; just as frequently, in fact, the most competitive cars in the more traditional rallies take care to avoid the myriad pitfalls of the devastating African event.

The protagonist of the Safari's early years was Volkswagen, which won four editions between 1953 and 1962. Then came Peugeot, with six wins between 1963 and 1978. Datsun/Nissan scored a remarkable seven wins between 1970 and 1982, as did Toyota between 1984 and 1994.

The driver who has won the greatest number of Safari Rallies is the Ugandan legend Shekkar Metha with five, followed by Bjorn Waldegaard.

196 top left The effect may not be the same as that of the migration of a herd of wild animals, but the passage of a rally car nonetheless makes its mark on the savannah. This photograph shows Biasion in 1989, an edition he won at the wheel of a Lancia Delta Integrale along with the navigator Siviero. That year the Italian driver won his second championship title.

196 top right Even though Stig Blomqvist failed to score points in the 1984 Safari Rally, he nonetheless finished the season as World Champion.

196-197 top This evocative aerial shot shows one of the Safari special stages. The African rally is staged in the region surrounding the Kenyan capital, Nairobi.

HONOR ROLL

The Winners of the Safari Rally

YEAR	CAR	CREW
1953	Volkswagen	Dix-Larsen
1954	Volkswagen	Preston Sr.-Marthava
1955	Ford Zephyr	Preston Sr.-Marthava
1956	DKW	Cicil-Vickers
1957	Volkswagen	Burton-Hoffman
1958	Ford Zephyr	Kopperud-Kopperud
1959	Mercedes 219	Frichy-Ellis
1960	Mercedes 219	Frichy-Ellis
1961	Mercedes 220	Manussis-Wolderidge
1962	Volkswagen 1.2	Fjastad-Schneider
1963	Peugeot 404	Novicky-Cliff
1964	Ford Cortina GT	Hugh-Yough
1965	Volvo PV544	Singh-Singh
1966	Peugeot 404	Shankland-Rothwall
1967	Peugeot 404	Shankland-Rothwall
1968	Peugeot 404	Novicky-Cliff
1969	Ford 20M	Illyard-Haird
1970	Datsun 1.6 SSS	Hermann-Schuller

YEAR	CAR	CREW
1971	Datsun 240Z	Hermann-Schuller
1972	Ford Escort RS 1.6	Mikkola-Palm
1973	Datsun 240Z	Metha-Drews
1974	Mitsubishi Colt Lancer	Singh-Doig
1975	Peugeot 504	Andersson-Hertz
1976	Mitsubishi Colt Lancer	Singh-Doig
1977	Ford Escort RS 1.8	Waldegård-Thorszelius
1978	Peugeot 504 Coupé V6	Nicolas-Lefevre
1979	Datsun 160 J	Metha-Doughty
1980	Datsun 160 J	Metha-Doughty
1981	Datsun 160 J	Metha-Doughty
1982	Datsun 160 J	Metha-Doughty
1983	Opel Ascona 400	Vatanen-Harryman
1984	Toyota Celica Turbo	Waldegård-Thorszelius
1985	Toyota Celica Turbo	Kankkunen-Gallagher
1986	Toyota Celica Turbo	Waldegård-Gallagher
1987	Audi 200 Quattro	Mikkola-Hertz
1988	Lancia Delta Integrale	Biasion-Siviero
1989	Lancia Delta Integrale	Biasion-Siviero
1990	Toyota Celica GT4	Waldegård-Gallagher
1991	Lancia Delta Integrale	Kankkunen-Piironen
1992	Toyota Celica Turbo 4WD	Sainz-Moya
1993	Toyota Celica Turbo 4WD	Kankkunen-Piironen
1994	Toyota Celica Turbo 4WD	Duncan-Williamson
1996	Mitsubishi Lancer Evo III	Mäkinen-Harjanne
1997	Subaru Impreza WRC 97	Liatti-Pons
1998	Mitsubishi Carisma	Burns-Reid

196 center left Nineteen ninety is to be remembered for the bitter struggle in the championship between Lancia at the height of its power and the young contender Toyota. The Japanese marque claimed the Safari Rally, Waldegård's Celica coming home first with Ericsson and Sainz in third and fourth.

196 center right Together with Metha, Kankkunnen can be considered one of the kings of the Safari Rally. Here we see him during the 1991 edition in which he triumphed with a Lancia Delta Integrale that could do with a wash.

196-197 bottom Didier Auriol, the works Toyota driver, seen here during the 1994 edition of the rally. That year the Frenchman won the World Rally Championship but was only third in the Safari, behind the Toyota of Duncan and Williamson and the Mitsubishi of Shinozuka and Kuukkala.

197 top left Nineteen ninety-three was an exceptional year: Toyota scored an historic victory with four cars filling the first four places. This photograph shows the winner, Kankkunen, negotiating a spectacular ford.

197 top right The 1994 edition of the African rally saw the spotlights turned on an unexpected winner, Duncan in the Toyota Celica Turbo 4WD.

197 bottom This picture immortalized Carlos Sainz during the 1998 edition of the Safari Rally aboard a Toyota Corolla.

THE SANREMO RALLY

The Sanremo Rally's progenitor, the Rally dei Fiori, was staged for the first time in 1928 and only ran for two years. It wasn't until the 1960s that the reborn event aroused any real interest, thanks in large part to its very demanding stages. Most of these snake through the harsh, hilly region of Liguria, which arches between the Mediterranean and the Alps and links up at its western extremity with the Côte d'Azur.

The Sanremo Rally has evolved continually, moving toward Tuscany in search of spectacular special stages and finding routes in areas of rare natural beauty that attract enthusiastic crowds.

The organizers of the Sanremo are credited with the introduction of the concept of special stages on unsurfaced tracks. In reality this was a fallback measure, given that the local 50-kph (30-mph) speed limits prevented anything else. The organizers thus opted for old bridle paths and military tracks that on the one hand were so grueling that they decimated the field, and on the

other created an extremely exciting style of rallying that was quickly adopted worldwide.

The Sanremo Rally can boast a unique record: it was here in 1981 that a woman won a World Rally Championship event for the first time, Michelle Mouton at the wheel of an Audi Quattro. Another curiosity concerns the annulment of the 1986 edition some months after the championship had finished, a FISA decision that took the title away from Alén and assigned it to Kankkunen.

The model that has distinguished itself most frequently in the Sanremo Rally is Lancia, a winner with the Flavia, the Fulvia, the Stratos, the 037 and the Delta—that is to say each and every one of the works team's World Championship cars—for a grand total of 19 victories.

The Italian driver Biasion has won three consecutive editions, and Markku Alén has also won three. However, the most successful driver is the Frenchman Auriol, with four victories.

HONOR ROLL

The Winners of the Sanremo Rally

YEAR	CAR	CREW
1928	Fiat 520	Urdareanu
1929	Fiat 521	Urdareanu
1961	Alfa Romeo Giulietta Ti	De Villa-De Villa
1962	Lancia Flavia	Frescobaldi-Malinconi
1963	Lancia Flavia	Patria-Orengo
1964	Saab 96 Sport	Carlsson-Palm
1965	Lancia Fulvia 2C	Cella-Gamenara
1966	Lancia Fulvia Coupé	Cella- Lombardini
1967	Renault 12 Gordini	Piot-Roure
1968	Porsche 911T	Toivonen-Tukkanen
1969	Lancia Fulvia HF 1.6	Källström-Haggbom
1970	Alpine-Renault A110	Therier-Callewaert
1971	Alpine-Renault A110	Andersson-Nash
1972	Lancia Fulvia HF 1.6	Ballestrieri-Bernacchini
1973	Alpine-Renault A110S	Therier-Jaubert
1974	Lancia Stratos	Munari-Mannucci
1975	Lancia Stratos	Waldegård-Thorszelius
1976	Lancia Stratos	Waldegård-Thorszelius
1977	Fiat Abarth 131	Andruet-Delferrier
1978	Lancia Stratos	Alen-Kivimaki
1979	Lancia Stratos	Fassina-Mannini
1980	Fiat Abarth 131	Röhrl-Geistorfer
1981	Audi Quattro	Mouton-Pons
1982	Audi Quattro	Blomqvist-Cederberg
1983	Lancia Rally 037	Alén-Kivimaki

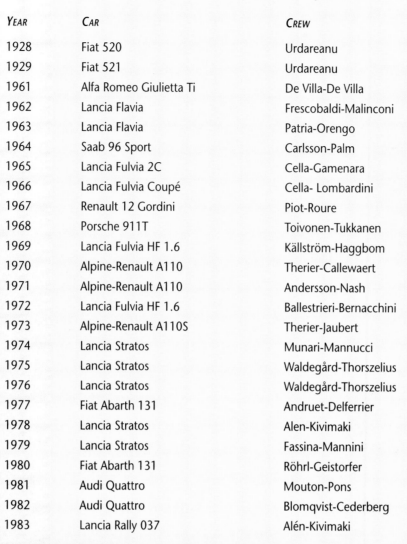

YEAR	CAR	CREW
1984	Peugeot 205 T16	Vatanen-Harryman
1985	Audi Quattro Sport S1	Röhrl-Geistorfer
1986	Lancia Delta S4	Alén-Kivimaki
1987	Lancia Delta HF 4WD	Biasion-Siviero
1988	Lancia Delta Integrale	Biasion-Siviero
1989	Lancia Delta Integrale	Biasion-Siviero
1990	Lancia Delta Integrale	Auriol-Occelli
1991	Lancia Delta Integrale	Auriol-Occelli
1992	Lancia Delta HF Integrale	Auriol-Occelli
1993	Ford Escort RS Cosworth	Cunico-Evangelisti
1994	Toyota Celica Turbo 4WD	Auriol-Occelli
1995	Subaru Impreza WRX	Liatti-Alessandrini
1996	Subaru Impreza WRX	McRae-Ringer
1997	Subaru Impreza WRC 97	McRae-Grist
1998	Mitsubishi Lancer Evo	Mäkinen-Mannisenmäki

199 left Tommi Mäkinen tackling the tortuous, narrow roads of the Sanremo Rally. In 1997, the edition shown here, the Finn was third behind a pair of Subarus. The previous year the talented driver had retired after hitting a concrete manhole cover that had been left askew. His co-driver Harjanne was slightly hurt as the car rolled.

199 top right The history of the Sanremo Rally revolves around a number of cardinal elements: the special stages of Langan, Monte Ceppo, Colle d'Oppio and Baiardo and a number in the Ligurian interior toward the Apennines. The transits are also memorable, with roads that frequently offer spectacular landscapes seemingly unchanged since the Middle Ages. The village acting as the backdrop to this shot is Baiardo.

199 bottom right. The 1990 Sanremo Rally marked a triumphant display by Lancia with four cars (Auriol, Kankkunen, Cerrato and Liatti) in the first five places. But why is the Toyota crew celebrating? Because the third-placed Sainz and Moya have just won the Drivers' Championship with a number of events still to go. At the end of the season, Lancia's Delta would win the Constructors' Championship by just six points from Toyota.

199

THE 1000 LAKES - THE RALLY OF FINLAND

Since 1997 this event has been known as the Rally of Finland, but rally fans will always think of it as the "1000 Lakes." This is one of the World Rally Championship's most prestigious events, a test of extraordinary severity and so technically demanding that the slightest distraction may be fatal. In these conditions the home drivers familiar with the terrain clearly enjoy a huge advantage, especially as the 1000 Lakes' route barely changes over the years.

The rally headquarters are located in a town called Jyväskylä, to the north of the capital Helsinki. The event is generally held in the last week of

200 The 1983 edition of the 1000 Lakes is to be remembered for Hannu Mikkola's great drive. That year he won the World Championship in his Audi in spite of the pressure from the very strong Lancia team featuring Röhrl and Alén. Mikkola won from his teammate Blomqvist, marking his fourth and last victory of the season. This was still sufficient to keep his extremely talented rivals at bay.

August, thus avoiding snow but with the entire rally staged on loose-surfaced tracks.

The first victory for a driver born outside Scandinavia did not come until 1990, Carlos Sainz breaking with tradition. The feat was subsequently repeated by the equally talented Auriol.

The history of the 1000 Lakes is also composed of series and sequences. Three consecutive victories have all been scored by the the Mini-Cooper, the

Ford Escort, the Fiat Abarth 131, the mighty Group B Peugeot 205 Turbo 16, and Mitsubishi's Lancer Evolution models.

The king of the Rally of Finland in the late 1990s is still Hannu Mikkola with seven victories, followed by Marku Alén with six. Among the current drivers only Tommi Mäkinen, the winner of the last four editions, comes close to threatening the great Hannu's primacy.

200-201 A classic World Championship rally traditionally dominated by Scandinavian drivers, in 1990 the 1000 Lakes was won by a Spaniard, Carlos Sainz, aboard a Toyota Celica GT4. Sainz finished 19 seconds ahead of Ari Vatanen.

201 center left Kankkunen and Piironen fly toward victory in the 1991 1000 Lakes aboard their Lancia Delta Integrale. The Finn regained the World Championship title after a four-year wait. He is the driver who has competed in the most WRC events.

201 bottom left A great shot of Didier Auriol's Toyota Celica from the 1994 edition. The Frenchman finished second to Mäkinen in the Ford Escort RS Cosworth. In 1999 the long-lived Escort gave way to the new Ford Focus, which has the unenviable task of challenging the Japanese machines of Mitsubishi, Subaru and Toyota.

201 bottom right The 1000 Lakes changed its name in 1997, officially becoming known as the Rally of Finland (or "Jyväskylän Suurajot" in Finland's remarkably complex language). That edition was won by Mäkinen with a Mitsubishi Lancer Evolution IV; the car seen here is a Toyota Celica of the latest generation.

The Winners of The 1000 Lakes - The Rally of Finland

YEAR	CAR	CREW
1959	Volvo	Calbo-Nurimaa
1960	Saab 96	Bremer-Lampi
1961	Mercedes 220SE	Aaltonen-Nurimaa
1962	Citroën DS19	Toivonen-Kalio
1963	Saab 96 Sport	Lampinen-Ahava
1964	Saab 96 Sport	Lampinen-Ahava
1965	Mini-Cooper	Mäkinen-Kaskitalo
1966	Mini-Cooper	Mäkinen-Kaskitalo
1967	Mini-Cooper	Mäkinen-Kaskitalo
1968	Ford Escort TC	Mikkola-Järvi
1969	Ford Escort TC	Mikkola-Järvi
1970	Ford Escort TC	Mikkola-Palm
1971	Saab 96 V4	Blomqvist-Hertz
1972	Saab 96 V4	Lampinen-Sholberg
1973	Ford Escort RS 1.6	Mäkinen-Liddon
1974	Ford Escort RS 1.6	Mikkola-Davenport
1975	Toyota Corolla 1.6	Mikkola-Aho
1976	Fiat Abarth 131	Alén-Kivimäki
1977	Ford Escort RS 1.8	Hamalainen-Tukkanen
1978	Fiat Abarth 131	Alén-Kivimäki
1979	Fiat Abarth 131	Alén-Kivimäki
1980	Fiat Abarth 131	Alén-Kivimäki
1981	Ford Escort RS	Vatanen-Richards
1982	Audi Quattro	Mikkola-Hertz
1983	Audi Quattro	Mikkola-Hertz
1984	Peugeot 205 T16	Vatanen-Harryman
1985	Peugeot 205 T16 E2	Salonen-Harjanne
1986	Peugeot 205 T16 E2	Salonen-Harjanne
1987	Lancia Delta HF 4WD	Alén-Kivimäki
1988	Lancia Delta Integrale	Alén-Kivimäki
1989	Mitsubishi Galant VR4	Ericsson-Billstam
1990	Toyota Celica GT4	Sainz-Moya
1991	Lancia Delta Integrale	Kankkunen-Piironen
1992	Lancia HF Integrale	Auriol-Occelli
1993	Toyota Celica Turbo 4WD	Kankkunen-Giraudet
1994	Ford Escort RS Cosworth	Mäkinen-Harjanne
1996	Mitsubishi Lancer Evo III	Mäkinen-Harjanne
1997	Mitsubishi Lancer Evo IV	Mäkinen-Harjanne
1998	Mitsubishi Lancer Evo IV	Mäkinen-Harjanne

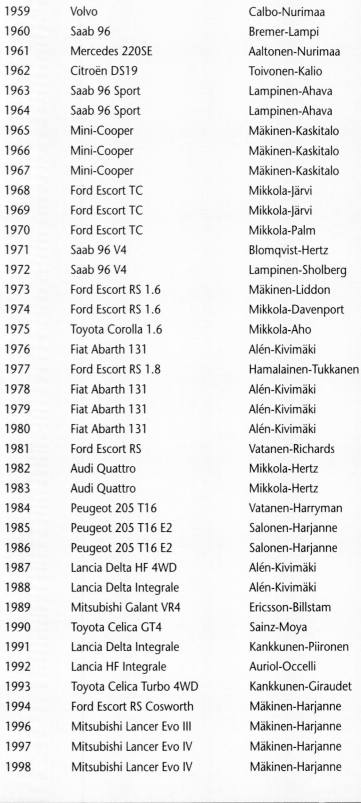

THE ACROPOLIS RALLY

The harder the going, the more the rally crews enjoy themselves—which is why at each edition of the Acropolis Rally their complaints regarding its severity and the unpredictability of the conditions sound more like self-satisfied grumbling than true protests. The Acropolis Rally is actually popular because of, rather than in spite of, the improbable rock-strewn transit tracks and special stages, each seemingly a rally in itself. In some cases, a kilometer on the Acropolis is harder on the cars and drivers than a kilometer on the Safari. If an edition of the Greek rally has taken place in which at least half of the crews who started made it to the finish, we certainly can't recall which one.

Staged entirely on unsurfaced tracks—if stones and boulders can be considered as such—the Acropolis is one of the most eagerly awaited events in the World Rally Championship calendar. Currently the rally is based at Athens, while in the past it has started from Lagonissi, a smaller coastal town to the south of the capital.

The history of the rally features three victories for Mercedes in the 1960s and the same number for Alpine-Renault and Ford. But the most frequent winner in Greece has been Lancia with seven victories, three of which came consecutively. Only two drivers, Walter Röhrl and Carlos Sainz, have managed to win three times.

202 top In 1981, a season also as triumphant as that of 1983, Ari Vatanen won the Acropolis Rally: here we see him on the coast with his Ford Escort RS. His contemporaries regarded the Finnish driver as unbeatable when driving a competitive car—and this in a period very rich in driving talents.

202-203 From 1985, a shot of the Peugeot 205 Turbo 16 driven by the eventual winner Timo Salonen. The bespectacled future World Champion had a cool, calm exterior and was a true ace who rarely committed errors.

202 bottom Kankkunen at the start of the 1986 Acropolis Rally, an event he won before Biasion. Kankkunen can be considered a model rally driver, combining innate talent, consistency and outstanding nerves and endurance. His general aplomb is accentuated by an old-fashioned moustache, but once behind the wheel he's transformed into a cold, calculating driver with a remarkable ability to handle critical situations. In spite of his fine record, he only managed two wins in the Acropolis Rally, in 1986 and 1991.

203 top Miki Biasion in an evocative photograph taken in 1988. This was a triumphal episode for Lancia with four cars filling the first four places— following Biasion were Ericsson, Florio and Alén. The following year Biasion repeated his success, this time in front of Auriol and Florio. The Biasion/Auriol duel was also a feature of the '92 edition, the final result being inverted. Biasion won again in '93, however, at the wheel of a Ford Cosworth (the car he drove in '92 as well).

203 center A symbolic image of the Acropolis Rally with the timeless monastery acting as a backdrop to one of the special stages of this gruelling World Championship event. Due to the severity of the terrain the Acropolis is also known as the "Mini-Safari." Some of the special stages held on shale are as hard on the cars as those of the African rally.

203 bottom In 1988, Nissan tried to rekindle the rally magic of the 240Z with the 200SX, but the team accumulated only enough points for eighth place in the Constructors' Championship. Despite being the first Japanese company to take international rallying seriously, Nissan has since fallen behind rival marques such as Subaru and Toyota in the sport.

HONOR ROLL

The Winners of the Acropolis Rally

YEAR	CAR	CREW
1952	Chevrolet	Pesmazoglou-Papamichael
1953	Opel Rekord	Papamichael-Dimitrakos
1954	Opel Kapitan	Papadopoulos-Dimitrakos
1955	Opel Kapitan	Pesmazoglou-Dimitrakos
1956	Mercedes 300SL	Schock-Moll
1957	Ferrari 250GT	Estager-Estager
1958	Lancia Aurelia GT	Villoresi-Basadonna
1959	Auto Union 1000	Levy-Wencher
1960	Mercedes 220SE	Schock-Moll
1961	Saab 96	Carlsson-Carlsson
1962	Mercedes 220SE	Borhinger-Lang
1963	Mercedes 220SE	Borhinger-Knoll
1964	Volvo PV544	Trana-Thermaenius
1965	Volvo 122S	Skogh-Tandlaskare
1966	Ford Cortina Lotus	Söderström-Palm
1967	Mini-Cooper	Hopkirk-Crelin
1968	Ford Escort TC	Clark-Porter
1969	Porsche 911S	Toivonen-Kalari
1970	Alpine-Renault A110	Therier-Callewaert
1971	Alpine-Renault A110	Andersson-Hertz
1972	Fiat Abarth 124 Spider	Lindberg-Eisendle
1973	Alpine-Renault A110S	Therier-Delferrier
1975	Opel Ascona 1.9	Röhrl-Geistorfer
1976	Datsun 160 J	Kallstrom-Andersson
1977	Ford Escort RS 1.8	Waldegård-Thorszellius
1978	Fiat 131 Abarth	Röhrl-Geistorfer
1979	Ford Escort RS 1.8	Waldegård-Thorszellius
1980	Ford Escort RS 1.8	Vatanen-Richards
1981	Ford Escort RS 1.8	Vatanen-Richards
1982	Audi Quattro	Mouton-Pons
1983	Lancia Rally 037	Röhrl-Geistorfer
1984	Audi Quattro	Blomqvist-Cederberg
1985	Peugeot 205 T16	Salonen-Harjanne
1986	Peugeot 205 T16 E2	Kankkunen- Piironen
1987	Lancia Delta HF 4WD	Alén-Kivimäki
1988	Lancia Delta Integrale	Biasion-Siviero
1989	Lancia Delta Integrale	Biasion-Siviero
1990	Toyota Celica GT4	Sainz-Moya
1991	Lancia Delta Integrale	Kankkunen-Piironen
1992	Lancia HF Integrale	Auriol-Occelli
1993	Ford Escort RS Cosworth	Biasion-Siviero
1994	Subaru Impreza WRX	Sainz-Moya
1996	Subaru Impreza WRX	McRae-Ringer
1997	Ford Escort WRC	Sainz-Moya
1998	Subaru Impreza 555	McRae-Grist

THE RAC AND THE INTERNATIONAL SWEDISH RALLIES

The WRC calendar changes from year to year. The classic, well-established events are ever-present, but others have been dropped—the interesting Ivory Coast Rally, for example.

For reasons of space we have been obliged to condense our accounts of some rallies that are from a technical and sporting point of view at least as important as those discussed above, but which are perhaps slightly less popular amongst rally fans worldwide. This is perhaps a somewhat harsh judgement against the RAC Rally—Britain's WRC event, which as the last round on the calendar is frequently close-fought—and the International Swedish Rally. These events are of course as significant and well established as the Sanremo, the Safari or the Acropolis, and their rolls of honor feature all the great champions of modern rallying. Both events are also characterized by climactic conditions: the RAC is frequently drenched with rain if not by ice and snow, and the Swedish Rally is certainly the coldest event on the calendar. Temperatures as low as -15°C are common, and the virtually guaranteed presence of ice and snow makes this rally doubly challenging. No driver born outside Scandinavia has ever won the event, and only in 1981—when Mikkola the Finn came first—have the Swedes themselves lost.

204 bottom left The 1992 RAC Rally was no walkover for Carlos Sainz, as this photograph documents: the Spanish driver staged a fine battle with reigning champion Kankkunen.

HONOR ROLL

The Winners of the RAC Rally

Year	Car	Crew	Year	Car	Crew
1951	Jaguar XK120	Appleyard-Appleyard	1976	Ford Escort RS 1.8	Clark-Pegg
1952	Allard-Cadillac	Imhof-Frayling	1977	Ford Escort RS 1.8	Waldegård-Thorszellius
1953	Jaguar XK120	Appleyard-Appleyard	1978	Ford Escort RS 1.8	Mikkola-Hertz
1954	Triumph TR3	Waalwork-Brooks	1979	Ford Escort RS 1.8	Mikkola-Hertz
1955	Standard Ten	Eayle-Harrocks	1980	Talbot Sunbeam Lotus	Toivonen-White
1956	Aston Martin DB2	Sims-Ambrose Jones	1981	Audi Quattro	Mikkola-Hertz
1958	Sunbeam-Rapier	Harper-Deane	1982	Audi Quattro	Mikkola-Hertz
1959	Ford Zephyr	Burgees-Pearson	1983	Audi Quattro	Blomqvist-Cederberg
1960	Saab 96	Carlsson-Turner	1984	Peugeot 205 T16	Vatanen-Harryman
1961	Saab 96	Carlsson-Brown	1985	Lancia Delta S4	Toivonen-Wilson
1962	Saab 96	Carlsson-Turner	1986	Peugeot 205 T16 E2	Salonen-Harjanne
1963	Volvo PV544	Trana-Thermaenius	1987	Lancia Delta 4WD	Kankkunen- Piironen
1964	Volvo PV544	Trana-Thermaenius	1988	Lancia Delta Integrale	Alén-Kivimäki
1965	Mini-Cooper	Aaltonen-Ambrose	1989	Mitsubishi Galant VR4	Airkkala-McNamee
1966	Ford Cortina Lotus	Söderström-Palm	1990	Toyota Celica GT4	Sainz-Moya
1968	Saab 96	Lampinen-Davenport	1991	Lancia Delta Integrale	Kankkunen- Piironen
1969	Lancia Fulvia HF	Kallström-Haggbon	1992	Toyota Celica GT4	Sainz-Moya
1970	Lancia Fulvia HF	Kallström-Haggbon	1993	Toyota Celica Turbo 4WD	Kankkunen-Grist
1971	Lancia Fulvia HF	Kallström-Haggbon	1994	Subaru Impreza WRX	McRae-Ringer
1972	Saab 96 V4	Blomqvist-Hertz	1995	Subaru Impreza WRX	McRae-Ringer
1973	Ford Escort RS 1.6	Mäkinen-Liddon	1996	Toyota Celica ST 205	Schwartz-Graudet
1974	Ford Escort RS 1.6	Mäkinen-Liddon	1997	Subaru Impreza WRC 97	McRae-Grist
1975	Ford Escort RS 1.6	Mäkinen-Liddon	1998	Mitsubishi Carisma	Burns-Reid

The Winners of the International Swedish Rally

YEAR	CAR	CREW
1950	BMW	Colerbaum
1951	Talbot-Lago	Bengtsson
1952	Porsche	Persson
1953	Porsche	Nottorp
1954	Porsche	Hammarlund
1955	Porsche	Borgefors
1956	Volkswagen	Bengtsson
1957	Volvo	Jansson
1958	Volvo	Andersson
1959	Saab 93	Carlsson
1960	Saab 96	Skogh-Skogh
1962	Mini-Cooper	Olsson-Söderström
1963	Porsche Carrera	Jansson-Petterson
1964	Volvo	Trana-Thermaenius
1965	Volvo	Trana-Thermaenius
1966	Saab 96	Andersson-Svedberg
1967	Ford Cortina Lotus	Soderstrom-Palm
1968	Porsche 911T	Waldegård-Helmer
1969	Porsche 911T/E	Waldegård-Helmer
1970	Porsche 911S	Waldegård-Thorszellius
1971	Saab 96	Blomqvist-Hertz
1972	Saab 96	Blomqvist-Hertz
1973	Saab 96	Blomqvist-Hertz
1975	Lancia Stratos	Waldegård-Thorszellius
1976	Saab 96	Eklund-Cederberg
1977	Saab 99	Blomqvist-Sylvan
1978	Ford Escort RS	Waldegård-Thorszellius
1979	Saab 99 Turbo	Blomqvist-Cederberg
1980	Opel Ascona 400	Kulläng-Berglund
1981	Audi Quattro	Mikkola-Hertz
1982	Audi Quattro	Blomqvist-Cederberg
1983	Audi Quattro	Mikkola-Hertz
1984	Audi Quattro	Blomqvist-Cederberg
1985	Peugeot 205 T16	Vatanen-Harryman
1986	Peugeot 205 T16 E2	Kankkunen- Piironen
1987	Mazda 323 GTX	Salonen-Harjanne
1988	Lancia Delta HF 4WD	Alén-Kivimäki
1989	Mazda 323 GTX	Carlsson-Carlsson
1991	Mitsubishi Galant VR4	Eriksson-Parmander
1992	Toyota Celica GT4	Jonsson-Bäckman
1993	Toyota Celica Turbo 4WD	Jonsson-Bäckman
1994	Toyota Celica Turbo 4WD	Radstrom-Bäckman
1995	Mitsubishi Lancer Evo II	Eriksson-Parmander
1996	Mitsubishi Lancer Evo III	Mäkinen-Harjanne
1997	Subaru Impreza WRC 97	Eriksson-Parmander
1998	Mitsubishi Lancer Evo IV	Mäkinen-Mannisenmäki

THE CORSE RALLY

Rallies of a certain fame are held on all three of the major islands in the western Mediterranean: the Targa Florio in Sicily, an event that has sadly declined; the Costa Smeralda in Sardinia; and the Tour de Corse in Corsica. Only the latter has World Championship status, and it is held on rough asphalt roads. Its principal characteristic is the vertiginous precipices dropping up to 300 meters from the edge of the special-stage roads. The Corsican rally is also sadly famous for the tragic accidents in which Lancia team members Attilio Bettega (1980), Henri Toivonen (1985) and Sergio Cresto (1985) were killed.

The Winners of the Tour de Corse

YEAR	CAR	CREW
1956	Renault Dauphine	Thiriou-Ferrier
1957	Alfa Romeo Giulietta SV	Nicol-Delageneste
1958	Renault Dauphine	Feret-Monraisse
1959	Renault Dauphine	Orsini-Canonici
1960	Porsche Carrera	Strahle-Linge
1961	Citroën DS19	Trautmann-Ogier
1962	Renault Dauphine	Orsini-Canonici
1963	Citroën DS19	Trautmann-Chabert
1964	Renault 8 Gordini	Vinatier-Masson
1965	Renault 8 Gordini	Orsini-Canonici
1966	Renault 8 Gordini	Piot-Jacob
1967	Lancia Fulvia HF	Munari-Lombardini
1968	Alpine Renault A110	Andruet-Gelin
1969	Porsche 911R	Larrouse-Gelin
1970	Alpine Renault A110	Darniche-Mahe
1972	Alpine Renault A110	Andruet-"Biche"
1973	Alpine Renault A110S	Nicolas-Vial
1975	Lancia Stratos	Darniche-Mahe
1976	Lancia Stratos	Munari-Maiga
1977	Lancia Stratos	Darniche-Mahe
1978	Lancia Stratos	Darniche-Mahe
1979	Lancia Stratos	Darniche-Mahe
1980	Porsche 911SC	Therier-Vial
1981	Lancia Stratos	Darniche-Mahe
1982	Renault 5 Turbo	Ragnotti-Andrié
1983	Lancia Rally 037	Alén- Kivimäki
1984	Lancia Rally 037	Alén- Kivimäki
1985	Renault 5 Turbo	Ragnotti-Andrié
1986	Peugeot 205 T16 E2	Saby-Fauchille
1987	BMW M3	Beguin-Lenne
1988	Ford Sierra Cosworth	Auriol-Occelli
1989	Lancia Delta Integrale	Auriol-Occelli
1990	Lancia Delta Integrale	Auriol-Occelli
1991	Toyota Celica 4WD	Sainz-Moya
1992	Lancia HF Integrale	Auriol-Occelli
1993	Ford Escort RS Cosworth	Delecour-Grataloup
1994	Toyota Celica 4WD	Auriol-Occelli
1995	Toyota Celica 4WD	Auriol-Giraudet
1996	Renault Mégane	Bulgaski-Chiaroni
1997	Subaru Impreza WRC	McRae-Grist
1998	Subaru Impreza 555	McRae-Grist

204 top right Second place in the last rally of '83 earned Mikkola the World Championship title. Here his navigator, Hertz, tries to act as a counterweight for more grip.

204 center right McRae during the 1995 Swedish Rally at the wheel of a works Subaru Impreza. The British champion had to wait until midway through the season before he scored his first championship points, this round going to the Scandinavian drivers and Mitsubishi.

204 bottom right It was an all-Scandinavian podium at the 1985 Swedish Rally. Seen here is Salonen with the Peugeot 205 T16; the race was won by his teammate Vatanen, before the Audi Quattro of local driver Blomqvist.

205 bottom left The Tour de Corse, a difficult, dangerous rally: this photograph shows Sainz tackling a narrow, damp, rough track with a precipice a few centimeters away and no barriers.

205 right A "tranquil" section of the Tour de Corse meets a Lancia Delta, probably that of Saby.

THE IBERIAN PENINSULA RALLIES

Two World Championship rallies are staged on the Iberian Peninsula. The first, oldest and most famous is the TAP Rally de Portugal, while the second is the Championship's newest event, the Catalunya Rally held in the Barcelona region. In Portugal a number of stages are held on loose surfaces, while the Spanish event is run on asphalt. Not surprisingly, the Catalunya has twice been won by one of the most popular and successful drivers of the 1990s, the Spaniard Carlos Sainz.

206 top For a number of years the Iberian Peninsula has been represented in the World Rally Championship by the Portuguese Rally. This picture is from the 1992 edition, with Carlos Sainz third at the finish. Some years earlier the success of the Spanish driver in this event had helped establish the Rally of Catalunya, which was won by Sainz himself that year.

HONOR ROLL

The Winners of the TAP Rallye de Portugal

YEAR	CAR	CREW
1967	Renault Gordini	Carpinteiro-Silva Perreira
1968	Lancia Fulvia HF	Fall-Crellin
1969	Citroën DS21	Romaozinho-Jocames
1970	Lancia Fulvia HF	Lampinen-Davenport
1971	Alpine-Renault A110	Nicolas-Todt
1972	BMW 2002	Warmblod-Davenport
1973	Alpine-Renault A110	Therier-Jaubert
1974	Fiat Abarth 124	Pinto-Bernacchini
1975	Fiat Abarth 124	Alén-Kivimäki
1976	Lancia Stratos	Munari-Maiga
1977	Fiat 131 Abarth	Alén-Kivimäki
1978	Fiat 131 Abarth	Alén-Kivimäki
1979	Ford Escort RS 1.8	Mikkola-Hertz
1980	Fiat 131 Abarth	Röhrl-Geistorfer
1981	Fiat 131 Abarth	Alén-Kivimäki
1982	Audi Quattro	Mouton-Pons
1983	Audi Quattro	Mikkola-Hertz
1984	Audi Quattro	Mikkola-Hertz
1985	Peugeot 205 T16	Salonen-Harjanne
1986	Renault 5 Turbo	Moutinho-Fortes
1987	Lancia Delta HF 4WD	Alén-Kivimäki
1988	Lancia Delta Integrale	Biasion-Cassina
1989	Lancia Delta Integrale	Biasion-Siviero
1990	Lancia Delta Integrale	Biasion-Siviero
1991	Toyota Celica 4WD	Sainz-Moya
1992	Lancia HF Integrale	Kankkunen-Piironen
1993	Ford Escort RS Cosworth	Delecour-Grataloup
1994	Toyota Celica 4WD	Kankkunen-Grist
1995	Subaru Impreza WRX	Sainz-Moya
1996	Toyota Celica ST 205	Madeira-Silva
1997	Mitsubishi Lancer Evo IV	Mäkinen-Harjanne
1998	Subaru Impreza 555	McRae-Grist

HONOR ROLL

The Winners of the Catalunya Rally

YEAR	CAR	CREW
1991*	Toyota Celica GT4	Schwarz-Hertz
1992*	Toyota Celica Turbo 4WD	Sainz-Moya
1993	Ford Escort RS Cosworth	Delecour-Grataloup
1995	Subaru Impreza WRX	Sainz-Moya
1996	Subaru Impreza WRX	McRae-Ringer
1997	Mitsubishi Lancer Evo IV	Mäkinen-Harjanne
1998	Toyota Corolla WRC	Auriol-Graudet

Drivers' World Championship only.

206 center A classic Portuguese Rally stage in 1997. Humps are very frequent on the tarmac rallies, Portugal being no exception—the driver is Mäkinen, the car a Mitsubishi.

206 bottom An evocative image of the 1991 Rally of Australia. Seen applying plenty of opposite lock is the

winner Kankkunen at the wheel of a Lancia Delta Integrale.

207 top Mäkinen does not hesitate to plunge his Mitsubishi into one of the many torrents encountered during the Rally Australia. The rough terrain and violent storms transform the so-called "highways" into a sequence of humps and pools.

THE AUSTRALIAN RALLY AND PACIFIC RALLY

THE ARGENTINE RALLY

Two World Rally Championship rounds are held in Oceania. The oldest is the Rally New Zealand, while Australia's event is a more recent addition. Both are held on beaten earth tracks, but the surfaces present very different characteristics, particularly in case of rain.

It is curious that the API Rally Australia is held in the largest country among those staging championship events but is concentrated in the smallest area.

207 center There is no lack of running water in Argentina, too. This photograph is from 1990 and the car is the Toyota Corolla driven by Carlos Sainz who finished second.

207 bottom Land, dust and solitude, characteristic elements of Patagonia. Mäkinen races toward victory in the 1997 edition of the Rally of Argentina.

This is the only World Championship rally held on the continent that has produced such road-racing greats as Fangio, Senna, Piquet and Fittipaldi but has yet to see equally regarded international rally drivers. The event, which has only enjoyed World Championship status since 1987, is based in Cordoba and held mostly on unsurfaced tracks.

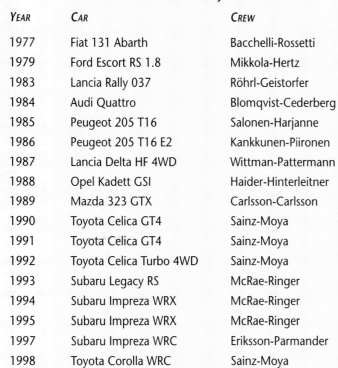

HONOR ROLL

The Winners of the Rally New Zealand

Year	Car	Crew
1977	Fiat 131 Abarth	Bacchelli-Rossetti
1979	Ford Escort RS 1.8	Mikkola-Hertz
1983	Lancia Rally 037	Röhrl-Geistorfer
1984	Audi Quattro	Blomqvist-Cederberg
1985	Peugeot 205 T16	Salonen-Harjanne
1986	Peugeot 205 T16 E2	Kankkunen-Piironen
1987	Lancia Delta HF 4WD	Wittman-Pattermann
1988	Opel Kadett GSI	Haider-Hinterleitner
1989	Mazda 323 GTX	Carlsson-Carlsson
1990	Toyota Celica GT4	Sainz-Moya
1991	Toyota Celica GT4	Sainz-Moya
1992	Toyota Celica Turbo 4WD	Sainz-Moya
1993	Subaru Legacy RS	McRae-Ringer
1994	Subaru Impreza WRX	McRae-Ringer
1995	Subaru Impreza WRX	McRae-Ringer
1997	Subaru Impreza WRC	Eriksson-Parmander
1998	Toyota Corolla WRC	Sainz-Moya

HONOR ROLL

The Winners of the API Rally Australia

Year	Car	Crew
1989	Toyota Celica GT4	Kankkunen-Piironen
1990	Lancia Delta Integrale	Kankkunen-Piironen
1991	Lancia Delta Integrale	Kankkunen-Piironen
1992	Lancia HF Integrale	Auriol-Occelli
1993	Toyota Celica Turbo 4WD	Kankkunen-Grist
1994	Mitsubishi Lancer Evo. III	Eriksson-Parmander
1995	Mitsubishi Lancer Evo. III	Eriksson-Parmander
1996	Mitsubishi Lancer Evo. III	Mäkinen-Harjanne
1997	Subaru Impreza WRC97	McRae-Grist
1998	Mitsubishi Lancer Evo V	Mäkinen-Mannisenmäki

HONOR ROLL

The Winners of the Rally Argentina

Year	Car	Crew
1981	Talbot Sunbeam Lotus	Fréquelin-Todt
1983	Audi Quattro	Mikkola-Hertz
1984	Audi Quattro	Blomqvist-Cederberg
1985	Peugeot 205 T16	Salonen-Harjanne
1986	Lancia Delta S4	Biasion-Siviero
1987	Lancia Delta HF 4WD	Biasion-Siviero
1988	Lancia Delta Integrale	Recalde-del Buono
1989	Lancia Delta Integrale	Ericsson-Billstam
1990	Lancia Delta Integrale	Biasion-Siviero
1991	Toyota Celica GT4	Sainz-Moya
1992	Lancia HF Integrale	Auriol-Occelli
1993	Toyota Celica Turbo 4WD	Kankkunen-Grist
1994	Toyota Celica Turbo 4WD	Auriol-Occelli
1996	Mitsubishi Lancer Evo. III	Mäkinen-Harjanne
1997	Mitsubishi Lancer Evo. IV	Mäkinen-Harjanne
1998	Mitsubishi Lancer Evo V	Mäkinen-Mannisenmäki

SPORTS-PROTOTYPES

Sports-prototypes are the link between sports cars and Formula 1 single-seaters, the link that in the evolution of the racing car unites Grand Prix machines with cars derived from normal production models. Sports-prototypes have played a fundamental role in the history of motor racing and in fact represent a point of equilibrium. In the mid-1970s, after a long period of maturation, these two-seater machines with bodywork that over the decades had been transformed from a cabriolet to barchetta to coupé style appeared to have succeeded in matching Formula 1 in terms of resources, drivers and public interest. However, while Formula 1 continued to consolidate its position, the uncertainties surrounding a Sports-Prototype Championship blighted by cancelations, reinstatements and variations in name and regulations led to disaffection and confusion.

Fortunately, certain individually renowned endurance races have continued to provide the category with prestigious settings in which to display its worth—Le Mans, Daytona and Sebring to name the most important, but also similar events staged at Spa-Francorchamps, Laguna Seca and the Nürburgring. Then there are the celebrated Mille Miglia, Targa Florio, Carrera Panamericana and Tourist Trophy events, now staged for historic cars and the late lamented Temporada Argentina, all endurance races meriting separate chapters in this book. The 6-, 12- or 24-hour races, the Mille Miglia, the Paris-Dakar and so on, are all events that have provided sterner tests for men and machines than even Formula 1. It should come as no surprise to see the names of F1's leading lights among the drivers competing in sports-prototype events: the appeal

and difficulty of the races have always attracted the leading drivers, many of whom have concluded their careers in the category.

This section devoted to sports-prototype racing has been divided into two parts. The first is purely historical, looking at the evolution of the category from its origins in the 1920s to the first World Championship in 1953 and through to the present day (with the hope that the FIA continues to provide adequate support). The second part is instead devoted to the endurance races *par excellence*, the Le Mans 24 Hours and its American counterparts, the Daytona 24 Hours and the Sebring 12 Hours.

208 bottom left Endurance races have attracted enthusiasts since the turn of the century: this picture shows Bob Burman tackling the loose-surfaced curves at Daytona Beach in his Benz 220 PS. This was 1910 and the American driver set the new world speed record of 211.4 kph (131 mph).

208-209 and 209 top Ready, steady, GO... on foot, though! Up until the 1970s the start of some sports prototype races was like this, with the drivers sprinting to their cars and leaping in through the window or over the side, a procedure that was certainly more spectacular than the present system—and was also illustrated in promotional posters such as this one for the 1963 Sebring 12 Hours. The photograph instead shows the start of the 1968 Le Mans 24 Hours.

209 bottom Porsche has long dominated the category reserved for sports-prototypes, a cross between production sports cars and Formula 1 single-seaters. This photograph shows three 956Cs crewed by Ickx and Bell (car number 1), Mass and Schuppan (No. 2) and Haywood and Holbert/Barth (No. 3) during the 1982 Le Mans 24 Hours.

THE HISTORY OF THE SPORTS-PROTOTYPE WORLD CHAMPIONSHIP

Even though the first Sports-Prototype World Championship was not held until 1953, the origins of this kind of racing date back to the 1920s and the first edition of the Le Mans 24 Hours. The first and most famous endurance race for sports cars—later somewhat ambiguously renamed sports-prototypes—was the concrete response to a demand that had actually arisen in the first decade of the 20th century.

The proliferation of motor racing events—the fruit of the innate spirit of human competition that saw in the new means of transport yet another challenge and opportunity for sport—had induced manufacturers to build increasingly extreme, Grand Prix-type racing cars that bore precious little resemblance to ordinary mass-produced models. This situation led to the

organization of events reserved for touring or sports cars that for half a century have represented a valid and frequently more attractive alternative to Grand Prix single-seaters. Up to the 1950s sports car events enjoyed international status and were often even more popular than Grands Prix, attracting the leading constructors and most talented drivers.

It should be remembered that the regulations for the first edition of the Le Mans 24 Hours held in 1923 accepted only cars appearing in manufacturer's catalogues and on sale to the public. The models of certain dimensions were to have four seats, doors of a specified size, a roof (that had to be raised during the race for a certain period), ballast corresponding to the appropriate number of passengers and a small quantity of spare parts. The drivers started with this

210 top left Earl Howe attempting to repair his Bugatti during the Brooklands Double Twelve in 1930: he was running at an average of 160 kph (99 mph) but was obliged to stop because the marshals signaled that he was losing a rear wheel.

210 bottom right John "Jock" Horsfall and Leslie Johnson drove an Aston Martin to victory in the 1948 Spa 24 Hours, the first post-war edition. The winners' average speed of 116 kph (72 mph) was slower than that of the previous editions: you have to go back to 1931 to find a lower average.

210-211 OSCA (right) participated in the 1500-cc class of the sports-prototype category in the 1950s, producing cars capable of challenging the Porsches. Here Cabianca is seen at the start of the Modena GP Sport of 1956, second on the grid behind a Stanguellini.

211 top Group photograph of team Jaguar before the 1951 Le Mans 24 Hours: from the left, C-Types No. 22 of Moss and Fairman, No. 23 of Johnson and Biondetti and No. 20 of Walker and Whitehead. This last car won the race, 3611.2 km (2242 mi.) at an average speed of 150.466 kph (93 mph).

*211 bottom Barchettas or coupés,
Porsches were always among the
protagonists of endurance races. The left
photograph shows the 1500 RSK Sebring
Spyder (race number 20) of Jean Behra,
characterized by its small rear fins. On the
right, the 356 (No. 52) of Hahnl and Zick
during the 1958 Nürburgring 1000 km
(621 mi.) staged on the classic 22.835-
kilometer German circuit, one of the
longest in the history of motor racing.*

Sports-Prototypes

equipment and raced for the next 24 hours,
alternating spells at the wheel with one or more co-
drivers and dealing with all refueling and repairs.
The pits were only able to supply spare tires, oil and
fuel (in pre-defined quantities), while batteries and
other electrical components could not be replaced
during the race.

It was probably the rigour and complexity of
the race that led to Le Mans becoming the greatest
expression of sports-prototype racing and
stimulated the birth of other celebrated endurance
races such as the Tourist Trophy and the Brooklands
6 and 12 Hours in England, the Spa-Francorchamps
24 Hours in Belgium and the Mille Miglia in Italy.

It was but a short step from the birth of a
number of races to the organization of a
championship: the Sports Prototype World
Championship was first staged in 1953 and for a
quarter of a century represented a valid alternative
to Formula 1. However, it then slowly declined until
the FIA attempted to revive its former glory by
promoting the GT Championship that at the end of
the millennium has become the IPC (International
Prototype Cup).

212 top right The start of a race is always thrilling: this image shows the 1964 Nürburgring 1000 km (621 mi.) with the cars lined up diagonally and Surtees the first away in the Ferrari 275P. Ferrari won, but with Scarfiotti and Vaccarella rather than the English driver.

212 center right A frightening accident for Klass at Mugello in 1967, when the circuit still featured a road route with a number of mountain passes. The Ferrari crashed into a tree and the trunk split the car in two at the cockpit.

212 bottom right The Porsche 908 of Toivonen and Larrousse at Mugello in 1969: the German car had made its debut the previous year at Monza but its first victory came in the Nürburgring 1000 km (621 mi.) with Jo Siffert and Vic Elford at the wheel.

This change, one of the many that have characterized the history of sports-prototype racing, can perhaps be identified as one of the causes of the ultimate failure of the category, despite its undoubted sporting and technological merits. There is no other explanation as to why the individual events mentioned above and those that were instituted from the 1950s on (the Daytona 24 Hours, the Sebring 12 Hours, the Monza and Brands Hatch 1,000 km (621 mi.) races and the Carrera Panamericana, most of which are still being staged), have always been better known than the Championship itself—or why certain manufacturers are prepared to invest all their resources in a single race, for example Le Mans, in which victory is worth far more than a complete Championship title.

On the other hand, the chronology of the World Championship speaks very clearly. After its debut in 1953 as the World Sports Car Championship, it was canceled in 1961 due to the superiority of Ferrari. It only returned sporadically, in 1976 and '77 and 1991 and '92. In 1962 it was replaced by the Speed World Challenge, organized for prototypes and GT cars with cylinder capacities of up to four liters in 1962 and unrestricted capacities the following year. From 1964 the FIA returned with the International Championship for Makes, which became the World Championship in 1972 and lasted until 1981.

212 top left Heading for victory in his Porsche RS 60/1600 spider is the Swiss driver Heini Walter, the European Mountain Champion in 1961.

212 bottom left Porsche stunned the world with the presentation of the 917 in 1969. Designed and built in just eight months, the car was powered by a 4.5-liter V12 producing 560 hp. This picture shows the German car crewed by Piper and Gardner in the Nürburgring 1000 km (621 mi.), in which it finished eighth.

213 top The international regulations were further modified in 1972, the new norms outlawing the five-liter prototypes with total displacement being restricted to three liters. Ferrari benefited and enjoyed a golden season with the 312PB and drivers mostly from Formula 1 such as the celebrated Ickx, who won this race with Mario Andretti.

213 center Waiting for the start of the 1965 Nürburgring 1000 km (621 mi.) with the Porsche 904s on the front row of the grid. However, the best placing the German cars could manage was third with Rindt and Bonnier; victory went to the Ferrari 275P2 driven by Surtees and Scarfiotti.

213 bottom left New regulations introduced in the late Sixties led to the institution in 1968 of the International Championship for Makes. The ICM allowed three-liter prototypes and five-liter homologated sports cars (those built in runs of at least 50 examples). The rulings had the effect of temporarily eliminating the main protagonists of sports-prototype racing in that era, such as the prestigious Ferraris and Fords, leaving the field free for the challenger Porsche.

213 bottom right Lorenzo Bandini drives the Ferrari 330 P4 to victory in the Monza 1000 km, a race valid for the 1967 Sports Prototype World Championship. The Italian driver, with the New Zealander Chris Amon, won at an average speed of 194.984 kph (121 mph).

In the two-year period 1976-77 when the World Sports Car Championships and the ICM coexisted, the cars were divided into Groups five and six and further subdivided according to engine capacity. In 1976 the World Championship was reserved for cars derived from production models (although by the time they reached the track they had little in common with showroom cars). The sports-prototypes thus competed in a minor championship, a sign of the waning interest in this category: the major manufacturers now concentrated on Formula 1 or alternatively competed only in the most important sports-prototype races such as Le Mans—those which guaranteed maximum exposure. The decline of the category continued and by 1979 it had been abandoned, the cars still active being restricted to hillclimbs or non-championship races.

In order to try to revive interest, a Drivers' Championship was introduced in 1981, and between 1982 and 1985 the series was renamed the World Endurance Championship. Finally, in the late 1980s the series was enlivened by Mercedes' and Jaguar's attempts to challenge the Porsche supremacy. From 1986 to 1990, racing was carried out under the name World Sports Prototype Championship.

But none of these solutions really took hold, and after 1992 the FIA decided to abandon the championship altogether. Following a break in 1993 and a transitional year in 1994 with seven races for GT cars, in 1995 the BPR organized the BPR GT Championship with 12 races around the world.

BPR is a private British concern whose name derives from the initials of its three founders, all respected figures within motor-racing circles: Jürgen Barth (13 times a competitor at Le Mans, a victory in 1977 with Jacky Ickx, and manager of the Porsche competition department); Patrick Peter (promoter of French races such as the Paris 1,000 km (621 mi.) and the Tour de France); and Stephane Ratel (founder of the Gentlemen Venturi Trophy and organizer of the Philippe Charriol Supersport Trophy). Within two years the FIA revived the Sports Prototype category once again, and in 1997 and 1998 organized the FIA World GT Championship in two divisions, GT1 and GT2.

Yet the many sports-prototype championships have generated a number of interesting themes despite their organizational vicissitudes; for example, the eternal Porsche-Ferrari challenge with the two marques each conquering 13 titles in eras in which one or the other were dominant. Following Porsche's first string in 1969-71, the German marque ruled from 1976 through to 1986, the only exceptions being the 1977 and 1981 seasons. Ferrari essentially ruled the roost from 1953 to 1967 before being publicly deposed by the upstarts at Ford.

The domination of the drivers' championship inaugurated in 1982 is less clearcut, with only Derek Bell, the Le Mans specialist Jacky Ickx and Jean-Louis Schlesser winning two titles each.

215 center Arturo Merzario celebrating victory at Imola in 1971 with his team: his Ferrari 312PB was powered by a 12-cylinder horizontally-opposed engine derived from the firm's Formula 1 unit. The structure of the car was also developed from the single-seater.

215 bottom These photographs are a tribute to one of the great protagonists of racing in the Seventies, Porsche. The bottom picture portrays the 935 of Belgian Jacky Ickx and German Jochen Mass, which won the Silverstone 6 Hours in 1978; the 935 had already won the previous edition of the race and would go on to victory in 1979 and 1981, too.

The top image it evokes the atmosphere of night racing: the powerful lights of Rolf Stommelen's Porsche 936 Turbo pierce the foggy dark of the Nürburgring 300 km (186 mi.) during the 1976 season. The German finished fifth, a placing sufficient to allow Porsche to conquer the sports-prototype series' World Championship.

HONOR ROLL

Winners of the Sports Prototype World Championship—Constructors and Teams

Year	Championship	Constructor-Team
1953	World Sports Car Championship	Ferrari
1954	World Sports Car Championship	Ferrari
1955	World Sports Car Championship	Mercedes-Benz
1956	World Sports Car Championship	Ferrari
1957	World Sports Car Championship	Ferrari
1958	World Sports Car Championship	Ferrari
1959	World Sports Car Championship	Aston Martin
1960	World Sports Car Championship	Ferrari
1961	World Sports Car Championship	Ferrari
1962	Speed World Challenge	Ferrari
1963	Speed World Challenge	Ferrari
1964	International Championship for Makes	Ferrari
1965	International Championship for Makes	Ferrari
1966	International Championship for Makes	Ford
1967	International Championship for Makes	Ferrari
1968	International Championship for Makes	Ford
1969	International Championship for Makes	Porsche
1970	International Championship for Makes	Porsche
1971	International Championship for Makes	Porsche
1972	International Championship for Makes	Ferrari
1973	International Championship for Makes	Matra-Simca

216 top Mercedes has never enjoyed consistent success in the Le Mans 24 Hours. The Stuttgart firm's two wins came in the 1952 edition with Lang and Riess and 37 years later in 1989 with Mass, Reuter and Dickens.

216 center Race stewards in the middle of the track send the cars lined up in two rows on their way. The procedure was changed in the Seventies with the drivers no longer required to sprint to their cars to start the race.

216 bottom A tire change in the Mazda pits during the 1991 Le Mans 24 Hours, an historic edition in that a Japanese car with spinning engine (driven by Europeans Weidler, Herbert and Gachot) won for the first time.

1974	International Championship for Makes	Matra-Simca
1975	International Championship for Makes	Alfa Romeo
1976	International Championship for Makes / World Sports Car Championship	Porsche/Porsche
1977	International Championship for Makes / World Sports Car Championship	Porsche/Alfa Romeo
1978	International Championship for Makes	Porsche
1979	International Championship for Makes	Porsche
1980	International Championship for Makes	Porsche
1981	World Sports Car Championship	Lancia
1982	World Endurance Championship	Porsche
1983	World Endurance Championship	Porsche
1984	World Endurance Championship	Porsche
1985	World Endurance Championship for Teams	Rothmans-Porsche
1986	World Sports Prototype Championship for Teams	Brun-Motorsport-Porsche
1987	World Sports Prototype Championship for Teams	Silk Cut Jaguar (TWR)
1988	World Sports Prototype Championship for Teams	Silk Cut Jaguar (TWR)
1989	World Sports Prototype Championship for Teams	Team Sauber Mercedes
1990	World Sports Prototype Championship for Teams	Team Sauber Mercedes
1991	World Sports Prototype Championship for Teams	Silk Cut Jaguar (TWR)
1992	World Sports Prototype Championship for Teams	Peugeot Talbot Sport
1995	BPR	West Competition
1996	BPR	Gulf Team
1997	FIA GT	AMG Mercedes
1998	FIA GT	AMG Mercedes

Winner of the World Sports Prototype Championship—Drivers

YEAR	DRIVER	TEAM	CAR
1981	Bob Garretson	Cooke-Woods Racing/ Garretson Racing/Varde Racing	Porsche 935/Porsche 935K3/Mazda RX3
1982	Jacky Ickx	Rothmans-Porsche	Porsche 956
1983	Jacky Ickx	Rothmans-Porsche	Porsche 956
1984	Stefan Bellof	Rothmans-Porsche	Porsche 956
1985	D. Bell-H.J. Stuck	Rothmans-Porsche	Porsche 962
1986	Derek Bell	Rothmans-Porsche	Porsche 962
1987	Raul Boesel	Silk Cut Jaguar (TWR)	Jaguar XJR8
1988	Martin Brundle	Silk Cut Jaguar (TWR)	Jaguar XJR9
1989	Jean-Louis Schlesser	Team Sauber Mercedes	Sauber C9/88-Mercedes-Benz
1990	M. Baldi/J. L. Schlesser	Team Sauber Mercedes	Sauber C9/88-Mercedes-Benz C 11
1991	Teo Fabi	Silk Cut Jaguar (TWR)	Jaguar XJR14/Jaguar XJR12
1992	Y. Dalmas-D. Warwick	Peugeot Talbot Sport	Peugeot 905B
1995	J. Nielsen-T. Bscher	West Competition	McLaren F1GTR
1996	R. Bellm-J. Weaver	Gulf Team	McLaren F1GTR
1997	Bernd Schneider (GT1)	AMG Mercedes	Mercedes CLK
	Justin Bell (GT2)	Viper Team Oreca	Chrysler Viper
1998	K. Ludwig-R. Zonta (GT1)	AMG Mercedes	Mercedes CLK
	O. Beretta-P. Lamy (GT2)	Viper Team Oreca	Chrysler Viper

216-217 A Porsche 911 GT1 during qualifying for the 1998 edition of the Le Mans 24 Hours. The German car won the race for the third year in a row, finishing at an average speed of 199.3 kph (123.8 mph) with a crew composed of McNish, Ortelli and Ajello.

217 top Aston Martin, photographed here during the 1989 edition, has only managed one Le Mans victory: in 1959 the car driven by Carroll Shelby and Roy Salvadori was first across the line after covering 4,347.9 km (2,700 mi.) at an average speed of 181.2 kph (112.5 mph).

217 bottom After having raced day and night the crews still have the energy to celebrate and perhaps enjoy a champagne rinse: this photograph shows the podium at Hungary's Hungaroring on the occasion of the fifth round of the 1998 FIA GT1 championship.

Drivers who have won the greatest number of titles

DRIVER	NUMBER OF TITLES
Derek Bell	2
Jacky Ickx	2
Jean-Louis Schlesser	2

Constructors who have won the greatest number of titles

CONSTRUCTOR	NUMBER OF TITLES
Porsche	13
Ferrari	13
Mercedes-Benz	5
Jaguar	3

THE SEBRING 12 HOURS

The Sebring 12 Hours has a place of honor in the roller-coaster history of the sports-prototype World Championship, as it was the first round of the first edition in 1953, anticipating other celebrated and eagerly-awaited events such as the Mille Miglia, the Le Mans 24 Hours, the Tourist Trophy and the Carrera Panamericana. The circuit, located around 150 km from Tampa and Orlando, had been in use since 1950 and was also the venue for the first United States Formula 1 Grand Prix in 1959. It has not been distinguished in terms of continuity, however, as it only staged sports-prototype championship events until 1972, and then once again in 1981. After 1959 it never again hosted the Grand Prix circuit.

The track has been modified on a number of occasions with the total length gradually being increased up to the 1980s, then reduced to the virtually identical length of the original layout, roughly six kilometres. In 1987 the track surface itself was renewed, as it had proven too abrasive.

In contrast with other endurance races, there is no one true Sebring 12 Hours specialist. The Belgian driver Olivier Gendebien and the German Hans-Joachim Stuck both won the race three times, as did the local heroes Mario Andretti and Phil Hill, two of the latter's victories being with Gendebien. These hat-tricks were all scored in a two-decade period between 1958 and 1975 with the exception of that of Stuck, who claimed his third victory in 1988 at the venerable age (for a racing driver) of 37. In recent times no other driver has managed to match these feats. It is curious to note the same great name at the top and bottom of the roll of 69-: Fangio, who won the 1956 and 1957 editions, also appears in 1992 and 1993. The surname is identical as are the forenames, Juan Manuel, but the Roman numeral "II" accompanying the recent results clears up any possible misunderstanding and denote that the Fangio in question is the nephew of the great "chueco," a driver who has yet to enjoy the international success of his uncle.

Porsche has instead dominated the results at Sebring in the sports-prototype category, winning no fewer than 17 editions and utterly monopolizing the event between 1976 and 1988, when the German firm came home first 13 years in a row.

HONOR ROLL

Year	Car	Crew	Av. Speed kph (mph)	Distance covered km (mi)
1952	Frazer-Nash	Gray-Kulok	101.115 (62.8)	1213.38 (753.5)
1953	Cunningham C4R-Chrysler	Fitch-Walters	120.638 (74.9)	1447.76 (899.1)
1954	OSCA MT4	Moss-Lloyd	116.468 (72.3)	1405.92 (873.1)
1955	Jaguar D-Type	Hawthorn-Walters	126.913 (78.8)	1523.08 (945.8)
1956	Ferrari 860 Monza	Fangio-Castellotti	135.292 (84)	1623.50 (1008.2)
1957	Maserati 450S	Fangio-Behra	137.373 (85)	1648.61 (1023.8)
1958	Ferrari 250TR	Collins-Hill	139.477 (86.6)	1673.71 (1039.4)
1959	Ferrari 250TR	Gurney-Daigh-Hill-Gendebien	131.108 (81.4)	1573.29 (977)
1960	Porsche 718RSK	Gendebien-Herrmann	136.678 (84.88)	1640.24 (1018.6)
1961	Ferrari 250TR	Hill-Gendebien	145.967 (90.64)	1757.40 (1091.3)
1962	Ferrari 250TR	Bonnier-Bianchi	143.460 (89.1)	1723.93 (1070.6)
1963	Ferrari 250P	Surtees-Scarfiotti	145.468 (90.33)	1749.03 (1086.1)
1964	Ferrari 275P	Parkes-Maglioli	148.643 (92.3)	1790.87 (1112.1)
1965	Chaparral 2D-Chevrolet	Hall-Sharp	136.343 (84.67)	1640.24 (1018.6)
1966	Ford GTX1	Ruby-Miles	158.723 (98.57)	1908.03 (1184.9)

218 Spectators, cars and drivers in two images that portray the most thrilling and evocative moment in motor racing, the start of the race when everyone is out to win. Up until the 1960s the start took place with the drivers sprinting in helmets and gloves toward their cars, parked herringbone-fashion at the side of the track. Success in the race could in part be due to the athletic prowess of the driver, as the faster they ran, the sooner they started.

219 top Fear, panic and confusion in the pits with the darkness emphasizing the flames and making the scene even more dramatic: the photograph dates from the 1962 edition of the Sebring 12 Hours with the Alfa Romeo TZ1 of Giunti bursting into flames after the start. Fortunately the Italian driver was not seriously injured.

219 center The 1996 edition of the Sebring 12 Hours, then still part of the IMSA category, saw 58 cars start but only 34 cross the finishing line after the hour hand had completed a full circle. The blue and yellow Riley & Scott Oldsmobile Mk3 (top) crewed by Taylor, Pace and Van de Poele won the race. This win interrupted Ferrari's victorious sequence that saw it triumphant in 1995, 1997 and 1998 with the 333SP entered by Gianpiero Moretti's team.

219 bottom A night stop for a Ferrari during the Sebring 12 Hours of 1962. The Ferrari 250TR driven by Jo Bonnier and Lucien Bianchi won the American endurance race at an average speed of 143.460 kph (89.1 mph).

1967	Ford GT40 MkIV	Andretti-McLaren	165.603 (102.84)	1991.72 (1236.86)
1968	Porsche 907/8	Herrmann-Siffert	164.977 (102.45)	1983.35 (1231.86)
1969	Ford-Mirage	Ickx-Oliver	166.346 (103.3)	2000.09 (1242.1)
1970	Ferrari 512S	Giunti-Vaccarella-Andretti	172.666 (107.23)	2075.40 (1288.82)
1971	Porsche 917K	Elford-Larrousse	181.052 (112.43)	2175.83 (1351.2)
1972	Ferrari 312P	Ickx-Andretti	179.459 (111.44)	2167.46 (1345.99)
1973	Porsche Carrera	Gregg-Haywood-Helmick	157.480 (97.78)	1889.76 (1173.54)
1975	BMW 3.0 CIL	Redman-Moffat-Posey-Stuck	165.183 (102.58)	1982.20 (1230.95)
1976	Porsche 911 Carrera RSR	Holbert-Keyser	160.398 (99.61)	1924.77 (1195.28)
1977	Porsche 911 Carrera RSR	Dyer-Frisselle	163.062 (101.26)	1956.75 (1215.14)
1978	Porsche 935	Redman-Mendez-Garretson	167.336 (103.92)	2008.03 (1246.99)
1979	Porsche 935	Akin-McFarlin-Woods	166.512 (103.4)	1998.14 (1240.85)
1980	Porsche 935	Barbour-Fitzpatrick	176.255 (109.45)	2115.06 (1313.45)
1981	Porsche 935	Leven-Haywood-Holbert	170.661 (105.98)	2050.30 (1273.24)
1982	Porsche 935	Paul-Paul Jr.	169.626 (105.34)	2359.51 (1465.26)
1983	Porsche 934	Baker-Muller-Nielop	146.889 (91.22)	1762.67 (1094.62)
1984	Porsche 935	de Narvaez-Heyer-Johansson	171.176 (106.3)	2054.11 (1275.60)
1985	Porsche 962	Wollek-Foyt	183.122 (113.72)	2197.46 (1364.62)
1986	Porsche 962	Akin-Stuck-Gartner	186.445 (115.78)	2237.34 (1389.39)
1987	Porsche 962	Mass-Rahal	163.926 (101.79)	1967.11 (1221.58)
1988	Porsche 962	Ludwig-Stuck	175.067 (108.72)	2100.80 (1304.59)
1989	Nissan GTP ZX-T	Brabham-Robinson-Luyendyk	181.440 (112.67)	2177.28 (1352.1)
1990	Nissan GTP ZX-T	Daly-Earl	165.751 (102.93)	1989.01 (1235.17)
1991	Nissan NPT 90	Brabham-Daly-Brabham	147.457 (91.57)	1769.48 (1098.85)
1992	Eagle Mk3-Toyota	Fangio II-Wallace	178.193 (110.66)	2138.32 (1327.89)
1993	Eagle Mk3-Toyota	Fangio II-Wallace	113.779 (70.66)	1365.35 (847.88)
1994	Nissan 300ZX	Millen-O'Connell-Morton	161.954 (100.57)	1943.45 (1206.882)
1995	Ferrari 333SP	Velez-Evans-Van de Poele	128.812 (79.99)	1548.19 (961.426)
1996	Oldsmobile R&S	Taylor-Pace-Van de Poele	161.191 (100.1)	1934.3 (1201.2)
1997	Ferrari 333SP	Evans-Velez-Dalmas-Johansson	161.191 (100.1)	1934.3 (1201.2)
1998	Ferrari 333SP	Moretti-Baldi-Theys-Luyendyk	158.230 (98.26)	1898.7 (1179.1)

The Drivers Who Have Won the Most Editions

DRIVER	NUMBER OF WINS
Mario Andretti	3
Olivier Gendebien	3
Phil Hill	3
Hans-Joachim Stuck	3

The Constructors Who Have Won the Most Editions

CONSTRUCTOR	NUMBER OF WINS
Porsche	17
Ferrari	9
Nissan	4
Ford	3

Daytona

Together with Indianapolis, Sebring, Watkins Glen and Laguna Seca, Daytona represents the pulsing heart of automotive speed in the United States. Daytona Beach, a celebrated coastal resort in southern Florida, has hosted the famous 24 Hours race since 1966, a race that up to 1981 (with the exception of 1976) was part of the Sports-Prototype World Championship. The fame of Daytona is not, however, restricted to that single endurance race, the United States' only major 24-hour event (Sebring being a 12-hour race). The American town is also the spiritual home of NASCAR racing, as the championship headquarters are based there and the track is the venue for the famous Daytona 500.

The 2.5 mi. (4 km) oval track has been in use since 1959: it was lengthened to 3.8 mi. (6.1 km) in 1961 for sports-car racing but the later addition of a chicane and various other modifications reduced it again to the present-day 3.5 mi. (5.7 km).

As with the other endurance races, Porsche is the great Daytona specialist, winning no fewer than

18 editions: Weissach's first victory came in 1968, after which there was a crescendo with wins in 1970, '71, '73 and '75 and a peak with seven consecutive triumphs between 1977 and 1983. Trailing far behind Porsche is Ferrari with three wins, followed by Jaguar and Nissan with two each. The Prancing Horse regained its winning ways in 1998 after a wait of 31 years (1967, Lorenzo Bandini and Chris Amon with the 330P4).

The merit for Ferrari's successful comeback is to be attributed to a veteran of American motor racing, the Italian Gianpiero Moretti, who persuaded the firm to construct the 333SP and to return to the sports-prototype category in 1993 after having abandoned it in the early 1970s to

concentrate on Formula 1. Moretti's Momo Racing Team took this car to victory at the Daytona 24 Hours with a crew composed of Gianpiero himself, Mauro Baldi (a winner at Le Mans in 1994) and Didier Theys. Such was Moretti's satisfaction that he was able to retire from the sport a happy man after a career spanning 20 years.

The greatest Daytona ace was, however, Hurley Haywood, the American driver who won five editions with Porsche, four in the 1970s and the last in 1991. Behind him with four wins comes another American, Peter Gregg (two of his wins were with Haywood) and a German, Rolf Stommelen.

220 left Alfa Romeo's participation in the 1968 Daytona 24 Hours was eagerly awaited: Andretti and Bianchi's Tipo 33/2 number 22 is lined up on the grid with the photographers taking their last shots before being ushered away from the track.

220-221 An aerial view of the chestnut-shaped Daytona circuit. Built in 1959, this track is the spiritual home of NASCAR, the American form of saloon racing, but since '61 it has also seen the country's most celebrated endurance race for sports-prototypes.

221 top It would be difficult not to notice Phil Hill and his Chaparral with an improbably high wing at the '67 Daytona 24 Hours. The American driver led the race early on but later had to give way to the Ferrari team, with Chris Amon and Lorenzo Bandini finally winning.

221 bottom The Daytona 24 Hours was staged from the early Sixties (this shot is from the 1968 edition). Porsche won only once in that decade, along with Ford, Ferrari and Lola, but in the Seventies the German firm dominated with its 917, 911 Carrera and 935 models, winning every edition of the American race except those in 1972 and 1976.

221

HONOR ROLL

YEAR	CAR	CREW	AV. SPEED KPH (MPH)	DISTANCE COVERED KM (MI.)
1966	Ford GT40 MkII	Miles-Ruby	172.82 (107.32)	4157.21 (2581.63)
1967	Ferrari 330P4	Bandini-Amon	170.077 (105.62)	4083.64 (2535.94)
1968	Porsche 907/8	Elford-Neerpasch-Stommelen Siffert-Herrmannn	171.712 (106.63)	4126.56 (2562.59)
1969	Lola T70 MkIIIB-Chevrolet	Donohue-Parsons	160.334 (99.57)	3838.37 (2383.63)
1970	Porsche 917	Rodriguez-Kinnunen	184.858 (114.8)	4439.27 (2756.79)
1971	Porsche 917K	Rodriguez-Oliver	175.745 109.14)	4218.53 (2619.71)
1972	Ferrari 312P (4-HOUR)	Ickx-Andretti	197.374 (122.57)	1189.53 (738.7)
1973	Porsche 911 Carrera RS	Gregg-Haywood	171.031 (106.21)	4108.16 (2551.17)
1975	Porsche 911 Carrera RS	Gregg-Haywood	176.126 (109.37)	4227.03 (2624.99)
1976	BMW 3.0 CSL	Gregg-Redman-Fitzpatrick	167.439 (103.98)	4018.54 (2495.51)
1977	Porsche 911 Carrera RSR	Graves-Haywood-Helmick	175.098 (108.74)	4208.49 (2613.47)
1978	Porsche 935	Stommelen-Hezemans-Gregg	175.005 (108.68)	4202.31 (2609.63)
1979	Porsche 935	Ongais-Haywood-Field	176.076 (109.34)	4227.03 (2624.99)
1980	Porsche 935	Stommelen-Jöst-Merl	183.952 (114.23)	4418.60 (2743.95)
1981	Porsche 935	Garretson-Rahal-Redman	182.102 (113.09)	4375.34 (2717.09)
1982	Porsche 935	Paul-Paul Jr.-Stommelen	184.743 (114.73)	4433.83 (2753.41)
1983	Porsche 935	Henn-Wollek-Ballot/Lena-Foyt	158.972 (98.72)	3815.33 (2369.32)
1984	March 83G-Porsche	Van der Merwe-Martin-Duxbury	165.953 (103.06)	3982.87 (2473.36)
1985	Porsche 956	Foyt-Wollek-Al Unser Jr-Boutsen	167.632 (104.10)	4023.17 (249.39)
1986	Porsche 962	Holbert-Bell-Al Unser Jr.	169.760 (105.42)	4074.24 (2498.39)
1987	Porsche 962	Robinson-Bell-Al Unser Jr.-Holbert	179.601 (111.53)	4310.42 (2676.77)
1988	Jaguar XJR-9	Brundle-Nielsen-Boesel-Lammers	173.717 (107.88)	4169.21 (2589.08)
1989	Porsche 962	Andretti-Bell-Wollek	148.074 (91.95)	3553.77 (2206.89)
1990	Jaguar XJR-12	Jones-Lammers-Wallace	181.625 (112.79)	4359.00 (2706.94)
1991	Porsche 962	Winter-Jelinski-Pescarolo-Haywood-Wollek	171.609 (106.57)	4118.62 (2557.66)
1992	Nissan R91CP	Hasemi-Hoshino-Suzuki	181.690 (112.83)	4360.56 (2707.91)
1993	Eagle Mk3-Toyota	Jones-Dismore-Moran	166.573 (103.44)	3997.75 (2482.6)
1994	Nissan 300 ZX	Pruett-Gentilozzi-Leitzinger-Millen	168.659 (104.74)	4047.82 (2513.7)
1995	Porsche	Lassig-Bouchut-Lavaggi-Werner	164.618 (102.23)	3950.827 (2453.46)
1996	Ford R&S	Leitzinger-Paul Jr.	161.739 (100.44)	3881.728 (2410.55)
1997	Ford R&S	Weaver-Leitzinger-Dyson-Wallace-Paul Jr.-Forbes-Robinson	164.623 (102.23)	3950.943 (2453.54)
1998	Ferrari 333SP	Moretti-Baldi-Theys-Luyendyk	181.690 (112.83)	4365.689 (2711.09)

222 An awesome Ferrari at the 1998 edition of the Daytona 24 Hours left adversaries of the caliber of Porsche in its wake as it returned to success in the 24-hour race after 31 years. Back in 1967 Maranello had won with the 330P4 driven by Lorenzo Bandini and Chris Amon. Merit for the 1998 victory goes to Gianpiero Moretti and his team who also took the 333SP to victory in the other two American endurance races par excellence, the Watkins Glen 6 Hours and

the Sebring 12 Hours. Moretti won at Daytona with Mauro Baldi, Didier Theys and Arie Luyendyk. The Italian driver and team owner, who at the end of the season retired from racing after having competed in the States for over 20 years, is owed a debt of gratitude by Ferrari: it was he who convinced the company to return to the American sports-prototype scene in 1993.

223 top A quartet of cars battling it out during the Daytona 24 Hours: the red, white, and blue Riley & Scott driven by Wallace, Leitzinger and Robinson had to better its great rivals—the Ferrari 333SP of the Moretti team, which had won the 1998 edition—to clinch the last 20th-century edition of the great American endurance race.

223 center The 1999 Daytona 24 Hours was the first major event for the sports-prototype category that season but the 33th edition of the race, which now ranks with Le Mans, Sebring, Spa-Francorchamps, and Reims in the canon of the sport.

The Drivers Who Have Won the Most Editions

DRIVER	NUMBER OF WINS
Hurley Haywood	5
Peter Gregg	4
Rolf Stommelen	4

The Constructors Who Have Won the Most Editions

CONSTRUCTOR	NUMBER OF WINS
Porsche	18
Ferrari	3
Riley & Scott	2
Jaguar	2
Nissan	2

223 bottom An American... in America. The Dodge (badged as a Chrysler in Europe) Viper GTS seen here during the Daytona 24 Hours of 1999. The Daimler-Chrysler musclecar was fresh from its triumph in the '98 FIA GT2 championship, part of the world series for sports-prototypes.

THE LE MANS 24 HOURS

The Le Mans 24 Hours is the motor race *par excellence*, a marathon for four-wheeled rockets lapping at remarkable average speeds for a day and a night, not stopping until the short hand of the timer's stopwatch has completed two complete revolutions. It is a race that has rightly become the stuff of legends, a cult so famous as to have been transformed into a memorable Hollywood film starring Steve McQueen, who would have loved to have taken part in the actual 1971 race but was prevented from doing so by his insurers. In 1979, with no film-making duties in his way, another actor/driver, Paul "PJ" Newman, not only competed but actually finished second.

While cinema was unable to resist the appeal and attraction of the world's most famous endurance race, for car manufacturers the French epic staged at La Sarthe is a veritable Siren call. Budgets running into the millions of dollars are the norm for those who take up the challenge, sums that would be sufficient to fund a team for an entire season in the minor championships. F

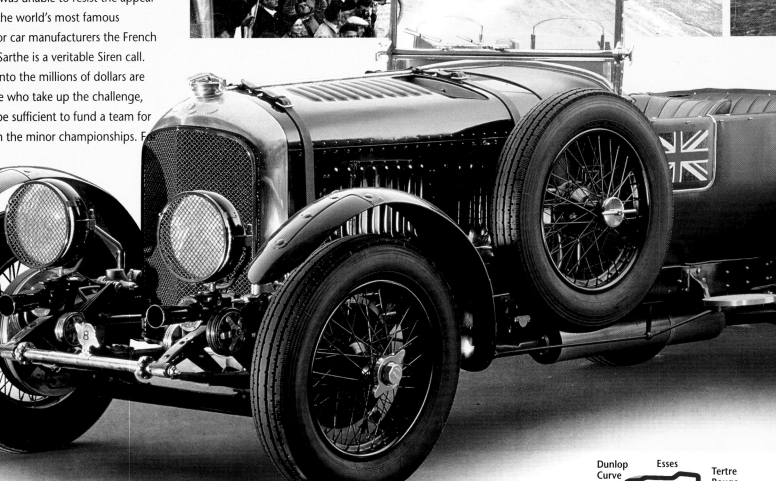

the drivers the race provides a unique experience. Winning at Le Mans demands the whole range of motor racing skills: innate talent, boldness, technical ability and a clear head capable of handling high levels of stress for the whole race. There is little rest to be had during the 24-hour period. It should therefore come as no surprise that some of the greatest names in motor racing, many coming from the world of Formula 1, have made their mark at Le Mans.

Nuvolari, Hawthorn, Phil Hill, Étancelin, Chinetti, Rindt, Pironi, Pescarolo, Bell and Scarfiotti are just a few of the drivers who have contributed to the history of the 24-hour race. Strangely, the greatest Grand Prix driver of all time, Juan Manuel Fangio, never drove here.

Special mention should be made of the great specialist, the Belgian Jacky Ickx who won the race on no fewer than six occasions, three times consecutively between 1975 and 1977.

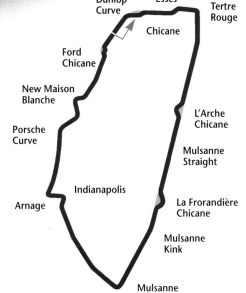

224 top The 1935 edition of the Le Mans 24 Hours went to Hindmarsh and Fontes (in Lagonda) who crossed the line first after completing 3006.8 km (1,867.2 mi.) at an average speed of 125.28 kph (77.8 mph). This was to be Lagonda's first and only win in the French race.

224 bottom and 225 bottom right It was Bentley that played the leading role in the first eight editions of the Le Mans 24 Hours—those from 1923 to the end of the decade, in which the celebrated event gained its repu-

tation as the endurance race par excellence. The British make won the 24-hour race in 1924 with Duff and Clemente and then from 1927 to 1930, first with Banjafield and Davids and then with the brilliant Woolf Barnato,

who won three consecutive editions paired with Rubin, Birkin and Kidston. The first great Le Mans car was a three-liter, four-seat open tourer with huge headlamps for the overnight phase of the race.

The first edition of the Le Mans 24 Hours was held in 1923 and in retrospect marked the birth of sports-car, later renamed sports-prototype, racing. Proclaimed as the "24 Hour Endurance Grand Prix Reserved for Production Touring Cars," the race was organized by the Automobile Club de l'Ouest. The idea for an event of this kind had been put forward the previous year during the Paris Motor Show and originally was commercially motivated. This explains why the cars competing in the race had to be identical in all respects to those in the manufacturers' sales catalogues.

225 top A thrilling moment in the 1935 edition of the Le Mans 24 Hours: this trio of cars racing through the esses includes the Lagonda number 14 of Banjafield and Gunter followed by the two Aston Martins (numbers 29 and 27) of Martin and Brackenbury and Elwes and Goodall.

225 bottom left Sammy Davis refueling his Sunbeam three-liter during the 1925 Le Mans 24 Hours. The wire mesh over the headlamps and the radiator grille protected them from the gravel thrown up from the poor road surface.

The commercial objectives were achieved in full, but it is unlikely that the ACO was prepared for the far-reaching international success of the race. The promotional value of the event for car manufacturers was immense, above all for those from neighboring Great Britain. Generally reluctant to invest time, money and technology in Grand Prix racing, the British manufacturers were quick to recognize the potential returns that could be provided by a Le Mans victory with a car identical to those they were trying to sell to their clientele.

Thirty-three cars from 17 different makes lined up for the start. The first names to be inscribed on the roll of honor were those of Lagache and Léonard who were first across the finishing line in their Chenard-Walcker after having completed 2209 km and 540 m (1,372 mi., 591 ft.) at an average speed of 92.065 kph (57.2 mph). The performance of the three-liter Bentley driven personally by its owner John F. Duff is worthy of note: the car finished in fourth place overall despite two hours having been lost while a split in the fuel tank was repaired. This misfortune was forgotten the following year when the latest version of the Bentley three-liter, with drum brakes on all four wheels, was driven to victory by Duff and Frank Clement. The prestigious British make won a further four consecutive editions of the 24-hour race from 1927 to 1930 before Alfa Romeo began to make its presence felt, winning four editions prior to the outbreak of the Second World War. This despite the fact that the Italian make did not enjoy the happiest of debuts at Le Mans: in 1928 an Alfa Romeo 1500 was rejected by the scrutineers because it was felt to be too sporting in appearance and lacking in any form of comfort.

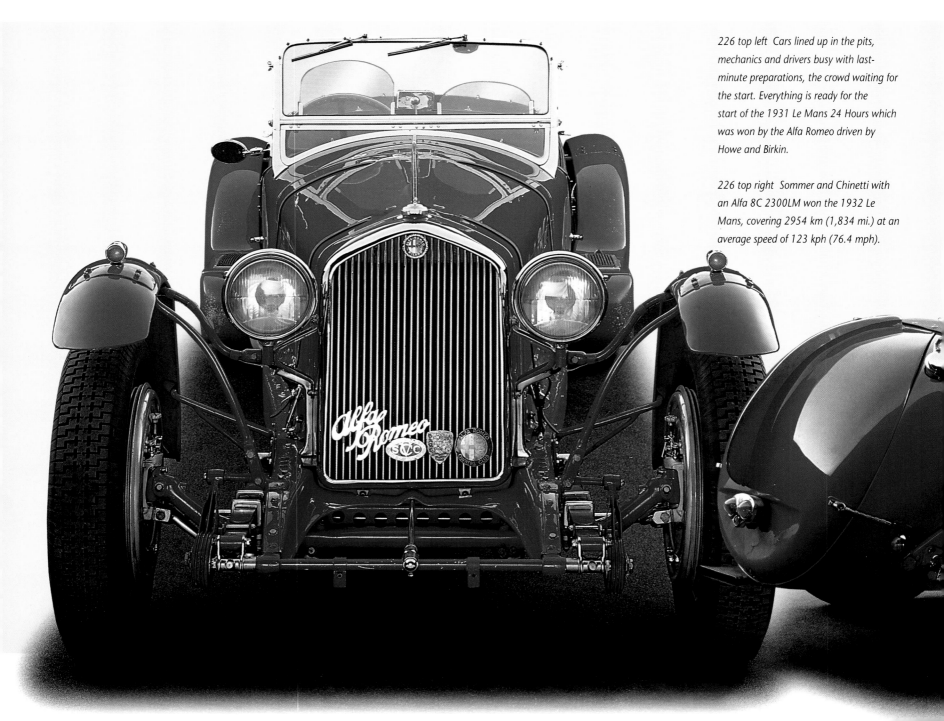

226 top left Cars lined up in the pits, mechanics and drivers busy with last-minute preparations, the crowd waiting for the start. Everything is ready for the start of the 1931 Le Mans 24 Hours which was won by the Alfa Romeo driven by Howe and Birkin.

226 top right Sommer and Chinetti with an Alfa 8C 2300LM won the 1932 Le Mans, covering 2954 km (1,834 mi.) at an average speed of 123 kph (76.4 mph).

226 bottom and 227 bottom The Alfa Romeo 8C 2300 Le Mans was one of Alfa's most successful competition models during the Thirties. In order to continue to dominate the sports car category Alfa had commissioned Vittorio Jano to design a new engine in 1930; the 8C 2300, a development of the 6C 1750, first saw the light of day in 1931. The bodywork and chassis were based on those of the 6C, as were the bore and stroke dimensions of the eight-cylinder engine. The total displacement naturally increased to 2300 cc and inevitable changes were made to components such as the camshaft drive, the two light-alloy cylinder blocks with steel liners and the light-alloy cylinder head. The supercharger was mounted on the right of the engine. As indicated by the name of the model, this car was specifically developed for Le Mans, an event that the 8C 2300 won four years in succession from 1931, with Howe and Birkin, Sommer and Chinetti, Sommer and Nuvolari, and Chinetti and Étancelin. The two- or four-seater open bodies were built by Zagato or Touring while the engine was taken from the Spider Corsa, the power output being increased from 155 to 165 hp. Alfa Romeo was never to win another edition of the 24-hour race after 1934.

227 top The Alfa Romeo 8C 2900B in open-top, long-wheelbase form during the 1937 edition of the Le Mans 24 Hours with Guidotti and Sommer. The car was a less powerful version of the 8C 2900A Corsa.

227 center left Nuvolari, in the car to the left, and Sommer, right, celebrating Alfa Romeo's third consecutive Le Mans victory in 1933 together with their mechanics.

227 center right Wimille and Veyron won the 1939 Le Mans 24 Hours, the last pre-war edition, with a Bugatti. This was the make's second and last victory, following its first in 1937.

228 top Its windshield broken, Rolt and Hamilton's C-Type Jaguar number 18 heading for victory in the 1953 edition of the Le Mans 24 Hours, the second of the British firm's seven wins. The car covered 4088 km (2,538 mi.) at an average speed of 170.3 kph (105.7 mph).

228 center left Trintignant, partnering Gonzales, preparing to tackle the 1954 Le Mans 24 Hours at the wheel of a Ferrari 375 Plus. Last-minute preparations before racing for an entire day and a night until the small hand had completed two complete revolutions paid off with victory, Ferrari's second in the French race.

The history of the French race is rich in illustrious rejections such as this: in 1958 the flying Rodriguez brothers intended to race together but the younger of the two, Ricardo, was only 16 at the time and was refused permission to partner Pedro, the Mexican Formula 1 ace adored by the local people for his fearless driving style. Four years later none other than Jim Clark was rejected: the wheelbolts of his Lotus were judged to be fragile and unsafe. Colin Chapman never forgave the organizers for this exclusion and took his revenge by forbidding any works Lotus participation in future editions.

With the exception of 1936 (a moment of crisis for the French automotive industry) and the war and immediate post-war years 1940-48, the Le Mans race has been staged annually. Up to the 1970s it retained the spectacular start in which the drivers sprinted across the track to reach their cars, jumped in and belted up as they shot away.

Porsche is the undisputed queen of Le Mans: the Weissach manufacturer has won 16 times and dominated the event between 1976 and 1987, giving way only twice, in 1978 to Renault and in 1980 to the Rondeau, a car built and driven by French specialist Jean Rondeau.

228 bottom right The French driver Pierre Levegh at the wheel of his Mercedes 300SLR number 20 during the night of the edition of the 24-hour race that will always be remembered for the terrible consequences of the accident Levegh allegedly provoked: his car left the track and plunged into the crowd, sowing death like a bomb in wartime. Eighty-three spectators were killed and another 75 hospitalized.

229 top left The tragic 1955 edition: Levegh's Mercedes crashed into the barriers and broke apart, ploughing into the crowd and killing 83 spectators and injuring at least 75. Le Mans came very close to being abandoned, but the show must go on—as, of course, must business.

229 top right Two E-Type Jaguars competing in the 1963 Le Mans 24 Hours, an edition won by the Ferrari driven by Bandini and Scarfiotti. The Coventry firm had not won the French marathon since 1957 and had to wait 31 years for its sixth victory.

229 center A do-it-yourself race: up until the Sixties it was by no means rare to see drivers doing their own refueling and cleaning their own windshields, like Lorenzo Bandini in this photograph— the Ferrari driver who won the 1963 Le Mans 24 Hours.

229 bottom Speed and accidents, an indivisible combination that is a part of endurance races such as the Le Mans 24 Hours, too. This picture shows three crashed cars, the one in the center being a Ferrari, from the 1966 edition won by Amon and McLaren at the wheel of a Ford GT40 MkII.

Ferrari is, of course, the other protagonist of the postwar epoch at Le Mans with nine wins, the majority coming in the Sixties. These victories consecrated the talent of Gendebien and brought forth drivers such as Rindt (the posthumous Formula 1 World Champion in 1970) and Vaccarella.

Jaguar, Alfa Romeo, Peugeot and Mercedes complete the group of great Le Mans makes. Mercedes deserted the 24-hour race for 34 years, during which time it tried to forget the tragedy of 1955 in what threatened to be the last edition of the race after Levegh's Mercedes ploughed into the crowd, killing 83 spectators. The Silver Arrows were not to return to the Sarthe until 1989 (and then only entered as Saubers), but these made up for lost time with a victory for Mass, Reuter and Dickens.

The Japanese have so far managed only one Le Mans victory, Mazda's 1991 win with the rotary-powered Type 787B. This was also the first victory for a Wankel engine (and, due to some hasty French rule changes, probably the last). Toyota came close to repeating that feat in '98, its works team arriving with three cars, nine drivers, and a staff of 120. After dominating most of the race and with less than 90 minutes to go the leading Toyota GT-One of Boutsen, Lees and Kelleners retired with transmission problems, thus handing the win to Porsche's 911-GT1, in reality a thinly-veiled prototype. Nissan/TWR's R391s also performed magnificently, the true GT racers falling only to the philosophically questionable Porsches.

230 center Alfa Romeo entered the 1968 edition of the Le Mans 24 Hours with the 33/2, among the fastest and best of the cars produced by the Italian firm in the modern period and a worthy heir to the great cars of the past that brought the make so many sports, Grand Prix and Formula 1 victories. Still, the 33 and its variants never managed to win Le Mans.

230 bottom This photograph shows Le Mans at night with the lights of the cars like streaks of flame and the evocative floodlighting around the circuit. This is the principal appeal of endurance racing: watching cars competing over a full 24 hours, a period long enough for plots to develop and surprises to be sprung right at the end.

231 top, center and bottom right The early Seventies: the decade having opened with Porsche victories in the Le Mans 24 Hours of 1970 and '71 with the Hermann-Attwood and Marko-van Lennep crews, the foundations were laid for the success the German firm enjoyed in the years to come. Matra-Simca (top photograph, the blue car on the right alongside a BMW) took center stage with wins from 1972 to '74. The next French victory came in 1978 with the Renault driven by Pironi and Jaussaud.

231 bottom left In 1966 Porsche introduced the Carrera 6, alias the 906, the heir to the 904 that had brought the make so much success. The 906 was powered by a two-liter, six-cylinder boxer engine.

232-233 Start of the 60th anniversary edition of the Le Mans 24 Hours in 1983: Porsche won the race (as in the previous two editions) with the Holbert-Haywood-Schuppan crew, who completed 5047.9 km (3,134.7 mi.) at an average speed of 210.3 kph (130.6 mph).

232 top left The 1981 edition of the 24 Hours has just started. The race was won by Ickx and Bell at the wheel of a Porsche 936.

232 center left Joyous celebrations with the customary bottle of champagne. In this image Henri Pescarolo and Klaus Ludwig are seen in the podium as winners of the 1984 Le Mans 24 Hours in a Porsche.

232 bottom left Four Ferrari 333SP prototypes were entered for prequalifying for the '98 edition of the Le Mans 24 Hours held during the month preceding the race. This picture shows one of the two Momo Racing cars.

HONOR ROLL

Year	Car	Crew	Av. Speed kph (mph)	Distance covered km (mi.)
1923	Chenard & Walker Sport	Lagache-Leonard	92.065 (57.2)	2209.54 (1372.1)
1924	Bentley Sport	Duff-Clement	86.555 (53.7)	2077.34 (1290.0)
1925	La Lorraine-Dietrich B3-6	De Courcelles-Rossignol	93.082 (57.8)	2233.98 (1387.3)
1926	La Lorraine-Dietrich B3-6	Bloch-Rossignol	106.350 (66.0)	2552.41 (1585.0)
1927	Bentley Sport	Banjafield-Davis	98.740 (61.3)	2369.81 (1471.6)
1928	Bentley 4.4	Barnato-Rubin	111.219 (69.0)	2669.27 (1657.6)
1929	Bentley Speed Six	Barnato-Birkin	118.492 (73.6)	2843.83 (1766.0)
1930	Bentley Speed Six	Barnato-Kidston	122.111 (75.8)	2930.66 (1819.9)
1931	Alfa Romeo 8C	Howe-Birkin	118.492 (73.6)	2843.83 (1766.0)
1932	Alfa Romeo 8C	Sommer-Chinetti	123.084 (76.4)	2954.04 (1834.4)
1933	Alfa Romeo 8C	Sommer-Nuvolari	131.001 (81.3)	3144.04 (1952.4)
1934	Alfa Romeo 8C	Chinetti-Étancelin	120.289 (74.7)	2886.94 (1792.8)
1935	Lagonda Rapide	Hindmarsh-Fontes	125.283 (77.8)	3006.80 (1867.2)
1937	Bugatti T57G	Wimille-Benoist	136.997 (85.1)	3287.94 (2014.8)
1938	Delahaye 135S	Chaboud-Tremoulet	132.539 (82.3)	3180.94 (1975.3)
1939	Bugatti T57C	Wimille-Veyron	139.781 (86.8)	3354.76 (2083.3)
1949	Ferrari 166MM	Chinetti-Selsdon	133.420 (82.8)	3178.28 (1973.7)
1950	Talbot Lago T26C-GS	Rosier-Rosier	144.380 (89.6)	3465.12 (2151.8)
1951	Jaguar C-Type	Walker-Whitehead	150.466 (93.4)	3611.19 (2242.5)
1952	Mercedes-Benz 300SL	Lang-Riess	155.575 (96.6)	3733.80 (2318.7)
1953	Jaguar C-Type	Rolt-Hamilton	170.366 (105.8)	4088.06 (2538.7)

YEAR	CAR	CREW	AV. SPEED KPH (MPH)	DISTANCE COVERED KM (MI.)
1954	Ferrari 375 Plus	Gonzales-Trintignant	169.215 (105.0)	4061.15 (2521.9)
1955	Jaguar D-Type	Hawthorn-Blueb	172.308 (107.0)	4135.38 (2568.1)
1956	Jaguar D-Type	Flockhart-Sanderson	168.122 (104.4)	4034.93 (2505.7)
1957	Jaguar D-Type	Flockhart-Blueb	183.217 (113.7)	4397.11 (2730.6)
1958	Ferrari 250TR	Gendebien-Hill	170.914 (106.1)	4101.93 (2547.3)
1959	Aston Martin DBR1	Shelby-Salvadori	181.163 (112.5)	4347.90 (2700.0)
1960	Ferrari 250TR	Frere-Gendebien	175.730 (109.1)	4217.53 (2619.1)
1961	Ferrari 250TR	Gendebien-Hill	186.527 (115.8)	4476.58 (2779.9)
1962	Ferrari 330LM	Gendebien-Hill	185.469 (115.1)	4451.26 (2764.2)
1963	Ferrari 250P	Scarfiotti-Bandini	190.071 (118.0)	4561.00 (2832.4)
1964	Ferrari 275P	Guichet-Vaccarella	196.638 (122.1)	4695.31 (2915.8)
1965	Ferrari 275LM	Rindt-Gregory	194.880 (121.0)	4677.11 (2904.5)
1966	Ford GT40 MkII	Amon-McLaren	201.795 (125.3)	4843.09 (3007.5)
1967	Ford GT40 MkIV	Gurney-Foyt	218.038 (135.4)	5232.90 (3249.6)
1968	Ford GT40	Rodriguez-Bianchi	185.536 (115.2)	4452.88 (2765.2)
1969	Ford GT40	Ickx-Oliver	208.250 (129.3)	4998.00 (3103.7)
1970	Porsche 917K	Herrmann-Atwood	191.992 (119.2)	4607.81 (2861.4)
1971	Porsche 917K	Marko-Van Lennep	222.304 (138.0)	5335.31 (3313.2)
1972	Matra-Simca MS670	Pescarolo-Hill	195.472 (121.3)	4691.34 (2913.3)
1973	Matra-Simca MS670B	Pescarolo-Larrousse	202.247 (125.6)	4853.95 (3014.3)

233 left Two Porsche 911 GT1s from the Porsche AG team follow each other along the prestigious Le Mans circuit during the 24 Hours in 1998: one of the two was to cross the line first, the car driven by McNish, Ortelli and Ajello, which after an entire day's racing had covered 4775.3 km at an average speed of 199.326 kph.

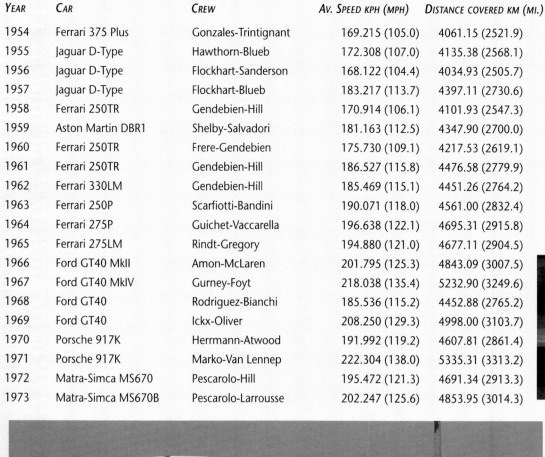

The Drivers Who Have Won the Most Editions

DRIVERS	NUMBER OF WINS
Jacky Ickx	6
Derek Bell	5
Olivier Gendebien	4
Henri Pescarolo	4
Woolf Barnato	3
Luigi Chinetti	3
Yannick Dalmas	3
Hurley Haywood	3
Phil Hill	3
Al Holbert	3
Klaus Ludwig	3

YEAR	CAR	CREW	AV. SPEED KPH (MPH)	DISTANCE COVERED KM (MI.)
1974	Matra-Simca MS670B	Pescarolo-Larrousse	191.940 (119.2)	4606.57 (2860.7)
1975	Gulf-Mirage GR8 Ford	Ickx-Van Lennep	191.484 (118.9)	4595.58 (2853.8)
1976	Porsche 936	Ickx-Barth-Haywood	198.748 (123.4)	4769.92 (2962.1)
1977	Porsche 936	Ickx-Bell	194.651 (120.8)	4671.73 (2901.1)
1978	Renault 369-Alpine A442B	Pironi-Jaussaud	210.189 (130.5)	5044.53 (3132.6)
1979	Porsche 935-K3	Ludwig-Whittington	173.913 (107.9)	4179.93 (2595.7)
1980	Rondeau M379B-Ford	Rondeau-Jaussaud	192.000 (119.2)	4608.02 (2861.6)
1981	Porsche 936	Ickx-Bell	201.056 (124.8)	4825.35 (2996.5)
1982	Porsche 956	Ickx-Bell	204.128 (126.8)	4899.09 (3042.3)
1983	Porsche 956	Holbert-Haywood-Schuppan	210.330 (130.6)	5047.93 (3134.8)
1984	Porsche 956	Pescarolo-Ludwig	204.178 (126.8)	4900.28 (3043.1)
1985	Porsche 956	Ludwig-Barilla-Winter	212.021 (131.8)	5088.51 (3159.9)
1986	Porsche 962	Stuck-Bell-Holbert	207.197 (128.7)	4972.73 (3088.1)
1987	Porsche 962	Stuck-Bell-Holbert	199.657 (123.9)	4791.78 (2975.7)
1988	Jaguar XJR9LM	Lammers-Dumfries-Wallace	221.665 (137.6)	5332.79 (3311.7)
1989	Sauber C9/88-Mercedes	Mass-Reuter-Dickens	219.990 (136.6)	5265.12 (3269.6)
1990	Jaguar XJR12	Nielsen-Cobb-Brundle	204.036 (126.7)	4882.40 (3031.9)
1991	Mazda 787B	Weidler-Herbert-Gachot	205.333 (127.5)	4922.81 (3057.1)
1992	Peugeot 905B	Warwick-Dalmas-Blundell	199.340 (123.8)	4787.20 (2972.8)
1993	Peugeot 905B	Brabham-Helary-Bouchut	213.358 (132.5)	5100.00 (3167.1)
1994	Dauer 962LM-Porsche 344	Dalmas-Baldi-Haywood	195.238 (121.2)	4685.70 (2909.8)
1995	McLaren F1 GTR	Dalmas-Lehto-Sekiya	168.992 (104.9)	4055.80 (2518.6)
1996	Joest-Porsche	Reuter-Wurz-Jones	200.600 (124.6)	4814.40 (2989.7)
1997	Joest-Porsche 911-GT1/97	Alboreto-Johansson-Kristensen	204.186 (126.8)	4909.60 (3048.8)
1998	Joest-Porsche 911-GT1/98	McNish-Ortelli-Aiello	199.326 (123.8)	4775.33 (2965.5)

The Constructors Who Have Won the Most Editions

CONSTRUCTOR	NUMBER OF WINS
Porsche	16
Ferrari	9
Jaguar	7
Alfa Romeo	4
Matra-Simca	3

233 right The Ferrari 333SP of the Jabouille-Bouresche team during the 24-hour race's night phase: The car, driven by the Franco-Italian crew of Policard, Bouillion and Sospiri, failed to make it through the night, being forced to retire with gearbox problems.

THE GREAT US CHAMPIONSHIPS

The Great US Championships

234 top left The CART championship, in spite of the opinion to the contrary expressed by those behind the IRL, does not rely wholly on the Indianapolis 500. This is shown by the crowded grandstands at the 1991 Denver race won by Al Unser Jr. in a season dominated by Chevrolet engines and Lola chassis.

234-235 One of the most thrilling moments of the American motor racing season, the start of the Daytona 500 in Florida—the key event in the NASCAR championship.

234 bottom This photograph shows Al Unser Jr. during the Road America event held at Elkhart Lake in Wisconsin over a distance of 200 miles. In 1998, the year this picture was taken, the youngest of the Unser dynasty started from the fifth row but was eliminated after a crash with Patrick Carpenter, who started from the eighth row.

Motor races in the United States soon differentiated from their European contemporaries. There were two fundamental differences that became apparent very early in the history of the sport. First and foremost, roads with decent surfaces were proportionally few and far between in the USA early this century compared with, for example, France and Germany. Moreover, the American spectators soon showed a preference for the spectacular rather than the epic; that is to say for circuits designed to offer continuous action with comfortable grandstands offering an optimal view over the whole of the track.

Indianapolis-style ovals met these requirements perfectly. Events such as the Vanderbilt Cup (organized along the lines of what was happening in France at the turn of the century) had the merit of revealing the potential inherent in motor racing to business entrepreneurs, car manufacturers, sportsmen and spectators, but were soon overtaken by events held on extremely fast, spectacular closed circuits, the grandstands bulging with spectators eager to pay for services such as car parking, refreshments, franchising and a seat that allowed them to follow the race in its entirety with no interruptions or variations in rhythm.

In theory the reduced dimensions of the tracks should have contributed to increased safety, as all points were easily reached by rescue services; in theory *only*, because in practice the extremely high speeds that were very soon achieved meant that accidents, many of them fatal, were not only frequent but were (and still are) one of the few variables, together with pit stops, affecting the never-ending changes of leadership and the outcome of races. This was especially true of Indy-style events, which frequently proved to be demolition derbies rather than true races.

Racing in the United States has developed in myriad different directions, as befits a population inclined to accept a challenge and eager for spectacle. While in Europe motor racing adopted classical canons (single-seater Grands Prix, endurance racing on road and track, hillclimbs and rallies) with relatively little attention being paid to championships for cars resembling production models, in the United States literally anything on wheels has been used for racing, from pickups to dune buggies to hotrods, to say nothing of dragsters and their ilk.

With regard to the most prestigious championships—those particularly rich in history and technical interest—three main sectors can be identified: Indy and CART, with single-seaters outwardly similar to Grand Prix cars; the NASCAR championship for modified touring cars, which attracts huge audiences and whose spiritual home at Daytona is to the series as Indianapolis was to CART; and races for sports and sports-prototypes similar to those used in the World Championship for Makes, aggressive cars with monstrously powerful engines.

The most famous championships organized for these latter machines are the Can-Am Challenge, which died in the 1980s after an influential period with great cars and drivers, and Trans-Am, which is still very popular and rather similar to today's European GT events.

One aspect in particular is shared by all these championships and makes them very different from those organized by the FIA: they are profoundly American, and therefore fans tend not to attach their allegiances to a driver or a car of a particular nationality. What galvanizes the public are the character and driving style of the individual competitors, the cars of the various teams frequently using identical chassis and engines.

This subject deserves not a chapter but a series of volumes for its variety and vastness. We have restricted ourselves to describing the main features and histories of the various series.

235 top Neighboring Canada, then Brazil, Japan and Australia, have all been gripped by the passion for single-seater CART racing. This is the pit lane of the Toronto circuit.

235 bottom The American automotive Oscars are assigned during an afternoon of fire at the Indianapolis Motor Speedway. And speaking of cinema, seen here is one of the great stars, racing enthusiast and team owner Paul Newman, talking to the Formula 1 World Champion and 1993 CART champion Nigel Mansell; this particular race was instead won by Emerson Fittipaldi.

The world's oldest and probably most famous motor racing championship is today known as CART (Championship Auto Racing Teams), but over the course of its nearly 100-year history it has changed its name and face frequently. Finally, in 1996, came the dramatic secession of the Indy World Series' most precious jewel, which broke away to form its own championship under the IRL (Indy Racing League) name. This was, of course, the world's most famous race, the Indianapolis 500.

This story, revolving around the concept of pure speed, increasingly frequently on oval circuits, could fill entire volumes and involve reams of the statistics beloved of American sport. We have restricted ourselves, however, to those events we consider to be the most significant in the history of the championship and which can be grouped into clearly defined eras: from 1902 to 1919, an embryonic championship and numerous historical controversies; from 1920 to 1955 under the AAA (American Automobile Association) National Championship banner (perhaps improperly also used for the races between 1909 and 1919); from 1956 to 1979 as the USAC title; and from 1979 to 1995 as the CART (later CART/IndyCar) World Series. As mentioned above, from 1996 the IRL has been run independent of the CART series.

We have already discussed the very early history of American motor racing with regards to the Vanderbilt Cup, an unsuccessful attempt to transplant European-style racing to the US but significant in that it awakened the passion and interest of industrialists, investors, drivers and fans.

None of the reports from the early part of this century speak of an organized championship, but during the 1950s the historian Russ Catlin drew up a classification in which, as well as indicating the annual champion for the races organized by the AAA from 1902 to 1908, he assigned the 1909 title to George Robertson rather than the accepted victor Bert Dingley (only fifth in the revised standings), until then officially recognized as champion. The same occurred with the 1920 results, Gaston Chevrolet (third) being deprived of the title in favour of Tommy Milton.

A vague echo remains of these distant events that had begun to gain strength in 1895 with the birth of the world's first automotive association, the American Motor League, at the same time as the first race held on the 28th of November in which six vehicles took part: an electric motorcycle, an electric car, a Duryea and three cars powered by Benz engines. Under a thick blanket of snow, the race was won by the Duryea driven by Frank Duryea himself, from the Muller-Benz of Muller, who crossed the line in a state of semi-consciousness due to exposure.

236 top One of the oldest of the North American circuits is that at Playa del Rey in California. Note the track surface made of wood. Of the four drivers seen here, three won National Championship events on several occasions during the first 15 years of the century: Lou Disbrow (4), Howdy Wilcox (10) and, behind, Bert Dingley who won at Santa Monica in 1909. In the center is Dave Lewis.

236 bottom Little trace remains of the American races of the early 20th century (this photograph is in all probability from 1904), partly because there was no organized championship at the time. Only in the 1950s did the historian Russ Catlin reconstruct, on the basis of the race results, hypothetical championship standings for the seasons 1902 through 1909. The 1904 champion was George Heath, immortalized here. Heath also won the 1904 Vanderbilt Cup at the wheel of a Panhard 90 hp.

237 left Bert Dingley, who in 1909 won at Portland and Santa Monica at the wheel of a Chalmers-Detroit. He was named season champion by AAA secretary Val Haresnape, a choice later disputed by historian Russ Catlin.

As early as 1901 racing was staged on an oval track, that of the Detroit Driving Club, with a classic statutory mile lap. Henry Ford beat a Winton here, ensuring enduring publicity for his cars. Then came the birth of the AAA and with it the controversies over the assignation of the title: were results in the field or the opinions of experts to decide the destination of the national title? The question remained unresolved for some time, leading to heated polemics and internal schisms that culminated in 1909 in open warfare between the AAA and the ACA (Automobile Club of America).

understanding in 1910, founding the Motor Holdings Company, to which was delegated the organization of two events of international stature, the American Grand Prize and the Vanderbilt Cup. This initiative was never taken any further, however.

However, there was room for all within American motor racing, even for a new circuit. Inaugurated on the 19th of August at the Indiana state capital, the Indianapolis oval was soon to catalyze the interest of enthusiasts throughout the country, becoming the Mecca of speed that Daytona is for the NASCAR series and Le Mans is for

The Early AAA Champions

Year	Driver
1902	H. Arkness
1903	B. Oldfield
1904	G. Heath
1905	V. Hémery
1906	J. Tracy
1907	E. Bald
1908	L. Strang
1909	G. Robertson

The two sporting bodies had very different opinions regarding racing. The AAA was the most popular of the two, well known to the general public for its organization of the Vanderbilt Cup (to which it applied arbitrary modifications to the regulations). The opposing forces gathered around the ACA complained about the AAA's overly simplistic and mismanaged organization and would have preferred to follow the example set by the European clubs with regard to the organization of motor racing: the ACA's American Grand Prize, in fact, respected the regulations in force in Europe. The two associations attempted to come to an

endurance racing. In that period, new tracks appeared almost overnight and the first banked board track, the Playa del Rey Motordrome, was constructed at Los Angeles.

Whilst in Europe the First World War interrupted all forms of motor racing, events continued to be held in the United States, the absence of European drivers making life easier for the local heroes who won every edition of what was still an unofficial championship. The AAA had finally decided to award the title of national champion on the basis of results on the track rather than questionable opinions, but in this case too the roll of honour was revised in 1927 by AAA secretary Val Haresnape; otherwise the first title to be taken into consideration would be that of 1916, with the series then being interrupted by the war until 1920.

The "Haresnape" champions are well known figures famous for their feats on both sides of the Atlantic: de Palma, Resta, Mulford and Chevrolet. The cars that were used in the races also belonged to established makes: Benz, Mercedes, Fiat and

237 center One of the most popular drivers in the early years of the sport in the United States was undoubtedly the Italian American Ralph de Palma, seen here adjusting his car prior to a championship race.

237 right This image speaks for itself: the smiling but dirt-blackened face is that of Barney Oldfield, whose best season was in 1915 when on two consecutive occasions (Venice and Tucson) he managed to get the better of drivers of the caliber of Dario Resta, Ralph de Palma, Bob Burman and Eddie Rickenbacker.

Peugeot from Europe and Stutz, Buick, Duesenberg, Marmon, Cadillac and Frontenac from the USA. The Frontenac was designed by the talented but unfortunate Louis Chevrolet together with his brother Gaston.

It should not be thought that winning the title was an easy matter: throughout this early period there were never fewer than 14 races in the calendar, and in 1909 there were 24. Frequently, however, they were races held on the same circuit on the same day. In 1909 there were 11 championship venues, 15 the following year and just six in 1918, even though seven new tracks had been inaugurated between 1915 and 1916. There was an increasing preference for oval tracks, and in 1917 all 14 national championship races were held on circuits of this type.

The first modifications to the regulations after the AAA had introduced the maximum weight limit of 1200 kg in (2646 lb.) 1908 came in 1911 with a maximum cylinder capacity of 9800 cc, reduced in 1913 to 7400 cc and again in 1915 to 4900 cc.

The AAA "Haresnape" Champions

YEAR	DRIVER	CAR
1909	B. Dingley	Chalmers-Detroit
1910	R. Harroun	Marmon
1911	R. Mulford	Lozier
1912	R. de Palma	Mercedes
1913	E. Cooper	Stutz
1914	R. de Palma	Mercedes
1915	E. Cooper	Stutz
1917	E. Cooper	Stutz
1918	R. Mulford	Frontenac
1919	H. Wilcox	Peugeot
1920	T. Milton	Dues.-Frontenac

238 left Peter de Paolo, portrayed here prior to the California race at Culver City in 1924. This talented driver came to the fore the following season when, despite driving a Duesenberg rather than the all-conquering Miller, he managed to win four races.

238-239 The Pikes Peak circuit, particularly famous in the 1950s for its unpredictable and harsh surface, is seen here in 1955 testing a single-seater to the limit.

The progressive reduction in engine size continued into the 1920s. In 1924 Jimmy Murphy, who in the meantime had won the 1922 national title and was leading the championship, was killed at the Syracuse circuit, becoming the first posthumous National Champion. The rest of the decade was marked by the manifest superiority of Harry Miller's machines, unbeaten up to 1935 and frequently entered with double make names: Stevens, Summers and subsequently Offenhauser. The latter was a member of the Miller staff who took over the firm when Harry Miller went bankrupt. Given the overwhelming success of the Offy engines in the post-war period and the following decades it can be said that the Miller dynasty actually endured until the mid-1970s and the advent of the Ford Cosworth engines. Subsequently the Offenhauser factory was acquired by Louis Meyer, the first man to win the Indy 500 three times, and his mechanic Dale Drake.

Among the drivers, following the double victories of Milton, Murphy, de Paolo and Meyer, the 1930s saw a series of championship wins by drivers who were subsequently unable to repeat the feat. This can be largely attributed to the widespread availability of cars of similar performance, all deriving from the Millers. Only Wilbur Shaw towards the end of the decade managed to take the title on two occasions, the second in 1939 at the wheel of a Maserati—the first non-American make to win the national championship since 1919. Shaw, who lived at Indianapolis, had temporarily retired from racing in 1927, distraught after the death of his wife.

In 1941 motor racing suffered a loss that was as great as it was ignored, a story that would be the ideal plot for a film. The victim was Louis Chevrolet, an extremely talented driver and ingenious designer. His death was apparently due to the hardships he had suffered during the Depression, a period in which he worked in a factory. Nothing out of the ordinary here, given that many rich and famous men had suffered a similar fate. The cruel twist was that Louis actually worked in the Chevrolet factory founded in 1911 by Billy Durant, who had asked the popular racing champion to design a new car. Chevrolet presented a prototype for an attractive and luxurious machine, quite the opposite of what Durant had in mind. The project was taken no further, but the entrepreneur cleverly associated the fortunes of his make with the popular driver and designer. Chevrolet is still today one of the great names of the automotive world, despite the fact that Louis died in poverty.

Two years later cancer of the face led to the

death of Harry Miller, engineering genius of the 1920s and undisputed master of the Indianapolis single-seater, he too in conditions of relative obscurity.

Before the outbreak of the war Rex Mays matched the feats of Wilbur Shaw by winning two championships. These were, however, second-class editions staged at just three circuits (Indianapolis, Springfield and Syracuse in 1940 and Indianapolis, Milwaukee and Syracuse the following year).

The championship was revived in 1946 and was won three times in succession by Ted Horn, who raced Horn-Offenhausers and Maseratis. Despite this

triple national championship success, Horn never managed to win at Indianapolis. Apart from Horn's serial wins, the first hat trick in the history of the championship, the most significant factor was the definitive success of the Offenhauser engines, now fitted with fuel-injection, especially when mounted in the asymmetric tubular chassis (the engine being located to the left) being increasingly used in the left-turn-only series.

These new cars became extremely popular, winning the majority of events up to the end of the AAA National Championship era. Those that were not built by Kurtis were usually Kuzmas or Epperlys or Watsons. Two statistics are sufficient to give an idea of the magnitude of the Offenhauser

domination: in the 1950s almost all the cars running at Indianapolis and the other American circuits were powered by Offy engines, and from 1947 to 1964 only five out of 223 events were won by cars with different power units (Maserati at Pikes Peak in 1947; Lincoln at Pikes Peak in 1955; Lotus-Ford at Milwaukee in 1963-64 and at Trenton 1964). This was a monopoly rather than mere supremacy, just as between 1923 and 1934 the Miller engines (from which the Offenhauser units were derived) had monopolized American racing. Offenhauser engines enjoyed a second youth in the 1970s, dominating once again until 1976.

Chassis and engines were thus the protagonists of 1950s American racing, with no one driver managing to prevail over his peers during the long AAA series that began in 1916 and finished in 1955. In reality, a new generation of enthusiastic drivers were learning their craft on the dirt tracks found throughout the country.

The AAA National Champions

Year	Driver	Car
1916	D. Resta	Peugeot
1920	T. Milton	Duesenberg
1921	T. Milton	Durant-Duesenberg/Durant-Miller/Frontenac
1922	J. Murphy	Duesenberg-Miller
1923	E. Hearne	Miller
1924	J. Murphy	Miller
1925	P. de Paolo	Duesenberg
1926	H. Hartz	Miller
1927	P. de Paolo	Miller
1928	L. Meyer	Miller
1929	L. Meyer	Miller
1930	B. Arnold	Summers-Miller
1931	L. Schneider	Stevens-Miller
1932	B. Carey	Stevens-Miller
1933	L. Meyer	Miller
1934	B. Cummings	Miller
1935	K. Petillo	Wetteroth-Offenhauser
1936	M. Rose	Miller-Offenhauser
1937	W. Shaw	Shaw/Stevens-Offenhauser
1938	F. Roberts	Wetteroth-Offenhauser
1939	W. Shaw	Maserati
1940	R. Mays	Stevens-Winfield
1941	R. Mays	Stevens-Winfield
1946	T. Horn	Horn-Offenhauser/Maserati
1947	T. Horn	Horn-Offenhauser/Maserati
1948	T. Horn	Horn-Offenhauser/Maserati
1949	J. Parsons	Kurtis-Offenhauser
1950	H. Banks	Maserati-Offenhauser/Moore-Offenhauser
1951	T. Bettenhausen	Deidt-Offenhauser/Kurtis-Offenhauser
1952	C. Stevenson	Kurtis KK4000-Offenhauser
1953	S. Hanks	Kurtis KK4000-Offenhauser
1954	J. Bryan	Kuzma-Offenhauser
1955	B. Sweikert	Kurtis KK500D-Offenhauser/Watson-Offenhauser

239 top left The year is 1958: six drivers tackle a corner under opposite lock. They are champion Rodger Ward, Don Bronson, Jud Larson (the eventual winner of this edition of the Atlanta 100), George Amick, Johnny Thomson and Earl Metter.

239 bottom left The start line for the Indianapolis race held over 100 miles in September 1959. The winner, Rodger Ward, is in pole position with the

Watson-Offenhauser number 5. Alongside is Don Bronson and, behind with race number 10, A. J. Foyt.

239 right One of the four aces of the Unser dynasty, CART and Indy racing's royal family; Louis, Al, Bobby and Al Jr. fought as hard against each other as they did their other rivals. Bobby is here portrayed after his victory at Pikes Peak in 1966.

240 top There were close similarities during the 1960s between the cars used in the Formula 1 World Championship and those of the USAC series. This photograph is of the last race of the season, the 1969 Phoenix 200 won by Mario Andretti, seen here in a close-fought duel with Bobby Unser, left. Unser was driving one of his own Chevrolet-powered cars while the Italo-American, who won the

National Championship that year, was at the wheel of a Brawner/ Hawk-Ford.

240 center In 1972 Bobby Unser gained his revenge over his brother Al, seen here racing with Mike Mosley, by winning the opening round of the championship, the Phoenix 150. In spite of Bobby's four victories that season, the title went to Joe Leonard.

240-241 An action photograph of the participants in the 1964 Milwaukee 100. Carrying race number 1 is A. J. Foyt, who dominated the season by winning no fewer than seven consecutive races and ten in total. Foyt was paired with a famous car, the Watson-Offenhauser with which he had also dominated the 1961 and 1963 championships. Only in 1962 did Rodger Ward, seen here with number 2, manage to break the cast-iron grip of the great American champion, who still boasts the highest number of Indy-car victories.

240 bottom This image was taken at Phoenix before the Arizona circuit had joined up with the Indy secessionists. The year was 1971, the driver portrayed Bobby Unser. The winner of that year's race was instead his brother Al with a Colt-Ford. Bobby won only the penultimate round that season, the Trenton 300 Miles.

In 1956, organization of the national championship passed into the hands of the United States Auto Club (USAC), which maintained undisputed control until 1979. From 1956 the championship-winning team was also recognized. Chassis and engines were frequently similar or identical and the differences therefore lay in the teams' race and logistical management qualities, especially in the attracting of sponsors. (In Europe instead it was generally the manufacturers of the cars themselves who entered the teams.) The races remained substantially unchanged, 12 or 13 to a season, peaking in the mid-1960s with 18.

That first championship was won by the Dean Van Lines team who followed up with a repeat win the following year, Jimmy Bryan driving on both occasions. Nineteen fifty-six saw the death at 73 years of age of one of the great pioneer drivers, Ralph de Palma; certainly one of the few AAA champions to die of natural causes.

The championship was profoundly shaken up in the 1960s when the engine was relocated from the front to the rear of the car. The first modern American single-seater built along these lines came from innovator Mickey Thompson, but it was England's Cooper and Lotus which really led the way.

Among the drivers a group of élite champions began to develop after Jimmy Bryan had won one AAA and two USAC titles. Among these multiple champions were A. J. Foyt (7 USAC titles), Mario Andretti (3), and Bobby Unser, Rodger Ward, Joe Leonard and Tom Sneva with two each. The rest of the pack were left with mere crumbs as in the meantime the racing dynasties began to arise, the Andrettis and Unsers moving to the fore.

Toward the end of the decade Drake, the owner of the Offenhauser factory, attempted to compete with the successful Ford V8 engines and in part succeeded, developing a new four-cylinder, turbocharged Offy producing 650+ hp. Until the mid-1970s, the turbo Offy remained viable as an Indianapolis powerplant.

A number of changes to the regulations were introduced in 1969: a weight limit was imposed, while the engines of forced-induction cars were restricted to a capacity of 2.65 liters. These modifications were intended to defend the national racing scene from the importation of European technology and innovations such as wings and turbocharging, but there was no way of stopping the invasion of British chassis and engines.

During the 1970s, however, it was notable that there was a greater number of chassis manufacturers in particular; following the mid-engine revolution that took place in the the decade before, the championship saw cars built by Colt, Eagle, King, McLaren, Coyote, Parnelli, Wildcat (one of the few truly American cars) and Penske, a British chassis concern founded and guided by the American Roger Penske, the leader of the most successful team at Indianapolis and of the championship overall. (Roger Penske is to Indianapolis what Bernie Ecclestone is to Formula 1; he was one of those behind the revolt of the teams against USAC that led to the creation of CART in 1978. No other team can rival Penske's ongoing string of titles and victories in other series

241 right The 1972 edition of the Michigan 150: on the left is Tom Sneva, on the right Bobby Unser, one of the season's protagonists with four victories. This race and the national title (this was still in the USAC period, prior to the arrival of CART) were won by Joe Leonard.

such as Can-Am, IndyCar, Formula 1, NASCAR and sports-prototypes. Penske Motorsports is even quoted on New York's NASDAQ exchange.)

With regard to engines, the Offy ultimately succumbed to the Ford-Cosworth, which wholly dominated the championship by decade's end.

In 1978 the teams decided that the time was right for them to assume greater responsibility within the organizational structure of the Indy championship. Eighteen team owners decided to found Championship Auto Racing Teams (CART) with Pat Patrick as president and six commissioners, including Roger Penske and A. J. Foyt. CART organized its first event in 1979, a 150-mile race at Phoenix. That year the CART championship was run virtually parallel with the official USAC series, and the affair ended up in court: representatives of the teams claimed that the USAC monopoly "deprived them of the means of earning a living." They won their case and were free to organize a new championship that was staged regularly until 1995. In 1980 an unsuccessful attempt was made to unify the two structures.

HONOR ROLL

The National USAC Champions

YEAR	DRIVER	TEAM	CAR
1956	J. Bryan	Dean Van Lines	Kuzma-Offenhauser
1957	J. Bryan	Dean Van Lines	Kuzma-Offenhauser
1958	T. Bettenhausen	John Zink Jr	Epperly/Kurtis KK4000/Watson-Offenhauser
1959	R. Ward	Leader Card	Watson-Offenhauser
1960	A. J. Foyt	Bowes Seal Fast	Meskowski-Offenhauser
1961	A. J. Foyt	Bowes Seal Fast	Watson/Meskowski-Offenhauser/Trevis-Offenhauser
1962	R. Ward	Leader Card	Watson-Offenhauser
1963	A. J. Foyt	Sheraton-Thompson	Watson/Meskowski-Offenhauser/Trevis-Offenhauser
1964	A. J. Foyt	Sheraton-Thompson	Watson-Offenhauser/Meskowski-Offenhauser
1965	Ma. Andretti	Dean Racing Ent.	Hawk-Ford/Kuzma-Offenhauser
1966	Ma. Andretti	Dean Racing Ent.	Hawk-Ford/Kuzma-Offenhauser
1967	A. J. Foyt	Sheraton-Thompson	Coyote-Ford/Meskowski-Offenhauser
1968	B. Unser	Leader Card	Eagle 68-Ford/Unser-Chevrolet/Eagle 68-Offenhauser
1969	Ma. Andretti	STP Granatelli	Hawk-Ford/Kuzma-Offenhauser
1970	A. Unser	Vel's Parnelli Jones	Colt 70-Ford/King-Ford
1971	J. Leonard	Vel's Parnelli Jones	Colt 71-Ford
1972	J. Leonard	Vel's Parnelli Jones	Parnelli-Offenhauser
1973	R. McCluskey	Lindsey Hopkins	McLaren M168-Offenhauser
1974	B. Unser	All-American Racers	Eagle 74-Offenhauser
1975	A. J. Foyt	Gilmore-Foyt Racing	Coyote-Ford
1976	G. Johncock	Patrick Racing	Wildcat-Offenhauser
1977	T. Sneva	Penske Racing	McLaren M24-Cosworth
1978	T. Sneva	Penske Racing	Penske PC6-Cosworth
1979	A. J. Foyt	Gilmore-Foyt Racing	Parnelli VPJ6C-Cosworth/Coyote-Ford

242 top Life in pit lane is always exciting, especially during the refuelling operations. In this case however, the pumps are not in action and clearly there is some problem with the car. The venue is the Meadowlands circuit.

242 bottom As the cars line up for the start, the colors give an indication of the prevalence of one team over another.

In 1979, therefore, two parallel championships were staged. Despite being one of the leading lights of the rebel CART movement, Foyt won the last edition of the Indy-USAC Championship whilst Rick Mears conquered the first of a trio of early CART titles. As for the teams, Penske immediately established its primacy on the oval tracks, winning seven of the 16 editions of the CART series between 1979 and 1994 with Mears, Al Unser father and son, and Danny Sullivan.

The new championship officially began in 1980, sponsored by the automotive paints colossus PPG, whose name was linked with CART in the official championship denomination.

For some years the Offenhauser engines had been struggling to compete for the title with the powerful Cosworth eight-cylinder units that only in

firm Ilmor Engineering) that replaced it, despite pressure from a well-developed six-cylinder Buick stock-block unit and the first Honda-Judd. Ironically Ilmor was founded by two former Cosworth engineers, a fact that bears remarkable similarity to the Miller-Offenhauser episode of 50 years earlier.

The Chevrolet engine was in its prime the following year, leaving just a single race to the Honda-Judd unit and powering Mario Andretti to his 50th Indy win and Formula 1 champion Emerson Fittipaldi to the CART title in 1989, a feat repeated by Nigel Mansell in 1993.

After having staged the championship for many years in 1996, CART was faced with a major crisis with the breakaway of Indianapolis and a number of other circuits. Basically, the owners of the Indianapolis circuit refused to accept a role subordinate to that of CART, claiming that the Indy 500 was by far the most prestigious event and more important than the championship series itself.

The CART championship continued with new protagonists and undamaged credibility. The Reynard-Hondas dominated the championship table for three consecutive seasons, the last two titles being taken by the Italian Alex Zanardi.

242-243 The dominator of the 1997 season, Alex Zanardi at the wheel of a Reynard-Honda, leads Paul Tracy in a Penske-Mercedes. The photograph was taken during one of the CART series races, but the circuit is not to be found in America: this is the Australian race at Surfer's Paradise in Queensland, the tropical resort to the north of Sydney.

243 right This image highlights how at the rear the traditionally round helmet has been modified with an aerodynamic profile that blends in with the flanks of the car. In the foreground, the steering wheel has been removed to facilitate access to the cockpit.

1988 gave way to Chevrolet. The name Offenhauser eventually disappeared from the starting grids in 1981 and one of the great champions, Bobby Unser, also hung up his driving gloves after three Indy 500 wins, two national championship titles and 35 victories in the general series.

The 1985 championship season was unusual in that winner Al Unser took the title by a single point from the second-place driver, none other than his son of the same name; clearly the proud father had no intention of giving way to his heir just yet. Bobby Rahal, one of the most talented drivers of the period, then won the title in 1986 and 1987, driving firstly a March and then a Lola for the Truesports team. He was also the first driver to win more than a million dollars in prize money (excluding sponsorship) in a single season, over half of the sum ($580,000) coming from his Indianapolis win. On that occasion the Chevrolet Corvette pace car was driven by the first man to break the sound barrier, jet pilot Chuck Yeager.

Nineteen eighty-seven was a year to remember as it marked the last year of the eight-cylinder Cosworth domination; it was the potent Chevy V8 turbo developing 720 hp (developed by the British

While the CART Championship continued as if nothing had happened, replacing Indianapolis and the other rebel circuits, a new structure was taking shape. In effect, the seed of rebellion had been sowed in 1995 when Indianapolis Motor Speedway president Tony George had announced the creation of a new series for 1996, a year of transition and preparation for the new championship which was to be inaugurated at the nascent DisneyWorld circuit at Orlando, Florida. Apart from this venue and, of course, Indianapolis itself, the new championship could count on events at Las Vegas, Phoenix and New Hampshire, while the technical specifications of the engines to be used, primarily the eight-cylinder, four-liter Aurora Oldsmobile, were being defined. With regards to the chassis, in 1997 the teams could choose between those produced by the Italian Dallara and British G-Force teams.

The first race was held on the 27th of January, 1996 at Orlando and was won by the rookie Buzz Calkins, who went on to take the championship title together with Scott Sharp. In 1997 it was officially decreed that the cars of CART could no longer use the "Indy-car" denomination—a decree instantly challenged (and beaten) in court, after which CART happily changed its working name to "IndyCar."

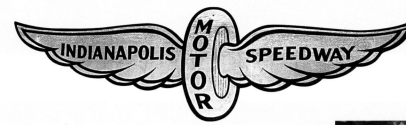

The Indianapolis story began on the ninth of February, 1909, when Mr. Carl Graham Fisher, the distinguished owner of Prest-O-Lite, a company producing carbide lamps, together with his partner James Allison, Arthur Newby of National Motors and Frank Wheeler of Wheeler-Schleber, a carburettor manufacturer, founded the Indianapolis Motor Speedway Corporation with the declared intent of constructing and managing a track suitable for racing and new-vehicle testing. Six months later the track was ready. A two and a half mile oval (just over 4 km/ 2.5 mi.) was leveled and roughly paved with asphalt and gravel. This precarious surface broke up during the inaugural race (won by a Fiat) causing numerous accidents, some of them fatal.

The organizers were anything but discouraged and threw themselves into the onerous task of laying 3,200,000 bricks as a new surface for the oval, hence the "Brickyard" nickname given to the circuit.

In 1910 Indianapolis hosted motor racing on the occasion of three national holidays, Memorial Day, Independence Day and Labor Day. The events were run over distances of ten, 50, 100 and 200 miles. It was Fisher who suggested that it would be more profitable to stage a single major event disputed over a distance of 500 miles, a formula that was adopted from 1911.

The first running of the "Indy 500" was a resounding success: some 70,000 spectators watched 40 cars driven by stars of the caliber[of de Palma, Bruce-Brown, Burman, Spenser, Wishart, Dawson, Wilcox, Anderson, Chevrolet and the winner Ray Harroun, the reigning national champion. Harroun's victory was disputed by Ralph Mulford, who claimed that the timing officials had failed to register one of his laps following the fatal accident involving Sam Dickson, Griener's mechanic, on the 13th lap. The fervently religious Mulford, who even refused to race on Sundays, subsequently gained his revenge by winning the 1918 national championship, but never managed to win the 500, a fact that rankled him for the rest of his life.

That first winner was driving a Marmon Wasp fitted with a rearview mirror, a feature as useful as it was innovative as it allowed the driver to check on the actions and distance of his rivals behind him.

The names of the car manufacturers racing at Indianapolis in the early years had much closer links with the world of racing than that of mass production: Mercer, Stutz (which later began to produce high-quality torpedoes and roadsters) and Mason. This last marque was named after a financier while the car was actually prepared by the Duesenberg brothers, Fred and August.

The crowds that flocked to Indiana in 1913 were given a bitter pill to swallow: Jules Goux, one of the famous Charlatans—the trio who had been commissioned to design the racing Peugeots at the expense of Ettore Bugatti—landed in America and went on to win the exciting race. Fiat had already come close to achieving the same feat, having finished third in 1911 and second in 1912. From then until 1919, European cars dominated the event: Peugeot won a further two editions while Mercedes and Delage took one each. Between 1915 and 1919 the key drivers were de Palma (famous for crossing the finish line with his engine in flames), Resta (winner of the 1916 edition, which was

244 top A winged motif, very frequent in the iconography of the early 20th century and used for automotive logos such as those of Duesenberg and Bentley, was also adopted by the Indianapolis speedway.

244 center This 1912 photograph portrays a car speeding past the podium at the celebrated Indianapolis circuit.

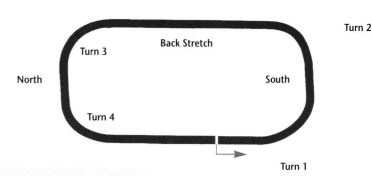

244-245 There are just a few minutes before the start of the race on the new high-speed circuit. The width of the track allowed six cars to start abreast, among which in the foreground here are three Buicks and two Marmons. In 1909 the race was run over a distance of 100 miles.

244 bottom right This is one of the first posters for the Indianapolis Motor Speedway, with the Indiana circuit already claiming to be the home of the world's most important race.

245 right Victory in the third edition of the race on the brick-paved oval went to Ray Harroun with a Marmon. This was the first edition to be run over 500 miles, the two previous races being shorter. Carl Fisher, the President of the company managing the track, came up with the idea of a single major race rather than a series of lesser events. This car, known as the Marmon Wasp, was the only six-cylinder machine to win a major race up to 1914.

reduced to 300 miles), and the crowd-pleasing ace Howdy Wilcox.

In 1916 Eddie Rickenbacker and Pete Anderson became the first two drivers to make a practice of wearing rigid (rather than cloth or leather) helmets on the track. Rickenbacker subsequently became a quintuple-ace fighter pilot during World War One and was awarded the Medal of Honor by the United States Congress and decorated with the Croix de Guerre by the French government. In 1927 he went on to buy the Indianapolis Motor Speedway from Carl Fisher for $70,000.

From 1920 prize money of $100 was awarded to the leading driver on each lap. The prospect of rich winnings clearly inspired the local drivers who, in spite of the presence of the powerful overhead-cam Peugeots driven mainly by Goux and Wilcox, succeeded in reviving American fortunes with a win for Gaston Chevrolet at the wheel of a car he had himself designed but which carried the name of the governor of the French colonies in the 17th century, Frontenac. (The car was alternatively known as the Monroe, after the team's financier.) During the same race de Palma's Ballot caught fire no fewer than six times as a result of a defective magneto.

Three years later came the first non-competing victim at the Brickyard when a spectator watching through a crack in the fencing was struck by a car that skidded into the barriers. That edition of the race also saw the first supercharged cars including the Mercedes 10/40/60 PS. From 1925 the Indy 500 was included among the races valid for the World Championship organized in a very haphazard fashion by the Automobile Club of Italy; the other events were initially the Italian, French and Belgian GPs. There was never a significant flow of drivers or teams from one side of the Atlantic to the other, each preferring to compete on home turf.

In the 1920s unusual cars appeared at Indianapolis

designed by Harry Miller of Los Angeles, whose
mechanical creations were to dominate the national
championship and the Indy 500 from 1922 to 1936.
Jimmy Murphy, the winner in 1922, was determined
to score back-to-back wins and asked Miller to
design a car that would be faster through the corners.

Miller considered the problem and mounted a
more powerful, supercharged engine but
recognized that the key lay in lowering the car's
center of gravity. But how?

The answer was simple: by relocating the
transmission and driving the front wheels, the
"hump" below the cockpit was eliminated. Murphy
received the solution enthusiastically but did not
have time to test the car before he was killed in an
accident on the banking at Syracuse.

As well as offering superchargers to the owners
of his cars (17 in this edition of the race) at the
symbolic price of one dollar, Miller also offered two

Norman Batten's Car on Fire.

of his revolutionary front-wheel-drive cars to Bennett
Hill. The offer was refused by Hill, who was wary of
the new technology, but a problem with his
traditional Miller obliged him to take over one of the
new cars. He immediately adjusted to the necessary
driving style and managed to make up a complete
lap and finish immediately behind the Duesenberg of
de Paolo and Batten, which for the first time at Indy
broke the 100 mph average speed barrier.

The need for the reporters to follow the action in
that maelstrom of dust, smoke, wheels and engines
led to the adoption of a singular strategy whereby
from 1927 each car was paired with a race official
who wore the same number on his back. The officials
sat alongside each other and each time the race

positions changed the officials concerned exchanged
seats—living lap counters no less!

A number of dramatic coincidences involved the
drivers. A vicious circle was triggered in 1926 when
the race was won by Lockhart, a driver with a
background in dirt track racing. Lockhart was then
killed in 1928 during an attempt to beat the Land
Speed Record of 207.5 mph that Keech had set 15
days earlier. Keech in turn died 15 days later, after
having won the Indy 500 of 1929. And in 1931 a
truly incredible accident occurred, by no means the
last of an infinite series in a race to forget. A wheel
flew out of the circuit into a garden where it killed a
child playing on the lawn. The Depression had in the
meantime struck the United States economy and the

Indianapolis race, like others throughout the country, took note and adapted. A new formula was adopted that made the widest possible use of stock engines and chassis. Rather inelegantly but very aptly this became known as the Junk Formula. Unfortunately the major victim was Harry Miller, who went bankrupt despite the excellence of his single-seaters. Paradoxically, his cars continued to dominate at Indianapolis and elsewhere, suitably modified and adapted to meet the new regulations which included the absurd obligation to carry a riding mechanic. In 1932 Studebaker challenged the Millers with a racing car developing almost 200 hp and derived from its extremely capable production models; the attempt was unsuccessful, however, with the best placed Studebaker finishing third.

Two years later the field was restricted to a maximum of 33 cars, whilst in 1936 the Speedway was substantially modernized with wider corners, a re-laid track and rebuilt retaining walls. Meyer won his third edition, a record soon matched by the local driver Wilbur Shaw, who won in 1937, '39 and '40.

Shaw returned home after the war to find his beloved track in a state of complete abandon. He asked Rickenbacker for an explanation and learned that the former ace intended to sell the complex. Shaw could hardly let such an opportunity escape him, and found in Tony Hulman the financier capable of paying $70,000 for the track while at the same time investing various millions in restoring it. Shaw became president of the new company.

247 right Jules Goux shakes hands with his mechanic after victory in the 1913 edition of the Indy 500. The Frenchman shocked a crowd unaccustomed to seeing a European driver beat their local heroes. Goux was one of the Charlatans, the team that designed and raced the Peugeot competition cars.

In 1946 no lesser a figure than Rudolf Caracciola, the greatest of the pre-war Mercedes drivers, honored the circuit with his presence. Caracciola would have liked to have raced with his faithful W165 hidden in Switzerland, but bureaucratic delays prevented him from doing so and he had to settle for the Thorne Special—hardly a great sacrifice, as it was identical to the car driven by the eventual winner. Caracciola himself was forced to retire while the winner Robson took advantage of the determined Mauri Rose's crash. The latter recovered to win the next two editions.

Some fascinating experiments appeared at Indy the same year as Caracciola, most notably the Fageol Twin Coach Special (powered by two supercharged Offys, one in the front and one at the rear); the mid-engined Miller reborn as the Tucker Torpedo Special to promote Preston Tucker's doomed startup carmaker; and the brilliantly sleek and fast Novi Governor Special, which in Ralph Hepburn's hands qualified for the race at a staggering 134.45 mph.

The latter was instead killed in a 1956 accident at the short circuit of Salem.

Indianapolis would hardly be Indianapolis without the pronouncement of the classic phrase, "Gentlemen, start your engines." Yet this tradition dates only to '57, the first edition won by an Epperly with a horizontally canted (a.k.a. "laydown") engine, a solution that allowed the center of gravity to be lowered still further. The Epperly was actually a development of the Kurtis- and Kuzma-type chassis, with the engine set even further to the left. In 1958, a year in which 13 cars were involved in a multiple pile-up that led to the death of one driver and serious injuries to another two, independent suspension was also seriously embraced. The year was additionally marked by the debut of one of the three drivers to have won four Indy 500s, Anthony Joseph Foyt Junior.

The 1960s opened with the relocation of the engine behind the driver but in front of the rear axle. The USAC that had taken on the honor of organizing the championship and modifying the

In that period the rule restricting the race to cars with naturally aspirated engines of up to 4.5 liters or supercharged units of up to three liters was retained, but the maximum weight limit was reduced to attract the young semi-professional drivers who competed on dirt tracks with lighter cars. In 1951, the year in which the first disc brakes were introduced, one of these roughneck drivers, Lee Wallard, was the first both to complete the 500 miles in less than four hours and to break the 200 kph average speed barrier. Four days later he was involved in a serious off-roading accident and was never able to race again.

The popularity of the Indy 500 increased and with it the prestige in terms of ever greater prize money: in 1953 the record-breaking total reached $246,300 and was pocketed by Bill Vukovich, who the previous year had been sidelined by a broken steering link when the race was seemingly his for the taking. "The Mad Russian" also won in 1954 but was killed in the '55 edition won by Bob Sweikert.

regulations reduced the maximum cylinder capacity once again, but by a rather insignificant margin: from 4.5 to 4.2 liters. In the meantime, on the occasion of the 50th anniversary edition of the 500, the Indianapolis speedway lost almost all of the bricks that had characterized its surface since 1911.

Foyt could hardly have chosen a better time to win his first Indy 500 after a thrilling struggle (in part played out in the pits) with Eddie Sachs. He was not yet the king of the ovals, the title still belonging to Rodger Ward who in 1962 won his second 500 setting a record as unusual as it was admirable: he was the first driver to complete six consecutive editions of the race. Another protagonist in this period was Parnelli Jones, who was the first driver to exceed an average speed of 150 mph (241.4 kph) during qualifying.

The monotonous supremacy of Kurtis-derived chassis and Offenhauser engines could hardly last forever, but while in Europe the major racing teams competed in a climate of feverish technological

248 left The Formula 1 World Champion, Jack Brabham, photographed during the 1961 Indy 500. The race was won for the first time that year by A. J. Foyt, one of three drivers to boast four wins at Indianapolis.

248 top right One of the leading lights of CART/Indy racing, Mario Andretti is seen here at the wheel of the Hawk-Ford with which he won the 1969 Indy 500. Surprisingly this was Andretti's sole Indianapolis victory in his remarkable open-wheel career.

revolution, at Indianapolis and the other great oval-track races changes were modest, probably due to the widespread standardization of the engines and chassis used. The teams combined the two elements in an attempt to achieve an optimum balance, a job for mechanics rather than designers. In 1962, however, Indianapolis hosted a number of unusual guests, including Colin Chapman. The owner of the English firm Lotus was surprised by the low-tech approach of Indy racing, and Ford engineers were simultaneously investigating the possibility of developing their production Falcon V8 into a power unit capable of blowing away the Offenhausers.

As early as 1963 Jim Clark came within a whisker of victory with his Lotus-Ford and eventually won the race in 1965, following a fierce battle with A. J. Foyt at average lap speeds in the order of 160 mph (260.6 kph). This was a victory that traumatized an American crowd unaccustomed to seeing the great trophy in the hands of foreign drivers, never mind in a British car. The following year another Briton, Graham Hill, repeated the feat at the wheel of a Ford-powered Lola with Clark second (although both he and his team were convinced he had won). The leading Italo-American, Mario Andretti, was only third. An accident involved

no fewer than 16 cars, but miraculously there were no serious injuries.

The 1964 edition of the race had instead been a tragic event despite the fact that for the first time the total prize money exceeded half a million dollars. A dramatic crash led to Dave MacDonald losing his life in the flames and Eddie Sachs dying later of his burns.

That great Indianapolis warhorse, the Offenhauser engine, was by now obsolete and Drake (the co-owner of the factory) attempted to face up to the Ford challenge with the introduction of a 600 hp turbocharged variant in 1968, a unit immediately

248-249 This image shows the start of the 1989 race won by Emerson Fittipaldi at the wheel of the Penske-Chevy (number 20); on the inside, in pole position with the Penske-Chevy (number 4) is Rick Mears, while Al Unser is in the centre with the Lola-Chevy (number 25). On the second row, from left to right: Crawford, Andretti and Brayton.

249 bottom left This photograph shows the dynamics of the car of Al Unser, the winner of four editions of the Indy 500 between 1970 and 1987. Al, Bobby and Al Unser Jr. have scored no fewer than nine Indy wins between them.

249 bottom right An evocative picture of the helmet of Emerson Fittipaldi. The Brazilian Formula 1 ace also won the CART championship in 1989.

chosen by 13 out of the field of 33 cars. Chapman had in the meantime assembled a team of four Lotus 56s with turbine engines and four-wheel drive, one of which was to have been driven by the recently deceased Jim Clark. The car was instead assigned to Mike Spence, who one month after Clark's death also perished in an accident. The three remaining cars were entrusted to Graham Hill, Joe Leonard and Art Pollard, all drivers of proven ability. The race was won, however, by Bobby Unser, one of the drivers who had kept faith with Drake and the Offenhauser engine.

In the meantime the prize money available at Indianapolis and for the other races in the

interruption. The stewards decided enough was enough after 332.5 miles.

Partly as a result of the dramatic events of the previous edition, in 1974 the quantity of fuel available to each car was reduced to 280 gallons (1060 liters), while the cars' fuel tanks had a maximum capacity of 40 gallons (151 liters); this meant that the cars could make up to seven pit stops. Moreover, the fuel filler was located on the side of the car furthest from the spectators.

In 1976 the sports pages were full of the bitter rivalry between teams and drivers. This was the moment in which one of the great Indy pro-tagonists, the Offenhauser engine, took its last bow

After a high-flying decade the Cosworth, too, was nearing the end of its domination. By 1987 the principal teams had already written it off, with the Indy wizard Penske opting for the Ilmor-Chevy unit for his cars. However, during qualifying—partly as a result of Danny Ongais' accident and partly because of the Chevy's disappointing performance—Penske took the drastic steps of going back to the Cosworth engine of the previous season and signing veteran Al Unser Sr. to drive the car. Things could hardly have worked out better, with Unser scoring his fourth Indy victory to bring him level with Foyt. Only Mears was to match this feat, scoring his own fourth victory in 1991, the year in which Foyt celebrated

championship increased year by year. In 1971 it reached the million-dollar threshold but by 1982 was already worth twice that. In 1985 no less than $3,217,000 were up for grabs, while the 75th anniversary edition in 1986 boasted a prize fund of around $4,000,000. Another significant off-track event was the death, at 83 years of age, of Eddie Rickenbacker, the WWI flying ace who had bought the Speedway from Carl Fisher in 1927, managed it until the outbreak of WWII, and then sold it to Shaw and Hulman. Hulman himself died in 1977, but had already handed over the privilege of pronouncing the famous phrase "Gentlemen, start your engines" to his wife Mary in 1975.

The 1973 edition of the Indy 500 was one to forget. Once again Indianapolis had fallen into the trap of failing to provide adequate competition in terms of chassis and engines. In recompense there was a great number of teams, veteran drivers and rookies. The race was immediately marred by the death of one of those veterans, Pollard, and then an accident involving 14 cars saw 13 spectators burned as fuel sprayed from a ruptured tank. The race was restarted some days later and this time the driver Swede Savage and a mechanic run over by the pace car lost their lives. Another suspension, another restart and then pouring rain led to another

as winner; for some years it had shown difficulty competing equally with the Ford-Cosworth V8. (Its last appearance on Indy's top-three podium would come in 1980.) Meanwhile, Johnny Rutherford joined the all-time greats with his third 500 victory. Bobby Unser was to match this feat the following year with a victory initially awarded to Andretti before being restored to Unser. Then came a brief revival of national pride in 1982 when an American driver, Gordon Johncock, won the Indy 500 with an American chassis, the Wildcat Mk8-B.

We have to wait until 1985 for a new generation of champions to make its mark at Indianapolis: Danny Sullivan, Bobby Rahal, Arie Luyendyk and Al Unser Jr. filled the gaps left by Al Unser Sr., Mario Andretti and A. J. Foyt, not to mention the less fortunate drivers who have not yet managed to win such as Roberto Guerrero and Michael Andretti. Moreover, the public had to applaud Formula 1 stars such as Emerson Fittipaldi and Jacques Villeneuve (who, at 21, was the youngest-ever 500 winner) as they enjoyed success in America's temple of speed.

In 1986 the old circuit was subjected to a radical program of renovation: Spiffy new garages were installed on the legendary Gasoline Alley, which had traditionally been a corridor of open shops and Spartan, tumbledown support facilities.

his record-breaking 35th Indy 500 start. (The 1993 edition of the race was in fact the first since 1958 in which Foyt was missing from the grid.) In recompense, Fittipaldi achieved the unique feat of winning his second 500 after twice taking the Formula 1 title and once the CART championship.

Another forgettable edition was that of 1988: there were so many accidents that 68 of the 200 laps were completed at reduced speed and only two drivers actually managed to complete the full race distance—Mears and Fittipaldi, both at the wheel of Chevrolet-powered cars. Average qualifying speeds, however, of 360 kph (224 mph) were recorded.

Albeit less rapidly than in Formula 1, the performance of the cars and engines used at Indy also improved. In 1990 Al Unser Jr. approached an

average speed of 368 kph (229 mph) in qualifying
while the winner, the Dutchman Arie Luyendyk who
was also to win in 1997, recorded the record-
breaking average speed of 299 kph (185.7 mph).

Nepotism remains one of Indy's ingrained vices.
In the 1992 edition, the Unser and Andretti
dynasties had no fewer than six entries between
them; victory went to the third of the Unsers (a win
repeated in 1994), while Mario Andretti and his son
Jeff both ended up in the hospital. Michael led for
much of the race but was sidelined just before the

end with a fuel-system problem. Al Unser Sr., the
father of Al Jr., finished third behind the interloper
Scott Goodyear. In this edition there was the
smallest-ever gap between first and second place:
just 43 *thousandths* of a second.

The last year that Indianapolis formed part of the
CART series esd 1995. It broke away together with
other satellite circuits to form the Indy Racing
League. Following a statement on March 11, 1995 wherein
Indianapolis Motor Speedway president Tony
George announced the organization of a new

championship, the following years' edition was the
first Indianapolis 500 held under the exclusive
auspices of a new sanctioning body: the Indy Racing
League, or IRL. The race winner in 1996 was Buddy
Lazier of Hemelgarn Racing, while in 1997 the
talented Dutchman Luyendyk, one of the fastest
drivers of all time and a two-time Indy winner, took
the record qualifying lap speed to 381 kph (237
mph). One year later, what is still widely considered
to be the world's most prestigious single race was
won by Eddie Cheever Jr.

HONOR ROLL

Winners of the Indianapolis 500

YEAR	CAR	DRIVER	AV. KPH (MPH)
1911	Marmon Wasp	R. Harroun-C.Patshke	120.1 (74.6)
1912	National	J. Dawson-D. Herr	126.7 (78.7)
1913	Peugeot L76	J. Goux	122.2 (75.9)
1914	Delage	R. Thomas	132.7 (82.4)
1915	Mercedes	R. de Palma	144.7 (89.8)
1916	Peugeot	D. Resta	135.2 (83.9)
1919	Peugeot	H. Wilcox	141.7 (87.9)
1920	Frontenac	G. Chevrolet	141.9 (88.1)
1921	Frontenac	T. Milton	144.2 (89.5)
1922	Duesenberg-Miller	J. Murphy	152.1 (94.4)
1923	Miller	T. Milton-H. Wilcox	146.4 (90.9)
1924	Duesenberg	L.Corum-J.Boyer	158.1 (98.2)
1925	Duesenberg	P. de Paolo-N. Batten	162.7 (101.1)
1926	Miller	F. Lockhart	154.3 (95.8)
1927	Duesenberg	G. Souders	157 (97.5)
1928	Miller	L. Meyer	160.1 (99.4)
1929	Miller	R. Keech	154.1 (95.7)
1930	Summers-Miller	B. Arnold	161.7 (100.4)
1931	Stevens-Miller	L. Schneider	154.9 (96.2)
1932	Wetteroth FD-Miller	F. Frame	167.6 (104.0)
1933	Miller	L. Meyer	167.6 (104.0)
1934	Miller	B. Cummings	168.8 (104.8)
1935	Wetteroth-Offenhauser	K. Petillo	171 (106.2)
1936	Stevens-Miller	L. Meyer	175.5 (108.9)
1937	Shaw-Stevens-Offenhauser	W. Shaw	182.8 (113.5)
1938	Wetteroth-Offenhauser	F. Roberts	188.6 (117.1)
1939	Maserati SC	W. Shaw	185.1 (114.9)
1940	Maserati SC	W. Shaw	183.9 (114.2)
1941	Wetteroth-Offenhauser	S. Davis-M. Rose	185.3 (115.1)
1946	Adams-Sparks	G. Robson	184.7 (114.7)
1947	Deidt-Offenhauser	M. Rose	187.2 (116.3)
1948	Deidt-Offenhauser	M. Rose	192.8 (119.7)
1949	Deidt-Offenhauser	B. Holland	195.3 (121.3)
1950	Kurtis-Offenhauser	J. Parsons	199.6 (123.9)
1951	Kurtis-Offenhauser	L. Wallard	203.2 (126.2)
1952	Kuzma-Offenhauser	T. Ruttman	207.5 (128.8)
1953	Kurtis KK500A-Offenhauser	B. Vukovich	207.2 (128.7)
1954	Kurtis KK500A-Offenhauser	B. Vukovich	210.6 (130.8)
1955	Kurtis KK500D-Offenhauser	B. Sweikert	206.3 (128.1)
1956	Watson-Offenhauser	P. Flaherty	206.8 (128.4)
1957	Epperly-Offenhauser	S. Hanks	218.2 (135.7)
1958	Kuzma-Offenhauser	J. Bryan	215.3 (133.7)
1959	Watson-Offenhauser	R. Ward	218.6 (135.5)
1960	Watson-Offenhauser	J. Rathmann	223.3 (138.7)
1961	Watson-Trevis-Offenhauser	A. J. Foyt	223.9 (139.1)
1962	Watson-Offenhauser	R. Ward	225.8 (140.2)
1963	Watson-Offenhauser	P. Jones	225.5 (140.0)
1964	Watson-Offenhauser	A. J. Foyt	225.9 (140.3)
1965	Lotus 38-Ford	J. Clark	242.5 (150.6)
1966	Lola T90-Ford	G. Hill	232.3 (144.2)
1967	Coyote/Lotus 34 Ford	A. J. Foyt	243.3 (151.1)
1968	Eagle 68-Drake-Offenhauser	B. Unser	250.9 (155.8)

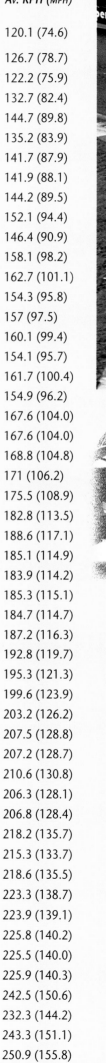

252 top This photograph shows a situation that occurs frequently during the Indy 500: this spectacular accident took place during the 1994 edition won by Al Unser Jr. for Team Penske.

252 bottom The undisputed symbol of Indianapolis is this imposing trophy that since early this century has entered the dreams of all the drivers who have participated in the Indy 500. The metal plaques carry the faces and names of all the winners from 1911 to the present day.

252-253 A gaggle of CART cars at the exit of a chicane. As in the Formula 1 World Championship, immediately after the start on the so-called "road tracks" (the non-oval circuits) this type of accident is fairly frequent—and undoubtedly preferable, in that the speeds are relatively modest and the risks for the drivers minimal.

253 top It even happens to the noble Speedway in Indiana: the 500 is occasionally struck by torrential rain that wrecks all strategies. This photograph was taken in 1997 a few minutes before the cars were fired up on the starting grid.

253 bottom In the foreground, one of the fastest Indianapolis drivers of all time, Arie Luyendyk, the Flying Dutchman, who won the 500 in both 1990 and in 1997 following the CART/IRL separation.

Year	Car	Driver	Av. KPH (MPH)
1969	Brawner/Hawk III-Ford	Ma. Andretti	252.4 (156.7)
1970	Colt 70-Ford	A. Unser	250.6 (155.6)
1971	Colt 71-Ford	A. Unser	253.8 (157.6)
1972	McLaren M16B-Offenhauser	M. Donohue	262.3 (162.9)
1973	Eagle 73-Offenhauser	G. Johncock	255.9 (158.9)
1974	McLaren M16 C/D-Offenhauser	J. Rutherford	255.2 (158.9)
1975	Eagle 75-Offenhauser	B. Unser	240.1 (149.1)
1976	McLaren M16E-Offenhauser	J. Rutherford	239.3 (148.6)
1977	Coyote-Foyt-Ford	A. J. Foyt	259.6 (161.2)
1978	Lola T500-Cosworth	A. Unser	259.6 (161.2)
1979	Penske PC6-Cosworth	R. Mears	255.7 (158.8)
1980	Chaparral 2K-Cosworth	J. Rutherford	229.9 (142.7)
1981	Penske PC9B-Cosworth	B. Unser	223.8 (138.9)
1982	Wildcat Mk88-Cosworth	G. Johncock	260.8 (161.9)
1983	March 83C-Cosworth	T. Sneva	260.9 (162)
1984	March 84C-Cosworth	R. Mears	263.3 (163.5)
1985	March 85C-Cosworth	D. Sullivan	246.2 (152,9)
1986	March 86C-Cosworth	B. Rahal	274.7 (170.6)
1987	March 86C-Cosworth	A. Unser	261 (162.1)
1988	Penske PC 17-Chevrolet	R. Mears	233 (144.7)
1989	Penske PC 18-Chevrolet	E. Fittipaldi	269.7 (167)
1990	Lola T90/00-Chevrolet	A. Luyendyk	299.2 (185)
1991	Penske PC 20-Chevrolet	R. Mears	284 (176.4)
1992	Galmer G92-Chevrolet	A. Unser Jr	216.4 (134.4)
1993	Penske PC 22-Chevrolet	E. Fittipaldi	253 (157.1)
1994	Penske PC 23-Mercedes Benz	A. Unser Jr	258.9 (160.8)
1995	Reynard-Ford Cosworth	J. Villeneuve	247.2 (153.5)
1996	Hemelgarn Racing	B. Lazier	238.1 (147.8)
1997	Treadway Racing	A. Luyendyk	234.7 (145.7)
1998	Rachel's Potato Chips	E. Cheever Jr.	233.6 (145.1)

The Most Frequent Winners at Indianapolis

Driver	Wins
A. J. Foyt, R. Mears, A. Unser Sr.	4
L. Meyer, J. Rutherford, W. Shaw, B. Unser	3
E. Fittipaldi, G. Johncock, A. Luyendyk, M. Rose, A. Unser Jr, R. Ward	2

THE CIRCUITS OF THE CART AND INDY CHAMPIONSHIPS

While Indianapolis may be the world's temple of speed, the American circuit is not the only stage on which Indy cars have done (and continue to do) battle. In fact, the geographical vastness of the North American continent inevitably led to events being widely scattered (especially prior to the advent of television), thus allowing thrill-seekers the opportunity to prove themselves at the wheel of single-seaters and motor racing fans to gather for automotive festivals that, unfortunately, were

Mid-Ohio, Portland, Southport, Toronto and Vancouver.

The IRL circus is instead staged at the nine ovals of Atlanta, Charlotte, Dover Downs, Indianapolis, Las Vegas, Phoenix, Pikes Peak, Longhorn and DisneyWorld. Lacking sufficient space to describe them all we have selected the most famous, those with a lengthy history. For the same reason we have restricted ourselves to recording the winners from the CART/IRL period only.

frequently the theatre of tragedies—not surprising, when one considers that races are traditionally held on circuits where speeds in excess of 400 kph (248 mph) are not infrequent.

CART can certainly boast a more widespread audience, particularly as it has expanded its horizons with races in Australia on the Queensland coast, in Brazil at Rio de Janeiro and in Japan at Motegi close to Tokyo. The most important events in the IRL calendar apart from Indianapolis are those at Phoenix in Arizona (one of motor racing's oldest homes) and DisneyWorld at Orlando, Florida, where the new championship's inaugural race was held.

The American circuits can be divided into ovals and road courses similar to the European tracks, and races are either measured in terms of hundreds of miles or laps. The CART ovals are often not geometrically perfect and in certain cases they are elongated on one side to form an almost triangular shape. The eight ovals currently used in the late Nineties are those of Fontana, Madison, Miami, Brooklyn (Michigan), Milwaukee, Motegi, Nazareth and Rio, and they are complemented by the road or city-street circuits of Cleveland, Detroit, Houston, Elkhart Lake, Laguna Seca, Long Beach,

MICHIGAN INTERNATIONAL SPEEDWAY

This circuit can be considered as the CART championship's replacement for Indianapolis, the race held there being known as the US 500. The Michigan International Speedway, as it is named, has a total length of 3.2 km (2 mi.). Between 1968 and 1986 the standard length of races was 200 miles, but by 1981 the classic 500-mile format, the longest for this type of race, had been adopted.

HONOR ROLL

Winners of the Michigan 500

YEAR	CAR	DRIVER	AV. SPEED (MPH)
1981	Penske PC7-Cosworth	P. Carter	132.89
1982	Wildcat Mk88-Cosworth	G. Johncock	153.925
1983	Penske PC10-Cosworth	J. Paul Jr.	134.862
1984	Lola T800-Cosworth	Ma. Andretti	133.482
1985	March 85C-Cosworth	E. Fittipaldi	128.22
1986	March 86C-Cosworth	J. Rutherford	137.14
1987	March 87C-Cosworth	Mi. Andretti	171.493
1988	Penske PC17-Cosworth	D. Sullivan	180.654
1989	Lola T89/00-Chevrolet	Mi. Andretti	160.21
1990	Lola T90/00-Chevrolet	A. Unser Jr.	189.727
1991	Penske PC20-Chevrolet	R. Mears	167.23
1992	Lola T92/00-Chevrolet	S. Goodyear	177.625
1993	Lola T93/00	N. Mansell	188.203
1994	Lola T94/00	S. Goodyear	159.8
1995	Lola-Ford Cosworth	S. Pruett	159.676
1996	Lola-Honda	A. Ribeiro	152.627
1997	Reynard-Honda	A. Zanardi	167.044
1998	Reynard-Mercedes	G. Moore	166.9

254-255 Jacques Villeneuve takes on fuel and tires. The circuit is that of Michigan which, following the defection of Indianapolis, hosted the most prestigious race in CART, the United States 500. Paradoxically, it was sponsored by Toyota in 1998.

255 bottom Milwaukee, 1998: Jimmy Vasser in a Reynard-Honda racing wheel to wheel with Mark Blundell in a similar car powered by a Mercedes-Ilmor engine. At the end of the day it was Vasser who was first to complete the 200 laps, while Blundell (well known to Formula 1 fans, too) finished in 12th place, four laps down on the winner.

CART & Indy

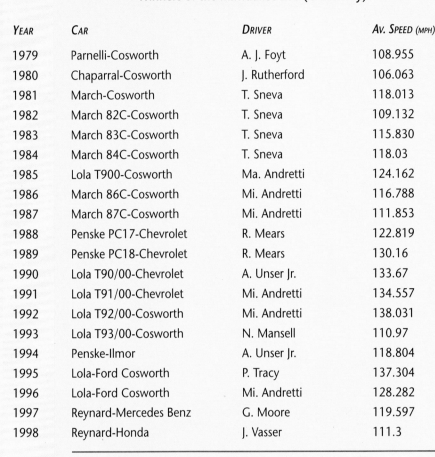

MILWAUKEE MILE

This is the world's oldest existing motor racing track, having been inaugurated before even Brooklands in England. It has hosted Indy-style races over the classic one-mile lap distance since 1903. The circuit is a perfect oval with a slight slope. When Indianapolis was part of the CART championship the Milwaukee 200 was held the following week. This is Michael Andretti's home circuit—he was born just two miles away and has won five editions of the Milwaukee 200 to Tom Sneva's four. Curiously, both Formula 1 champions Jim Clark and Nigel Mansell won their first Indy races here.

HONOR ROLL

Winners of the Milwaukee 200 (CART only)

Year	Car	Driver	Av. Speed (mph)
1979	Parnelli-Cosworth	A. J. Foyt	108.955
1980	Chaparral-Cosworth	J. Rutherford	106.063
1981	March-Cosworth	T. Sneva	118.013
1982	March 82C-Cosworth	T. Sneva	109.132
1983	March 83C-Cosworth	T. Sneva	115.830
1984	March 84C-Cosworth	T. Sneva	118.03
1985	Lola T900-Cosworth	Ma. Andretti	124.162
1986	March 86C-Cosworth	Mi. Andretti	116.788
1987	March 87C-Cosworth	Mi. Andretti	111.853
1988	Penske PC17-Chevrolet	R. Mears	122.819
1989	Penske PC18-Chevrolet	R. Mears	130.16
1990	Lola T90/00-Chevrolet	A. Unser Jr.	133.67
1991	Lola T91/00-Chevrolet	Mi. Andretti	134.557
1992	Lola T92/00-Cosworth	Mi. Andretti	138.031
1993	Lola T93/00-Cosworth	N. Mansell	110.97
1994	Penske-Ilmor	A. Unser Jr.	118.804
1995	Lola-Ford Cosworth	P. Tracy	137.304
1996	Lola-Ford Cosworth	Mi. Andretti	128.282
1997	Reynard-Mercedes Benz	G. Moore	119.597
1998	Reynard-Honda	J. Vasser	111.3

256 top The 1990 season was one of the most exciting in the history of the CART series; Michael Andretti (seen here at Laguna Seca) scored five wins, the same as Al Unser Jr. who nonetheless took the national title by 210 points to 181. Both drivers are sons of racing families and were racing with Lola-Chevrolets in 1990.

256-257 Paul Tracy slows coming into the pits at Long Beach.

257 top Emerson Fittipaldi is seen here racing in 1989. It was from 1985 that the Brazilian, the greatest of the second generation of South American aces, had been enjoying great success in the American championship. In 1989 he set his personal record of five wins in a season, three of them consecutive, which was sufficient for him to take the title.

ELKHART LAKE

This appealing road course has hosted all kinds of racing, including Can-Am events in which the cars could display all their awesome power in a spectacular setting. With regard to Indy-type championships, the race was known up to 1994 as the Elkhart Lake 200 before being re-baptized as Road America. During the Fifties the circuit ran around the lake of the same name. It is considered to be the United States' most attractive road circuit with the sole limitation of an extremely variable climate. Look carefully at the table of winners: in 1985 the race was won by a certain Jacques Villeneuve. Rather than Gilles' famous son, however, this was Gilles' brother. Villeneuve the Younger won at Elkhart in 1994 and 1995.

HONOR ROLL

Winners of the Elkhart Lake 200/Road America

Year	Car	Driver	Av. Speed (mph)
1982	March 82C-Cosworth	H. Rebaque	109.132
1983	March 83C-Cosworth	Ma. Andretti	99.41
1984	Lola T800-Cosworth	Ma. Andretti	116.347
1985	March 85C-Cosworth	J. Villeneuve	114.066
1986	March 86C-Cosworth	E. Fittipaldi	81.833
1987	Lola T87/00-Chevrolet	Ma. Andretti	120.155
1988	Penske PC18-Chevrolet	E. Fittipaldi	122.215
1989	Penske PC18-Chevrolet	D. Sullivan	122.803
1990	Lola T90/00-Chevrolet	Mi. Andretti	106.192
1991	Lola T91/00-Chevrolet	Mi. Andretti	126.205
1992	Penske PC 21-Chevrolet	E. Fittipaldi	110.656
1993	Penske PC 22-Chevrolet	P. Tracy	118.408
1994	Reynard 94I-Ford	J. Villeneuve Jr.	114.634
1995	Reynard-Ford Cosworth	J. Villeneuve Jr.	103.901
1996	Lola-Ford Cosworth	Mi. Andretti	102.947
1997	Reynard-Honda	A. Zanardi	102.995
1998	Reynard-Honda	D. Franchetti	104.6

LAGUNA SECA

A famous California circuit laid out near the former Fort Ord military base, up until 1987 the circuit was a little less than two miles (3 km) in length and resembled the United States' shield-shaped road markers in plan. A deep loop was then added to skirt around the infield lake and the total length was extended to a Formula 1-eligible 2.2 miles (3.5 km). This circuit close to Monterey has also hosted Can-Am, Formula 5000, sports-prototype, and GT racing in its day.

257 bottom Mansell had a great season in 1993, conquering the CART title. This photograph shows him at the wheel of his Ford Cosworth-powered Lola smoking the rear tires off the line.

HONOR ROLL

Winners of Laguna Seca 200

YEAR	CAR	DRIVER	AV. SPEED (MPH)
1979*	Prophet/Lola-Chevrolet	B. Rahal	113.211
1980*	Frisbee GR3-Chevrolet	A. Unser Sr.	108.728
1981*	March 817-Chevrolet	T. Fabi	115.895
1982*	Frisbee GR3-Chevrolet	A. Unser Jr.	114.151
1983	March 83C-Cosworth	T. Fabi	106.943
1984	March 84C-Cosworth	B. Rahal	119.105
1985	March 85C-Cosworth	B. Rahal	112.923
1986	March 86C-Cosworth	B. Rahal	119.693
1987	Lola T87/00-Chevrolet	B. Rahal	118.879
1988	Penske PC17-Chevrolet	D. Sullivan	94.090
1989	Penske PC18-Chevrolet	R. Mears	122.803
1990	Penske PC18-Chevrolet	D. Sullivan	103.556
1991	Lola T91/00-Chevrolet	Mi. Andretti	103.604
1992	Lola T92/00-Chevrolet	Mi. Andretti	99.996
1993	Penske PC22-Chevrolet	P. Tracy	118.408
1994	Penske PC23-Ilmor	P. Tracy	92.978
1995	Reynard-Mercedes-Benz	G. de Ferran	98.493
1996	Reynard-Honda	A. Zanardi	102.687
1997	Reynard-Honda	J. Vasser	109.647
1998	Reynard-Ford Cosworth	B. Herta	105.6

(CART drivers in SCCA Can-Am races and SCCA Can-Am cars)

HONOR ROLL

PHOENIX

As early as 1915 the circuit of the state capital of Arizona was hosting Indy-style races and Phoenix has always represented one of the most important events of the season. The defection from the CART championship in favour of the IRL was thus a clamorous decision. Like the tracks at Daytona, Nazareth and Michigan, Phoenix is an irregular oval with the back straight interrupted by a sharp but very fast left-hander. The third turn, opposite the first, is thus very gentle compared with the rest of the circuit. The Phoenix oval is also a mile in length.

Winners of the Phoenix 150-200 (CART and IRL only)

YEAR	CAR	DRIVER	AV. SPEED (MPH)
1979	Chaparral 2K-Cosworth	A. Unser	123.023
1980	Phoenix-Cosworth	T. Sneva	99.926
1981	March 81C-Cosworth	T. Sneva	118.727
1982	March 82C-Cosworth	T. Sneva	110.997
1983	March 83C-Cosworth	T. Fabi	126.671
1984	March 84C-Cosworth	B. Rahal	98.48
1985	March 85C-Cosworth	A. Unser	120.644
1986	March 86C-Cosworth	Mi. Andretti	134.676
1987	March 87C-Cosworth	R. Guerrero	138.02
1988	Lola T88/00-Chevrolet	Ma. Andretti	121.993
1989	Penske PC18-Chevrolet	R. Mears	126.112
1990	Penske PC19-Chevrolet	R. Mears	126.291
1991	Lola T91/00-Chevrolet	A. Luyendyk	129.988
1992	Lola T92/00-Chevrolet	B. Rahal	130.526
1993	Lola T92/00-Chevrolet	Ma. Andretti	123.847
1994	Penske PC 23-Ilmor	E. Fittipaldi	107.437
1995	Reynard-Ford Cosworth	R. Gordon	133.98
1996	Reynard-Cosworth	A. Luyendyk	117.368
1997	Dallara-Aurora	J. Guthrie	89.190
1998	Dallara-Aurora	S. Sharp	98.110

NASCAR WINSTON CUP

258 top left There were still 13 years to go before the first NASCAR championship, but stock car racing was already very popular in the 1930s. This photograph shows the 1936 race at Daytona Beach, the track laid out on the sands. The winner was Milt Marion at the wheel of a Ford V8; in sixth place was the young Bill France, a name that was to become famous.

258 top right All the cars that take part in the NASCAR championship have

to be decorated with the official decals: that of 1955 is shown here, two checkered flags and two stylized cars.

258 bottom Everything is set for the start of the Daytona 500 in 1993: the cars are lined up on the grid, the mechanics and technicians are making last-minute adjustments and checks and journalists and photographers are roaming amongst the cars, capturing the atmosphere. Dale Jarret was to win this edition in a Chevrolet.

The NASCAR Winston Cup is the most popular of the American motor racing championships, polarizing the attention of sponsors, the media and the public: at every race between 100 and 150 thousand people crowd the grandstands at the oval circuits in order to watch the "stock cars"—purportedly ordinary production models that the average American might use to drive to work, do the shopping or take the kids to school. In truth, these are pure-race monsters capable of mind-blowing average speeds of up to 360 kph (224 mph). They lap continuously, covering distances of between 400 and 800 km (248–497 mi.), even at night. Herein lies the success of the stock formula which finds its greatest expression in the NASCAR (National Association for Stock Car Auto Racing) Winston Cup.

This overwhelming success in the United States ever since the formula's debut in 1949 has no equals in Europe: on the Continent the corresponding touring-car championships and the GT series for sports-prototypes have never enjoyed the same kind of mass appeal, sponsorship and media interest. The causes are to be found not so much in the quality of the two championships, as the resources and technology devoted to both are of the highest levels, but rather in the lack of continuity and homogeneity in the European regulations. The European touring car races lack an international championship and the experimental ITCC (International Touring Car Championship) of the late Nineties—which was in part linked to races valid for the most famous national series, the German championship—proved to be a failure. This means that only the national championships survive and attract any interest: the BTCC (British Touring Car Championship); the aforementioned German series (the STW or *Super Touren Wagen,* better known under the old name of DTM or *Deutsche*

Tourenwagen Meisterschaft); and the Italian *Superturismo* championship.

The situation regarding the sports-prototype championship is even more delicate, as the FIA has continually shuffled the pack regarding the official international series. Only towards the end of the century has it in part restored the sports car championship to its former glories of the 1970s, carefully regulating this form of competition. In the meantime, like the national championships for touring cars, the individual races (the 24-hour races at Daytona, Spa-Francorchamps and Le Mans and the Sebring 12 Hours) have kept the category alive, acting as a magnet for constructors and sponsors. To all this has to be added the strong competition from Formula 1 and the World Rally Championship.

The origins of NASCAR in effect coincide with those of Formula 1: while in Europe the circus was being established in 1950 with Grand Prix-type cars, on the far side of the Atlantic the first birthday of the Winston Cup stock-car championship was being celebrated. The series was strictly reserved for

cars deriving from genuine production models, and at stake was a trophy named after the sponsoring tobacco brand, Winston.

Stock-car racing has been in existence since the 1930s and has its epicenter on the Atlantic coast, principally at Daytona Beach, Florida—the coastal resort that, as well as a temple of sports-prototype racing with a 24-hour race similar to that held at Le Mans, has become the headquarters and beating heart of NASCAR racing. At first a circuit was created on the beach of the Florida resort that snaked across the hard sand close to the edge of the ocean. Sand was also banked up to form a kind of guardrail preventing the spectators from invading the dusty track that also incorporated part of the main beach highway. On that improvised track, constructed and dismantled within a matter of days like the big top of a circus, all kinds of essentially stock cars gave battle: convertibles, classic four-door sedans, pick-ups and even station wagons. These were, in the main, road vehicles transformed into racing cars by the removal of extra

seats, the application of go-fast stripes to the sides and hand-painted numbers to the doors and the addition of metal guards—frequently made of chicken wire—mounted over the headlights, front grill and windshield to protect them from gravel, stones and other debris that might be found on the rudimentary track.

Among those who raced on the dusty tracks—those lovers of speed eager to put their driving talent to the test—was one Bill France, a mechanic by training who immediately caught the eye as one of the youngest drivers in the category in the 1930s: he contested his first races at just 16 years of age.

After the Second World War, "Big" Bill France was keen to try regulating these informal challenges, creating a championship with its own venues, regulations and safety measures that could attract the interest of the public and investors alike. France realized that if he was to have a future in motor racing he had to plan beyond his immediate career as a driver. Perhaps the only racer to have competed on all of the era's major stock-car circuits, he was

NASCAR

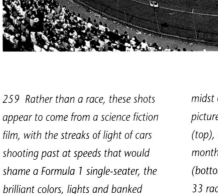

259 Rather than a race, these shots appear to come from a science fiction film, with the streaks of light of cars shooting past at speeds that would shame a Formula 1 single-seater, the brilliant colors, lights and banked curves of the speedway bowl that looks like a spaceship about to land in the midst of the crowd. Instead the pictures show the circuits of Richmond (top), completely rebuilt in eight months in 1988, and Martinsville (bottom). The latter held two of the 33 races in the 1998 Winston Cup series, one in September and one in April.

also perhaps the only man forceful and visionary enough to organize a stock-car championship.

In spite of his experience it was no easy task. Immediately after the end of the war France began working on an idea for a championship series but was obstructed by those who ought instead to have been on his side: the American Automobile Association, the United States' most powerful automotive body. The AAA had no faith in the future of stock-car racing held on improvised, dusty tracks. They were considered second-rate, unprofitable events and France's scheme was thus rejected. However, "Big" Bill refused to admit defeat and, in 1946 with the help of his wife, organized the first National Championship Stock Car Circuit (NCSCC) with headquarters close to the Halifax river at Daytona Beach, Florida.

The races were held primarily in Florida, Georgia, the Carolinas and Virginia, plus a few sporadic appearances in the northwest. The winner of what may be considered as the forerunner of the NASCAR Winston Cup series was Fonty Flock, who received a prize of $3,000.

The newborn championship had yet to gain national status, a situation that Bill France was determined to change. He was encouraged by the positive reaction to the first edition, repeated the following year, and thus felt ready to attempt something that had never before been achieved.

The meeting at Daytona's Streamline Hotel in December of 1947 can be considered as the foundation stone of what was to become the United States' most popular motor racing championship. Such was the birth of the NASCAR series, in a hotel room to which Bill France invited friends, ex-drivers, promoters, lawyers and businessmen, explaining to them the aims, organization, regulations, calendars and potential profits of the new championship. He convinced them all and immediately formed an

260 The 40th edition of the Daytona 500: since 1959 the most famous of the oval speedways has been the home of the Winston Cup and has hosted its most celebrated race. The father of the championship, Bill France Sr., moved here in order to develop his idea for a stock-car championship. Before the speedway was built, a temporary track was laid out on the sands and incorporated a section of public highway.

organizing committee. The president, elected unanimously of course, was Bill France, who continued to epitomize the spirit of NASCAR. He believed in the formula wholeheartedly and even moved to Daytona Beach with his family so as to be able to follow its development firsthand. He also transmitted this belief to his sons, Bill Jr. and Jim, who became, respectively, president and vice-president on his retirement in 1972.

After an 18-month period of gestation the first NASCAR championship got under way in June, 1949. There were eight races in the calendar, the first at Charlotte in which 33 cars took part. The size of the crowd exceeded all expectations: 13,000 spectators! This success attracted new investors, above all concessionaires who scented guaranteed economic returns from sponsoring the initiative. The second race was held on the beach at Daytona with 28 cars starting.

No driver took part in all eight races, but eight out of 50 participated in six. The championship saw

born. The Grand Prix series attempted to bring the United States into its fold by including the Indianapolis 500 as one of the races valid for the championship, but this was an experiment destined for failure in that the European drivers never came to race in the States except on rare occasions and the Americans were reluctant to travel to Europe. Furthermore, the American public demonstrated a clear preference for the NASCAR series which that season staged no less than 51 races, over six times the number of the previous year. This was confirmation of the success being enjoyed by the "strictly stock" cars.

The 1950s were golden years for NASCAR racing with a championship that in its second edition was already faced with a fundamental decision: whether to abandon the improvised dirt tracks, frequently built on farmland or incorporating sections of public highway, in favor of purpose-built facilities with asphalt circuits. This idea came to a businessman, Harold Brasington, who recognized

261 top These photographs illustrate the eighth (left) and the 27th (right) rounds of the 1998 NASCAR Winston Cup, held five months apart (in April and September) at Martinsville. The cars have just started and, in a triumph of brilliant colors, prepare to join battle to the last fender. During the race, in fact, there will be no lack of accidents. Note in the picture to the left the Ford Taurus number 21 which already sports a damaged rear end. On the occasion of the 1998 championship the two-door Taurus facsimile replaced the glorious Thunderbird, which was pensioned off after many years of honorable service.

261 bottom Great celebrations for Dale Jarret's victory. The driver in the black overalls with a magnum of champagne in his hands climbed onto the top step of the podium after crossing the line first in his Ford Taurus.

its first woman driver in that first season, Sara Christina, who was to finish 13th.

Red Byron in an Oldsmobile was the first driver to inscribe his name on the NASCAR roll of honor: he won two races, followed by Bob Flock, the NCSCC champion. However, Byron saw all the points he had accumulated annulled at the start of the following season as in the meantime he had competed in events outside the NASCAR championship.

NASCAR inaugurated its second season in 1950, the year in which in Europe the Formula 1 series was

261

262 top Frenetic tension-filled moments in the pits during which every hundredth of a second saved could be vital: the tyres consumed by the continuous lapping on the oval circuits are changed and the vehicles are topped up with dozens of liters of fuel via the unusual red tanks resembling enormous syringes. This picture shows Jeff Gordon at the wheel of a Chevrolet Monte Carlo at New Hampshire.

262-263 In this photograph the driver Jeff Gordon is hunkered into the cockpit of his Chevrolet Monte Carlo. The car has been suitably prepared for NASCAR Winston Cup championship; it is in fact a purpose-built racing machine, sharing virtually no components or even dimensions with the street car it is intended to represent. Gordon dominated the '98 season, collecting 13 wins and taking the title for the third time as well as pocketing a check for $2,000,000. Gordon is NASCAR racing's great young star and enters the new millennium as the series' leader, having earned a place alongside the heroes such as Earnhardt, Waltrip, Yarborough and the Pettys.

the potential earnings after seeing the crowds (and above all the financial income) generated by the Indianapolis Motor Speedway on the occasion of the Indy 500. The construction of the first asphalt circuit for the NASCAR championship took place at Darlington in South Carolina. The location was strategic: the peaceful village of Darlington was at a crossroads for the tourist traffic between New York and Florida, while 40 miles away one found the highway leading to the state's capital city, Columbia.

Darlington thus hosted the south's first NASCAR 500-mile race. It was a great success, with 25,000 people crowding the grandstands to watch the 51 cars fight it out side-by-side on the oval track for 500 miles (over 804 km). Johnny Mantz won in a Plymouth.

In the 1960s no less than six of the 18 speedways currently hosting NASCAR races became asphalt circuits: Charlotte, Atlanta, North Carolina, Michigan, Dover and Alabama joined the most famous of them all, Daytona, built in 1959.

The motive that lay behind the construction of these American temples of speed was simple: business. The public interest in the series was enormous and in 1950 there were a record 56 races each season with Lee Petty winning the championship three times in 1954, '58 and '59 and becoming the first great NASCAR hero. He was also the head of a family that for four generations has played a leading role in stock car racing. Following the successes of Lee, it was Richard who went on to better his father's achievements and established himself as the undisputed NASCAR king.

Richard raced from 1958 to 1992, conquering seven titles in the 1960s (two) and 1970s (five) in Plymouths, Dodges and Chevrolets, taking part in 1157 races, winning 200 and setting 57 pole-

262 bottom A car comes in for one of the many pit stops that are such a feature of the NASCAR championship: the car receiving the attention of the mechanics is a Pontiac; at the wheel is Dick Trickle, a driver from Wisconsin who joined the United States' most popular series in 1989 after having raced for many years in the national ASA series.

position times. He conquered Daytona on no fewer than 12 occasions and earned $1,000,000 during the 1970 season alone.

After Richard, sons Adam and Kyle joined the "family business"—part of a nepotistic tradition that is stronger in NASCAR than in any other form of motor sport. Apart from the Pettys there are the Flocks, the Waltrips, the Wallaces, the Pearsons, the Earnhardts, the Woods, plus many more—including of course the Frances, who set the example for all these NASCAR dynasties.

The 1980s were dominated by Darrell Waltrip and Dale Earnhardt (six titles between them), with Earnhardt continuing to play a leading role into the Nineties (winning titles in 1990, '91, '93 and '94), until his mantle was taken over by the new rising star Jeff Gordon, who seems set to be the new Richard Petty: he has already won three titles, the first in '95 and two consecutively in '97 and '98, this last with two races to spare. Gordon has already entered the NASCAR record books as the youngest

driver (at 27) to have conquered three Winston Cup championship titles. The 1998 win consecrated his passage from young promise to established legend because apart from taking the title he also scored numerous high placings. The NASCAR regulations, in fact, reward not only those with the good fortune to win a race but also those who place consistently: the Winston Cup title has in fact been clinched many times by drivers with relatively few outright wins to their name.

This is a championship with a very strong human factor, thanks above all to its family basis and the succession of generations, surnames that have in practice monopolized the roll of honour for decades, or individual drivers who have been racing for decades such as Dave Marcis, still taking part in the NASCAR series after making his debut in 1968. This kind of situation is rare in other championships, and is the sort of phenomenon that can relegate the cars to a supporting role behind the drivers.

The national constructors have made the series their own, of course, greatly aided by the rulebook. There has never been a legitimate foreign attempt to invade the protected territory of the American V8s. This is perhaps another reason why it is the men, rather than the cars, that have made NASCAR history. The battles have always been fought out among Chevrolet, Ford, Dodge, Oldsmobile, Plymouth, Mercury and Pontiac, the cream of the US industry. Chevrolet, the country's largest selling brand, has taken the lion's share of glory by carrying a driver to the title 21 times since its first win in 1955. The Chevy hegemony, with the Monte Carlo in particular, has been especially apparent since the early 1980s: from 1984 to 1998 Chevy has won 12 titles, with six consecutively (1993–98).

263 top All the crews of the various teams are ready to receive their cars for the pits stops: the circuit is Darlington, the first asphalt venue for the NASCAR Winston Cup. Among the cars in the pits is the Chevrolet Monte Carlo that dominated the 1998 season with Jeff Gordon.

263 bottom Roy Johns, better known to NASCAR fans as Roy Buckshot, is portrayed here during the Kroker 200 at Indianapolis Raceway Park.

264 Crash tests for the American
NASCAR racers that reach maximum
speeds of over 350 kph (217 mph).
In this shot Mike Skinner aboard a
Chevrolet Monte Carlo (number 31) has
collided with Chad Little (car number
97) and Bobby Labonte (number 18) at
Bristol during the 1998 championship.

265 top left and 265 bottom Accidents
are frequent and spectacular:
fortunately, in the majority of cases the
consequences are not serious and the
cars can often be repaired in time to
rejoin the race.

265 top right Dale Earnhardt seen here
at the wheel of his Chevrolet Monte
Carlo with conspicuous damage to the
flanks. The American driver—the
protagonist of the Winston Cup series in
the early Nineties before passing on the
baton to the emergent Jeff Gordon—is,
together with Richard Petty, the driver
who has won the greatest number of
NASCAR titles: seven.

HONOR ROLL

YEAR	DRIVER	TEAM	CAR
1949	Red Byron	Parks Novelty	Oldsmobile
1950	Bill Rexford	Julian Buesink	Oldsmobile
1951	Herb Thomas	Thomas-Sandford Motors/Fabulous	Plymouth/Oldsmobile/Hudson
1952	Tim Flock	Ted Chester	Hudson
1953	Herb Thomas	Fabulous	Hudson
1954	Lee Petty	Petty Engineering	Dodge/Chrysler
1955	Tim Flock	Mercury Outboards Westmoreland	Chrysler/Chevrolet
1956	Buck Baker	Satcher Motors	Ford/Chrysler/Dodge
1957	Buck Baker	Hugh Babb/Buck Baker	Chevrolet
1958	Lee Petty	Petty Engineering	Oldsmobile
1959	Lee Petty	Petty Engineering	Oldsmobile/Plymouth
1960	Rex White	Piedmont/Friendly	Ford/Chevrolet
1961	Ned Jarret	Courtesy/BG Holloway	Ford/Chevrolet
1962	Joe Weatherly	Bud Moore	Pontiac
1963	Joe Weatherly	Bud Moore	Pontiac/Chrysler/Dodge/Plymouth/Mercury
1964	Richard Petty	Petty Engineering	Plymouth
1965	Ned Jarret	Bondy Long	Ford
1966	David Pearson	Cotton Owens	Dodge
1967	Richard Petty	Petty Enterprises	Plymouth
1968	David Pearson	Holman & Moody	Ford
1969	David Pearson	Holman & Moody	Ford
1970	Bobby Isaac	K&K Insurance	Dodge
1971	Richard Petty	Petty Enterprises	Plymouth
1972	Richard Petty	Petty Enterprises	Plymouth/Dodge
1973	Benny Parsons	LG de Witt	Chevrolet

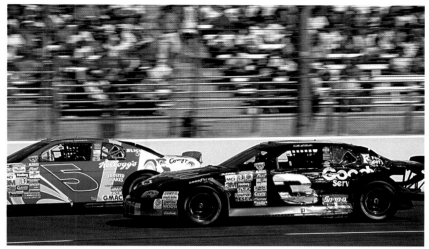

265 center right Four crackerjack mechanics deal with the nose of a Ford Taurus at the NASCAR Brickyard race held on the Indianapolis Motor Speedway.

Year	Driver	Team	Car
1974	Richard Petty	Petty Enterprises	Dodge
1975	Richard Petty	Petty Enterprises	Dodge
1976	Cale Yarborough	Junior Johnson	Chevrolet
1977	Cale Yarborough	Junior Johnson	Chevrolet
1978	Cale Yarborough	Junior Johnson	Oldsmobile
1979	Richard Petty	Petty Enterprises	Chevrolet
1980	Dale Earnhardt	Osterlund Racing	Chevrolet
1981	Darrell Waltrip	Junior Johnson	Buick
1982	Darrell Waltrip	Junior Johnson	Buick
1983	Bobby Allison	Di Gard Racing	Buick
1984	Terry Labonte	Billy Hagan	Chevrolet
1985	Darrell Waltrip	Junior Johnson	Chevrolet
1986	Dale Earnhardt	Richard Childress Racing	Chevrolet
1987	Dale Earnhardt	Richard Childress Racing	Chevrolet
1988	Bill Elliott	Elliott Brothers	Ford
1989	Rusty Wallace	Raymond Beadle	Pontiac
1990	Dale Earnhardt	Richard Childress Racing	Chevrolet
1991	Dale Earnhardt	Richard Childress Racing	Chevrolet
1992	Alan Kulwicki	Alan Kulwicki	Ford
1993	Dale Earnhardt	Richard Childress Racing	Chevrolet
1994	Dale Earnhardt	Richard Childress Racing	Chevrolet
1995	Jeff Gordon	Rick Hendrick Racing	Chevrolet
1996	Terry Labonte	Rick Hendrick Racing	Chevrolet
1997	Jeff Gordon	Rick Hendrick Racing	Chevrolet
1998	Jeff Gordon	Rick Hendrick Racing	Chevrolet

Drivers who have won the most titles

Driver	Number of titles
Dale Earnhardt	7
Richard Petty	7
Jeff Gordon	3
Lee Petty	3
David Pearson	3
Cale Yarborough	3
Darrell Waltrip	3

Constructors who have won the most titles

Constructor	Number of titles
Chevrolet	21
Ford	8
Plymouth	7
Dodge	7
Oldsmobile	6
Chrysler	4
Buick, Hudson, Pontiac	3

THE CAN-AM CHALLENGE

The story of the Can-Am cars, the most awesome beasts in the history of sports-car racing, intolerant of engine capacity and power-output rules, and in fact most regulations, was brief but intense. The Can-Am machines were in some ways similar to those employed in the sports-prototype category of the Sixties, and they shared the same fate. Certainly, the emotions stirred by these mega-powered monsters—sanctioned by the Sports Car Club of America (SCCA) but classified as Group 7 by the FIA—have rarely been matched. It is for this reason that many of the great champions were keen to test themselves in the open-cockpit Lolas, Porsches and McLarens.

The Canadian-American Challenge was born in 1966 under the auspices of the Canadian Automobile Sport Clubs (CASC) and the Sports Car Club of America (SCCA). Can-Am purists consider the Golden Age to have been over as early as 1974 when, after nine editions, the championship was integrated with Formula 5000 before returning in a lower key and with a reduced calendar from 1977

a distant country, New Zealand, that exported great drivers such as Denny Hulme and Bruce McLaren: the pair dominated Can-Am, the latter above all as a team owner (five titles). In the final part of the first period, however, two titles were won by an equally famous team from the United States, Penske, which raced the incredibly powerful Porsche 917s.

In 1969 the number of championship races was increased to nine with important circuits such as Elkhart Lake, Watkins Glen and Michigan being represented. The McLaren M8B-Chevrolet won every race. In reality McLaren's cars remained unbeaten from September 1968 through September 1970—that is to say for 22 consecutive races; a statistic that would have been all the more impressive had it not been for Hulme's retirement in the last race of '67 after the team had already claimed the title with five wins out of six. That race instead went to the indefatigable Surtees at the wheel of another great car, the Lola T70-Chevrolet.

The McLaren domination drew to a close in 1971, and by 1972 the European Porsches were

superiority proved to be counterproductive and lacking in promotional value.

Nonetheless, the unrestricted monsters made a return in 1977 and once again there was a clear dominator, this time a Lola with Chevy power (in practice the American engine manufacturer won every edition of the championship with the exception of the two Porsche wins). Lola went on to become the marque with the greatest number of Can-Am titles: six in total, one more than McLaren.

The late Seventies saw the participation of VIPs from the international automotive circus. From Formula 1 there was Jackie Stewart, Alan Jones, Keke Rosberg and Jacques Villeneuve (along with Patrick Tambay, second only to Hulme for the number of victories); from CART/Indy there were Al Unser Sr. and

through 1986. Bearing this in mind, it is easy to identify the protagonists of the two eras.

The first Can-Am race was staged on 11 September 1966 at St. Jovite and was won by John Surtees who, with his own team, also won the six-event championship (St. Jovite, Bridgehampton, Mosport, Laguna Seca, Riverside, Las Vegas). However, the great car and motorcycling champion, the only man to win world titles in both sports, was soon obliged to give way to two great colleagues and a great team. It is curious to note that one of the rare bi-national championships (Canada and the United States) came to be dominated by racers from

already putting up a successful challenge to the orange racers. The turbocharged, 12-cylinder Porsche 917s were simply too powerful for their rivals to handle, Lola and Chaparral included, and also won every race in 1973, again in the Penske colors. The baton then passed to the Chevrolet-powered Shadow.

It was this season-long domination by individual teams with the outcome of each race and the championship title in little doubt that signaled the end for the Can-Am series, just as happened in sports-prototype racing in which Ferrari, Mercedes and Porsche frequently abandoned the category after triumphant seasons because their manifest

Jr., Danny Sullivan, and Teo Fabi; while Jacky Ickx and the Holberts, father and son, came over from their sports- and endurance-racing duties. Phil Hill also ventured into the Challenge at its start.

But just as they had increased, the number of races and the size of the crowds progressively diminished. There was a return to six rounds in 1983 while just four were staged in 1986, the series' last season. This extreme category was effectively replaced by the IMSA GTP championship (which, since as early as 1981, had seen Porsche, March and Nissan all taking turns coming to the fore) and the SCCA Trans-Am. Also born in '66, the Trans-Am series has survived to this day thanks to the greater interest shown by the constructors, sponsors and public. This series has featured cars such as the Chevy Camaro and Corvette, Ford Mustang and the Porsche 911. Thus the production-based Trans-Am series survives, while the Can-Am Challenge—perhaps the freest, most unrestricted sports-car championship ever seen—has died out.

266 left The starting grid at Bridgehampton in 1968. England's Stirling Moss is driving the Aston Martin DBS pace car; the marque was made famous in America by James Bond and the earlier DB5.

266 top right A fine view of the Road Atlanta circuit, the home of important motor racing events including this round of the Can-Am Challenge. This picture dates from 1973: in the lead are two Porsche 917/30s, the first of which is driven by Mark Donohue, winner of the overall championship for Team Penske.

Can-Am

HONOR ROLL

YEAR	DRIVER	TEAM	CAR
1966	John Surtees	Surtees	Lola T70-Chevrolet
1967	Bruce McLaren	McLaren Motor Racing	McLaren M6A-Chevrolet
1968	Denny Hulme	McLaren Motor Racing	McLaren M8A-Chevrolet
1969	Bruce McLaren	McLaren Motor Racing	McLaren M8B-Chevrolet
1970	Denny Hulme	McLaren Motor Racing	McLaren M8D-Chevrolet
1971	Peter Revson	McLaren Motor Racing	McLaren M8F-Chevrolet
1972	George Follmer	Penske Racing	Porsche 917/10
1973	Mark Donohue	Penske Racing	Porsche 917/30
1974	Jackie Oliver	Shadow Racing Team	Shadow DN4A-Chevrolet
1977	Patrick Tambay	Haas-Hall Racing	Lola T333CS-Chevrolet
1978	Alan Jones	Haas-Hall Racing	Lola T333CS-Chevrolet
1979	Jacky Ickx	Carl Haas Racing	Lola T333CS-Chevrolet
1980	Patrick Tambay	Carl Haas Racing	Lola T530-Chevrolet
1981	Geoff Brabham	Team VDS	Lola T530-Chevrolet/VDS 001
1982	Al Unser Jr	Galles Racing	Frisbee GR3-Chevrolet
1983	Jacques Villeneuve	Canadian Tire	Frisbee GR3-Chevrolet
1984	Michael Roe	Don Walker	VDS 002/004-Chevrolet
1985	Rick Miaskiewicz	Mosquitto Autosport	Frisbee-Chevrolet
1986	Horst Kroll	Kroll Racing	Frisbee KR3-Chevrolet

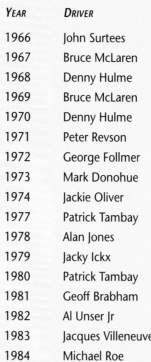

Drivers with the greatest number of wins

DRIVER	WINS
Denny Hulme	22
Patrick Tambay	12
Al Holbert	10
Bruce McLaren	9
Mark Donohue	7
George Follmer	7
Alan Jones	7
Jim Crawford	5
Jacky Ickx	5
Peter Revson	5

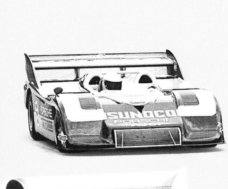

Constructors with the greatest number of wins

CONSTRUCTOR	WINS
McLaren	40 (5)
Lola	37 (6)
Porsche	16 (2)
Frisbee	12 (4)
Vds	12 (1)
March	11
CAC	5
Spyder	5
Shadow	4 (1)

(Number of championship titles in brackets)

266-267 A dynamic image of the starter Ted Hopkins as the McLaren M8B-Chevrolet of Bruce McLaren crosses the line in the Watkins Glen 200, the third round of the 1969 Can-Am Championship. The title was won that year by McLaren himself.

267 bottom center This photograph taken at Laguna Seca in 1980 shows an unusual hybrid combining an open-wheel Formula-type car with a faired sports-style machine. This is a Tiga at its debut in the hands of Vern Schuppan. The wing, open at either end and mounted on two vertical struts, is typical of the late Seventies.

267 bottom right Two McLaren M8s racing in convoy during a 1969 race. The first is driven by the team owner, Bruce McLaren.

ROAD RACES

268 top This photograph shows one of the very first cars to carry the Anonima Lombarda Fabbrica Automobili (Alfa) badge; the factory had earlier assembled French Darracqs under license. The image dates from 1912 and the couple sitting at the front are Baldoni and Nasi; the car is a 24 hp and the occasion the Tour of Sicily, better known as the Targa Florio.

268 center left An unusual shot of Nino Vaccarella climbing out of his Alfa Romeo 33/2 Daytona on the occasion of the 1968 Targa Florio. In spite of the best efforts of the Sicilian driver (the 1965 winner), victory that year went to a Porsche (that of Elford and Maglioli), one of the swarm of powerful 907s the Stuttgart firm entered for the '68 race.

268 center right Had Stirling Moss won even half of the races that he dominated he would have retired with a quite remarkable record. Instead the English driver managed to lose numerous events that he had already almost won. Not on this occasion, though: In 1955 the Englishman won the first Targa Florio valid for the World Sports Car Championship with his Mercedes. This photograph shows how close Moss came to not finishing this race. His teammate was the equally talented and sporting Collins, while the car was a variant of the beautiful 300SLR.

Clearly the origins of motor racing are to be found on the roads because at the birth of the automobile the only circuits in existence were those reserved for horses and dogs. In fact the road was the best promotional setting from which to publicize the inherent virtues of the motor car (its reliability and convenience) by means of exciting and demanding trials. It should not be forgotten that the marriage between cars and industry had been immediate: industry promptly appropriated this precious new means of transport that promised enormous potential expansion, the aperture of new markets and vast profits. The marketing value of road races throughout the globe should not, therefore, be underestimated, especially in the first two decades of their existence.

In the epic period motor races were simply organized city-to-city raids that were occasionally transformed into endurance races—especially in the United States, where the generally less sophisticated road surfaces than those found in Europe justified and reinforced the idea of a challenge fought out not only against rival competitors but even against nature, conditions and the "institutions."

268 bottom The Ferrari of Vaccarella and Bandini, seen in this picture, won the Targa Florio in 1965. Lorenzo then perished at Monte Carlo in a GP Ferrari whilst the Sicilian driver became headmaster of a private school after having become the driver with the greatest number of Targa victories. Note the graffiti urging on Vaccarella.

268-269 The 1907 Targa Florio: Felice Nazzaro aboard a Fiat 28/40 hp (subsequently homologated as a 60 hp) passes through the village of Petralia Soprana.

269 top right An historic driver, Campari, with two victories in the Mille Miglia (1928 *and 1929) seen here with Marinoni. An historic car, the Alfa 1750S had two victories, with Campari in 1929 and with Nuvolari in 1930. This photograph dates from 1931 when Mercedes shattered the dreams of the Italian drivers by winning with the SSKL of Caracciola.*

With the advent of closed circuits, increasingly necessary as a result of the growing speeds of the racing machines, the nature of road racing mutated and assumed a more populist approach, with the races becoming purely sporting events.

Open-road racing can thus be said to have differentiated from GP-type races with the maturation of the Tourist Trophy (an event born in 1905) and the Targa Florio (organized since 1906) and reached its apotheosis with the Mille Miglia, the lifespan of which coincides with the fabled "Golden Age" of Grand Prix between the second half of the 1920s and the decade immediately after the Second World War. These two generations were dominated respectively by Tazio Nuvolari and Juan Manuel Fangio; thus, it is a curious fact that the Italian driver won the open-road Targa Florio, Mille Miglia and Tourist Trophy while Fangio never enjoyed success in any of these events. Even the Le Mans 24-hour circuit race was won by Nuvolari but not Fangio.

In this period the careers of many great drivers were made thanks to the open-road races; no mean feat, given that these events were particularly insidious. Above all the road surfaces were variable and frequently in poor condition. Then there were the logistical difficulties of dealing with servicing

and of communication, even on a visual level, with the pits. Lastly, the most important element was represented by the spectators: almost always ungovernable and perched in the most improbable places, for example the outside of a corner, or hanging from telegraph poles, trees, lampposts and billboards, flattened against walls, doorways or fences or sitting on dry-stone fences, their legs dangling just inches away from the cars' ideal racing line.... The drivers' most difficult task was actually that of finding a balance between audacity, daring, a natural propensity for extreme risk and a sense of responsibility towards the gaggle of fans (the Targa Florio attracted upwards of half a million spectators) who themselves were notably lacking in responsibility.

The official death of open-road racing can be placed in 1957 when, during the Mille Miglia, Alfonso de Portago's Ferrari suffered a blown tyre and crashed at 170 kph (105.6 mph), scything down nine people including five children. Far worse tragedies have happened in the history of motor racing (two years earlier at Le Mans, 83 people were killed when Levegh's Mercedes plowed into the crowd), but de Portago's accident gave the authorities the pretext to bring a halt to open-road

racing. Three more editions of the Mille were staged at Brescia as regularity trials, while the Targa returned to its original state after a suspension of just one year. (It would take another round of tragedies to bring the curtain down on its long and noble story.) The Carrera Panamericana, perhaps the most accident-plagued of them all, would run just five times.

As examples of an era these races still survive, now poorly commemorated as vintage events; pantomimes during which more or less illustrious figures attempt for a day to revive the emotions the true protagonists of those glorious years, now either dead or aging heroes, guard jealously.

269 bottom right In 1953, the year of this photograph, over 500 crews took part in the race that crossed the central and northern regions of Italy. Seen here at the start in Brescia is Stirling Moss, but victory went to the extremely elegant Count Marzotto. This edition is remembered above all for the display put on by Fangio in a severely disabled car.

LA CARRERA PANAMERICANA

Even though only five editions were ever held, *La Carrera Panamericana* (billed as "The Mexican Road Race" in the United States) has a special place in the history of racing thanks to the peculiarities of its route and the quality of the participating drivers and marques. This enthralling yet gruelling race which was over 3000 km (1863 mi.) long demanded total commitment from the competitors. Being fast, talented and daring was simply not enough; what was required was great physical stamina, an ability to concentrate for long periods and the capacity to adapt to the extreme climactic conditions caused by the great difference in height (from sea level up to 3200 m [10,502 ft.]) encountered along the way. This last factor was the root of considerable problems with the fuel/air mixture, which was inevitably poor at such an altitude. The Carrera can be thought of as a perfect and unrepeatable synthesis of conventional racing and raids.

Chryslers, Oldsmobiles and the favourites, the mighty, high-compression, V8-powered Cadillacs.

The sports cars that dominated the similar European events (the Mille Miglia, the Targa Florio and the Coppa d'Oro delle Dolomiti) were not even taken into consideration. After six exhausting days and 27.5 hours of actual racing the honours went to an Oldsmobile 88 powered by a five-liter V8 and driven by Hershal McGriff, who snatched victory on the last stage from Thomas Deal in a Cadillac. The average speed of 124.6 kph (77.4 mph) is hardly what one would expect of a mild-mannered touring machine. Much of the merit was due to the driver, of course, for his ability to get the best out of his car, but there was also an ever-present element of trickery: many of the North American participants had highly tuned engines, in clear contradiction of regulations that were theoretically strict but in practice ignored.

270 top Like the other road races, the Panamericana attracted huge numbers of local Mexican fans who lined the interminable route that crossed the entire country. Mexico was the first state to complete its section of the great highway intended to traverse the continent and the race was designed to celebrate this great achievement.

270 bottom A Lincoln Capri crosses the unusual finishing line of the 1952 Panamericana, the first year in which a classification for touring cars was compiled. The Carrera finished in the South, at Ciudad Juarez, after a race of eight stages and a total of over 3000 km (1,863 mi.).

270-271 Fabulous handpainting decorates a Lincoln participating in the fourth edition of La Carrera.

The Carrera was born out of Mexican national pride at being the first country to complete its section of a grandiose project initiated in the Twenties, the Panamerican Highway—an interminable paved road designed to unite the Americas from north to south. The idea of celebrating this imposing communications artery with a major sporting event was by no means mistaken. It had the desired effect of arousing the enthusiasm of the local population as well as of people all over the world.

The inaugural edition of 1950 was truly unique, above all in terms of the cars that took part: the majority were large American saloons that in some respects still echoed the rather inefficient models of the 1940s. There was a 1937 Cord, the model famous for its coffin-like bonnet and retracting headlights; a Studebaker Champion designed by the great stylist of French origins Raymond Loewy; a number of Packards and Buicks as well as Lincolns,

This was the only occasion on which the race was run from North (on the border with the United States) to South (the border with Guatemala); successive editions ran from South to North, but the start was never located on the Guatemalan border. The inversion was as a result of the need to thin out the field as soon as possible. As with the other great road races, after its brilliant debut and inclusion in the official international racing calendar, the élite car manufacturers began to plan assaults on La Carrera Panamericana.

This was the time of rising power for Ferrari's berlinettas and the Drake sent two teams to Mexico, one composed of Piero Taruffi and Luigi Chinetti and the other with Alberto Ascari and Luigi Villoresi. Both were equipped with magnificent 212 Inters. They finished in this order despite the desperate comeback by Ascari (who won four out of eight stages), and the two Italian cars were sold on the spot. The best of the Americans finished from third place downwards, with

the Chrysler Saratogas best—one was driven by Tony Bettenhausen to first place in the last two stages but only 16th overall, another by William Sterling to third place behind the Ferraris—followed by the Mercurys and Lincoln Cosmopolitans. A member of one of the world's most famous racing families, the Unsers, also took part: the tough and talented Jerry Unser was subsequently to be eclipsed by the fame of Louis, Al, Bobby and Al Junior, however....

The third edition again saw the American cars forced to bow to the strength of the European opposition in spite of Taruffi's "traitorous" move to Oldsmobile. Victory went to one of the most beautiful cars of all time, the Mercedes 300SL Gullwing with its upwards hinging doors. The 300SL had already won the Le Mans 24 Hours and was thus a worthy rival of the Lancia Aurelia B20 and Ferrari 340 "Mexico." Ferrari's and Lancia's best

271 top right The 1952 edition of the Carrera Panamericana saw the curiously named pairing of Kling and Klenk victorious in their Mercedes 300SL. During the course of the race the navigator was injured by a bird that smashed the windshield and finished up trapped in the rear deck.

271 bottom right This photograph shows the winners of the second edition of La Carrera Panamericana, which was held in 1951. After a low-key debut, the race attracted crews and teams from throughout the world. This was the first edition to run a shorter route that did not reach the Mexican borders but finished at Ciudad Juarez rather than El Ocotal. Seen here aboard a Vignale-bodied Ferrari 212 is the Italian pairing of Taruffi and Chinetti who, together with Ascari and Villoresi, were worthy representatives of the Drake. The two Ferraris were sold after the event.

HONOR ROLL

Year	Car	Crew	Av. Speed kph (mph)
1950	Oldsmobile	H. McGriff-R. Elliot	124.6 (77.4)
1951	Ferrari 212 Vignale	P. Taruffi-L. Chinetti	141.7 (86.7)
1952	Mercedes-Benz 300SL	K. Kling-H. Klenk	165.1 (102.5)
1953	Lancia D24	J.M. Fangio-G. Bronzoni	169.2 (105.1)
1954	Ferrari 375 Plus	U. Maglioli	173.7 (107.9)

The Carrera Stages (km/mi.)

The first edition featured nine rather than eight stages:

1 C. Juarez-Chihuahua (375/233)
2 Chihuahua-Parral (300/186)
3 Parral-Durango (404/250)
4 Durango-León (547/339)
5 León-Mexico City (448/278)
6 Mexico City-Puebla (135/84)
7 Puebla-Oaxaca (412/256)
8 Oaxaca-Tuxtla (540/335)
9 Tuxtla-El Ocotal (275/171).
Total: 3436 km (2133 mi.).

1 Tuxtla-Oaxaca (530/329)
2 Oaxaca-Puebla (407/253)
3 Puebla-Mexico City (128/80)
4 Mexico City-León (420/261)
5 León-Durango (530/329)
6 Durango-Parral (404/251)
7 Parral-Chihuahua (300/186)
8 Chihuahua-C. Juarez (358/222).

Total: 3077 km (1911 mi.).

efforts were in vain as the Kling/Klenk pairing came home 27 minutes ahead of the second-placed Mercedes of Hermann Lang. The winning navigator Klenk suffered injuries to the face when a bird smashed through the windshield and ended up, trapped and clawing madly, behind the seats. Although it was a closed coupé, this Mercedes gave birth to the SL roadster dynasty, unmatched for its longevity, class and prestige.

In 1952 a classification for touring cars was introduced and dominated by the Lincoln Capris (five filling the first five places). There were also two privately-entered Porsche 356s, one of which was driven to ninth place overall by Prince Metternich.

The Carrera immediately formed part of the World Sports Car Championship when it was instituted in 1953. After its fine performance the previous year, Lancia was looking for victory at all costs. The team was equipped with excellent cars,

the D23s and D24s, and exceptional drivers such as Fangio, Taruffi, Bonetto, Castellotti and Bracco. In fact the final podium was all-Lancia with Fangio (first without winning a single stage), Taruffi and Castellotti. It was a joyless podium though after the loss of the veteran Bonetto, who the previous year had completed the race despite having a crushed roof following a roll and in this edition suffered a terrible accident during the fourth stage: he had just managed to shake off Taruffi and went straight at a sharp corner when he failed to notice a "vado," a dip caused by a dry streambed. His D24 literally took off into the air, throwing Bonetto against the wall of a house. He died instantly.

That year there were four categories, of which two were for sports cars (over- or under-1.6 l); this was increased to five in 1954, including over- or under-1.5 l sports cars, 3.5+ l touring cars, "special" touring cars and "European" touring cars.

The Ferrari 375 Pluses re-appropriated the throne in what was to be the last edition of the Carrera. The race was won by the 26-year-old Umberto Maglioli from his fellow Ferrari driver Phil Hill, the two followed home by the Porsche 550s which, despite belonging to a lower category, got

the better of the 375MM and 250 Monza Ferraris. This edition was dominated by the private entrants, but the cars and drivers were of the highest quality.

A 1955 edition of the Carrera was planned for December, but in August the Mexican government vetoed the funds for the repair of the road surfaces. Behind the excuse of the event's danger probably lay a purely economic question; all the same, the end was nigh for the great open-road races.

THE MILLE MIGLIA

If you could unite the point of departure of the first edition of the Mille Miglia and the point of arrival of the last one with a colored ribbon you would obtain an inextricable cat's cradle given that the route of this classic race mutated over the years and significantly so. It would be useful to be able to circumscribe and define a three-decade automotive period of which the Mille Miglia was the spiritual essence thanks to the competitiveness, cunning, determination and healthy dose of madness displayed by the participants. These qualities combined chemically and transformed into the propellant required to tackle a race staged on roads open to traffic over a distance of around 1600 km (993 mi.) and strewn with hidden dangers and surprises.

Between 1927 and 1957 the 24 editions of the Mille Miglia were widely covered by the media and attracted fervent support thanks to feats performed by men and machines that were in strident contrast with everyday life.

The original route of the "MM" that wound through northern and central Italy started in Brescia, reached Bologna and then headed out to the Adriatic coast. From there it turned sharply inland to Rome, traversing the Apennines before heading north toward Lombardy (the region in which Brescia is located) by way of the heartland of Italian automotive culture, Emilia Romagna, the home of Ettore Bugatti, de Tomaso, Ferrari, Maserati, Lamborghini, OSCA, Stanguellini, ATS and Minardi and then, together with the neighboring Marche, the two-wheeled legends of Benelli, Bimota, Ducati, Malaguti, Marini and Morbidelli. Having passed Bologna, the speeding sports and touring cars homed in on their point of departure, Brescia. One of the first changes to the original route was the elimination of the first passage through Bologna, the city being visited on the return leg only.

The idea of organizing an event inspired by the turn of the century city-to-city races was that of Giovanni Canestrini, Renzo Castagneto, Aymo Maggi

272 top left This image records the delight of Gianbattista Guidotti, with his arm raised, alongside Tazio Nuvolari, for the 1930 victory that is remembered for the passing of Varzi with the headlights switched off.

272 top right A poster publicizing the 1954 edition of the Mille Miglia.

272 center In 1931 the Nuvolari-Guidotti pairing lined up at the start hoping to repeat the success of the previous year.

272 bottom left Rudolph Caracciola wins the 1931 Mille Miglia aboard an SSKL, the last version prepared by Mercedes for its wealthiest clientele.

272-273 The Alfa Romeo 8C 2300 Spider Touring won the Italian road race three years running between 1932 and '34. The racing versions were characterized by a shorter wheelbase than that of the standard model: there was a difference of 35 cm (14 in.) between the two. The eight-cylinder in-line power unit produced over 160 hp.

273 top This 1934 photograph testifies to the great interest aroused by the Mille Miglia and records one of the key moments of the race, the completion of the outward leg at the Rome checkpoint. Alfa celebrated Italian power with its third consecutive win in the race. This triumphant series continued through '39. Italy's prewar domination would have been complete if not for single wins by Mercedes and BMW.

273 center This image shows one of Alfa Romeo's true jewels, the 6C 1750GS from 1930, an extraordinarily versatile road and race machine. Many different versions were constructed allowing the coachbuilders of the era (Farina, Zagato and Touring) to create magnificent roadsters, cabriolets, torpedoes and saloons.

273 bottom left The tiny Fiat Balilla Coppa d'Oro at the Rome checkpoint in 1933. The success of the Mille Miglia can be attributed in part to the fact that all types of cars could participate and enjoy their moment of glory. For example, Fiat gained considerable publicity from the

participation of this minuscule roadster, and the relatively accessible price of the car meant that the dreams of Italian youngsters could become reality in much the same way as occurred with MG in Britain, Peugeot and Renault in France, DKW and BMW in Germany and Ford in America.

and Franco Mazzotti. Brescia was the obvious candidate to host such a race as, ever since the birth of the motorcar, it had closely and enthusiastically followed the evolution of the industry and as early as 1899 had staged a race for cars and motorcycles over 233 km (145 mi.) on the Lombardy roads between Brescia, Mantua and Cremona. In 1904 it had hosted one of the first motor shows and a race won by one of the stars of the day, Vincenzo Lancia with a Fiat. The following year Vincenzo Florio chose Brescia as the venue for his Coppa Florio, an event inspired by the Gordon Bennett Trophy, which was initially staged in France. Florio then turned his attention to the Targa Florio in his native Sicily. In 1921, on the nearby Fascia d'Oro circuit at Montichiari, Brescia had the honour of staging the first Italian Grand Prix, an event subsequently "stolen" by the Automobile Club of Milan which transferred it to the Parco Reale

in Monza. The city witnessed women racing drivers, among whom a true champion immediately caught the eye: Baroness D'Avanzo, who raced up to the Thirties. It also staged the Gran Premio Gentleman, a race reserved for private entrants and which was won by one of the finest amateur drivers of all time, Count Giulio Masetti, whose reputation was inextricably linked with Mercedes and the Targa.

From an industrial point of view Brescia had what it took to become an automotive capital: engineering culture, an industrious social fabric and numerous wealthy entrepreneurs. However this potential went untapped and the only car manufacturer of any size was OM (Officine Meccaniche) which won the first edition of the Mille Miglia before devoting itself to the production of highly esteemed commercial and industrial vehicles. What was lacking at Brescia was a man, a leader, a courageous entrepreneur such as

Agnelli in Turin or Romeo in Milan. Cheated of the national Grand Prix, in 1927 Brescia—the "Lioness of Italy"—once again found itself at the center of automotive attention with the first edition of a remarkable event much of whose popularity was due to it being open to cars of any type. The OM driven by Minoia and Morandi won that first Mille Miglia held between the 26th and the 27th of March, 1927, with the Isotta-Fraschini of Aymo Maggi the first car away.

Having seen the widespread interest and enthusiasm generated by the event, the Grand Prix stars were flocking to Brescia as early as 1928. Bordino was driving for Bugatti while there were also Brilli-Peri and Nuvolari with the works Alfa Romeo 6C 1500s while the firm also entered a "secret" supercharged model entrusted to Campari and Ramponi. This last was a pairing made in heaven

273 bottom right Alfa Romeo enjoyed a doubly sweet triumph in the 1934 Mille Miglia. First came the great Achille Varzi at the wheel of a Tipo C Monza gaining satisfying revenge over Nuvolari, who had beaten him the previous year and in 1930. In 1934 Tazio was second in front of another Alfista, Chiron of Monte Carlo, who was driving a 2600M.

Mille Miglia

274 top This photograph shows the "shroud" that characterized the rear of the Alfa Spider Touring. In this period the stylistic schools throughout the world, and particularly in France and Italy, were strongly influenced by aeronautic practice. The 8C's apparently wide track was in fact narrower than that of the 6C 1750, while the new car was longer overall by more than 1 m (3 ft.) (4.68 versus 3.65).

274 center The dashboard of the Alfa Romeo 8C 2900 Mille Miglia built between 1936 and '38. This version was in fact from 1938 and denominated the 2900B. Note the split windshield, the right-hand drive, the opposed instrument faces and the four-spoke steering wheel.

and scored back-to-back victories in 1928 and 1929. The 1928 Alfa 6C Sport was a magnificent machine that subsequently evolved into the 1750 and was built in six series and infinite variants; as well as saloons there were a number of absolute coachbuilding masterpieces in the form of spiders, torpedoes and cabriolets. Later it gave way to the eight-cylinder model that scored a hat-trick of wins between 1932 (seven Alfas in the first seven places) and 1934 when, in its turn, it handed over the baton to the 2900A (for a further three victories).

It was a 6C 1750 that won the 1930 Mille Miglia, probably the most celebrated of all time. Few are unaware of the reasons, which nonetheless we will briefly outline here. The leader Varzi was caught by Nuvolari and Guidotti. According to the only detailed account we have, that of Giovan Battista Guidotti, the pair switched off their headlights, tricking Varzi into thinking his rivals had

problems and were consequently easing up. Nuvolari took immediate advantage, sweeping past to win the race at an average speed that for the first time broke the 100 kph (62 mph) barrier. At the finish, to those who asked him how the race had gone Varzi angrily snapped *"They switched off their lights!"* The anecdote is undoubtedly reliable; what the history books, a little too inclined to mythology, forget to mention is that Varzi had started the race ten minutes earlier, and therefore Nuvolari and Guidotti were comfortably in the lead and assured of victory anyway. In all probability the Flying Mantuan could have avoided this risky, colorful piece of trickery and still gone on to a deserved win in the fourth edition of the Mille Miglia with what was in any case a bold and tenacious drive.

In our opinion too much has been made of the headlight episode. If that was so remarkable, what is there to be said about Brivio, who in 1936 led home

274 bottom The Alfa Romeo 8C Mille
Miglia Spider Touring features
streamlining characteristic of the styling
of the era. The 8C 2900A won three
editions of the Mille between 1936 and
1938 with, respectively, Brivio,
Pintacuda and Biondetti.

275 top left Varzi prepares to take
part in the 1930 Mille Miglia. An
extremely talented, fast and
courageous driver, shortly before his
death Varzi managed to overcome a
period of deep depression that saw
him addicted to cocaine.

a champion of Farina's caliber without any
headlights at all—not through choice, but rather due
to electrical failure? This is clearly a sporting episode
of greater merit experienced in that narrow,
unconscious band that divides courage from
foolhardiness and which represents the mental state
of racing drivers in battle.

However, the first full decade of the Mille Miglia
was an Alfa Romeo monologue, the only exception
coming in 1931 with one of the very rare foreign
victories in the Brescian race. It was the Mercedes
SSKL of Caracciola that got the better of the Italian
cars: the SSKL was the ultimate evolution of the
successful series of Mercedes K and SS models
destined for wealthy clients and the most important
races. Caracciola was a worthy rival for Nuvolari,
Campari and Varzi, both in terms of talent and
sporting character.

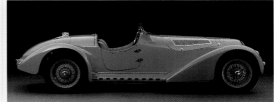

275 top right This image shows an Alfa
Romeo 8C Mille Miglia similar to the
one Brivio drove to victory in 1936 but
lacking aerodynamic mudguards
and generally plainer.

275 center This picture portrays the Alfa
Romeos that took part in the 1938 edition
of the Mille Miglia. From left to right: 142
of Pintacuda-Mambelli, second overall;
148 of Siena-Villoresi; 141 of Farina-
Meazza; 143 of Biondetti-Stefani, first
overall. The third placed car of Dusio-
Boninsegni is missing from the photograph.

275 bottom This rare photograph
shows the Alfa Corse service van
used on the 1938 Mille Miglia.
The car on which the mechanics
are changing the tyres is the 8C
2900B driven to second place by
Carlo Pintacuda.

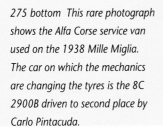

276 top left The BMW 328 of von Hanstein and Baumer prepares to start the 1940 Mille Miglia.

276 top right The 1940 BMW 328 Spider photographed on the reduced circuit used for the Mille Miglia of that year. The edition was won at the lightning-fast speed of 167.7 kph (104 mph). Portrayed here is the Brudes-Roese pairing with race number 74, while Wencher and Scholtz competed with number 71. BMW dominated the race, finishing first, third, fifth and sixth.

276 center This picture shows a rear three-quarters view of the 1940 BMW 328 spider bodied by the Italian coachbuilder Touring. The name Touring was subsequently used by the Munich-based firm to identify its station wagons. The 1971-cc engine of the standard model produced 80 hp, while the units sent to Brescia for the 1940 race developed up to 130 hp.

276-277 bottom The Mille Miglia had
not been won by a foreign car since
1931, but the Alfa Romeo monopoly was
broken in 1940 by a beautiful two-seater
from the Bavarian firm BMW. This was
the company's first major international
victory. The 328 was driven by Fritz

Huschke von Hanstein and navigated by
Walter Baumer in place of Count
Giovanni Lurani. (The latter had been
unnerved by the suicidal driving style of
von Hanstein, who wore the SS symbol
on his overalls.) After having driven like a
madman throughout the race, the

German aristocrat stopped the car a few
kilometers from the finish, got out and
walked round the car to the navigator's
door. To his teammate's astonishment he
then opened the door and invited him
to take the wheel and enjoy the honour
of driving across the finishing line.

277 top The BMW 328 berlinetta number
70 of the winner of the 1940 Mille Miglia
Fritz Huschke Von Hanstein passing in
front of the leader board. In the
foreground is the column of the number
70 with the operator about to insert the
time for the ninth and last passage.

277 center The front of the 328 spider
that took part in the 1940 Mille Miglia.
The winning car was a closed version
bodied by Touring. The works team was
composed of five cars: a prototype coupé,
the Touring coupé and three spiders. Roofs
apart, they were all very similar.

The second foreign victory was by BMW in 1940 with another historic car, the 328. The number one driver was Fritz Huschke von Hanstein while alongside him was to be Giovanni Lurani, himself a talented driver. However, after the practice sessions the Italian nobleman got out of the car determined that never again would he ride alongside the apparently insane von Hanstein. Walter Baumer took his place and the Bavarian crew streaked to a clear victory at the record average speed of almost 168 kph (104 mph), thus breaking the 100-mph threshold for the first time. This record was set on a reduced circuit, Brescia-Cremona-Mantua of 167 kilometers (103 mi.) which was lapped nine times.

The first thrilling period of the Mille Miglia saw victories for two German crews, with every other edition apart from the debut race going to Alfa Romeo. In 1935 it was actually the P3 that won in the hands of Carlo Pintacuda.

The first post-war edition was held in 1947 and passed through both Turin and Milan. It appeared that history was about to repeat itself as victory went to the 2900B, an elegant, prestigious Alfa Romeo of which just a few eagerly sought-after examples were constructed. The car was driven by Clemente Biondetti who had already won in 1938 (a tragic edition as at a level crossing near Bologna a Lancia crashed and ten people were killed, including seven children) and was to win again in 1948 and 1949, not for Alfa but for Ferrari, thus establishing himself as the most successful Mille Miglia driver. While Clemente Biondetti was deservedly the material winner of the MM, the moral victory that year went to Nuvolari in a rare episode in the history of motor racing in which the drama lay elsewhere, not on the track.

Nuvolari had lost his young children to illness in 1947 and 1948. Bowing to no man in terms of courage and daring, unscathed despite the insane feats of the Thirties, Tazio was finally defeated by a cruel destiny. A disease had weakened but failed to kill him, and even though his Grand Prix days were long gone the now 55-year-old driver challenged Death in every race, like those Scandinavian warriors for whom any death other than on the battlefield was unacceptable. Innate ability and an instinct for survival had perhaps so far protected him from suicidal impulses.

In 1948 Enzo Ferrari was in search of glory for the new cars carrying his name. He thus despatched his jewels to the Mille Miglia, entrusting them to the expert hands of Biondetti and Nuvolari. In that race, despite his poor physical condition and low morale, the great Tazio drove with the strength of desperation, accumulating a lead of 29 minutes over his teammate. His car began to suffer and even the driver's seat broke, obliging Nuvolari to replace it with a fruit crate. Ferrari was waiting for him at Maranello and seeing him so debilitated, physically wrecked, he tried to convince him to retire: a particularly rare event, as Ferrari was always reluctant to make any concessions to his drivers. (He was of the opinion that they were paid to give their all.) "You'll have other opportunities," he said in an attempt to persuade Tazio. Sadly, Nuvolari responded, "Dear Ferrari, at our age there aren't going to be many more opportunities." He restarted, still driving on the limit. The brakes failed between

Reggio Emilia and Parma. With the car sidelined the nervous tension drained away and he was unable even to climb out of the cockpit. He had to ask for help from a priest, who literally pulled him from the car and put him to bed where he slept like a child.

Death, so long awaited, tricked him yet again. It was not until 1 August 1953, that Nuvolari passed away in a hospital bed like any common mortal. He was buried with his leather helmet. In 1954 the Mille Miglia passed through Mantua in order to honor the driver who, like few others, had graced the event. The Nuvolari Prize was inaugurated for the fastest driver through the Cremona-Mantua section.

In the post-war period new protagonists appeared on the Grand Prix stage and also in the road races, especially the Mille Miglia. In fact, the automotive

world's latest star was already waiting in the wings. It appears that he never enjoyed a particularly happy relationship with open-road races, even though he never held back in them in South America. The Mille attracted him, and he was as sure of his ability to win—as Nuvolari, Campari, Caracciola and Varzi had before him—any kind of race, be it road or track, sprint or marathon, quick or slow. He was also eager to prove it; for Juan Manuel Fangio, there was no alternative.

Strangely enough, despite taking part in five editions of the Brescian race, the five-time World Champion never won a single Mille Miglia. He was twice second, once third and once fourth; nonetheless Fangio was the protagonist in two episodes worthy of mention, the equal of those involving Brivio and Nuvolari.

278-279 *The Cisitalia Nuvolari Spyder is recognizable thanks to the rear fins, which in those years had just begun to appear on American cars. They were more prominent in the closed rather than the open-top version. The design of the 1946 MM car that brought ephemeral glory to the marque created by Piero Dusio was the work of Dante Giacosa and Giovanni Savoruzzi. "Cisitalia" stood for Compagnia Industriale Sportiva Italia.*

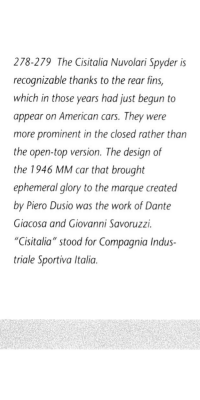

279 top *This shot allows us to admire the plan form and the cockpit of the production Cisitalia 202 inspired by the car driven by Nuvolari in the 1947 Mille Miglia. This small, light car was powered by an in-line, four-cylinder engine of 1089 cc producing a maximum power output of just 60 hp for a maximum speed of 180 kph (112 mph). Five Cisitalias took part in the 1947 Mille Miglia; apart from the two examples like the one portrayed here, entrusted to Nuvolari and Minetti, there were also a streamlined berlinetta driven by Taruffi, a short-wheelbase streamlined spider driven by Cisitalia boss Dusio and an enclosed berlinetta driven by Bernabè. Cisitalia enjoyed their moment of glory at the 1947 Mille Miglia thanks above all to Nuvolari, who put Clemente Biondetti's Alfa 2900 in its place and stretched out a lead of seven minutes at the Rome checkpoint. The other two Cisitalias still in the race finished third and fourth. The thrilling race in which Biondetti never gave up was eventually decided by a violent storm: the Alfa 2900 was a closed car while Nuvolari's was open. The Flying Mantuan was peppered with hailstones and obliged to slow. He eventually finished second but was the moral victor. After that glorious 1947 race Dusio asked for and received Nuvolari's permission to name a short production run of the 202 Sport MM as the Spyder Nuvolari in honor of the great driver. However, interest in the make had largely been extinguished by 1949.*

In 1953 the left-hand steering link on his Ferrari broke; in left-hand curves the car would behave normally but in those to the right it would inexorably tend to go straight. The use of the brakes worsened the situation so Fangio relied on engine braking. Despite driving in these seemingly impossible conditions the Argentine managed to bring his car home in second place behind Count Marzotto, who on that occasion consecrated his reputation as a driver after having won the 1950 25th anniversary edition (celebrated by no less that 730 entries) at the age of 22. Young, extremely wealthy and the heir to a textiles empire, Marzotto was accustomed to racing (and winning) in a dinner jacket and tie.

Another episode that had a profound effect on Fangio's career occurred during the 1956 Mille

Klemantaski, himself a co-driver on a number of occasions, instead developed pace notes contained within a windowed container that protected the roll of notes compiled during practice.

The all-too-common tragedy of open-road racing was repeated in 1957 when the Ferrari of the much loved driver Alfonso de Portago crashed at 250 kph (155 mph) following a burst tire near Mantua. Among the dead were five children, and the curtain thus fell on the Mille Miglia. In the following years regularity trials were organized but were of little interest. Since 1982 instead an historic Mille Miglia revival has been organized, a kind of parade for VIPs and owners of historic cars—those that once had given the best of themselves in the real race, and in the hands of real drivers; a different breed.

Miglia. On that occasion he decided to race alone, the only member of the Ferrari team to depart in an open car with no top. Beating rain tormented him throughout the race and the great driver later admitted that he had never suffered so much as on that occasion. He nevertheless came home fourth. Dogged by ill fortune he was never able to add a Mille Miglia crown to his remarkable career record.

Another curious anecdote concerns Villoresi's victory in 1951. His Ferrari crashed but the impact was absorbed by a Stanguellini parked at that point, having earlier retired from the race. Clearly the little car was badly damaged and the furious Stanguellini himself demanded—but apparently never received—adequate compensation from the victor. Villoresi is reputed to have crossed the line with only fourth gear working.

Between 1950 and 1957 the roll of honor demonstrates that Ferrari had laid claim to the popular race passing though its home territory, winning every edition except that of 1954 won by the Lancia D24 of Alberto Ascari and that of 1955 won by Stirling Moss. The Englishman was at the wheel of another classic Mercedes, the 300SLR, a model unfortunately associated with the cruelest tragedy ever to occur during a motor race that same year at Le Mans. Moss was accompanied on his epic drive by the journalist Denis Jenkinson, who read pace notes from a rudimentary road book of the entire route. The noted photographer Louis

280 top left The Rome checkpoint during the 1953 edition; immediately afterwards the cars headed for Bologna and on to Brescia. Seen here is Count Marzotto, the winner of this edition in a Ferrari 340MM as well as that of 1950. This gentleman driver was accustomed to racing in a jacket and tie.

280 top right The Italian road race was dominated by Ferrari during the 1950s. Portrayed here is Kling at the wheel of his Alfa Romeo 3000CM entered by the Milanese firm in a vain attempt to rival Maranello's success.

280 center While Alfa failed to repeat its prewar triumphs in the Mille, Lancia managed to beat the Ferraris thanks to Ascari and his D24—a brilliant car which foreshadowed Enzo's mighty 250 Testa Rossa by half a decade. Here the talented Alberto, son of Antonio, wins at Brescia in 1954.

280 bottom Farina and Parenti were involved in a dramatic accident near Verona during the 1954 edition. Farina, the former F1 World Champion, was killed in a road accident in 1966.

280-281 A thrilling moment during the 1953 edition of the Mille Miglia with the first appearance on Italian roads of the Mercedes 300SL Gullwing, a member of the magnificent line of sports cars of unequalled beauty, both coupés and roadsters.

281 top In 1955 Mercedes scored its second and last victory in the Italian race with the British ace Stirling Moss, seen here close to Ravenna on the Adriatic coast. This was the third time that a non-Italian car had won the race, the first coming in 1931 with Caracciola and the second in 1940 with von Hanstein. Moss was driving a 300SLR.

HONOR ROLL

YEAR	CAR	CREW	AV. SPEED KPH (MPH)
1927	OM	F. Minoia-G. Morandi	77.7 (48.2)
1928	Alfa Romeo 1500S	G. Campari-G. Ramponi	84.6 (52.5)
1929	Alfa Romeo 1750S	G. Campari-G. Ramponi	90.2 (56)
1930	Alfa Romeo 1750S	T. Nuvolari-G. B. Guidotti	101 (62.7)
1931	Mercedes-Benz SSKL	R. Caracciola-W. Sebastian	101.7 (63.1)
1932	Alfa Romeo 8C Monza	B. Borzacchini-A. Bignami	110.7 (68.7)
1933	Alfa Romeo 8C Monza	T. Nuvolari-D. Compagnoni	109.2 (67.8)
1934	Alfa Romeo 8C Monza	A. Varzi-A. Bignami	115 (71.4)
1935	Alfa Romeo Tipo B (P3)	C. Pintacuda- A. Della Stufa	115.4 (71.7)
1936	Alfa Romeo 2900A	A. Brivo-C. Ongaro	123.8 (76.9)
1937	Alfa Romeo 2900A	C. Pintacuda-P. Mambelli	115.4 (71.7)
1938	Alfa Romeo 2900A	C. Biondetti-A. Stefani	136.2 (84.6)
1940	BMW 328	H. von Hanstein-W. Baumer	167.7 (104.2)
1947	Alfa Romeo 2900B	C. Biondetti-E. Romano	112.9 (70.1)
1948	Ferrari 166S	C. Biondetti-G. Navone	121.4 (75.4)
1949	Ferrari 166 MM	C. Biondetti-E. Salani	132.1 (82)
1950	Ferrari 195S	G. Marzotto-M. Crosara	123.9 (76.9)
1951	Ferrari	L. Villoresi-P. Cassani	122.5 (76.1)
1952	Ferrari 225S	G. Bracco-A. Rolfo	129.3 (80.3)
1953	Ferrari 340MM	G. Marzotto-M. Crosara	130.3 (80.9)
1954	Lancia D24	A. Ascari	140.4 (87.2)
1955	Mercedes-Benz 300SLR	S. Moss-D. Jenkinson	158.6 (98.5)
1956	Ferrari 290MM	E. Castellotti	138.2 (85.8)
1957	Ferrari 315S	P. Taruffi.	153.5 (95.3)

281 bottom A truly sad photograph from the 1958 edition which was held as a regularity trial rather than a true race. The previous year 11 viewers, including five children, had lost their lives in de Portago's crash. The new formula was intended to test the drivers' ability to respect predetermined timings. While it was right to stop the Mille Miglia it was not so happy the idea of replacing it with a different event under the same name. This was also the fate that awaited the Targa Florio.

THE TARGA FLORIO

There are those who claim that the Targa Florio is the oldest race in the world. Such a statement is clearly mistaken, but perhaps derives from the great affection aroused by the event. The Targa—the *real* Targa Florio, that is—has been dead and buried since 1973, the last year it enjoyed World Sports Car Championship status, or at the latest since 1977, after four editions disputed in a lower key. Since then the Targa has become a mediocre Italian rally, a simulacrum that boasts only a noble heritage accumulated over the course of decades. Nevertheless, even as a rally the Targa could have continued as a major international event: very competitive routes, plenty of loose-surfaced roads and

282 right, top Bablot seen here at the wheel of a Berliet during the 1906 Targa Florio. Certain sources classify him in second place, others in third behind the pair of Italas.

282 right center In both 1907 (this photograph) and 1908 Vincenzo Lancia had to settle for second place, firstly behind Nazzaro and then behind the Isotta-Fraschini of Trucco. This shot is a splendid example of the synthesis of modernism and a traditional landscape.

a very warm public accustomed to high performance and prestigious structures, traditions and passion.

Why then has Vincenzo Florio's beloved race been allowed to decline into a third-rate rally, reaching the end of the millennium gasping for breath if not definitively dead? Perhaps the answer can be found in the sublime and unequalled art of the Sicilians, so talented at destroying what they have created from nothing, living the death as the extreme creative experience.

More prosaically, perhaps, it lies in the organizers' inability to match the standards of the race's founder, Vincenzo Florio, a flexible anticipator of trends. Crushed by jealousies, power plays and self-interests, the race collapsed under the weight of its own success after a three-year period between 1970 and 1972 during which the contemporary automotive élite put

282 left Fiat and Itala were not the only two marques represented in the first edition of the Targa Florio: this photograph shows the Le Blons' Hotchkiss in action on the infinite straight of Buonfornello which runs parallel to the

railway and leads into the rising finish at Cerda. As can be seen, this was actually a touring car with four seats and boat-tailed bodywork while those of the professional drivers were true race-prepared, two-seater roadsters.

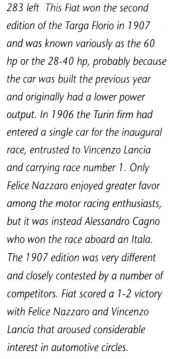

283 left This Fiat won the second edition of the Targa Florio in 1907 and was known variously as the 60 hp or the 28-40 hp, probably because the car was built the previous year and originally had a lower power output. In 1906 the Turin firm had entered a single car for the inaugural race, entrusted to Vincenzo Lancia and carrying race number 1. Only Felice Nazzaro enjoyed greater favor among the motor racing enthusiasts, but it was instead Alessandro Cagno who won the race aboard an Itala. The 1907 edition was very different and closely contested by a number of competitors. Fiat scored a 1-2 victory with Felice Nazzaro and Vincenzo Lancia that aroused considerable interest in automotive circles.

283 right This photograph shows one of the first Alfas in action, the 40-60 of 1913, subsequently revised in 1920, again for the Targa Florio. The three Tipo Corse were on that occasion entrusted to Giuseppe Campari, Enzo Ferrari and Giulio Ramponi.

on matchless displays witnessed by half a million spectators.

In 1986 the author had the honor of playing an active part on the Organizing Committee of the first Targa Florio *Storica*. As if by magic, the disintegrating and abandoned grandstands of Cerda, a small town outside Palermo, swarmed with people again. The pits, the timekeepers' huts, the race steward' and press quarters appeared to be crowded with specters from the past, reliving, even just for a day, the emotions of a what was once a major event. It was an unforgettable day. The great drivers came back, the true sports-prototypes, the protagonists of the Targa's greatest editions came back, the old Grand Prix racers of the beginning of the century came back, eager to claim the well deserved tribute reserved for pioneers. It was, however, an error to repeat the experience in the following years, degrading a moment that tasted of history into a banal meeting-place for bored rich people, collectors of period curios, a clown-like trimming for an equally insipid rally.

Automotive fans should once in their lives retrace, like pilgrims on the way to Jerusalem or Compostela, the Apennine passes of the Mille Miglia or the route of the old Nürburgring circuit,

distinguishable from the regular road by the differently graded asphalt. In the case of the Targa one could choose the Buonfornello straight leading into the arrival at Cerda or the Collesano descents.

The emotions that the asphalt and the dry-stone walls outside the old farmhouses arouse would still be strong. One can still read, faded in color as in memory, the graffiti urging on the second and last great sovereign of the Targa, Nino Vaccarella, the Flying Headmaster; a Sicilian gentleman driver who, although he has linked his name to impressive victories on the principal world circuits, is one with the history of the Targa because he was (and still is) the local hero—against his will perhaps. In reality Vaccarella was a fast driver more suited to closed circuits, but sometimes fate chooses for us.

Vaccarella *is* the Targa Florio. It is said, for example, that during a religious procession at

Collesano (one of the key passages of the Targa from which began the descent toward the Buonfornello straight), rumours began that he—Nino—had arrived to visit the local mayor. The faithful did not hesitate for a moment: having handed the understanding Madonna over to a few old women, the parish priest and those people who, as they were actually under the *fercolo* could hardly abandon it, the crowd set out to find Nino, preferring to carry the popular driver through the streets.

But Vaccarella was only the second king of Cerda; the first was Vincenzo Florio, head of an extremely wealthy family of entrepreneurs and tradesman that in the early years of this century was enjoying its moment of greatest splendor, thanks in part to a mercantile fleet of impressive tonnage. Florio, from one of the most high profile families in Europe and Vincenzo, was a dynamic and restless man who loved competition and innovation more than anything else. The automobile represented the ideal synthesis of both passions; here he was, like a Sicilian Count de Dion, ready to organize a major event for the already busy motoring calendar of the first decade of the century, despite the apparently insurmountable difficulties created by the prohibitive conditions of his native Sicily's roads.

In 1905 he had already organized the Coppa Florio, an event that was staged at Brescia in Lombardy to a formula that imitated the Gordon Bennett Trophy. It was held for the last time in 1925, after eight editions, with the definitive victory of Peugeot. Florio, however, was eager to bring racing to his home, that rugged western Sicily later sadly infamous as the cradle of the Mafia.

Thanks to its rich prize fund and the large number of aristocrats and important people that never failed to attend the race, the Targa Florio quickly became one of the most well-attended racing events, and an obligatory proving ground for any driver worthy of the name.

The circuit was traced at the desks of the authoritative *L'Auto*, a French specialist journal. Florio unfolded a map of Sicily, illustrating for the editors and photographers the salient points of the great circuit he had devised: 148 km (92 mi.) up and down the Madonie, the rugged hills that with the Nebrodi mountains run like the tendons of a hand across the tormented Sicilian soil.

This initial circuit was blighted by an elevated number of railway crossings and was thus reduced.

competition. But the massive crowds, a course that seemed made especially to forge heroes and to demonstrate the reliability of the cars, the sumptuous and festive reception of the master of the house in the salons of the Hotel Delle Terme at Termini Imerese, were such that the true winner was Don Vincenzo himself. From the following year the Targa adopted the exciting, elitist and competitive Grand Prix formula with victory going to another great figure of the day, Felice Nazzaro, as usual at the wheel of a Fiat, who succeeded in getting the better of the Isotta-Fraschinis and of his teammate Vincenzo Lancia.

From 1912 to 1914 the Targa was staged as the Giro di Sicilia to a different formula. It would be impossible not to refer to those events, rich with anecdotes.

The problem of the loose surfaces was resolved by spreading a bituminous compound across the "trazzere," as the Sicilian mule-tracks are called, the "fix" that helped to keep the road surface stable.

There is another curious anecdote linked to the physical realization of the Targa Florio. The Sicilian entrepreneur commissioned one of the most famous Art Nouveau artists, Lalique, noted for his admirable works in crystal, to make the large metal relief plaque that has remained unchanged throughout the decades. To the honor of the Targa was added the very appetizing prize fund of 50,000 Italian lire.

The first edition in 1906 was won by a daring driver of the time, Alessandro Cagno, in an Itala 115 hp, a touring model whose design was derived from conventional cars. Florio's great event ran the risk of being ruined by strikes by the stevedores at Genoa and by the French transport workers: of the 30 crews registered, only 10 succeeded in taking part in the

Targa Florio

In 1912 the Giro di Sicilia was run clockwise in a single stage. Cyril Snipe, the gentleman at the wheel of a SCAT, had gained two hours over his adversaries after 16 hours of grueling driving. It was a lead seemingly impossible to lose. However, such was his fatigue that he stopped the car, climbed out, lay down and fell asleep immediately. After almost two hours, his co-driver Pedrini tried in vain to waken him, until, exasperated, he made recourse to the classic slapstick bucket of cold water. Having woken, Snipe got back behind the wheel and, like a robot, drove off again, winning with a half hour to spare. Needless to say, the following editions were divided into two stages, with a parc fermé at Agrigento.

The outbreak of the First World War then interrupted all forms of European motor sport. When the Targa returned in 1919, it was to the Madonie and a shorter course of 108 km (67 mi.) which was retained until 1930. There was another rather comic event in 1919: Boillot, the winner, accidentally spun just before the winning post and actually crossed the line backward. Dismay among the judges: is it a valid maneuver? The issue was resolved in pantomime fashion. Boillot remounted and repeated the last few feet in the correct direction and was proclaimed the winner.

Before proceeding with the painful pruning of the effervescent and impassioned episodes of a sporting event whose confines go well beyond those of the mere race results, a work of synthesis demanded by the insurmountable physical limits such as the dimensions of this book, we conceded ourselves a brief statistical parenthesis.

Looking at the roll of honor, it would appear that for the drivers the Targa was a kind of drug. Accumulating participations is something like adding military campaign ribbons to one's uniform; moreover, to win means nothing if one does not win again, and straight away. In fact, the series of 1-2s reported in the annals of the Automobil Club di Palermo is incredible: Giulio Masetti, a private entrant of great technical and human qualities (1921-22) with Fiat and Mercedes (a nobleman adopted by the local fans for his courage and great feeling for the Targa roads, he was tragically to die in 1926 on a cursed hairpin curve); Bartolomeo Costantini (1925-26) and Albert Divo (1928-29), principal artificers of the magnificent Bugatti

286 top left *The Targa Florio was a fascinating race because it allowed the pinnacles of modern technology to be combined with the ruins of a decadent civilization. Achille Varzi is seen here in a P2 passing through one of the many villages whose remains are testimony to a distant past. In the Sixties and Seventies this context was the setting for the ultra-modern sports prototypes that shot past ancient dry-stone walls and ruined churches.*

sequence of five consecutive wins; Tazio Nuvolari (1931-32) scored the only back-to-back driver's victories during the record-breaking Alfa Romeo series of six consecutive wins between 1930 and 1935, but the nonconsecutive wins of Varzi (1930 and '34) and Brivio (1933 and '35) must be mentioned; Luigi Villoresi (1939-40) with Maserati; Clemente Biondetti (1948-49) with Ferrari; and Olivier Gendebien (1961-62), also with Ferrari. The Belgian driver had already won in 1958 and therefore deserves mention in the roll of honor as much as Nino Vaccarella and Umberto Maglioli, the only other drivers to score three wins. Felice Nazzaro, Jo Siffert, Herbert Müller and Arturio Merzario also boast of two wins, albeit not consecutively.

What is curious is that in spite of so many double wins, no one was ever been able to win three times in a row, as if there were a limit to the creation of local deities. An equally curious fact concerns not a win but an absence: the greatest of all racing drivers, Juan Manuel Fangio, never went beyond his 1955 placing of second. The roll of honor should also contain the name of Elisabeth Junek, a noblewoman who in 1928 led drivers of the caliber of Campari, Divo and Varzi before fatigue obliged her to surrender the lead and victory.

Cold statistics cannot, however, describe to us the victorious arrival of Varzi in 1930, with his mechanic trying to put out a fire whose flames had already surrounded the entire car, or the success of Nuvolari who the following year had to tackle a dreadful road surface made impassable by rain (Florio, facing the possibility of canceling the race, opted for the old, longer course) that turned the race into a sort of knock-out contest with cars and drivers unrecognizable beneath a layer of mud.

These were the years of the now famous works of the driver and illustrator Gordon Crosby, who rendered the key moments of overtaking maneuvers, generally between the red and blue Alfas and Bugattis that dominated the period, in his paintings. Such realism in those subjects: one would think that the artist boasted of a fervid imagination and a great capacity to recreate situations of enormous emphasis and tension, but nothing could be further from the truth. In reality Vincenzo Florio, who attributed great

286 top right *In 1930 Alfa Romeo finally had a car capable of breaking the Bugatti stranglehold, the P2 driven to victory by Varzi. The more domesticated 6C 1750 Sport also took part in the race and is seen here before the start with Gasparini and Arcangeli.*

286 center This photograph portrays two of the automotive greats, on the left Don Vincenzo Florio, a determined, stubborn Sicilian nobleman, patron of the race of the same name and a lover of challenges and speed; on the right the greatest motor racing champion of his time, Tazio Nuvolari.

286 bottom Achille Varzi wins the 21st Targa Florio with an Alfa Romeo and is saluted by his mechanics.

287 top The great Alfa Romeo P3 was successful in the Targa Florio, too. It was driven to victory in 1934 and 1935 by Varzi and Brivio-Sforza (in the photograph taken immediately after the end of the race).

287 bottom A magnificent sequence of Alfa Romeo victories began with Varzi's win in 1930. In 1931 and 1932 Nuvolari made the Sicilian race his own, with the 8C Monza on both occasions. The marque scored six consecutive victories in the Thirties.

importance to means of communication, had thought well to make available to journalists, illustrators and photographers vehicles authorized to take to the track: the reporters really were "in" the race—the dream of any sportswriter.

From 1932 the Targa shrank, and the 72-km (45 mi.) Piccolo Circuito delle Madonie was born, to be lapped 11 times (previously the race had generally been run over three laps).

Shortly afterward the Florio family entered a phase of decline, its empire crumbling, and in 1937 the Targa Florio was taken over by the Automobil Club di Palermo. The race headquarters was moved within the Parco della Favorita, a fabulous green space between the provincial capital and the sea. This was the Maserati era, interrupted only by the second tolling of the bells of war.

In 1948 the effervescence of a group of important and aristocratic young people, automobile enthusiasts with the economic potential of the most prosperous landowners, relaunched the Giro di Sicilia, which was staged for three years and first saw Ferrari then Alfa prevail. However the old lion had yet to be tamed, and in 1951 Don Vincenzo succeeded in taking his race back to it its original circuit, increasingly lined by enthusiastic crowds mindful of pre-war emotions. The return of the Piccolo Circuito delle Madonie proved congenial to Lancia for three consecutive years with victories for three drivers of great talent: Felice Bonetto, Umberto Maglioli and Piero Taruffi. The second epic period of the Targa was about to begin, the very essence of international racing: an open-air laboratory of winning cars and a great crucible of champions. Fitting recognition of

the status of the race came in 1955 with its inclusion in the calendar of races valid for the World Sports Car Championship. Thus began the great battles between utterly unforgettable cars.

There was the Mercedes 300SLR that carried Stirling Moss to victory in 1955. There were the Ferrari 250 Testa Rossa (1958), Dino 246SP (1961-62), 275S and the so-called P2 (1963) that brought wins for Luigi Musso, Olivier Gendebien, Wolfgang "Taffy" von Trips (who shortly after this 1961 win was to lose his life at Monza), and Willy Mairesse. And who could forget that the contest of 1963, all but wrapped up by Bandini and Scarfiotti, was instead gifted to Porsche because of a crash just before the finish, or how the "crazy" Ricardo Rodriguez inflamed the adoring crowd with his sideways style, just as his brother Pedro was to do soon afterward? These tales are the Targa Florio.

288 top left Peter Collins, paired with Stirling Moss, won the '55 Targa in Mercedes' barchetta variant of the 300SLR. Collins and Moss (one of the protagonists in the years to come) formed one of the most well-balanced pairings ever seen in the Sicilian race.

288 top right A beautiful car crosses the finishing line of the 1961 Targa Florio: the Ferrari 246SP, the first successful mid-engine Ferrari GT. This was the car's sole victory in 1961, but Ferrari won the World Championship thanks to the exploits of the venerable Testa Rossa. The drivers were von Trips and Gendebien.

There were also of course the Porsches, with the glorious series of nine victories between 1959 to 1970 including Jo Bonnier's two wins (first teamed with Graham Hill and Hans Hermann, then with Carlo Abate) and the success of drivers of the caliber of Jo Siffert, Umberto Maglioli, Vic Elford, and Rolf Stommelen. The series was interrupted only by Gendebien's back-to-back wins for Ferrari in 1961 and '62 and Nino Vaccarella's in 1965, a triumph he shared with Lorenzo Bandini. (The latter assumed even greater significance due to the fact that it was Vaccarella again, this time with Toine Hezemans in an Alfa T33/3, who later broke the domination of the mighty Porsche prototypes.)

In those years and in the years to come it was always the same story: the Porsches shot away from the start thanks to their great agility on the twisting

better of the European cars, in particular the beautiful Porsche 908 Barchetta (one of the all-time sacred icons of the Targa together with the Bugatti T35, the Alfa Romeo 8C Monza, the Maserati 6CM and the Ferrari 275P2). Ford, above all, had already been carrying the battle to Porsche with a good-looking, competitive car, the Mark IV powered by a seven-liter V8. One curious detail: the French ski champion Jean-Claude Killy also participated in the 1967 Targa.

With the exception of a 1957 edition reduced to a kind of gymkhana due to the tragic events that led to the interruption of the Mille Miglia, the period between 1955 and 1973 that coincided with the golden age of the sports-prototypes witnessed the apotheosis of the Targa. In those years the heights of competitiveness were reached on a circuit that was unmatched in its ability to generate pathos and emotions.

First came the long wait for dawn with the spectators scattered along the track, a swarming army that closed in on "enemies" and opened up as the favorites passed.

Thence the tension of the staggered start, with the first ones out streaking away to confront unknown dangers on a circuit whose first key moments were lived out immediately after the start thanks to curves and hairpins on which the powerful cars suffered while the lighter ones traced elegant trajectories.

288 bottom left Portrayed here is instead a wonderful car from one of the small-displacement categories, the Alfa Romeo TZ1 Zagato of Bianchi. This photograph is from 1965, the year in which Vaccarella and Bandini took the Targa Florio in a Ferrari 275P2.

roads, but at the first sign of a straight the Ferraris would angrily unleash all their power, rocketing to over 300 kph (186 mph) on the treacherous Buonfornello straight that was unforgiving of even the slightest slip or loss of concentration.

At the end of the Sixties the effective American cars employed in the World Championship began to make their presence felt. In 1967 the powerful seven-liter, 575-hp Chaparral was entered for the Targa, a monster that had just won at the Nürburgring but that in Sicily was unable to get the

After one reached Collesano there came a descent toward the sea that anyone in his right mind would refuse even to contemplate but which the racers would run through at insane speeds, their brakes about to give out from fatigue and heat.

After the heart-in-mouth descent with one's soul projected beyond the next curve came the Buonfornello straight, which may look like an interminable esplanade but is in reality an uneven strip that speeds of over 300 km (186 mph) per hour transformed into a dark tunnel from which not

288 bottom right *From the 1950s through to the 1960s there were infinite duels between Ferrari and Porsche, the true leitmotif of the Targa Florio (and of sports-prototype racing in general). In 1959 Porsche scored an important victory with the 1500 Spyder of Barth and Seidel. This picture instead shows the more powerful 1600 of Maglioli and Hermann, which was forced to retire along with the identical car of Bonnier and von Trips. Nonetheless, all three steps on the podium were occupied by Porsche drivers at race's end.*

288-289 *Amid the Italian and German cars the British marques also had opportunities to make their presence felt in the Targa Florio; seen here is the BRM of Konig. Note the graffiti on the road, frequently containing colorful phrases. Ironically in 1971 the Porsche ace Rodriguez skidded on graffiti that read "Porsche Kaput," his race ending with the car stranded on the pavement.*

infrequently one would be shot bullet-like toward the fields (as happened to Regazzoni in 1973; after a flight of 100 m (382 ft.) he ended upside-down in a ditch but miraculously alive). A firecracker let those in the grandstands slightly higher know that once the last three curves were negotiated, the car would be storming through toward the finishing line.

Porsche's domination during the Sixties was undoubtedly favored by Ferrari, which often did not show or at best sent a single works car. The reason was simple: Ferraris were designed for fast tracks

289 top right *This photograph portrays one of the two Chevron-BMWs in the 1969 Targa and entrusted to the British crew of Brown and Enever. That year the struggle among the cars with engines of up to five liters (not included in the sports-prototype category, which was restricted to three) saw a number of fascinating cars: the two Chevron-BMWs, a Porsche 910 (Nomex-Biscaldi), the Alfa Tipo 33 of Giunti and Galli (Vaccarella was racing in the three-liter category with de Adamich) and Bonnier's Lola T70.*

289 bottom right *The King of the Targa Florio, the "Flying Headmaster," Nino Vaccarella: he is seen here in the 1969 Targa, an edition dominated by Porsche due to the absence of Ferrari, which was concentrating on Formula 1. Vaccarella was to finish third the following year, and in 1971 scored his last victory in the Sicilian race.*

where they collected victory after victory while the Targa was too atypical a race.

As not even Ford had managed to worry Porsche, who would descend upon Sicily with strong and well-prepared teams, Carlo Chiti's Autodelta Alfa Romeos took up the challenge, triumphing with one of the most successful cars in the history of racing, the Tipo 33. Thanks to the Alfa 33, Vaccarella and Hezemans succeeded in stopping the Porsches in 1971. It was one of the most hard-fought editions, together with that of the preceding year in which victory went to another Targa great, Jo Siffert, in the company of Brian Redman.

Nineteen seventy also saw the setting of the fastest-ever lap by Leo Kinnunen (33'36", an average speed of almost 129 kph [80 mph]) in a Porsche, as well as another episode that was unusual to say the least. About 10 km (6.2 mi.) from the finish line Laine, in a Porsche 908/2, lost his right-front wheel and yet managed to continue as if nothing had happened, his times showing no reduction in speed.

The three-year period of grace closed with the very well-deserved victory of Arturo Merzario, another great ace, with the prudent Sandro Munari at the wheel of the revived Ferrari. In 1973 the last World Championship edition was won by Gijs van Lennep and Herbert Müller in a Porsche 911 Carrera RSR.

The international federation then wisely decided that the Sicilian race was no longer a stage on which 600-hp monsters could do battle without jeopardizing the excessive crowds lining the roads (in the last editions a tract of the local highway had

been closed and used as parking for the spectators, with shuttles to the circuit).

Shrewd administrators would have lost no time in building a circuit whose returns in economic, image and tourism terms were guaranteed. Instead, much was promised and nothing was done, and the Targa lived on for another four years as a national event that allowed Vaccarella to make it a three-of-a-kind. Then in 1977 the inevitable happened: a car went off the road, ploughing into a group of spectators. For the Targa this was the end, and it soon declined into a third-rate road rally.

It seems almost that the history of the Sicilian race with all its highs and lows traces, emphasizes and exasperates the vicissitudes experienced and suffered by automotive sport in general: is it perhaps wrong to consider the early Seventies, the last years of the Targa, as those in which motor racing began a profound process of transformation that will eventually debase its purely sporting nature, ultimately subjugating it to the demands of sponsors and of television?

290 top Vic Elford was one of the favorites for the 1969 Targa Florio but was delayed by a broken fan. He then proceeded to stage a magnificent comeback that included a perilous passing maneuver on the Cerda-Bivio Sclafani descent at the expense of Nanni Galli in an Alfa.

YEAR	CAR	CREW	AV. SPEED KPH (MPH)	
1948	Ferrari	C. Biondetti-I. Troubetzkoi	88.8	(55.1)
1949	Ferrari	C. Biondetti-A. Benedetti	81.5	(50.6)
1950	Alfa Romeo	M. Bornigia-G. Bornigia	86.9	(53.9)
1951	Frazer-Nash	F. Cortese	76.6	(47.5)
1952	Lancia	F. Bonetto	78.4	(48.7)
1953	Lancia	U. Maglioli	80	(49.7)
1954	Lancia	P. Taruffi	89.9	(55.8)
1955	Mercedes-Benz 300SLR	S. Moss-P. Collins	96.3	(59.8)
1956	Porsche	U. Maglioli-H. Von Hanstein	90.9	(56.4)
1957	Fiat	F. Colonna	-	
1958	Ferrari 250TR	L. Musso-O. Gendebien	94.8	(58.9)
1959	Porsche 718RSK	E. Barth-W. Seidel	91.3	(56.7)
1960	Porsche RS80	J. Bonnier-H. Hermann-G. Hill	95.3	(59.2)
1961	Ferrari Dino 246SP	W. von Trips-O. Gendebien	103.4	(64.2)
1962	Ferrari Dino 246SP	W. Mairesse-R. Rodriguez-O. Gendebien	102	(63.3)
1963	Porsche RS82	J. Bonnier-C. Abate	103.9	(64.5)
1964	Porsche 904GTS	A. Pucci-C. Davis	100.3	(62.3)
1965	Ferrari 275P2	N. Vaccarella-L. Bandini	102.6	(63.7)
1966	Porsche 906 Carrera	W. Mairesse-H. Müller	98.9	(61.4)
1967	Porsche 910/B	P. Hawkins-R. Stommelen	108.8	(67.6)
1968	Porsche 907/B	V. Elford-U. Maglioli	111.1	(69)
1969	Porsche 908/B	G. Mitter-U. Schutz	117.5	(73)
1970	Porsche 908/B	J. Siffert-B. Redman	120.1	(74.6)
1971	Alfa Romeo T33/3	N. Vaccarella-T. Hezemans	120.1	(74.6)
1972	Ferrari 312P	A. Merzario-S. Munari	122.5	(76.1)
1973	Porsche 911 Carrera	G. van Lennep- H. Müller	114.7	(71.2)
1974	Lancia Stratos	G. Larrousse-A. Ballestrieri	-	
1975	Alfa Romeo	N. Vaccarella-A. Merzario	-	
1976	Osella	"Amphicar"-A. Floridia	-	
1977	Chevron	R. Restivo-"Apache"	-	

291 top One of the most thrilling editions of the Targa Florio took place in 1971. Alfa Romeo and Porsche fought for a supremacy that went well beyond sporting merit: in play was the high technological profiles of two marques that had been responsible for glorious chapters in the history of the sports-prototype category. As in the best of scripts, the underdog (Alfa) emerged victorious with Vaccarella and Hezemans, followed 1' 11" behind by that of de Adamich and van Lennep (seen here), with the Lola of Bonnier/Attwood third. This proved an unfortunate race for Porsche, despite having drivers such as Elford, Rodriguez, Larousse, Siffert and Redman in its ranks.

291 bottom This picture shows the last edition of the Targa Florio as a World Championship race, that of 1973. Seen here is the Porsche 911 three-liter Carrera RSR, which won the race with Gijs van Lennep and Herbert Müller.

THE TOURIST TROPHY

Tourist Trophy

An atypical racing car industry, an atypical national automotive context and atypical races: once again Britain found opportunities to differentiate itself from the Continent with one of the oldest and most representative of motor races, the Tourist Trophy.

This is at least true up to the point when British engineers and racing teams began to take a serious and committed interest in Grand Prix-type races like those staged elsewhere in Europe and began to establish their reputations in that category. In the meantime, the Tourist Trophy, born way back in 1905, evolved in many different ways with modifications to the format, formula and venue. It is in fact an event that is difficult to categorize.

The accounts of the era prior to the first edition are full of the abolition in 1896 of the obligation for every car travelling in the UK to be preceded by a man carrying a red flag; unfortunately this liberation coincided with the first fatal accident in recorded automotive history, at Crystal Palace in London.

The first edition of the Tourist Trophy was staged on the 14th of September, 1905, on the Isle of Man and was not restricted to four-wheeled vehicles but open to motorcycles and, for a brief period, sidecar combinations (the origins of the famous Jaguars). In fact, today the Isle of Man TT races are motorcycling events and no longer involve cars.

The 1905 race—which earned its place in history not only as the first edition of the Tourist Trophy but also of organized British racing in general—was won by John Napier, whose name was later carried on the first British car to win a major race. (On this occasion he drove an Arrol-Johnston 18 hp.) The event was not a straight race but a form of regularity trial based on a fuel-consumption formula.

The second edition is also worthy of mention. It was won by the Honorable Charles Rolls at the wheel of a car he manufactured in partnership with Henry Royce, which at the finish had barely a drop of fuel left in its tank (0.131 gallons, just over half a liter). The third edition also consigned to history the

name of another manufacturer that was to become famous throughout the continent, Rover. Fuel consumption was still a fundamental parameter and Ernest Courtis covered 241 miles (387 km) on fewer than ten gallons of petrol (9.75, equal to around 45 liters) at an average speed of 46.3 kph.

The following year there was a drastic change in the regulations with normal production cars giving way to a Formula Libre. This time the name Napier appeared on the bonnet of the winning car as the

292 top left The unforgettable driver Alberto Ascari taking a corner at the wheel of his Lancia D24 during one of the Dundrod Tourist Trophy races held near Belfast, 1954.

victor, Watson, was at the wheel of a powerful four-cylinder Hutton prepared by Napier.

A series of intermittent editions takes us to 1928, but by this time everything had changed: the Tourist Trophy was no longer a Formula Libre event but a handicap race for sports cars. It was no longer staged on the Isle of Man either, but at Ards to the south of Belfast in Ireland, where nine editions were held. The ostracism from the British mainland was due to the ban on open-road racing

292 top right The Tourist Trophy was born in 1905 as a regularity trial based on fuel consumption. This unusual 1906 image shows nine participants attempting to negotiate one of the six ascents of Jasper Road in Sydenham. The well known car is a Rolls-Royce driven by Claude Johnson. The race was actually won by Charles Rolls himself in an identical car.

292-293 After the first six editions the Tourist Trophy was moved from the Isle of Man to the Ards circuit. Attracted by the race, many continental manufacturers sent teams to participate in an event that privileged cars of low power outputs and small engine capacities. This photograph shows an Alfa and a Talbot.

292 bottom The great Stirling Moss scored a number of TT victories. Here he is seen in the pits watching the mechanics working on his Jaguar C-Type on the occasion of the 20th Tourist Trophy, held at Dundrod in 1953.

293 top Juan Manuel Fangio's Mercedes 300SLR tackles a sweeping corner in the 1955 TT ahead of Mike Hawthorn's Jaguar D-Type.

293 center Jaguars had opportunities to enhance their reputation in the Tourist Trophy. This photograph, taken during the 1954 edition of the TT at Dundrod shows a short-nose D-Type with fairing driven by Stirling Moss.

293 bottom The Aston Martin team happily salute the winning car of the '58 Tourist Trophy, the DBR1 of Stirling Moss.

imposed by the safety-minded English government.

In spite of its unusual formula (and thanks to a generous prize fund), the event was honored by the presence of the greats of the era, among whom were Tazio Nuvolari (a two-time winner) and Rudolf Caracciola. The marques represented were also of great prestige, from Alfa Romeo to Mercedes and Bugatti as well as the local Bentleys and Vauxhalls. In the meantime a number of emergent marques had also begun to attract attention, including Sunbeam, Lea-Francis, Riley and above all MG, whose Magnette was driven to victory by Nuvolari with a time that was only beaten nearly 20 years later by Stirling Moss. (MG stands for *Morris Garages,* a small

firm that won its first race in 1925. The Magnette remains the most famous of the racing MGs, its reputation exceeding even that of the Midget thanks to an 1100-cc class victory in the 1933 Mille Miglia.) The Ulster era drew to a close in 1936 and the Tourist Trophy was staged at Donington Park for two years, still run to the sports car formula.

The "TT" however, had an itinerant destiny and subsequently moved back to Ireland and the Dundrod circuit. Dundrod was considered to be a difficult circuit, but the most entertaining and exciting in Britain during the early Fifties. That ended in 1955, when the death of three drivers in the Tourist Trophy led to its closure; only two years

earlier the race had been inserted in the World Sports Car Championship calendar.

The Tourist Trophy then moved to Goodwood, a circuit (like Silverstone) built on an old military airfield in Surrey and home to the Formula 1 Glover Trophy race as well as the TT.

The Stirling Moss era was celebrated between Dundrod and Goodwood, the great English driver winning no fewer than seven editions, either solo or with a teammate, at the wheel of Aston Martins, Ferraris and Jaguars. No other driver ever matched this feat, although remarkably Denny Hulme managed to win in 1965, 1966, 1968 and then again 18 years later in 1986 at the age of 50.

The TT lost its World Championship status in 1959 and the following editions were staged for GT cars. The event moved yet again in 1965 to the small Oulton Park circuit, which also staged the British Empire Trophy and the Gold Cup. The sports cars returned, with a parenthesis in 1967 when the race was staged for touring cars. This was also the formula adopted after 1970 when the race was moved to Silverstone, where it became a round of the national touring car championship. In 1994 the TT made a return to Donington as a round in the ephemeral World Touring Car Championship of that year and was won by the New Zealander Radish.

294 top left The start of the 1961
edition of the Tourist Trophy staged at
Goodwood, the fifth venue of the
British race. One of the Ferrari 250GTs
was driven to victory by the local
hero Stirling Moss.

294 top right Moss completed a series
of five consecutive victories in the Tourist
Trophy in 1961: this edition was very
similar to that of the previous
year and the winning car, seen here
during a refuelling stop, was again
a Ferrari 250GT. Note the Italian plates
from Modena, the capital of the
province in which Maranello, the home
of Ferrari, is located.

HONOR ROLL

YEAR	CIRCUIT	CAR	CREW	AV. SPEED KPH (MPH)
1905	Isle of Man	Arrol-Johnston	J. Napier	54.6 (33.9)
1906	Isle of Man	Rolls-Royce 20 hp	C. Rolls	63.4 (39.3)
1907	Isle of Man	Rover 20 hp	E. Courtis	46.3 (28.7)
1908	Isle of Man	Napier-Hutton	W. Watson	80.9 (50.2)
1914	Isle of Man	Sunbeam	K. L. Guinness	90.8 (56.4)
1922	Isle of Man	Sunbeam	J. Chassagne	89.8 (55.8)
1928	Ards	Lea-Francis	K. Don	101.5 (63)
1929	Ards	Mercedes-Benz SS	R. Caracciola	117.2 (72.8)
1930	Ards	Alfa Romeo 6C	T. Nuvolari	114.1 (70.9)
1931	Ards	MG Midget C-Type	N. Black	109.3 (67.9)
1932	Ards	Riley 9	C. R. Whitcroft	119.5 (74.2)
1933	Ards	MG Magnette K3	T. Nuvolari	126.6 (78.6)
1934	Ards	MG Magnette NE	C. Dodson	120.1 (74.6)
1935	Ards	Riley 1.5	F. Dixon	123.8 (76.9)
1936	Ards	Riley 1.5	F. Dixon-C. Dodson	125.5 (77.9)
1937	Donington Park	Talbot-Darracq	G. Comotti	110.6 (68.7)

YEAR	CIRCUIT	CAR	CREW	AV. SPEED KPH (MPH)
1938	Donington Park	Delage	L. Gérard	108.8 (67.6)
1950	Dundrod	Jaguar XK120	S. Moss	120.9 (75.1)
1951	Dundrod	Jaguar C-Type	S. Moss	134.5 (83.5)
1953	Dundrod	Aston Martin DB3S	P. Collins-P. Griffith	131.5 (81.7)
1954	Dundrod	DB-Panhard	P. Armagnac-G. Laureau	110.6 (68.7)
1955	Dundrod	Mercedes-Benz 300SLR	S. Moss-J. Fitch	142.1 (88.3)
1958	Goodwood	Aston Martin DBR1/300	S. Moss-T. Brooks	142.1 (88.3)
1959	Goodwood	Aston Martin DBR1/300	S. Moss-C. Shelby-J. Fairman	143.9 (89.4)
1960	Goodwood	Ferrari 250GT	S. Moss	137.7 (85.5)
1961	Goodwood	Ferrari 250GT	S. Moss	139.4 (86.6)
1962	Goodwood	Ferrari 250GTO	I. Ireland	153 (95)
1963	Goodwood	Ferrari 250GTO	G. Hill	153.1 (95.1)
1964	Goodwood	Ferrari 330P	G. Hill	161.4 (100.2)
1965	Oulton Park	Brabham BT8-Climax	D. Hulme	151.4 (94)

294-295 *A fine view of the grandstand straight at Goodwood, which hosted the TT between 1958 and 1964. The British ace Stirling Moss was first across the line this time in a Ferrari 250GT, winning at an average speed of 139.4 kph (87 mph).*

295 top *In 1965 the Tourist Trophy transferred once again, this time to Oulton Park. These were exceptional years for the sports-prototypes that also competed in the TT. This 1966 image shows the talented Denny Hulme aboard the winning Chevrolet-powered Lola T70 MkII.*

1966	Oulton Park	Lola T70MkII-Chevrolet	D. Hulme	153.2 (95.1)
1967	Oulton Park	Alfa Romeo Giulia GTA	A. de Adamich	129.8 (80.6)
1968	Oulton Park	Lola T70MkIII-Chevrolet	D. Hulme	159.4 (99)
1969	Oulton Park	Lola T70MkIIIB-Chevrolet	T. Taylor	155.8 (96.8)
1970	Silverstone	Chevrolet Camaro Z28	B. Muir	160.8 (99.9)
1972	Silverstone	Ford Capri RS600	J. Mass-D.Glemser	171.4 (106.5)
1973	Silverstone	BMW 3.0 CSL	D. Bell-H. Ertl	175.1 (108.8)
1974	Silverstone	Chevrolet Camaro Z28	S. Graham	156.6 (97.3)
1975	Silverstone	Chevrolet Camaro Z28	S. Graham	157.2 (97.6)
1976	Silverstone	BMW 3.0 CSL	J. Xhenceval-P. Dieudonné-H. de Fierland	163.1 (101.3)
1977	Silverstone	BMW 3.0 CSL	D. Quester-T. Walkinshaw	169.8 (105.5)
1978	Silverstone	BMW 3.0 CSL	R. V. Hove-E. Joosen	165.5 (102.8)
1979	Silverstone	BMW 3.0 CSL	M. Finotto-C. Facetti	167.3 (103.9)
1980	Silverstone	BMW 635 CSi	U. Grano-H. Neger-H. Werginz	164.5 (102.2)
1981	Silverstone	Mazda RX7	T. Walkinshaw-C. Nicholson	166 (103.1)
1982	Silverstone	Jaguar XJS	T. Walkinshaw-C. Nicholson	161.7 (100.4)
1983	Silverstone	Rover Vitesse	R. Metge-S. Soper	159.8 (99.2)
1984	Silverstone	BMW 635 CSi	H. Kelleners-G. Brancatelli	149.6 (92.9)
1985	Silverstone	Rover Vitesse	T. Walkinshaw-W. Percy	167.2 (103.8)
1986	Silverstone	Rover Vitesse	D. Hulme-J. Allam	165.5 (102.8)
1987	Silverstone	BMW M3	E. Calderai-F. Mancini	162.3 (100.8)
1988	Silverstone	Ford Sierra RS500	A. Rouse-A. Ferté	167.3 (103.9)
1994	Donington Park	Ford Mondeo Ghia	P. Radish	143.9 (89.4)

295 bottom left *During the Seventies the Tourist Trophy continued to attract touring cars used in the various national championships for this category. SCCA-type Camaros Z28s ruled the early part of the decade, winning three of first five races.*

295 bottom right *Although it has lost its international standing, the TT still survives as a national race for touring cars. This photograph dates from 1997, the year in which the race was won by Alain Menu in a* Renault Laguna.

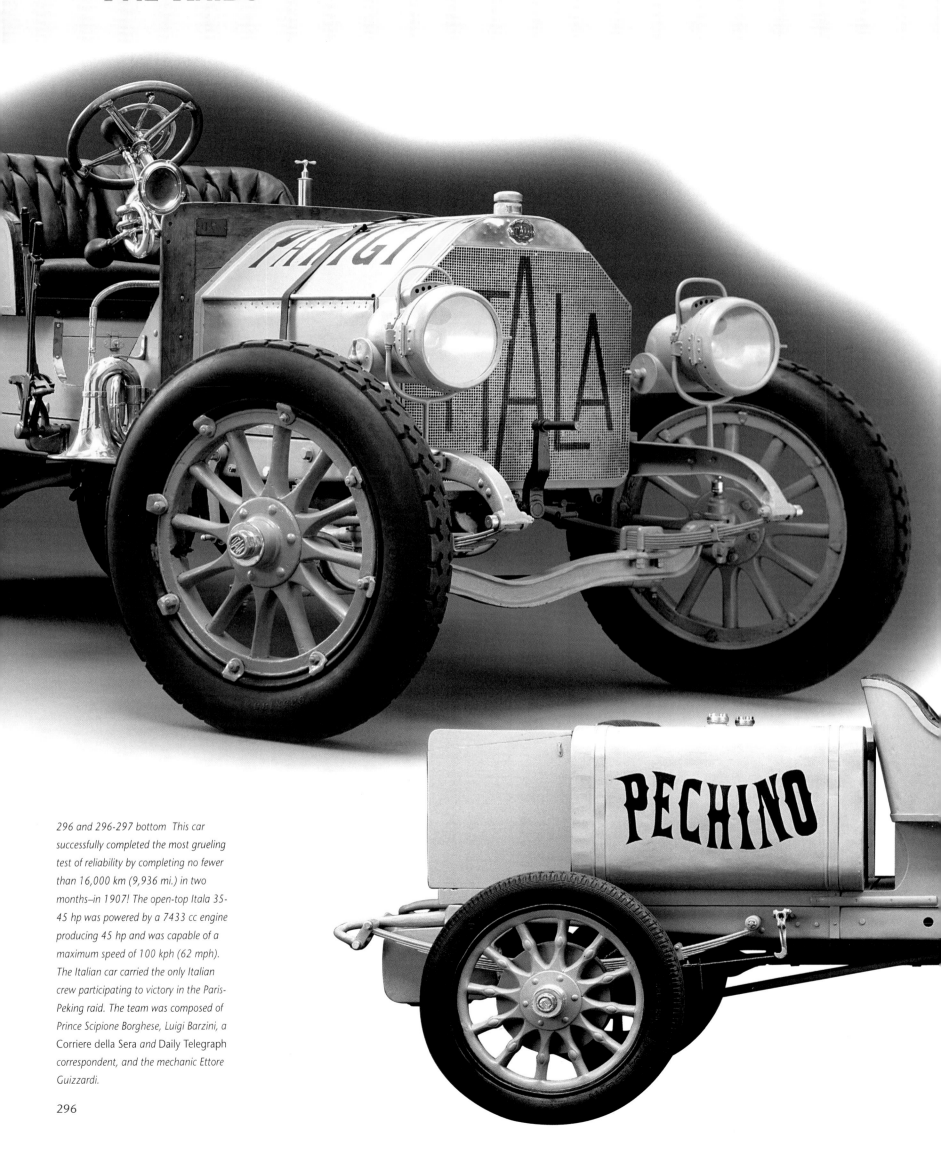

THE RAIDS

296 and 296-297 bottom This car successfully completed the most grueling test of reliability by completing no fewer than 16,000 km (9,936 mi.) in two months–in 1907! The open-top Itala 35-45 hp was powered by a 7433 cc engine producing 45 hp and was capable of a maximum speed of 100 kph (62 mph). The Italian car carried the only Italian crew participating to victory in the Paris-Peking raid. The team was composed of Prince Scipione Borghese, Luigi Barzini, a Corriere della Sera *and* Daily Telegraph *correspondent, and the mechanic Ettore Guizzardi.*

Paris Peking

The automobile, man, raids; that is to say the means, the mind and the goal. The invention of the horseless carriage allowed man to undertake long journeys; when these journeys developed into competitive raids then the circle was squared: find the courage, accept the challenge, test your stamina. The raids were born soon after the motor car first turned a wheel: Paris-Rouen (1894, 127 km/79 mi.), Paris-Marseilles-Paris (1896, 1700 km/106 mi.), Paris-Toulouse-Paris (1900, 1347 km/106 mi.), New York-Portland (1905, 6437 km/4,000 mi.).

The sporting nature of the raids can be traced back to two automotive phenomena: the raid as a long transfer, perhaps without any classification based on time, and raids as events staged over very demanding and unpredictable terrain. In the pioneering phase of motor sport the former prevailed, closer to the concept of "adventure," while in recent times raids have developed as tests of the crews and the robustness of their vehicles with extreme events such as the Paris-Dakar (or as it has recently been rebaptized, the Granada-Dakar),

9000 km (5,589 mi.) through the African desert.

"Is there anyone who will accept to travel next summer from Peking to Paris by automobile? The greatest test of stamina ever undertaken by motor cars over a distance of 16,000 km [9,936 mi.]." With this challenge launched on the 31st of January, 1907, by the Parisian daily newspaper *Le Matin* began one of the most memorable automotive feats of all time. Twenty-five crews responded to the call including a single Italian entry composed of Prince Scipione Borghese, the mechanic Ettore Guizzardi and the *Corriere della Sera* and *Daily Telegraph* correspondent Luigi Barzini with an Itala 35-45 hp. Just five cars actually started from Peking on the 10th of June, 1907; among them was the Itala. Borghese and Guizzardi soon established a convincing lead and on the 10th of August, two months after starting, drove victoriously into Paris.

The following year the longest race of all time was organized, the New York-Paris via Siberia, won after drawn-out arguments, by the Roberts-Shuster crew aboard a Thomas Flyer. In the 1960s instead, along with the Alpine, African (such as the trans-Africa event) and South American raids, élite events such as the Rome-Liege-Rome and later the London-Monaco were organized. However, 72 years after the Peking-Paris, it was still the French capital which was the mother of all raids thanks to Thierry Sabine, the organizer of the first Paris-Dakar. The event started from Versailles and crossed the

297 top and center These photographs portray the team that won the Paris-Peking raid. In the center photograph, the protagonists are seen during the Berlin stage; in the top photograph, after exactly two months' racing, can be recognized, from the left, Borghese, Barzini and Guizzardi. Of the 25 teams who entered the devastating race organized by the Parisian daily paper Le Matin, *only five actually started on the 10th of June, 1907.*

Paris Dakar

country by way of the N20, while the loose-surface special stages on the slopes of the Pyrenees provided the first severe test. The third stage ran through Spain to Granada, before the cars embarked for Morocco. After traveling overnight the competitors tackled the Moroccan scree slopes of the Atlas plateau and then the Sahara of Mauritania and Mali, the setting for the longest stages that decided the race.

The physical and mental preparation of the crews is fundamental in these conditions while the power output of the vehicle is of secondary importance; what counts is the cool head of a driver capable of dealing with 100-m (328 ft.) high dunes, the navigator's sense of direction, tactical

intelligence and self-control. After completing over 9000 km (5,589 mi.) of dust, sand, rocks, sunburn, red eyes and blistered hands, the sea and the warm colors of Senegal are a mirage for those few crews who actually cross the finishing line and can truly say "we made it."

Despite the controversy it arouses, the Paris-Dakar has become legendary for these very reasons; it provides a challenge and an opportunity to measure one's psycho-physical strength. Jacky Ickx, Jacques Lafitte, Henri Pescarolo, Mark Thatcher (son of the former British Prime Minister), Jean-Loup Chretien (a French astronaut) and the various winners such as Neveau, Auriol, Orioli and Peterhansel have all eagerly accepted this challenge.

298 Tracks through the sand, passages through villages composed of a few huts and beneath the gaze of the locals, dunes up to a 100 m (328 ft.) high concealing potential hazards. This is the Paris-Dakar, first organized by Thierry Sabine in 1979 and involving, among other things, cars derived from mass-production models that have been specially prepared to cope with the African desert conditions, such as the 1987 Citroën Visa (top) and the Peugeot 205 Turbo (bottom) of '88.

298-299 *The arid dunes of the desert act as a backdrop to the passage of a number of cars. After crossing France and Spain, the cars and drivers are severely tested by the African terrain. This image dates from 1988.*

299 right *As the race approaches its final destination the landscape of the Paris-Dakar is transformed, with the desert giving way to the beaches of Senegal. This picture shows other participants in the event including four-wheel drive industrial vehicles with power outputs that frequently exceed 500 hp, enough to give even a Formula 1 single-seater food for thought.*

299 bottom *Probably as a result of driver error—the dunes can be up to 100 m (328 ft.) high and difficult to judge—a vehicle sinks into the sand.*

BIBLIOGRAPHY

AA. VV., *Grand Prix Story*, Hellwag, 1990
AA. VV., *Daimler 1896-1996*, Jaguar Italia SpA, 1996
AA. VV., *Ferrari 1946-1990 Opera Omnia*, Automobilia, 1990
AA. VV., *Official Historical Championship Car Record Book*, CART Ind, 1998
AA. VV., *Tutte le Alfa Romeo 1910-1995*, Editoriale Domus, 1995
AA. VV., *Tutte le Fiat*, Editoriale Domus, 1970
AA.VV., *Le macchine Sport e Prototipo 1923-82*, Automobilia, 1982
Altieri, P., Lurani, G., *Alfa Romeo Catologue Raisonné 1910-1989*, Automobilia, 1988
Amatori, F., *Storia della Lancia 1906-1969*, Fabbri Editori, 1992
Brown, D, *Monaco Grand Prix*, Motor Racing Publications, 1989
Casamassima, P, *Storia della Formula 1*, Edizioni Calder, 1996

Cimarosti, A, *Carrera Panamericana "Mexico"*, Automobilia, 1987
Demaus, A. B., *Motor Sport in the 20s*, Alan Sutton, 1989
Flammang, J., *Chronicle of the American Automobile*, Publications International, 1994
Fusi, L., *Alfa Romeo, tutte le vetture dal 1910*, Emmeti Grafica Editrice, 1978
Hunter, D., *The Illustrated Story of Stock Car Racing*, MBI Publishing, 1998
Klein, R, *Rally*, Könemann, 1998
Lewandowski, J., *Mercedes Benz Catologue Raisonné 1886-1990*, Automobilia, 1990
Lyons, Pete, *Can-Am*, Motorbooks Int. P&W, 1995
Norris, I., *Jaguar Catologue Raisonné 1922-1992*, Automobilia, 1991
Raffaelli, F. & F., *Terra di piloti e di motori*, Artioli Editore, 1994

Rendall, I., *Bandiera a scacchi*, Vallardi & Associati, 1993
Requirez, S, *Targa Florio*, Flaccovio Editore, 1997
Schrader, H., *BMW Automobili*, Editoriale Semelfin, 1992
Seregni, Aldo, *Vita da rally*, Rino Fabbri Editore, 1975
Teissedre J.-M., *1998 Le Mans 24 Hours*, IHM Publishing, 1998
Verini, M., *Rally*, Longanesi & C., 1977

•Annuals
AA. VV, *Annuari Autosprint*, Conti Editore
AA. VV, *CART Media Guide*, CART Inc.
AA. VV, *Champ Car '98*, Racer
AA. VV., *Campionato del Mondo rally*, Massimo Baldini Editore
AA. VV., *Velocità e Rally*, Edizioni Studio Erre
Carmignani, F., *Rallyrama*, Edipromo

Deschenaux, J., *Marlboro Grand Prix Guide*, Charles Stewart & Co Ltc
Giordano, M., *Memorandum Rally*, Barbero Editori
Higham, P., *The Guinness Guide to International Motor Racing*, Guinness Publishing

• Specialist magazines and periodicals
Auto, Conti Editore SpA
AutoCapital, Editoriale Motori srl
Autosprint, Conti Editore
La Manovella e ruote a raggi, Giorgio Nada Editore
Le Grandi Automobili, Automobilia
Ruoteclassiche, Editoriale Internazionale Milano SpA
Guida all'acquisto di tutto, Edizioni Errezeta
Radar Coupé & Spider, Studio Zeta Editore

INDEX

PHOTOGRAPHIC CREDITS

Antonio Attini/Archivio White Star: pages 220-221.
Actualfoto: pages 62 left center, 70 bottom, 74 top, 76 right bottom, 78 center, 79 top, 82 bottom, 83 bottom, 84 left top and center, 84 right center, 84 bottom, 87 bottom right, 94-95, 95 center, 96 center, 97 bottom right, 99 right top, 101 right, 102-103, 103 top left, 103 bottom, 104 center right, 105 bottom, 108-109, 110 center right, 141 right top, 144 right, 145 top, 149 bottom, 152 left top, 152 right top, 152 bottom, 153 top, 208-209, 210-211, 212 center right, 212 bottom, 213 top, 213 bottom, 214, 214-215, 215 top, 215 center top, 218 top, 221 bottom, 226 top right, 227 center right, 230 center and bottom, 230-231, 278 bottom, 290 top.
AKG Photo: pages 19 bottom right, 21 center, 24-25, 44 right bottom, 45 left top, 46 center and bottom, 56-57, 61 top, 61 bottom, 65 right top, 68 left, 284-285.
Archivio Storico Alfa Romeo: pages 40 left bottom, 42 left bottom, 43 right top, 43 center, 50 center, 53 center, 53 right bottom, 54 center, 56 bottom, 58 right top, 58 bottom, 59 top, 59 left center, 60 center, 62 right center, 62 center bottom, 64 center top, 65 left top, 76 left, 76 right top, 77 center right and left, 77 bottom, 209 top, 220 left, 226 top left, 227 top, 268 top, 268 center left, 269 top, 272 top and center, 273 center, 273 right bottom, 275 center and bottom, 278 right top, 284, 285 right, 286 top, 287 top, 288 left bottom.
Archivio Autogerma: page 64 left top.
Archivio BMW: pages 276 bottom, 277 top.
Archivio Carli: pages 209 top, 297 top.
Archivio Ferrari: pages 6 center right, 69 right top, 280 left top.
Archivio Storico Fiat: page 176 bottom.
Archivio Porsche: pages 209 bottom, 211 bottom, 212 left top and bottom, 215 bottom, 266 top, 290 center.
Aububurn Cord Duesenberg Museum: pages 34 top, 35 bottom right, 37 bottom left, 244 center.
Ken Breslauer: pages 258 top right and left.
Neill Bruce: pages 44 left top, 45 left bottom, 81 right top, 82 right top, 85 bottom left, 86, 90 center left, 96-97, 97 top, 98 top, 98-99, 149 top and center right, 156 top, 157 right bottom, 178 bottom right, 179 center right, 181 right top, 183 top, 195 left, 210 left, 230 top destra, 283 left top, 284 center top.
The Bugatti Trust: pages 24 left top and bottom, 32 center bottom, 36 center and bottom, 38 center, 41 center bottom, 41 bottom, 47, 49 top and center.
Corbis: pages 22 left, 22 top, 133 bottom, 134 bottom, 135, 154-155.
Corbis Bettmann: page 23 top.
Upi Corbis: pages 61 right center, 87 bottom right, 166 top, 288 bottom, 228-229.

Upi Corbis Bettmann: pages 246-247 top, 247 right, 266-267.
Bruce Craig Photos: pages 236, 237, 238, 239, 270 top, 270 bottom, 270-271.
Daimler Benz Archives: pages 6 left top, 23 bottom, 35 center, 43 bottom, 44-45, 50 bottom, 57 top and center, 63 bottom, 64-65, 81 bottom, 82 left top, 82 right center, 152 left center, 162 top, 179 top, 268 center right, 285 top, 288 right top.
Joseph Emonts Pohl: pages 8-9, 234 top, 254 top, 254-255.
Mary Evans Picture Library: pages 13 center right, 15 bottom right, 16 bottom, 19 bottom left, 20 bottom, 24 right top, 25 left, 25 right top, 29 bottom left, 31 left bottom, 39 right bottom, 40 right bottom, 41 top, 42 right bottom, 46 top, 62 left top, 84 right top.
Farabolafoto: pages 2 left, 25 right center, 38 bottom right, 50 top, 52 left, 52-53, 53 left top, 53 left bottom, 53 left bottom, 54 top, 54-55, 59 bottom, 60 left top, 60 bottom, 60-61, 63 left top, 64 center, 64 right bottom, 65 center and bottom, 67 right, 69 left bottom, 78 bottom, 82-83, 83 right, 86-87, 91 top, 96 top, 98 left bottom, 100 left, 109 bottom right, 119 top left, 122 left center and bottom, 124 bottom, 138 top, 152 left center, 194 right top, 269 bottom, 272 bottom, 273 top, 273 left bottom, 275 left top, 280 center, 281 bottom, 282 left, 282 top, 286-287, 288 left top, 288 right bottom, 293 center, 297 center.
GM Media Archives: pages 218 bottom, 219 bottom.
GP Library: pages 6-7 bottom, 70 top, 73 left bottom, 83 top, 85 top and center, 90 center right, 90 bottom, 90-91, 92 top, 92 right center, 98 right bottom, 99 left top, 99 bottom, 100 top and bottom, 102 top, 102 left, 102-103, 103 top, 103 bottom, 104 top left, 105 top, 110 top right, 110-111, 114 fifth photograph from top, 120 left top, 145 bottom, 148 center left, 148-149, 158 left top, 168 top, 170 left bottom, 228 center, 267 bottom, 268 bottom, 290 bottom.
Kinrade/Sutton Motor Sport Images: pages 258-259, 259 bottom, 261, 262 top, 262-263, 263 top, 265 right top, 265 bottom.
Reinhard Klein: pages 176-177, 177 right, 178, 179, 180, 181, 182, 184 top right, 184 left bottom, 185, 186 top, 186 left center, 187 bottom, 190-191, 192 top and bottom, 193 top, 196-197, 203 bottom.
Lat: pages 217 bottom, 266 left, 267 top.
Ludvigsen Library: pages 292 bottom, 293 top and bottom.
The National Motor Museum Bealieau: pages 10 top, 11 center, 18 center left, 19 top, 20 top, 21 right top, 30 top, 96 left, 117 center, 151 left top.

Phipps Photographic: pages 296, 296-297, 297 top left bottom.
Sutton - Phipps Photographic: pages 297 bottom right.
Photo 4: pages 1 bottom, 7 top, 74 left center, 75 right, 87 right center, 90 center top left, 99 center right, 104 top left, 110 bottom right, 111 left center, 112 left top and bottom, 112 right, 112-113, 113 right top, 113, 114 third photograph from top, 115 top, 115 top, 114-115, 115 bottom right, 116, 118, 119 top right, 120 right top, 121 center, 122-123, 123 right center, 123 right bottom, 124 top left and right, 124-125, 125 top, 126, 126-127, 127, 128, 128-129, 129 center and bottom, 130-131, 131 center and bottom, 138-139, 139, 142 bottom, 142-143, 143 top left, 146 top, 146-147, 147 top and bottom, 150, 150-151, 151 right top, 151 bottom, 154 top, 154 left, 154 bottom, 155 top, 158 top, 158-159, 159, 163, 164, 164-165, 166-167, 166 bottom, 167, 168 bottom, 168-169, 169 right top, 169 center and bottom, 170 top, 170 center left, 170 right bottom, 170-171, 171 top, 171 bottom, 172 bottom, 173, 175 center and bottom, 176 top, 177 top, 183 center and bottom, 184 left top, 185 right bottom, 186-187, 187 top, 188, 188-189, 189, 190, 191 top and bottom, 192 center, 193 bottom, 194 bottom, 195 right, 196, 197, 198, 199, 200, 201, 202, 202-203, 203 top and bottom, 204, 205, 206, 207, 218-219, 219 center, 222, 223, 234-235, 235 bottom, 244 top, 248-249, 249, 251 center and bottom, 252, 253, 257 top, 258 bottom, 260-261, 262 bottom, 298, 299.
Private Collection: pages 6 bottom left, 12 bottom, 54 bottom, 285 center.
Joe Robbins: pages 263 bottom, 264-265, 265 center right.
The Peter Roberts Collection c/o Neill Bruce: pages 1 top, 8 bottom, 10-11, 11 bottom, 12 top, 12-13, 13 top, 13 center left, 13 bottom, 14 left, 14-15, 14 bottom, 15 bottom left, 15 top right, 16 top and center, 17, 18 top, 18 center right, 18 bottom, 20-21, 21 top left, 21 bottom, 22 right top and bottom, 22-23, 25 right and left bottom, 26, 27 center and bottom, 28 bottom, 28-29, 29 top, 29 bottom right, 30-31, 31 bottom, 32 top, 32 center, 33 right top, 33 bottom, 34 bottom, 35 top, 35 bottom left, 36 top, 37 top, 38 top left and right, 39 right center and bottom, 40 top, 41 right center, 42 center, 42-43, 44 left bottom, 49 right center, 49 left bottom, 51 bottom, 57 bottom, 58 left top, 59 right center, 61 left center, 62 right top, 63 right top, 64 left bottom, 65 bottom, 66 top, 69 left top, 74 bottom, 77 top, 79 bottom, 80 top, 81 left bottom, 81 right center and bottom, 82 left center, 85 right bottom, 87 top, 88 left and right top, 88-89, 89 top, 104 bottom, 138

bottom, 140, 140-141, 148 top, 148 center right, 148 bottom, 162 right center, 174 right top, 208, 210 bottom, 211 top, 225 bottom left, 227 center left, 228 top, 229 top, 230 alto left, 244 bottom, 244-245, 268-269, 271 right, 274 right top, 280-281, 281 top, 282 center, 282 bottom, 282-283, 284 center bottom, 285 bottom, 292 right top, 292-293.
Rainer W. Schlegelmich: pages 4-5, 8 top, 72, 72-73 top, 73 right bottom, 74-75, 75 left, 75 bottom, 88 top center, 88 right center, 88 bottom, 89 bottom, 90 top, 91 bottom, 92 left center, 92 bottom, 92-93, 93, 94 top, 94 bottom, 95 top, 95 bottom, 97 left bottom, 100-101, 101 top, 106, 107, 111 left top, 111 bottom, 125 left bottom, 129 top, 132, 132-133, 133 top and center, 136, 136-137, 137, 141 bottom, 142 top, 143 top right, 143 bottom left, 144 center and bottom, 145 top, 145 bottom left, 146 bottom, 152-153, 153 center and bottom, 155 center and bottom, 156 right bottom, 156-157, 157 center, 157 left bottom, 159 left center, 162 bottom, 164 right bottom, 169 left top, 170 center, 172 top center right, 172-173, 174 left top, 174 right bottom, 175 top, 212-213, 213 center, 216-217, 229 center and bottom, 224 top, 224-225 top, 231 top and right bottom, 232 center, 233, 288-289, 289 bottom, 291.
Nigel Snowdon: pages 242-243, 254 bottom, 255 bottom.
Sporting Pictures: pages 103 center left, 104 bottom right, 108 top, 108 center left, 108 bottom, 109 top, 109 center, 109 bottom left, 110 top left, 111 right top, 112 left center, 113 left top, 114 first, second and fourth photograph from top, 115 bottom left, 116 right bottom, 117 bottom, 118-119, 120 top, 120 center and bottom, 121 top, 121 bottom, 122 right top and bottom, 122 left center, 123 top, 123 left center, 123 left bottom, 124 center left and right, 125 left bottom, 130 bottom, 131 top, 143 bottom right, 147 center, 159 right bottom, 174 left bottom, 185 bottom, 186 bottom, 216, 217 top, 232-233, 232 bottom, 235 top, 242 top and bottom, 249, 250, 250-251, 251 top, 252-253, 256-257, 257 bottom, 265 top left.
Bob Tronolone Collection: pages 9 top, 248 left, 248 top, 256 top.
Frederick A. Usher Collection: pages 15 top left, 22 right center, 27 top, 31 top, 31 center, 31 bottom left, 32 bottom, 33 left top, 37 center, 37 bottom, 38-39, 41 left center, 42 top, 45 right bottom, 245 right, 286 bottom.
Foto Zumbrunn Zurigo: pages 2 right, 2-3, 28 top, 43 left top, 48, 48-49, 49 right bottom, 53 right top, 55 top, 67 left, 70-71, 71, 80 center, 80-81, 104-105, 224-225, 225 bottom right, 226 bottom, 226-227, 231 bottom left, 246-247 bottom, 272-273, 274 top and bottom, 275 right top, 276 center, 276-277, 277 bottom, 278-279, 279, 296, 296-297.

ACKNOWLEDGMENTS

The Authors would like to thank:
the Press Offices PPG CART, IRL, CSAI, Professional Sportcars;
the Archives of the Companies; the colleagues Giorgio Angeletti, Franco Carmignani, Guido Daelli, Marco Ragazzoni.
A special acknowledgment Anna Giudice.

The Publisher would like to thank: the Historical Archives of BMW, Ferrari, Fiat, Mercedes, Porsche, Indianapolis Motor Speedway;
Elvira Ruocco of Archivio Storico Alfa Romeo; Laura Mancini of GM Media Archives; Ken Breslauer and Bob Tronolone.